Contents and Index

BASIC STITCHES

Stockinette stitch

Work with number of stitches desired.
Row 1 (right side): Knit.
Row 2 (wrong side): Purl.
Repeat these 2 rows for pattern.

I = 1 knit stitch (k)
− = 1 purl stitch (p)

Twisted stockinette stitch

Work with number of stitches desired.
Row 1 (right side): Knit, inserting needle through back loop of each stitch.
Row 2: Purl as usual.
Repeat these 2 rows for pattern.

− = 1 purl stitch (p)
∪ = 1 twisted knit stitch (worked in back loop)

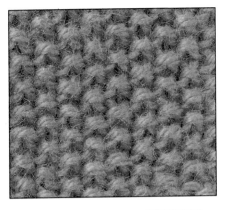

Moss stitch

Even number of stitches.
Row 1: * K 1, p 1 *; repeat from * to *.
Row 2: * P 1, k 1 *; repeat from * to *.
Repeat these 2 rows for pattern.

I = k 1
− = p 1

Uneven number of stitches.
Row 1: K 1, * p 1, k 1 *; repeat from * to *.
Repeat this row for pattern.
Note: Always work k over p (as sts face you) and p over k.

Reverse stockinette stitch

Work with number of stitches desired.
Row 1 (right side): Purl.
Row 2: Knit.
Repeat these 2 rows for pattern.

I = 1 knit stitch (k)
− = 1 purl stitch (p)

Garter stitch

Work with number of stitches desired.
Knit every row for pattern.

I = 1 knit stitch (k)

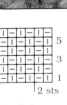

Double moss stitch

Work with an even number of stitches.
Rows 1 and 2: * K 1, p 1 *; repeat from * to *.
Rows 3 and 4: * P 1, k 1 *; repeat from * to *.
Repeat these 4 rows for pattern.

I = k 1
− = p 1

BASIC STITCHES

Rib stitch (k 1, p 1)

Even number of stitches.
Row 1: * P 1, k 1 *; repeat from * to *.
Repeat this row for pattern.

Uneven number of stitches.
Row 1: P 1, * k 1, p 1 *; repeat from * to *.
Row 2: K 1, * p 1, k 1 *; repeat from * to *.
Repeat these 2 rows for pattern.

ı = k 1
− = p 1

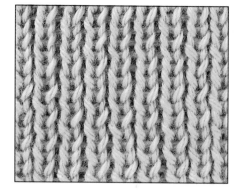

Rib stitch (k 2, p 2)

Work with a multiple of 4 stitches.
Row 1: * K 2, p 2 *; repeat from * to *.
Repeat this row for pattern.

For uneven number of stitches, see Rib stitch (k 1, p 1) above.

ı = k 1
− = p 1

Rib stitch (k 3, p 3)

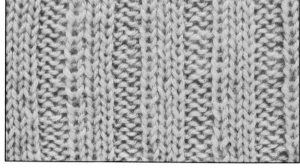

Work with a multiple of 6 stitches.
Row 1: * P 3, k 3 *; repeat from * to *.
Repeat this row for pattern.

For uneven number of stitches, see Rib stitch (k 1, p 1) above.

6 sts

ı = = k 1
− = = p 1

Brioche rib

Work with an even number of stitches, plus 2 for selvages (not shown on chart).
Row 1: Knit.
Row 2: K 1(selvage), * k 1, k 1 by inserting needle into center of next stitch of row below, then drop unworked stitch above off left needle without working it (k 1 below made) *; repeat from * to * across, k last stitch (selvage). Repeat Row 2 for pattern.

ı = k 1
V = k 1 below

Mock brioche rib

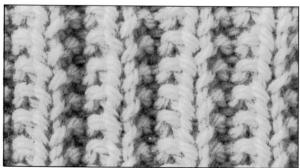

Work with a multiple of 4 stitches, plus 2.
Row 1: * K 3, p 1 *; repeat from * to *, ending with k 2.
Row 2: P 1, * k 3, p 1 *; repeat from * to *, ending with k 1.
Repeat these 2 rows for pattern.

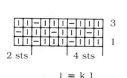

2 sts   4 sts

ı = k 1
− = p 1

CLASSIC STITCHES

Uneven rib

Work with a multiple of 4 stitches.
Row 1: * P 2, k 2 *; repeat from * to *.
Row 2: K 1, * p 2, k 2 *; repeat from * to * across, ending last repeat with k 1.
Repeat these 2 rows for pattern.

ı = k 1
– = p 1

ı = k 1
– = p 1

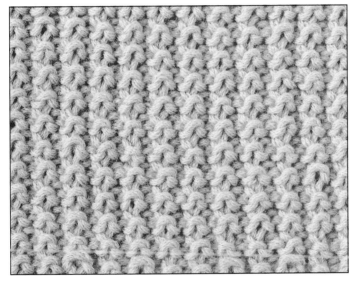

Sand stitch

Work with an even number of stitches.
Row 1 (right side as shown): * K 1, p 1 *; repeat from * to *.
Row 2: Knit.
Repeat these 2 rows for pattern.

Sand stitch with slip stitches

Work with an even number of stitches.
Row 1 (right side): * With yarn in back of work, slip 1 stitch as if to purl; with yarn in front, p 1 *; repeat from * to *.
Row 1: Purl.
Repeat these 2 rows for pattern.

– = p 1
v = slip stitch

CLASSIC STITCHES

Ladder rungs

Work with a multiple of 10 stitches, plus 7.
Row 1 (right side): * P 3, k 1, p 3, k 3 *; repeat from * to *, ending with p 3, k 1, p 3.
Row 2: K 3, p 1, k 3, * p 3, k 3, p 1, k 3 *; repeat from * to *.
Row 3: Repeat Row 1.
Row 4: K 3, p 1, * k 9, p 1 *; repeat from * to *, ending with k 3.
Repeat these 4 rows for pattern.

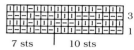

7 sts   10 sts

ı = k 1
− = p 1

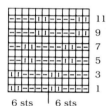

6 sts   6 sts

ı = k 1
− = p 1
□ = 1 st as shown

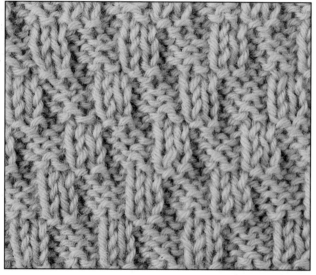

Little step stitch

Work with a multiple of 6 stitches.
Rows 1 and 3: * P 4, k 2 *; repeat from * to *.
Row 2 and all even-numbered rows: Work each stitch as it appears on this side of work (k the k sts and p the p sts).
Rows 5 and 7: P 2, *k 2, p 4 *; repeat from * to *, ending last repeat with p 2.
Rows 9 and 11: * K 2, p 4 *; repeat from * to *.
Repeat Rows 1 through 12 for pattern.

Seaside chain stitch

Work with a multiple of 7 stitches, plus 4.
Rows 1 and 3: P 5, * k 1, p 6 *; repeat from * to *, ending last repeat with p 5.
Row 2 and all even-numbered rows: Work each stitch as it appears on this side of work (k the k sts and p the p sts).
Rows 5 and 7: * P 4, k 1, p 1, k 1 *; repeat from * to *, ending p 4.
Repeat Rows 1 through 8 for pattern.

4 sts ı 7 sts

ı = k 1
− = p 1
□ = 1 st as shown

CLASSIC STITCHES

Mirrored triangle stitch

Work with a multiple of 7 stitches.
Row 1: * K 6, p 1 *; repeat from
* to *.
Row 2: * K 2, p 5 *; repeat from * to *.
Rows 3 and 4: * K 4, p 3 *; repeat
from * to *.
Row 5: Repeat Row 2.
Row 6: Repeat Row 1.
Row 7: * P 1, k 6 *; repeat from
* to *.
Row 8: * P 5, k 2 *; repeat from
* to *.
Rows 9 and 10: * P 3, k 4 *; repeat
from * to *.
Row 11: Repeat Row 8.
Row 12: Repeat Row 7.
Repeat these 12 rows for pattern.

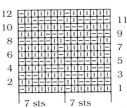

ı = k1
- = p 1

Little parallelograms

Work with a multiple of 10 stitches.
Row 1: P 1, * k 2, p 4, k 2, p 1 *;
repeat from * to *, ending last repeat
with p 1.
Row 2: K 1, * p 2, k 4, p 2, k 2 *;
repeat from * to *, ending last repeat
with k 1.
Row 3: * P 2, k 2 *; repeat from * to
*, ending p 2.
Row 4: * K 2, p 2 *; repeat from * to
*, ending k 2.
Row 5: Repeat Row 2.
Row 6: Repeat Row 1.
Row 7: Repeat Row 4.
Row 8: Repeat Row 3.
Row 9: Repeat Row 2.
Row 10: Repeat Row 1.
Row 11: Repeat Row 3.
Row 12: Repeat Row 4.
Repeat these 12 rows for pattern.

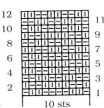

ı = k 1
- = p 1

CLASSIC STITCHES

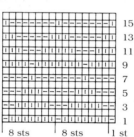

ı = k 1
− = p 1
▢ = 1 st as shown

```
I−−−−−−−I−−−−−−−I  15
III−−−−−IIIIII−−−−−  13
IIIII−−−IIIIIIII−−−  11
IIIIIII−IIIIIIIII−  9
−−−−−IIIIIII−−−−−I  7
−−−IIIIIII−−−IIIIIII  5
−IIIIIIIII−−IIIIIIII  3
−IIIIIII−−−IIIIIII  1
```
|← 8 sts →|← 8 sts →| 1 st

Pyramids

Work with a multiple of 8 stitches, plus 1.

Row 1: P 1, * k 7, p 1 *; repeat from * to *.

Row 2 and all even-numbered rows: Work each stitch as it appears on this side of work (k the k sts and p the p sts).

Row 3: P 2, * k 5, p 3 *; repeat from * to *, ending last repeat with p 2.

Row 5: P 3, * k 3, p 5 *; repeat from * to *, ending last repeat with p 3.

Row 7: P 4, * k 1, p 7 *; repeat from * to *, ending last repeat with p 4.

Row 9: K 4, * p 1, k 7 *; repeat from * to *, ending last repeat with k 4.

Row 11: K 3, * p 3, k 5 *; repeat from * to *, ending last repeat with k 3.

Row 13: K 2, * p 5, k 3 *; repeat from * to *, ending last repeat with k 2.

Row 15: K 1, * p 7, k 1 *; repeat from * to *.

Repeat Rows 1 through 16 for pattern.

Triangles

Work triangle pattern on 10 stitches. For pattern as shown, work with a multiple of 12 stitches, plus 10, worked with 2-st vertical stockinette stitch rib between each 10-stitch triangle pattern, charted below.

Rows 1, 5, 9, and 13: Work (p 2, k 2) twice, p 2 (pattern section), * k 2 for rib, repeat 10-st pattern section as before *; repeat from * to *.

Rows 2, 6, 8, and 12: P 1, work (k 2, p 2) twice, k 1 (pattern), * p 2, repeat 10-st pattern *; repeat from * to *.

Rows 3, 7, 11, and 15: Work (k 2, p 2) twice, k 2 (pattern), * k 2, repeat 10-st pattern *; repeat from * to *.

Rows 4, 10, 14, and 16: K 1, work (p 2, k 2) twice, k 1 (pattern), * p 2, repeat 10-st pattern *; repeat from * to *.

Repeat Rows 1 through 16 for pattern.

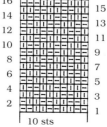

ı = k 1
− = p 1

CLASSIC STITCHES

Palladian stitch

Work with a multiple of 14 stitches, plus 1.

Row 1: K 3, * p 9, k 5 *; repeat from * to *, ending last repeat with k 3.

Rows 2 and 14: P 2, * work (k 3, p 1) twice, k 3, p 3 *; repeat from *, ending last repeat with p 2.

Rows 3 and 13: *K 1, p 3, k 3, p 1, k 3, p 3 *; repeat from * to *, ending k 1.

Rows 4 and 12: K 3, * p 3, k 3, p 3, k 5 *; repeat from * to *, ending last repeat with k 3.

Rows 5 and 11: P 2, * k 3, p 5, k 3, p 3 *; repeat from * to *, ending last repeat with p 2.

Rows 6 and 10: K 1, * p 3, k 3, p 1, k 3, p 3, k 1 *; repeat from * to *.

Rows 7 and 9: P 2, * k 1, p 3, k 3, p 3, k 1, p 3 *; repeat from * to *, ending last repeat with p 2.

Row 8: K 5, * p 5, k 9 *; repeat from * to *, ending last repeat with k 5.

Repeat Rows 1 through 14 for pattern.

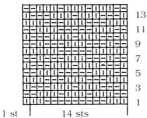

ı = k 1
− = p 1

Zigzag moss stitch

Work with a multiple of 10 stitches.

Row 1: * K 5, work (p 1, k 1) twice, p 1 *; repeat from * to *.

Rows 2 and 10: P 1, * work (k 1, p 1) twice, k 1, p 5 *; repeat from * to *, ending last repeat with p 4.

Rows 3 and 9: K 3, * work (p 1, k 1) twice, p 1, k 5 *; repeat from * to *, ending last repeat with k 2.

Rows 4 and 8: P 3, * work (k 1, p 1) twice, k 1, p 5 *; repeat from * to *, ending last repeat with p 2.

Rows 5 and 7: K 1, * work (p 1, k 1) twice, p 1, k 5 *; repeat from * to *, ending last repeat with k 4.

Row 6: * P 5, work (k 1, p 1) twice, k 1 *; repeat from * to *.

Repeat Rows 1 through 10 for pattern.

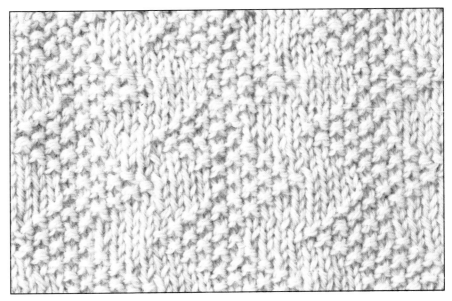

ı = k 1
− = p1

CLASSIC STITCHES

Concentric squares

Work with a multiple of 30 stitches, plus 2.

Rows 1, 3, 5, 7, 9, 23, 25, 27, 29, and 31: Knit.

Rows 2 and 32: Purl.

Rows 4, 6, 28, and 30: P 2, * k 28, p 2 *; repeat from * to *.

Rows 8, 10, 24, and 26: P 2, * k 4, p 20, k 4, p 2 *; repeat from * to *.

Rows 11, 13, 19, and 21: K 11, * work (p 1, k 1) 5 times, p 1, k 19 *; repeat from * to *, ending last repeat with k 10.

Rows 12, 14, 20, and 22: P 2, * k 4, p 5, work (k 1, p 1) 5 times, k 1, p 4, k 4, p 2 *; repeat from * to *.

Rows 15 and 17: K 11, * p 1, k 1, p 1, k 5, p 1, k 1, p 1, k 19 *; repeat from * to *, ending last repeat with k 10.

Rows 16 and 18: P 2, * k 4, p 5, k 1, p 1, k 1, p 5, k 1, p 1, k 1, p 4, k 4, p 2 *; repeat from * to *.

Repeat Rows 1 through 32 for pattern.

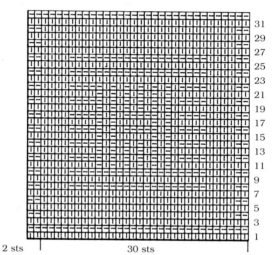

ı = k 1
– = p 1

Garter stitch columns

Work with a multiple of 8 stitches, plus 1.

Row 1 and all odd-numbered rows (right side): Knit.

Rows 2 and 10: K 2, * p 1, k 3 *; repeat from * to * across, ending last repeat with k 2.

Rows 4, 6, and 8: P 3, * k 3, p 5 *; repeat from * to *, ending last repeat with p 3.

Row 12: K 2, * p 5, k 3 *; repeat from * to *; ending last repeat with k 2.

Repeat Rows 1 through 12 for pattern.

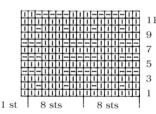

ı = k 1
– = p 1

CLASSIC STITCHES

Flowered meadow

Work with a multiple of 8 stitches, plus 2.

Rows 1, 3, 7, and 9 (right side): Knit.

Row 2 and all even-numbered rows: Purl.

Row 5: K 3, * work flower as follows: knit the next 3 stitches together and, without dropping them from the left needle, k the first stitch, then k the 2nd and the 3rd stitches together, dropping the original stitches from the left needle (flower made), k 5 *; repeat from * to *, ending last repeat with k 4.

Row 11: K 7, * make flower on 3 stitches as before, k 5 *; repeat from * to *, ending last repeat with k 8. Repeat Rows 1 through 12 for pattern.

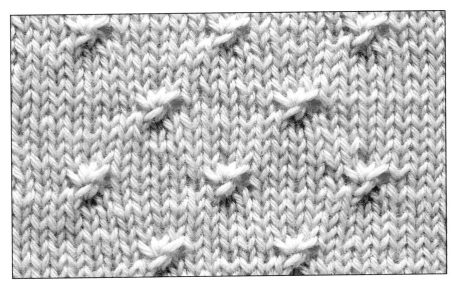

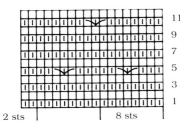

ı = k 1
∨ = 1 flower
□ = p 1

Embossed rib stitch

Work with an uneven number of stitches.

Row 1 (right side): Knit.

Row 2: P 1, * work double stitch as follows: insert needle below next stitch into the stitch of the previous row and knit, drop unworked stitch above from left needle (double stitch made), p 1 *; repeat from * to *. Repeat these 2 rows for pattern.

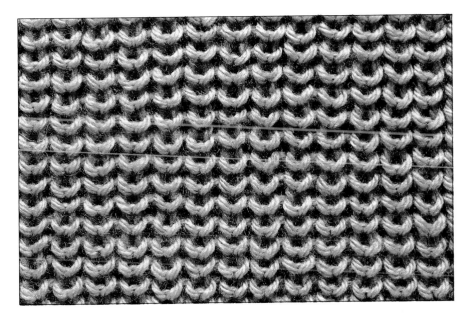

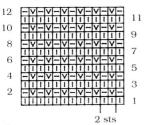

ı = k 1
– = p 1
∨ = 1 double st

13

CLASSIC STITCHES

Diagonal lines

Work with a multiple of 10 stitches.
Row 1: * K 5, p 5 *; repeat from * to *. *Note*: Chart indicates pattern, not individual knit or purl stitches.
Row 2: P 1, * k 5, p 5 *; repeat from * to *, ending last repeat with p 4.
Row 3: K 3, * p 5, k 5 *; repeat from * to *, ending last repeat with k 2.
Row 4: P 3, * k 5, p 5 *; repeat from * to *, ending last repeat with p 2.
Row 5: K 1, * p 5, k 5 *; repeat from * to *, ending last repeat with k 4.
Row 6: * P 5, k 5 *; repeat from * to *.
Row 7: P 4, * k 5, p 5 *; repeat from * to *, ending last repeat with p 1.
Row 8: K 2, * p 5, k 5 *; repeat from * to *, ending last repeat with k 3.
Row 9: P 2, * k 5, p 5 *; repeat from * to *, ending last repeat with p 3.
Row 10: K 4, * p 5, k 5 *; repeat from * to *, ending last repeat with k 1.
Repeat these 10 rows for pattern.

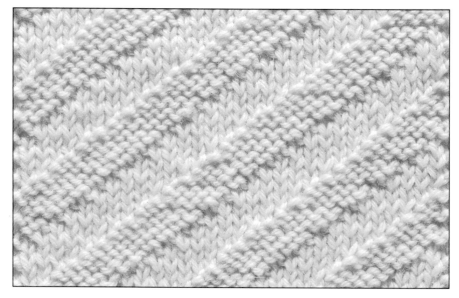

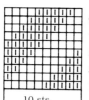

I = 1 st in stockinette st
□ = 1 st in reverse stockinette st

Rows of jewels

Work with multiple of 4 stitches, plus 3.
Row 1 (right side): P 3, * start jewel as follows: k in front loop of next stitch without dropping it from left needle, then k into back loop of same stitch, then into front loop, dropping original stitch from needle (3 sts worked in one st), p 3 *; repeat from * to *.
Row 2: K 3, * p 3, k 3 *; repeat from * to *.
Row 3: P 3, * k 3 stitches together as one (jewel completed), p 3 *; repeat from * to *.
Row 4: Knit.
Repeat these 4 rows for pattern.

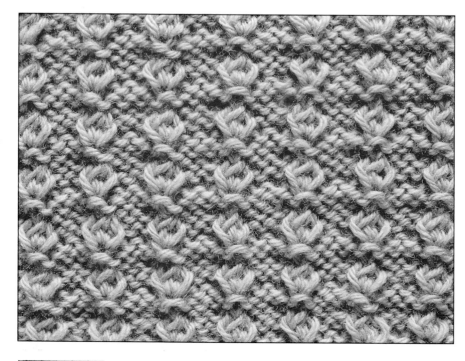

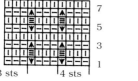

I = k 1
– = p 1
▼ = start of jewel
≡ = p 3
▲ = k 3 tog

CLASSIC STITCHES

Broken rib stitch

Work with a multiple of 4 stitches, plus 2.

Rows 1 and 3: P 2, * work (k 1 through back loop) twice, p 2 *; repeat from * to *.

Rows 2 and 4: K 2, * work (p 1 through back loop) twice, k 2 *; repeat from * to *.

Row 5: Purl.

Row 6: Knit.

Repeat these 6 rows for pattern.

ı = k 1
− = p 1
! = 1 twisted st (worked in back loop)

2 sts ¦ 4 sts ¦ 4 sts

Alternating seeds

Work with a multiple of 10 sts.

Row 1: K 1, * p 1, k 1, p 1, k 7 *; repeat from * to *, ending last repeat with k 6.

Row 2: * P 5, work (k 1, p 1) twice, k 1*; repeat from * to *.

Row 3: K 6, * p 1, k 1, p 1, k 7 *; repeat from * to *, ending last repeat with k 1.

Row 4: * Work (k 1, p 1) twice, k 1, p 5 *; repeat from * to *.

Repeat these 4 rows for pattern.

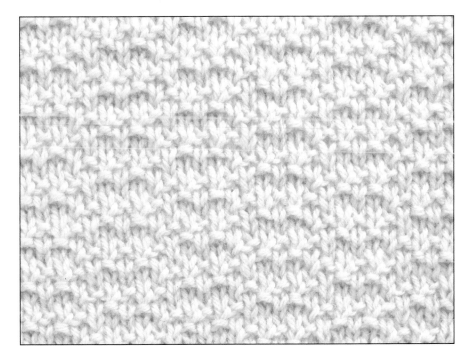

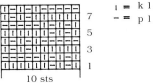

ı = k 1
− = p 1

10 sts

CLASSIC STITCHES

Arrows

Work with a multiple of 5 stitches, plus 2 for selvages.

Row 1 (right side): Knit.

Rows 2 and 14: Purl.

Rows 3 and 13: K 3, * bring yarn forward, slip 3 as if to purl, take yarn to back, k 2 *; repeat from * to *, ending last repeat with k 1.

Rows 4 and 12: P 1, take yarn to back, slip 2, bring yarn forward, * p 2, yarn back, slip 3, yarn forward *; repeat from * to *, ending last repeat with slip 1, yarn forward, p 1. *Note*: When slipping stitches, always carry the yarn across right side of work.

Rows 5 and 11: K 1, slip 2, * k 2, slip 3 *; repeat from * to *, ending last repeat with slip 1, k 1.

Rows 6 and 10: P 3, * slip 3, p 2 *; repeat from * to *, ending last repeat with p 1.

Rows 7 and 9: K 2, * slip 3, k 2 *; repeat from * to *.

Row 8: P 1, * slip 3, p 2 *; repeat from * to *; p last stitch.

Repeat Rows 1 through 14 for pattern.

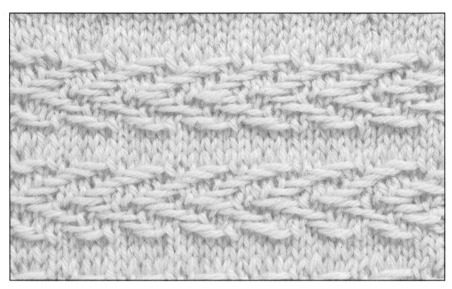

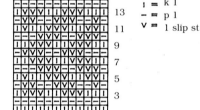

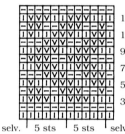

ı = k 1
− = p 1
V = 1 slip st

selv. 5 sts 5 sts selv.

Raised rib

Work with a multiple of 6 stitches, plus 2 for selvages.

Row 1 (right side): Knit.

Row 2: Purl.

Row 3: K 1(selvage), * p 5, work double stitch as follows: insert needle into stitch just below next stitch and knit, drop unworked stitch above from left needle (double stitch made) *; repeat from * to * across, ending k last stitch (selvage).

Row 4: P 1, k across to last st, p last stitch.

Repeat Rows 3 and 4 for pattern.

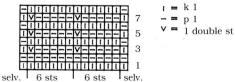

ı = k 1
− = p 1
V = 1 double st

selv. 6 sts 6 sts selv.

CLASSIC STITCHES

Little corners

Work with a multiple of 6 stitches.
Row 1: * P 3, k 3 by working in the back loop of each st (3 twisted k sts made) *; repeat from * to *.
Row 2 and all even-numbered rows: Work each stitch as it appears on this side of work (k the k sts, p the p sts).
Row 3: Work 1 twisted k st, * p 3, work 3 twisted k sts *; repeat from * to *; ending last repeat with 2 twisted k sts.
Row 5: Work 2 twisted k sts, * p 3, work 3 twisted k sts *; repeat from * to *, ending last repeat with 1 twisted k st.
Row 7: * Work 3 twisted k sts, p 3 *; repeat from * to *.
Row 9: Repeat Row 5.
Row 11: Repeat Row 3.
Repeat Rows 1 through 12 for pattern.

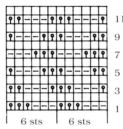

- = p 1
♀ = 1 twisted st (worked in back loop)
☐ = = 1 st as shown

Staggered little squares

Work with a multiple of 16 stitches, plus 1.

Rows 1 and 3: * K 1 by working in the back loop of stitch (twisted k st made), * work (k 3, then 1 twisted k st) 3 times, p 3 *; repeat from * to *, ending twisted k st in last st.
Row 2 and all even-numbered rows: Work each stitch as it appears on this side of work (k the k sts, p the p sts).
Rows 5 and 7: * Work 1 twisted k st, work (k 3, then 1 twisted k st) twice, p 3, 1 twisted k st, k 3 *; repeat from * to *, ending with twisted k st in last st.
Rows 9 and 11: * Work 1 twisted k st, k 3, 1 twisted k st, p 3, work (1 twisted k st, k 3) twice *; repeat from * to *, ending with twisted k st in last st.
Rows 13 and 15: * Work 1 twisted k st, p 3, work (1 twisted k st, k 3) 3 times *; repeat from * to *, ending with twisted k st in last st.
Repeat Rows 1 through 16 for pattern.

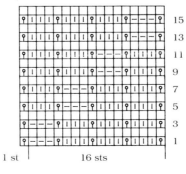

ı = k1
- = p 1
♀ = 1 twisted st (worked in back loop)
☐ = 1 st as shown

CLASSIC STITCHES

Layette stitch

Work with a multiple of 9 stitches, plus 3.

Row 1 (right side): * P 3, k 2, p 1, work 1 twisted k st by knitting in back loop of st, p 1, 1 twisted k st *; repeat from * to *, ending p last 3 sts.

Row 2: K 3, * bring yarn forward, slip 1, return yarn to back, k 1, yarn forward, slip 1, yarn back, k 1, yarn over, k 2, pass yarn-over over k 2 sts and drop it, k 3 *; repeat from * to *. Repeat these 2 rows for pattern.

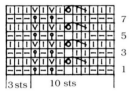

ı = k 1
– = p 1
ı̧ = 1 twisted st (worked in back loop)
v = 1 slip st
o = yarn over (dropped)
⌒ = yarn over passed over 2 k sts
☐ = empty square with no st indicated

Woven stitch

Work with a multiple of 12 stitches.

Rows 1, 3, 5, and 7: * K 2, p 2, k 2, work 6 sts in garter st (k on right and wrong side rows).

Row 2 and all even-numbered rows: K garter sts and work each remaining stitches as it appears on this side of work (k the k sts and p the p sts).

Rows 9, 11, 13, and 15: * Work 6 sts in garter st, k 1, p 2, k 2 *; repeat from * across.

Repeat Rows 1 through 16 for pattern.

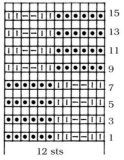

ı = k 1
– = p 1
• = garter st
☐ = 1 st as shown

18

CLASSIC STITCHES

Twisted rib stitch

Work with an uneven number of stitches.

Row 1 (right side): Work twisted k st by knitting into back loop of stitch, * p 1, work 1 twisted k st *; repeat from * to *.

Row 2: Work twisted p st by purling into back loop of stitch, * k 1, work 1 twisted p st *; repeat from * to *.

Repeat these 2 rows for pattern.

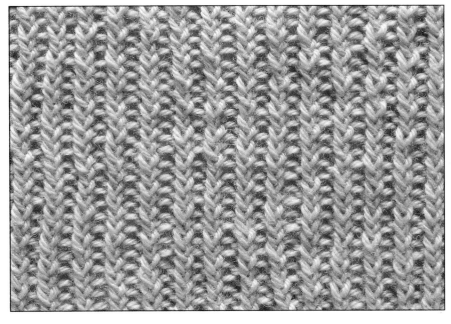

I = k 1
– = p 1
ℐ = 1 twisted k st
▲ = 1 twisted p st

Knotted rib stitch

Work with an uneven number of stitches.

Row 1 (right side): P 1, * k 1, p 1 *; repeat from * to *.

Row 2: K 1, * p 1, k 1 *; repeat from * to *.

Rows 3 through 6: Repeat Rows 1 and 2 twice more.

Row 7: P 1, * knit 3 sts in next st by knitting front loop, then back loop, then front loop, p 1 *; repeat from * to *.

Row 8: K 1, * p 3 sts together as 1, k 1 *; repeat from * to *.

Repeat these 8 rows for pattern.

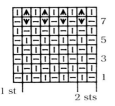

I = k 1
– = p 1
⋁ = 3 sts worked in one st
▲ = 3 sts tog

CLASSIC STITCHES

Little checker

Work with a multiple of 4 stitches.
Row 1: * K 2, p 2 *; repeat from
* to *.
Rows 2 and 4: Work each stitch as it
appears on this side of work (k the k
sts and p the p sts).
Row 3: * P 2, k 2 *; repeat from *
to *.
Repeat these 4 rows for pattern.

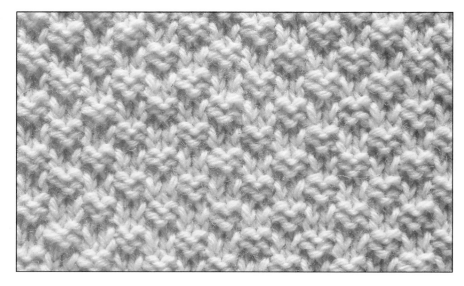

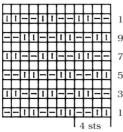

l = k 1
– = p 1
☐ = 1 st as shown

Fins

Work with a multiple of 14 stitches,
plus 2 for selvages.
Rows 1, 3, 7, and 9 (right side):
Knit.
Row 2 and all even-numbered rows:
Purl.
Row 5: K 5, * work right fin as follows:
skip next 2 sts on left needle and
insert needle into stitch 4 rows below
following st, draw up long loop and
place it on left needle at tip, k loop
and first st on left needle together as
one (right fin made); k 4, work left fin
as follows: reach back to draw up long
loop, 4 rows below, from next st after
the st where right fin loop originated
and place new loop on right needle, k
1, pass loop over this k st and drop it
(left fin made), k 8 *; repeat from * to
*, ending last repeat with k 5.
Row 11: K 12, * work right fin as
before, k 4, work left fin, k 8 *; repeat
from * to *, ending last repeat with
k 12.
Repeat Rows 1 through 12 for
pattern.

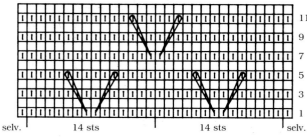

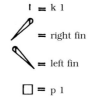

l = k 1

= right fin

= left fin

☐ = p 1

CLASSIC STITCHES

Mock braids

Even number of stitches.
Rows 1 and 3 (right side): K 1, * slip
1, k 1, yarn over, pass the slip st over
both k st and yarn-over and drop it *;
repeat from * to *, ending k last st.
Row 2 and all even-numbered rows:
Purl.
Row 5: Knit.
Repeat Rows 1 through 6 for pattern.

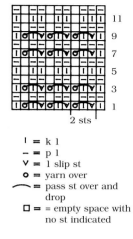

l = k 1
− = p 1
V = 1 slip st
o = yarn over
⌒ = pass st over and
drop
□ = empty space with
no st indicated

Woven squares

Work with a multiple of 9 stitches,
plus 3.
Rows 1, 3, and 5: K 3, * p 6, k 3 *;
repeat from * to *.
Row 2 and all even-numbered rows:
Work each stitch as it presents itself
on this side of work (k the k sts and
p the p sts).
Rows 7 and 9: P 3, * k 6, p 3 *;
repeat from * to *.
Repeat Rows 1 through 10 for
pattern.

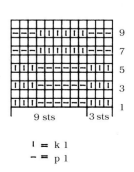

l = k 1
− = p 1

CLASSIC STITCHES

Garter stitch rib

Work on 3 stitches between 4- or
5-stitch panels of stockinette st.
Row 1: K 3.
Row 2: K 1, p 1, k 1.
Repeat these 2 rows for rib pattern.

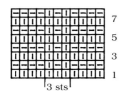

I = k 1
– = p 1

Stars

Work with a multiple of 8 stitches,
plus 2.
Rows 1 and 3 (right side): K 1, *
work (k 2 sts together) twice, k 4 *;
repeat from * to *, ending last repeat
with k 5.
Rows 2 and 4: P 5, * k 1, work
increase by picking up connecting
strand between stitches with tip of
needle and placing it on left needle to
knit a stitch on it (increase made),
k 1, make another increase as before,
p 4 *; repeat from * to *, ending last
repeat with p 1.
Rows 5 and 7: K 5, * work (k 2 sts
together) twice, k 4 *; repeat from * to
*, ending last repeat with k 1.
Rows 6 and 8: P 1, * work (k 1,
increase as before) twice, p 4 *; repeat
from * to *, ending last repeat with
p 5.
Repeat these 8 rows for pattern.

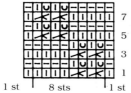

I = k 1
– = p 1
⌄ = k 2 tog

∪ = increase

CLASSIC STITCHES

Classic slip stitch rib

Work with a multiple of 3 stitches, plus 2.

Row 1: * P 2, k 1 *; repeat from * to *, ending p 2.

Row 2: K 2, * bring yarn forward, slip 1, return yarn to back, k 2 *; repeat from * to *.

Repeat these 2 rows for pattern.

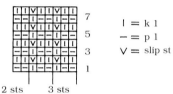

I = k 1
− = p 1
V = slip st

2 sts   3 sts

Raised bar stitch

Even number of stitches.

Rows 1 and 3: * K 1, p 1 *; repeat from * to *.

Row 2 and all even-numbered rows: Work each stitch as it appears on this side of work (k the k sts and p the p sts).

Rows 5 and 7: * P 1, k 1 *; repeat from * to *.

Repeat Rows 1 through 8 for pattern.

I = k 1
− = p 1
□ = 1 st as shown

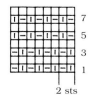

2 sts

CLASSIC STITCHES

Little peacock

Work with a multiple of 12 sts.
Row 1 (right side): Knit.
Rows 2 and 4: Purl.
Row 3: Work (k 2 sts together) twice,
* work (yarn over, k 1) 4 times, then
work (k 2 sts together) 4 times *;
repeat from * to *, ending last repeat
with k 2 sts together twice.
Row 5: Knit.
Repeat Rows 3 through 6 for pattern.

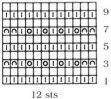

I = k 1
□ = p 1
O = yarn over
∩ = k 2 tog

12 sts

Diamond stitch

Work with a multiple of 3 stitches,
plus 2.
Row 1: * P 2, yarn over, k 1, yarn
over *; repeat from * to *, ending p
last 2 sts.
Row 2: Work yarn-over loops as
stitches. K 2, * p 3, k 2 *; repeat from
* to *.
Row 3: * P 2, k 3 *; repeat from * to
*, ending p last 2 sts.
Row 4: K 2, * p 3 sts together, k 2;
repeat from * to *.
Repeat these 4 rows for pattern.

I = k 1
— = p 1
O = yarn over
⌢ = = p 3 tog

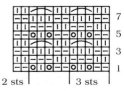

2 sts   3 sts

CLASSIC STITCHES

Creative stamps

Work with a multiple of 12 stitches, plus 7.

Rows 1 and 2 (moss stitch): K 1, * p 1, k 1 *; repeat from * to *.

Rows 3 and 4 (stockinette st): K 1 row, p 1 row.

Rows 5 and 11: K 7, * p 1, k 1, p 1, k 9 *; repeat from * to *, ending last repeat with k 8.

Rows 6 and 10: P 7, * work (k 1, p 1) twice, k 1, p 7 *; repeat from * to *.

Rows 7 and 9: K 6, * work (p 1, k 1) 3 times, p 1, k 5 *; repeat from * to *, ending last repeat with k 6.

Row 8: P 7, * work (k 1, p 1) twice, k 1, p 7 *; repeat from * to *.

Rows 12 and 16: Purl.

Rows 13 and 17: Knit.

Rows 14 and 15: Repeat Row 1.

Rows 18 and 24: P 2, *k 1, p 1, k 1, p 9 *; repeat from * to *, ending last repeat with p 2.

Rows 19 and 23: K 1, * work (p 1, k 1) twice, p 1, k 7 *; repeat from * to *, ending last repeat with k 1.

Rows 20 and 22: * Work (k 1, p 1) 3 times, k 1, p 5 *; repeat from * to *, ending last repeat with k 1.

Row 21: * Work (k 1, p 1) 3 times, * k 7, work (p 1, k 1) twice, p 1 *; repeat from * to *, ending k in last stitch.

Rows 25 and 26: Repeat Rows 3 and 4.

Repeat these 26 rows for pattern.

Little curls

Work with a multiple of 8 stitches, plus 1.

Rows 1, 3, 5, 9, and 11 (right side): Knit.

Row 2 and all even-numbered rows: Purl.

Row 7: K 3, * work curl on next 3 sts as follows: without dropping the stitches from left needle, p 3 together, then k the same 3 stitches together, then p them together again, drop the original stitches (curl made), k 5 *; repeat from * to *, ending last repeat with k 3.

Row 13: K 7, * work curl as before, k 5 *; repeat from * to *, ending last repeat with k 7.

Repeat Rows 3 through 14 for pattern.

1 = moss stitch
2 = stockinette st
l = k 1
− = p 1

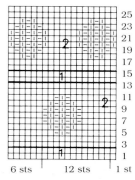

6 sts | 12 sts | 1 st

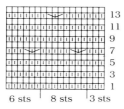

6 sts | 8 sts | 3 sts

l = k 1
⌣ = 1 curl
□ = p 1

CLASSIC STITCHES

Zigzag rib stitch

Work with a multiple of 10 stitches, plus 1.

Row 1: P 1, * k 1, p 1, work (k 2, p 1) twice, k 1, p 1 *; repeat from * to *.

Row 2: * K 1, p 2, work (k 1, p 1) twice, k 1, p 2 *; repeat from * to *, ending k in last st.

Row 3: P 1, * k 3, p 3, k 3, p 1 *; repeat from * to *.

Row 4: K 2, * p 3, k 1, p 3, k 3 *; repeat from * to *, ending last repeat with k 2.

Repeat these 4 rows for pattern.

```
7
5
3
1
```
10 sts   1 st

ı = k 1
− = p 1

Wedges

Work with a multiple of 8 stitches, plus 3.

Rows 1 and 5: P 3, * k 5, p 3 *; repeat from * to *.

Row 2 and all even-numbered rows: Work each stitch as it appears on this side of work (k the k sts and p the p sts).

Row 3: P 3, * k 2, p 1, k 2, p 3 *; repeat from * to *.

Rows 7 and 15: K 3, * p 1, k 3 *; repeat from * to *.

Rows 9 and 13: K 4, * p 3, k 5 *; repeat from * to *, ending last repeat with k 4.

Row 11: K 1, p 1, * k 2, p 3, k 2, p 1 *; repeat from * to *, k in last st. Repeat Rows 1 through 16 for pattern.

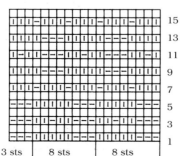

```
15
13
11
9
7
5
3
1
```
3 sts   8 sts   8 sts

ı = k 1
− = p 1
□ = 1 st as shown

CLASSIC STITCHES

Vertical columns of garter stitch

Work with a multiple of 6 stitches.
Row 1 (right side): * P 3, k 3 *;
repeat from * to *.
Row 2: Knit.
Repeat these 2 rows for pattern.

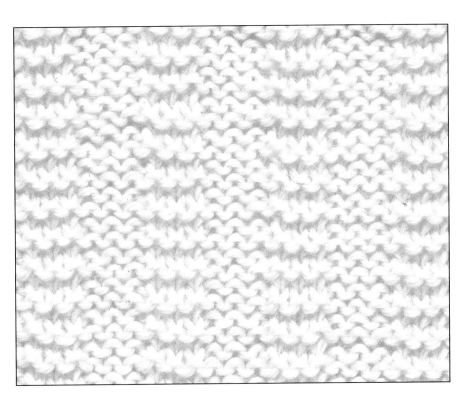

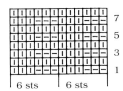

l = k 1
— = p 1

Diamonds

Work with multiple of 8 stitches, plus 1.
Row 1: Knit.
Row 2: Purl.
Row 3: K 4, * p 1, k 7 *; repeat from * to *, ending last repeat with k 4.
Rows 4 and 10: P 3, * k 1, p 1, k 1, p 5 *; repeat from * to *, ending last repeat with p 3.
Rows 5 and 9: K 2, * p 1, k 3 *; repeat from * to *; ending last repeat with k 2.
Rows 6 and 8: P 1, * k 1, p 5, k 1, p 1 *; repeat from * to *.
Row 7: P 1, * k 7, p 1 *; repeat from * to *.
Repeat Rows 3 through 10 for pattern.

l = k 1
— = p 1

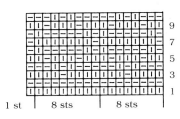

CLASSIC STITCHES

Heavy rain

Work with a multiple of 6 stitches, plus 4.

Row 1 (right side): P 4, * yarn over, p 2 sts together *; repeat from * to *.

Row 2 and all even-numbered rows: Work each as it appears on this side of work (k the k sts and p the p sts). Knit yarn-over loops.

Rows 3 and 5: P 4, * k 1, p 5 *; repeat from * to *.

Row 7: P 1, * yarn over, p 2 sts together, p 4 *; repeat from * to *, ending last repeat with p 1.

Rows 9 and 11: P 1, * k 1, p 5 *; repeat from * to *, ending last repeat with p 2.

Repeat Rows 1 through 12 for pattern.

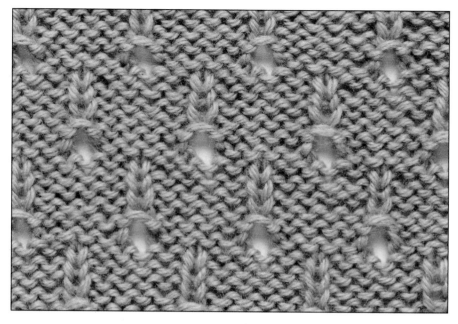

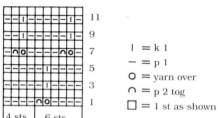

| = k 1
− = p 1
O = yarn over
∩ = p 2 tog
□ = 1 st as shown

Rods

Work with a multiple of 3 stitches.

Rows 1 and 3 (right side): Knit.

Row 2 and all even-numbered rows: Work each stitch as it appears on this side of work (k the k sts and p the p sts).

Rows 5 and 7: K 1, * p 1, k 2 *; repeat from * to *; ending last repeat with k 1.

Rows 9 and 11: * P 2, k 1 *; repeat from * to *.

Repeat Rows 1 through 12 for pattern.

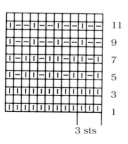

3 sts

| = k 1
− = p 1
□ = 1 st as shown

CLASSIC STITCHES

Labyrinth

Work with a multiple of 18 sts.
Rows 1 and 2 (stockinette st): K 1 row, p 1 row.
Rows 3, 5, 14, and 23: K 3, * p 3, k 15 *; repeat from * to *, ending last repeat with k 12.
Rows 4, 6, 13, 15, 22, and 24: P 12, * k 3, p 15 *; repeat from * to *, ending last repeat with p 3.
Rows 7, 9, 10, and 12: * K 3, p 15 *; repeat from * to *.
Rows 8 and 11: * K 15, p 3 *; repeat from * to *.
Rows 16, 18, 19, and 21: P 6, * k 3, p 15 *; repeat from * to *, ending last repeat with p 9.
Rows 17 and 20: K 9, * p 3, k 15 *; repeat from * to *, ending last repeat with k 6.
Repeat Rows 7 through 24 for pattern.

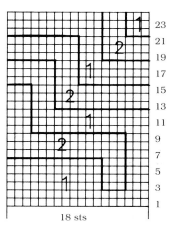

1 = stockinette stitch
2 = reverse stockinette st

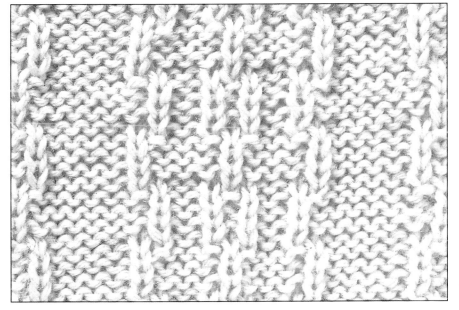

Triple chains

Work chains on 11 stitches. For pattern as shown, work chains between sections on reverse stockinette st.
Rows 1 and 3: P 1, k 1, p 2, k 1, p 1, k 1, p 2, k 1, p 1.
Rows 2, 4, and 10: K 1, p 1, k 2, p 1, k 1, p 1, k 2, p 1, k 1.
Rows 5 and 9: K 2, p 2, k 3, p 2, k 2.
Rows 6 and 8: P 1, work (k 4, p 1) twice.
Row 7: K 1, work (p 4, k 1) twice.
Repeat Rows 3 through 10 for pattern.

l = k 1
— = p 1

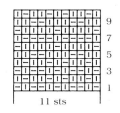

11 sts

CLASSIC STITCHES

Country flowers

Work with a multiple of 10 stitches, plus 3.

Row 1 (right side): P 5, * k 3, p 7 *; repeat from * to *, ending last repeat with p 7.

Row 2 and all even-numbered rows: Work each stitch as it appears on this side of work (k the k sts and p the p sts). Purl bobble st.

Row 3: P 4, * work right cross on 2 sts as follows: skip 1 st, k next st, then p skipped st, drop original sts from left needle, (right cross made), k 1, work left cross on 2 sts as follows: slip 1 st to dp needle and hold in front of work, p next st, then k from dp needle (left cross made), p 5 *; repeat from * to *, ending last repeat with p 4.

Row 5: P 3, * right cross, p 1, work bobble as follows: knit, purl, knit, purl, and knit all in next st; turn work, p 5 sts just made, turn, k 5, turn, p 5, turn, slip 4 sts to right needle without working them, k last bobble st, then pass slip sts one at a time over this last bobble st and drop them (one bobble st remains and bobble is made), p 1, left cross, p 3 *; repeat from * to *.

Row 7: K 3, * p 7, k 3 *; repeat from * to *.

Row 9: K 2, * left cross, p 5, right cross, k 1 *; repeat from * to *, ending last repeat with k 2.

Row 11: K 1, * work bobble, p 1, left cross, p 3, right cross, p 1 *; repeat

from * to *, ending with bobble, k last st.

Repeat Rows 1 through 12 for pattern.

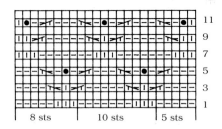

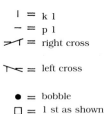

l	= k 1
−	= p 1
⊐⊤	= right cross
⊤⊏	= left cross
●	= bobble
□	= 1 st as shown

Bows in columns

Work with a multiple of 9 stitches, plus 2.

Row 1 (right side): Knit.

Row 2 and all even-numbered rows: K 2, * p 7, k 2 *; repeat from * to *.

Row 3: K 4, * work bow on 3 sts as follows: k 3 together without dropping them from left needle, yarn over and again k same 3 stitches together, dropping original sts (bow made), k 6 * repeat from * to *, ending last repeat with k 4.

Repeat Rows 1 through 4 for pattern.

l	= k 1
−	= p 1
⋎	= bow

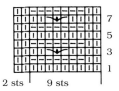

CLASSIC STITCHES

Flame motif

Work with a multiple of 8 stitches.
Row 1 (right side): * K 1, p 7 *; repeat from * to *.
Row 2 and all even-numbered rows: Work each stitch as it appears on this side of work (k the k sts and p the p sts).
Row 3: K 2, * p 5, k 3 *; repeat from * to *, ending last repeat with k 1.
Row 5: K 3, * p 3, k 5 *; repeat from * to *, ending last repeat with k 2.
Row 7: K 4, * p 1, k 7 *; repeat from * to *, ending last repeat with k 3.
Row 9: * P 1, k 7 *; repeat from * to *.
Row 11: P 2, * k 5, p 3 *; repeat from * to *, ending last repeat with p 1.
Row 13: P 3, * k 3, p 5 *; repeat from * to *, ending last repeat with p 2.
Row 15: P 4, * k 1, p 7 *; repeat from * to *, ending last repeat with p 3.
Repeat Rows 1 through 16 for pattern.

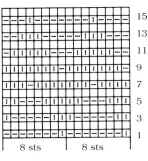

| = k 1
— = p 1
□ = 1 st as shown

Flat diamonds

Work with a multiple of 11 stitches.
Row 1 (right side): P 4, * k in back loop of next st (twisted k st made), work 2 more twisted k sts, p 8 *; repeat from * to *, ending last repeat with p 4.
Row 2 and all even-numbered rows: Work each stitch as it appears on this side of work (k the k sts and p the p sts). *Note*: Work each p st in back loop (twisted p st).
Rows 3 and 11: P 3, * k 5 twisted sts, p 6 *; repeat from * to *, ending last repeat with p 3.
Rows 5 and 9: P 2, * k 3 twisted sts, p 1, k 3 twisted sts, p 4 *; repeat from * to *, ending last repeat with p 2.
Row 7: P 1, * k 3 twisted sts, p 3, k 3 twisted sts, p 2 *; repeat from * to *, ending last repeat with p 1.
Repeat Rows 1 through 12 for pattern.

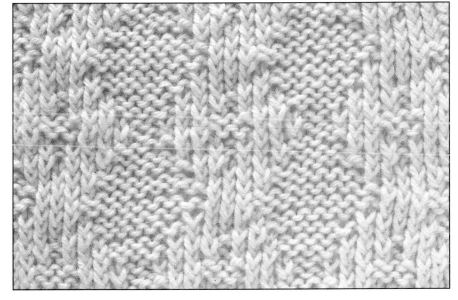

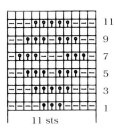

⚲ = 1 twisted st
— = p 1
□ = 1 st as shown

CLASSIC STITCHES

Pennants

Work with a multiple of 8 stitches.
Note: To work moss st, always p over k st (as it faces you) and k over p st.
Row 1 (right side): * P 1 (moss st), k 7 *; repeat from * to *.
Row 2: * P 6, k 1, p 1 (2 moss sts) *; repeat from * to *.
Row 3: * P 1, k 1, p 1 (3 moss sts), k 5 *; repeat from * to *.
Row 4: * P 4, work (k 1, p 1) twice (4 moss sts) *; repeat from * to *.
Row 5: * P1, work (k 1, p 1) twice (5 moss sts), k 3 *; repeat from * to *.
Row 6: * P 2, work (k 1, p 1) 3 times (6 moss sts) *; repeat from * to *.
Row 7: * P 1, work (k 1, p 1) 3 times (7 moss sts), k 1 *; repeat from * to *.
Row 8: * K 1, p 1 *; repeat from * to *.
Repeat these 8 rows for pattern.

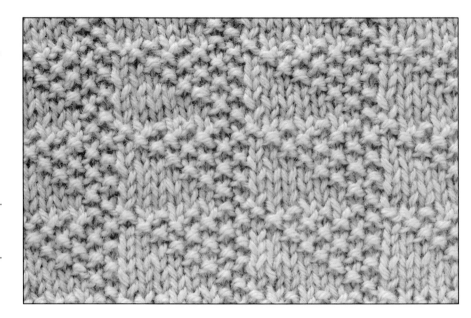

= k 1
= p 1
= moss st

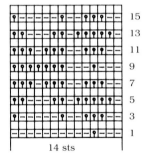

= 1 twisted st
= p 1
= 1 st as shown

Variations on a theme

Work on a multiple of 14 stitches.
Row 1 (right side): P 3, * k next st in back loop (twisted k st made), p 13 *; repeat from * to *, ending last repeat with p 10.
Row 2 and all even-numbered rows: Work each stitch as it appears on this side of work (k the k sts and p the p sts). *Note*: Work each p st in back loop (twisted p st).
Rows 3 and 15: * P 2, work 3 twisted k sts, p 2, work 1 twisted k st, p 5, work 1 twisted k st *; repeat from * to *.
Rows 5 and 13: * P 1, work 5 twisted k sts, p 1, work 2 twisted k sts, p 3, work 2 twisted k sts *; repeat from * to *.
Row 7 and 11: * P 2, work 3 twisted k sts, p 2, work 3 twisted k sts, p 1, work 3 twisted k sts *; repeat from * to *.
Row 9: * P 3, work 1 twisted k st, p 3, work 7 twisted k sts *; repeat from * to *.
Repeat Rows 1 through 16 for pattern.

CLASSIC STITCHES

Double pennants

Work with a multiple of 13 stitches.
Rows 1 and 9 (right side): K 1, *
p 4, k 3, p 4, k 2 *; repeat from * to *,
ending last repeat with k 1.
Rows 2 and 8: P 2, * k 3, p 3, k 3,
p 4 *; repeat from * to *, ending last
repeat with p 2.
Rows 3 and 7: K 3, * p 2, k 3, p 2,
k 6 *; repeat from * to *, ending last
repeat with k 3.
Rows 4 and 6: P 4, * k 1, p 3, k 1,
p 8 *; repeat from * to *, ending last
repeat with p 4.
Row 5: Knit.
Row 10: P 5, * p 3, k 10 *; repeat
from * to *, ending last repeat with
k 5.
Repeat these 10 rows for pattern.

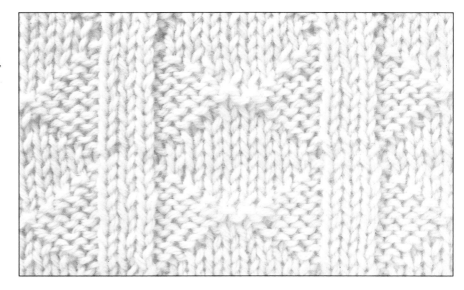

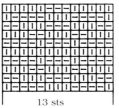

I = k 1
— = p 1

13 sts

Camping

Work with a multiple of 8 stitches.
Row 1: * K 1, p 3 *; repeat from * to
*.
Row 2: * K 1, p 5, k 1, p 1 *; repeat
from * to *.
Row 3: K 2, * p 1, k 3 *; repeat from
* to *, ending last repeat with k 1.
Row 4: P 2, * k 1, p 1, k 1, p 5 *;
repeat from * to *, ending last repeat
with k 3.
Repeat these 4 rows for pattern.

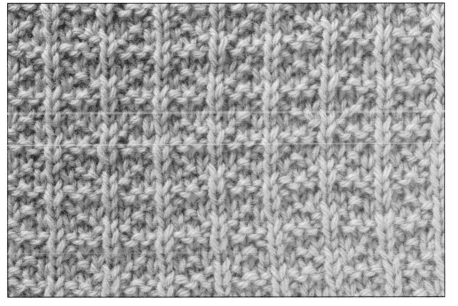

I = k 1
— = p 1

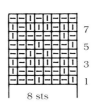

8 sts

CLASSIC STITCHES

Moving rib stitches

Work with a multiple of 5 stitches, plus 1.

Row 1 (wrong side): Knit.

Rows 2 and 4: * K 2, p 3 *; repeat from * to *, ending k in last st.

Row 3: P 1, * k 3, p 2 *; repeat from * to *.

Row 5: Knit.

Rows 6 and 8: P 1, * k 2, p 3 *; repeat from * to *.

Row 7: * K 3, p 2 *; repeat from * to *.

Repeat Rows 1 through 8 for pattern.

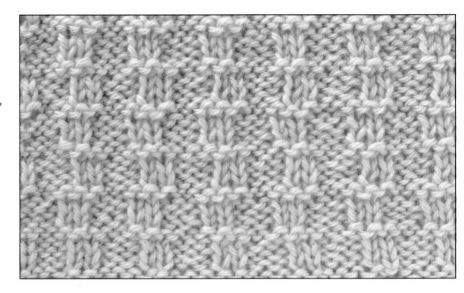

| = k 1
— = p 1

5 sts

| = k 1
⌣ = 1 knot
□ = p 1

Knotted butterflies

Work with a multiple of 12 stitches, plus 2.

Rows 1 and 9: K 2, * work knot on 2 sts as follows: p 2, then slip these 2 p sts back onto left needle, pass yarn to the left in front of same sts and return yarn to back of work, slip 2 sts back onto right needle (yarn will wrap around sts to make knot); k 6, make knot on 2 sts as before, k 2 *; repeat from * to *.

Row 2 and all even-numbered rows: Purl.

Rows 3 and 7: K 2, * work knot on 2 sts twice, k 2 *; repeat from * to *.

Row 5: * K 2, work knot on 2 sts 5 times *; repeat from * to *, ending k last 2 sts.

Row 11: Knit.

Repeat Rows 1 through 12 for pattern.

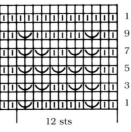

12 sts

CLASSIC STITCHES

Simple switchgear

Work with a multiple of 18 stitches, plus 9.

Rows 1 and 7 (right side): K 2, * work (p 1, k 1) twice, p 1, k 4, work (p 1, k 1) twice, p 1, k 4 *; repeat from * to *, ending (p 1, k 1) twice, p 1, k 2.

Row 2 and all even-numbered rows: Work each stitch as it appears on this side of work (k the k sts and p the p sts).

Rows 3 and 5: * K 2, work (p 1, k 1) twice, p 1, k 2, p 9 *; repeat from * to *, ending last repeat with k 2.

Rows 9 and 11: * P 9, k 2, work (p 1, k 1) twice, p 1, k 2 *; repeat from * to *, ending p 9.

Repeat Rows 1 through 12 for pattern.

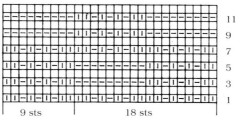

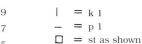

| = k 1
− = p 1
□ = st as shown

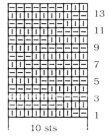

| = k 1
− = p 1

Steering sails

Work with a multiple of 10 stitches.

Row 1 (right side): * P 2, k 8 *; repeat from * to *.

Rows 2, 12, and 14: * P 7, k 3 *; repeat from * to *.

Rows 3 and 11: * P 4, k 6 *; repeat from * to *.

Rows 4 and 10: * P 5, k 5 *; repeat from * to *.

Rows 5 and 9: * P 6, k 4 *; repeat from * to *.

Rows 6 and 8: * P 3, k 7 *; repeat from * to *.

Row 7: * P 8, k 2 *; repeat from * to *.

Row 13: * P 2, k 8 *; repeat from * to *.

Repeat Rows 3 through 14 for pattern.

CLASSIC STITCHES

Mosaic

Work with a multiple of 22 stitches.
Rows 1, 4, 6, and 9: * P 5, k 1, p 5, k 2, p 7, k 2 *; repeat from * to *.
Rows 2, 3, 7, 8, and 10: * P 3, k 5, work (p 3, k 4) twice *; repeat from * to *.
Row 5: * P 1, k 9, p 1, k 11 *; repeat from * to *.
Repeat Rows 3 through 10 for pattern.

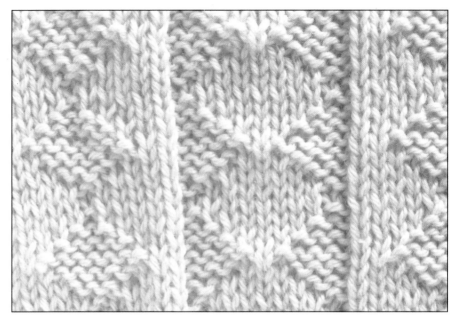

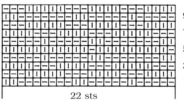

| = k 1
− = p 1

Furrows

Work with a multiple of 6 stitches, plus 3.
Rows 1 and 3: P 3, * k 1, slip 1, k 1, p 3 *; repeat from * to *.
Row 2 and all even-numbered rows: Work each stitch as it appears on this side of work (k the k sts and p the p sts).
Rows 5 and 7: K 4, * slip 1, k 5 *; repeat from * to *, ending last repeat with k 4.
Repeat Rows 1 through 8 for pattern.

| = k 1
− = p 1
V = 1 slip st
□ = 1 st as shown

CLASSIC STITCHES

Simple checker

Work with a multiple of 8 stitches.
Rows 1 through 5: * K 4, p 4 *;
repeat from * to *.
Rows 6 through 10: *P 4, k 4 *;
repeat from * to *.
Repeat these 10 rows for pattern.

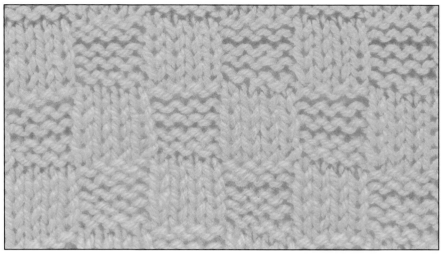

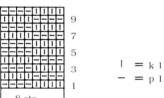

| = k 1
− = p 1

8 sts

Large tiles

Work with a multiple of 15 stitches.
Row 1: Purl.
Rows 2, 4, 6, 8, 10, 12, 14, and 18:
Work each stitch as it appears on this
side of work (k the k sts and p the p
sts).
Rows 3, 7, and 11: * K 2, work (p 1,
k 1) 4 times, p 1, k 2, p 2 *; repeat
from * to *.
Rows 5 and 9: * K 3, work (p 1, k 1)
3 times, p 1, k 3, p 2 *; repeat from *
to *.
Rows 13 and 15: * K 2, p 13 *;
repeat from * to *.
Rows 16 and 20: Purl.
Rows 17 and 19: P 11, * k 2, p 13 *;
repeat from * to *, ending last repeat
with p 2.
Repeat Rows 3 through 20 for
pattern.

| = k 1
− = p 1

15 sts

37

CLASSIC STITCHES

Mirrored bars

Work with a multiple of 8 stitches.
Row 1: Knit.
Row 2: * K 4, p 4 *; repeat from
* to *.
Row 3: K 3, * p 4, k 4 *; repeat from
* to *, ending last repeat with k 1.
Row 4: P 2, * k 4, p 4 *; repeat from
* to *, ending last repeat with p 2.
Row 5: K 1, * p 4, k 4 *; repeat from
* to *, ending last repeat with k 3.
Row 6: Purl.
Row 7: Knit.
Row 8: P 3, * k 4, p 4 *; repeat from
* to *, ending last repeat with p 1.
Row 9: K 2, * p 4, k 4 *; repeat from
* to *, ending last repeat with k 2.
Row 10: P 1 * k 4, p 4 *; repeat from
* to *, ending last repeat with p 3.
Row 11: * K 4, p 4 *; repeat from
* to *.
Row 12: Purl.
Repeat these 12 rows for pattern.

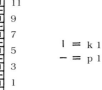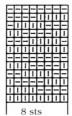

```
      ==-----IIIII  11
      =IIIII----==   9
      II==----=II    7
      IIII====III    5
      I==----=III    3
      IIIII----==    1
      IIIII----==
          8 sts
```

I = k 1
− = p 1

Squares and rectangles

Work with a multiple of 12 stitches.
Rows 1 and 11: K 2, * p 6, k 6 *;
repeat from * to *, ending last repeat
with k 4.
Row 2 and all even-numbered rows:
Work each stitch as it appears on this
side of work (k the k sts and p the p
sts).
Rows 3, 5, 7, and 9: * P 2, k 6, p 2,
k 2 *; repeat from * to *.
Row 13: Knit.
Repeat Rows 1 through 14 for
pattern.

I = k 1
− = p 1
□ = 1 st as shown

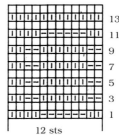

```
     IIIIIIIIIIII  13
     II==------II  11
     II==IIIIII==   9
     II==IIIIII==   7
     II==IIIIII==   5
     II==IIIIII==   3
     IIII======II   1
        12 sts
```

CLASSIC STITCHES

Stepped motifs

Work with a multiple of 16 stitches.

Rows 1 and 2 (stockinette st): K 1 row, p 1 row.

Row 3: K 3, * work 3-st right cross as follows: slip 1 st to dp needle and hold in back, p 2, k 1 from dp needle; k 13 *; repeat from * to *, ending with k 10.

Rows 4, 6, 8, and 10: Purl.

Row 5: K 2, * work right cross, k 13 *; repeat from * to *; ending with k 11.

Row 7: K 1, * right cross, k 13 *; repeat from * to *, ending with k 12.

Row 9: * Work right cross, k 13 *; repeat from * to *.

Rows 11 through 22: Work in stockinette st.

Row 23: K 11, * right cross, k 13 *; repeat from * to *, ending with k 2.

Rows 24, 26, 28, and 30: Purl.

Row 25: K 10, * right cross, k 13 *; repeat from * to *, ending with k 3.

Row 27: K 9, * right cross, k 13 *; repeat from * to *, ending with k 4.

Row 29: K 8 * right cross, k 13 *; repeat from * to *, ending with k 5.

Rows 31 through 40: Work in stockinette st.

Repeat these 40 rows for pattern.

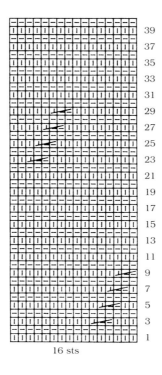

16 sts

| = k 1
− = p 1
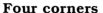 = 3-st right cross

Four corners

Work with a multiple of 10 stitches.

Rows 1 and 3: K 3, * p 2, k 8 *; repeat from * to *, ending last repeat with k 5.

Row 2 and all even-numbered rows: Work each stitch as it appears on this side of work (k the k sts and p the p sts).

Rows 5 and 7: * K 3, p 7 *; repeat from * to *.

Rows 9 and 11: * P 7, k 3 *; repeat from * to *.

Rows 13 and 15: K 5, * p 2, k 8 *; repeat from * to *, ending last repeat with k 3.

Row 17: Knit.

Repeat Rows 1 through 18 for pattern.

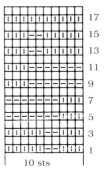

10 sts

| = k 1
− = p 1
☐ = 1 st as shown

CLASSIC STITCHES

Climbing

Work with a multiple of 8 stitches.
Row 1: * K 6, p 2 *; repeat from * to *.
Rows 2, 4, and 6: Work each stitch as it appears on this side of work (k the k sts and p the p sts).
Row 3: K 5, * p 2, k 6 *; repeat from * to *, ending last repeat with k 1.
Row 5: K 4, * p 2, k 6 *; repeat from * to *, ending last repeat with k 2.
Row 7: K 3, * p 2, k 6 *; repeat from * to *, ending last repeat with k 3.
Row 8: Knit.
Repeat these 8 rows for pattern.

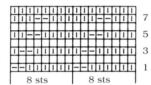

| = k 1
− = p 1
□ = 1 st as shown

Alternating wedges

Work with a multiple of 16 sts.
Note: To work moss st, always k over a p st (as it faces you) and p over a k st.
Row 1: P 1(moss st), k 7, work (p 1, k 1) 3 times, p 1 (7 moss sts), k 1.
Row 2: * P 2, work (k 1, p 1) 3 times (6 moss sts), p 6, k 1, p 1 (2 moss sts) *; repeat from * to *.
Rows 3 and 11: * Work moss st on 3 sts, k 5, moss st on 5 sts, k 3 *; repeat from * to *.
Rows 4 and 10: * P 4, moss st on 4 sts *; repeat from * to *.
Rows 5 and 9: * Moss st on 5 sts, k 3, moss st on 3 sts, k 5 * repeat from * to *.
Rows 6 and 8: * P 6, moss st on 2 sts, p 2, moss st on 6 sts *; repeat from * to *.
Row 7: * Moss st on 7 sts, k 1, moss st on 1 st, k 7 *; repeat from * to *.
Repeat Rows 1 through 12 for pattern.

| = k 1
− = p 1
● = 1 moss st

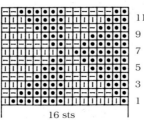

CLASSIC STITCHES

Twisted stitch pattern

Work with a multiple of 13 stitches, plus 10.

Note: K or p in back loop for twisted st.

Row 1: P 2, k 6, p 1, * work (2 twisted k sts, p 1) twice, k 6, p 1*; repeat from * to *, ending with p 2.

Rows 2 and 4: K 2, *work (bring yarn forward to slip 1, yarn over, k 1) twice, slip 1 as before, yarn over, k 2, work (2 twisted p sts, k 1) twice *; repeat from * to *, ending with k in last 3 sts.

Row 3: P 2, * k 1, work (k 2 sts together through back loops, k 1) twice, k 2 together through back loops, p 1, work (2 twisted k sts, p 1) twice *; repeat from * to *, ending with p in last 2 sts.

Repeat Rows 3 and 4 for pattern.

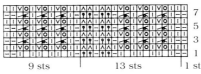

I = k 1	∧ = twisted p st
— = p 1	⊀ = k 2 tog
ⴹ = twisted k st	
O = yarn over	□ = empty square with
V = 1 slip st	no st indicated

9 sts   13 sts   1 st

Composition

Work with a multiple of 16 stitches, plus 1.

Note: To work moss st, always k over p st (as it faces you) and p over k st.

Row 1: K 1, * work (p 1, k 1) 3 times, p 1 (7 moss sts), k 1, p 7, k 1*; repeat from * to *.

Row 2 and all even-numbered rows: Working moss st over moss sts of previous row, work each remaining st as it appears (k the k sts and p the p sts).

Row 3: K 2, * work 5 moss sts, k 3, p 5, k 3 *; repeat from * to *, ending last repeat with k 2.

Row 5: K 3, * work 3 moss sts, k 5, p 3, k 5 *; repeat from * to *, ending k 3.

Row 7: K 4, * work 1 moss st, k 7, p 1, k 7 *; repeat from * to *, ending k 4.

Row 9: K 4 * p 1, k 7, p 1 (1 moss st), k 7 *; repeat from * to *, ending k 4.

Row 11: K 3, * p 3, k 5, work 3 moss sts, k 5 *; repeat from * to *, ending k 3.

Row 13: K 2, * p 5, k 3, work 5 moss sts, k 3 *; repeat from * to *, ending k 2.

Row 15: K 1, * p 7, k 1, work 7 moss sts, k 1 *; repeat from * to *.

Repeat Rows 1 through 16 for pattern.

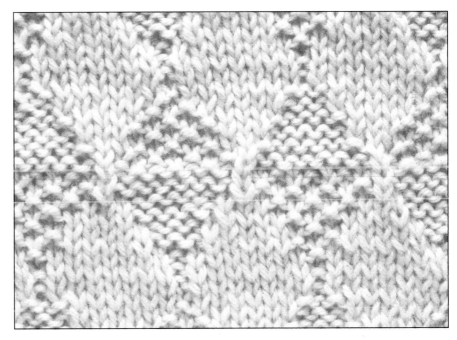

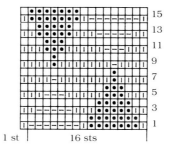

I = k 1	
— = p 1	
• = 1 moss st	
□ = 1 st as shown	

1 st   16 sts

CLASSIC STITCHES

Duet

Work with a multiple of 6 stitches.
Row 1: P 1, * work left cross on 2 sts as follows: take yarn to back of work, slip 2 sts, with tip of left needle pass first slipped st over the 2nd and drop it, return remaining st to left needle and k it through front loop, then back loop (left cross made); work right cross on 2 sts as follows: on left needle, pass 2nd st over first st keeping the passed st on tip of right needle, yarn over right needle, then pass first (which is the passed st from left needle) over the yarn-over loop to make a knit st on right needle, k next st on left needle (right cross made); p 2 *; repeat from * to *, ending last repeat with p 1.
Row 2: K 1, * p 4, k 2 *; repeat from * to *, ending last repeat with k 1. Repeat these 2 rows for pattern.

- = p 1
| = k 1
⋉ = left cross
⋊ = right cross

Mini tulips

Work with a multiple of 10 stitches, plus 1.
Note: To work moss st, k over p st (as it faces you) and p over k st.
Row 1: P 5, * k 1, p 9 *; repeat from * to *; ending last repeat with p 5.
Row 2 and all even-numbered rows: Working moss st over moss st, work each remaining stitch as it appears on this side of work (k the k sts and p the p sts).
Row 3: P 4, * k 3, p 7 *; repeat from * to *, ending with k 4.
Row 5: P 3, * k 5, p 5 *; repeat from * to *, ending with k 3.
Row 7: P 2, * k 3, p 1, k 3, p 3 *; repeat from * to *, ending with k 2.
Row 9: P 1, * k 3, p 3, k 3, p 1 *; repeat from * to *.
Row 11: K 3, * p 2, k 1 (moss st), p 2, k 5 * repeat from * to *, ending with k 3.
Row 13: P 1, k 1, p 2, work 3 moss sts, p 2, k 1 *; repeat from * to *, ending p 1.
Row 15: P 2, * k 1, work 5 moss sts, k 1, p 3 *; repeat from * to *, ending p 2.
Row 17: P 3, * k 1, work 3 moss sts, k 1, p 5 *; repeat from * to *, ending p 3.
Row 19: P 4, * k 1, work 1 moss st, k 1, p 7 *; repeat from * to *, ending p 4.
Repeat Rows 1 through 20 for pattern.

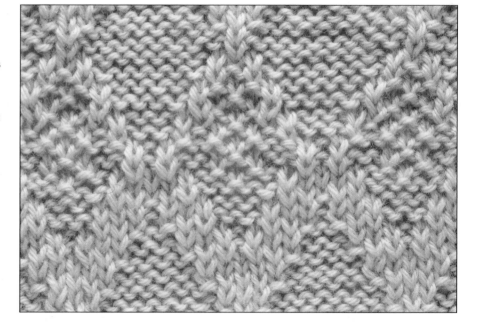

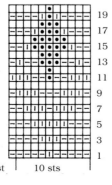

| = k 1
- = p 1
● = 1 moss st

☐ = 1 st as shown

CLASSIC STITCHES

Ears of corn

Work with a multiple of 6 stitches.
Rows 1 and 3: * K 3, p 3 *; repeat from * to *.
Row 2 and all even-numbered rows: Work each stitch as it appears on this side of work (k the k sts and p the p sts).
Row 5: * K 1, work left cross on 4 sts as follows: slip 2 sts to dp needle and hold in front of work, k next 2 sts, then p 2 sts from dp needle (left cross made); p 1 *; repeat from * to *.
Repeat Rows 1 through 6 for pattern.

| = k 1
− = p 1
4-st left cross
□ = 1 st as shown

Distant towers

Work with a multiple of 8 stitches, plus 1.
Row 1: K 1, * yarn over, p 2 sts together, p 6 *; repeat from * to *.
Rows 2, 4, 6, 12, 14 and 16: Work each stitch as it appears on this side of work (k the k sts and p the p sts).
Rows 3, 5, and 7: K 2, * p 7, k 1 *; repeat from * to *, ending last repeat with p 7.
Rows 8 and 18: Purl.
Rows 9 and 19: Knit.
Rows 10 and 20: Purl.
Row 11: K 1, p 4, * yarn over, p 2 together, p 6; repeat from * to *, ending last repeat with p 2.
Rows 13, 15, and 17: K 1, p 4, * k 1, p 7 *; repeat from * to *, ending last repeat with p 3.
Repeat Rows 1 through 20 for pattern.

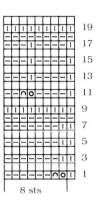

| = k 1
− = p 1
O = yarn over
∩ = p 2 tog

□ = 1 st as shown

CLASSIC STITCHES

Ribbons

Work with a multiple of 18 stitches, plus 9.

Rows 1 and 7: * K 9, p 9 *; repeat from * to *, ending k last 9 sts.

Row 2 and all even-numbered rows: Work each stitch as it appears on this side of work (k the k sts and p the p sts).

Rows 3, 5, 13, and 15: Knit.

Row 9: * K 13, work long loop as follows: insert right needle into stitch 8 rows below next stitch and k 1, drawing up long loop, transfer loop to left needle and knit it together with the next stitch on needle (long loop made); k 17 *; repeat from * to *, ending last repeat with k 13.

Rows 11 and 17: * P 9, k 9 *; repeat from * to *, ending p last 9 sts.

Row 19: K 4, * work long loop as before in next st, k 17 *; repeat from * to *, ending last repeat with k 4. Repeat Rows 1 through 20 for pattern.

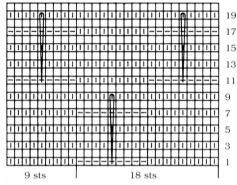

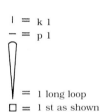

```
| = k 1
- = p 1
⌄ = 1 long loop
□ = 1 st as shown
```

Clasped rolls

Work with a multiple of 12 stitches, plus 2.

Rows 1, 3, 9, and 11 (right side of work): Purl.

Rows 2 and 10: Knit.

Rows 4, 6, and 8: * P 10, slip 2 with yarn forward *; repeat from * to *, ending p last 2 sts.

Rows 5 and 7: K 2, * slip 2 with yarn at back, k 10 *; repeat from * to *.

Rows 12, 14, and 16: P 4, * slip 2 with yarn forward, p 10 *; repeat from * to *, ending last repeat with p 8.

Rows 13 and 15: K 8, * slip 2 with yarn at back, k 10 *; repeat from * to *, ending last repeat with k 4. Repeat Rows 1 through 16 for pattern.

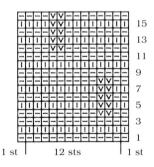

```
| = k 1
- = p 1
V = 1 slip st
```

44

CLASSIC STITCHES

Direction north

Work with a multiple of 24 stitches, plus 1.

Row 1 (right side): Knit.

Rows 2, 4, and 6: K 11, * p 3, k 21 *; repeat from * to *, ending last repeat with k 11.

Row 3 and all odd-numbered rows: K the k sts (as they face you) and p the p sts.

Row 8: K 7, * p 1, k 3, p 3, k 3, p 1, k 13 *; repeat from * to *, ending with k 7.

Row 10: K 7, * p 2, k 2, p 3, k 2, p 2, k 13 *; repeat from * to *, ending with k 7.

Row 12: K 7, * p 3, work (k 1, p 3) twice, k 13 *; repeat from * to *, ending with k 7.

Row 14: K 7, * p 4, k 1, p 1, k 1, p 4, k 13 *; repeat from * to *, ending with k 7.

Row 16: K 8, * p 3, k 1, p 1, k 1, p 3, k 15 *; repeat from * to *, ending with k 8.

Row 18: K 9, * p 3, k 1, p 3, k 17 *; repeat from * to *, ending with k 9.

Row 20: K 10, * p 5, k 19 *; repeat from * to *, ending with k 10.

Row 22: K 11, * p 3, k 21 *; repeat

from * to *, ending with k 11.

Row 24: K 12, * p 1, k 23 *; repeat from * to *, ending with k 12.

Rows 26 and 28: Knit.

Repeat these 28 rows for pattern.

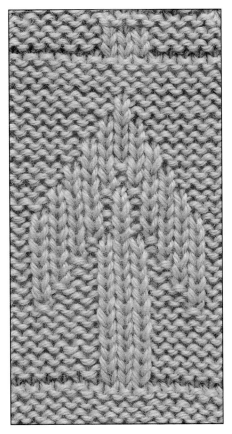

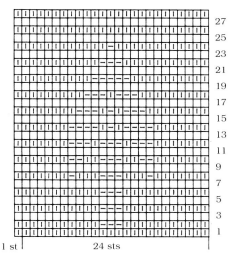

l = k 1

— = p 1

□ = 1 st as shown

Easy squares

Work with a multiple of 12 sts, plus 10.

Note: To work moss st, always k over p st (as it faces you) and p over k st.

Rows 1, 3, 5, 7, 9, and 11: K 10, * p 1, k 1 (2 moss sts), k 10 *; repeat from * to *.

Rows 2, 4, 6, 8, 10, and 12: P 10, * k 1, p 1 (2 moss sts), p 10 *; repeat from * to *.

Rows 13 and 14: Work in moss st.

Repeat these 14 rows for pattern.

l = k 1

• = moss st

□ = p 1

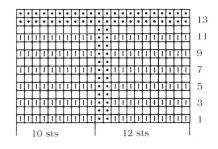

45

CLASSIC STITCHES

Jewel

Work with a multiple of 6 stitches, plus 5.

Rows 1, 3, 5, 11, 13, and 15: Knit.

Rows 2, 4, 6, 12, 14, and 16: Purl.

Rows 7 and 9: K 1, * p 1, slip 1 with yarn at back of work, p 1, k 3 *; repeat from * to *, ending last repeat with k 1.

Row 8: P 1, * k 3, p 3 *; repeat from * to *, ending k 3, p 1.

Row 10: Work (p 1, k 1) twice, * p 3, k 1, p 1, k 1 *; repeat from * to *, ending p 1.

Rows 17 and 19: P 1, k 3, p 1, * slip 1 with yarn at back, p 1, k 3, p 1 *; repeat from * to *.

Row 18: K 1, p 3, * k 3, p 3 *; repeat from * to *, ending k in last st.

Row 20: K 1, p 3, *k 1, p 1, k 1, p 3 *; repeat from * to *, ending k in last st.

Repeat these 20 rows for pattern.

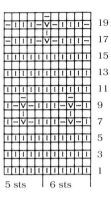

5 sts	6 sts

| = k 1
− = p 1
V = slip st
□ = 1 st as shown

Arabesque

Work with a multiple of 6 stitches, plus 1.

Rows 1 and 3: P 3, * k 1, p 5 *; repeat from * to *, ending k 1, p 3.

Row 2 and all even-numbered rows: Work each stitch as it appears on this side of work (k the k sts, p the p sts).

Rows 5, 7, 21, and 23: P 2, * k 1, p 1, k 1, p 3 *; repeat from * to *, ending last repeat with p 2.

Rows 9, 11, 17, and 19: P 1, * k 1, p 3, k 1, p 1 *; repeat from * to *.

Rows 13 and 15: K 1, * p 5, k 1 *; repeat from * to *.

Repeat Rows 1 through 24 for pattern.

1st	6 sts	6 sts

| = k 1
− = p 1
□ = 1 st as shown

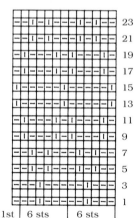

46

CLASSIC STITCHES

Staves

Work with a multiple of 18 stitches, plus 10.

Rows 1 and 5: K 11, * p 2, k 2 in back loop (k 2 twisted sts made), p 2, k 12 *; repeat from * to *, ending with k 11.

Rows 2 and 6: P 1, * k 8, p 2, k 2, p 2 in back loop (p 2 twisted sts made), k 2, p 2 *; repeat from * to *, ending k 8, p 1.

Rows 3 and 7: K 1, * p 8, k 2, p 2, k 2 twisted sts, p 2, k 2 *; repeat from * to *, ending p 8, k 1.

Rows 4 and 8: P 11, * k 2, p 2 twisted sts, k 2, p 12 *; repeat from * to *, ending last repeat with p 11.

Row 9: Knit.

Row 10: Work (p 2, k 2) twice, * p 12, k 2, p 2, k 2 *; repeat from * to *, ending with p 2.

Rows 11 and 15: * K 2, p 2, k 2 twisted sts, p 2, k 2, p 8 *; repeat from * to *, ending last repeat with k 2.

Rows 12 and 16: * P 2, k 2, p 2 twisted sts, k 2, p 2, k 8 *; repeat from * to *, ending last repeat with p 2.

Rows 13 and 17: * K 2, p 2, k 2 twisted sts, p 2, k 12 *; repeat from * to *, ending last repeat with k 2.

Row 14: P 2, * k 2, p 2 twisted sts, k 2, p 12 *; repeat from * to *, ending last repeat with p 2.

Row 18: Purl.
Repeat these 18 rows for pattern.

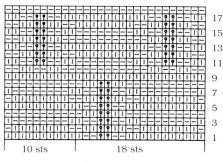

| | = k 1 |
| − = p 1 |
| ꝑ = 1 twisted st |

Quadrille

Work with a multiple of 16 stitches.
Note: To work moss st, always k over p st (as it faces you) and p over k st.

Rows 1, 7, 13, and 19: Knit.

Row 2 and all even-numbered rows: Working moss st over moss sts, work each remaining stitch as it appears on this side of work (k the k sts and p the p sts).

Rows 3 and 5: * K 5, work (p 1, k 1) 5 times, p 1 (11 sts worked in moss st) *; repeat from * to *.

Rows 9 and 11: Work (p 1, k 1) twice (4 moss sts), * k 5, work (k 1, p 1) 5 times, k 1 (11 moss sts) *; repeat from * to *, ending last repeat with 7 moss sts.

Rows 15 and 17: Work 8 moss sts, * k 5, work 11 moss sts *; repeat from * to *, ending k 5, work 3 moss sts.

Rows 21 and 23: K 1, * work 11 moss sts, k 5 *; repeat from * to *, ending last repeat with k 4.
Repeat Rows 1 through 24 for pattern.

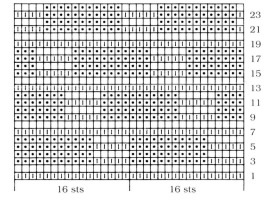

| | = k 1 |
| • = 1 moss st |
| □ = p 1 |

CLASSIC STITCHES

Foliage

Work with a multiple of 6 stitches.
Row 1: * K 4, p 2 *; repeat from
* to *.
Row 2 and all even-numbered rows:
Work each stitch as it appears on this
side of work (k the k sts and p the p
sts).
Row 3: * K 3, p 3 *; repeat from
* to *.
Row 5: * K 2, p 4 *; repeat from
* to *.
Row 7: K 1, * p 4, k 2 *; repeat from
* to *, ending last repeat with k 1.
Row 9: K 1, * p 3, k 3 *; repeat from
* to *, ending last repeat with k 2.
Row 11: K 1, * p 2, k 4 *; repeat from
* to *, ending last repeat with k 3.
Repeat Rows 1 through 12 for
pattern.

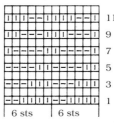

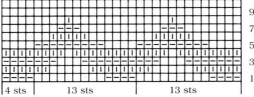

| = k 1
— = p 1
□ = 1 st as shown

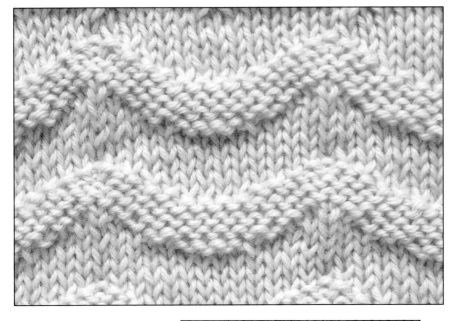

| = k 1
— = p 1
□ = stockinette st

Easy scallops

Work with a multiple on 13 stitches,
plus 4.
Note: For stockinette st, knit on right-
side rows, purl on wrong-side rows.
Row 1 (right side): P 4, * k 9, p 4 *;
repeat from * to *.
Row 2: K 6, * p 5, k 8 *; repeat from
* to *, ending p 5, k 6.
Row 3: P 7, * k 3, p 10 *; repeat from
* to *, ending k 3, p 7.
Row 4: K 8, * p 1, k 12 *; repeat from
* to *, ending p 1, k 8.
Row 5: K 4, * p 9, k 4 *; repeat from
* to *.
Row 6: P 6, * k 5, p 8 *; repeat from
* to *, ending k 5, p 6.
Row 7: K 7, *p 3, k 10 *; repeat from
* to *, ending p 3, k 7.
Row 8: P 8, * k 1, p 12 *; repeat from
* to *, ending k 1, p 8.
Row 9: Knit.
Row 10: Purl.
Repeat these 10 rows for pattern.

CLASSIC STITCHES

Variations in knit and purl

Work with a multiple of 10 stitches, plus 1.

Row 1 (right side): P 5, * k 1, p 9 *; repeat from * to *, ending k 1, p 5.

Row 2 and all even-numbered rows: Work each stitch as it appears on this side of work (k the k sts and p the p sts).

Rows 3 and 27: P 4, * k 1, p 1, k 1, p 7 *; repeat from * to *, ending last repeat with p 4.

Rows 5 and 25: P 3, * work (k 1, p 1) twice, k 1, p 5 *; repeat from * to *, ending last repeat with p 3.

Row 7: P 2, * work (k 1, p 1) twice, k 3, p 3 *; repeat from * to *, ending last repeat with p 2.

Row 9: * Work (p 1, k 1) twice, p 1, k 5 *; repeat from * to *, ending p 1.

Row 11: Work (k 1, p 1) 3 times, k 5, * work (p 1, k 1) twice, p 1, k 5 *; repeat from * to *.

Row 13: * Work (p 1, k 1) twice, p 3, k 3 *; repeat from * to *, ending p 1.

Row 15: K 1, p 1, k 1, * p 5, work (k 1, p 1) twice, k 1 *; repeat from * to *, ending last repeat with k 1, p 1, k 1.

Row 17: P 1, * k 3, p 3, work (k 1, p 1) twice *; repeat from * to *.

Row 19: * K 5, work (p 1, k 1) twice, p 1 *; repeat from * to *, ending k 1.

Row 21: P 1, * k 5, work (p 1, k 1) twice, p 1 *; repeat from * to *.

Row 23: P 2, * k 3, work (p 1, k 1) twice, p 3 *; repeat from * to *, ending last repeat with p 2.

Repeat Rows 1 through 28 for pattern.

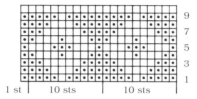

□ = stockinette st

● = moss st

Buttons

Work with a multiple of 10 stitches, plus 9.

Rows 1, 3, 9, and 11 (right side): Purl.

Rows 2, 4, 10, and 12: Knit.

Rows 5 and 7: P 2, * k 5, with yarn at back slip 5 *; repeat from * to *, ending k 5, p 2.

Rows 6 and 8: K 2, * p 5, with yarn in front slip 5 *; repeat from * to *, ending p 5, k 2.

Rows 13 and 15: P 2, * with yarn in back slip 5, k 5 *; repeat from * to *, ending slip 5, p 2.

Rows 14 and 16: K 2, * with yarn in front slip 5, p 5 *; repeat from * to *, ending slip 5, k 2.

Repeat these 16 rows for pattern.

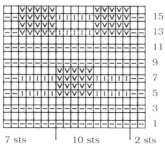

− = p 1

| = k 1

V = slip st

□ = 1 st as shown

CLASSIC STITCHES

Moss stitch diamonds

Work with a multiple of 10 sts,
plus 1.

Note: For stockinette st, knit on right-side rows, purl on wrong side. For moss st, always p over k sts (as they face you) and k over p sts.

Rows 1 and 9: P 1, work (k 1, p 1) twice (5 moss sts made), * k 1, work (p 1, k 1) 4 times, p 1 (9 moss sts) *; repeat from * to *, ending k 1, work 5 moss sts.

Rows 2 and 8: Work 4 moss sts, * p 3, work 7 moss sts *; repeat from * to *, ending p 3, work 4 moss sts.

Rows 3 and 7: Work 3 moss sts,

* k 5, work 5 moss sts *; repeat from * to *, ending k 5, work 3 moss sts.

Rows 4 and 6: Work 2 moss sts, * p 3, k 1 (moss st), p 3, work 3 moss sts *; repeat from * to *, ending last repeat with 2 moss sts.

Row 5: Work 1 moss st, * k 3, work 3 moss sts, k 3, work 1 moss st *; repeat from * to *.

Row 10: Purl.

Repeat these 10 rows for pattern.

```
I = k 1
− = p 1
□ = 1 st as shown
```

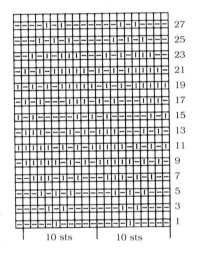

10 sts   10 sts

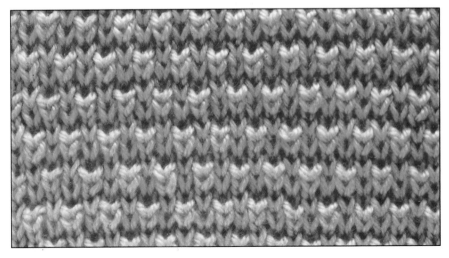

```
I = k 1
− = p 1
V = embossed st
```

2 sts

Embossed stitch

Work on an uneven number of stitches.

Rows 1 and 5: Knit.

Row 2 and all even-numbered rows: Purl.

Row 3: K 1, * work embossed st as follows: k in st 2 rows below next st, then k st above on left needle, with tip of left needle lift and pass the long stitch over the last st worked and drop it (embossed st made), k 1 *; repeat from * to *.

Row 7: K 2, * work embossed st as before, k 1 *; repeat from * to *, ending with k last 2 sts.

Repeat Rows 1 through 8 for pattern.

CLASSIC STITCHES

Spades

Work with a multiple of 10 stitches, plus 1.

Row 1: K 1, * p 4, k 1* repeat from * to *.

Row 2 and all even-numbered rows: Work each stitch as it appears on this side of work (k the k sts and p the p sts).

Row 3: K 1, * p 3, k 3, p 3, k 1 *; repeat from * to *.

Row 5: K 1, * p 2, k 5, p 2, k 1 *; repeat from * to *.

Row 7: K 1, * p 1, k 7, p 1, k 1 *; repeat from * to *.

Row 9: K 2, * p 3, k 1, p 3, k 3 *; repeat from * to *, ending last repeat with k 2.

Row 11: K 3, * p 2, k 1, p 2, k 5 *; repeat from * to *, ending last repeat with k 3.

Row 13: K 4, * p 1, k 1, p 1, k 7 *, repeat from * to *, ending last repeat with k 4.

Repeat Rows 1 through 14 for pattern.

I = k 1
− = p 1
□ = 1 st as shown

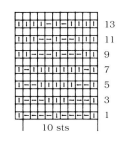

10 sts

Loom

Work with a multiple of 24 stitches, plus 5.

Row 1: K 1 (selvage), * k 1, p 1, k 1, p 3, work (k 1, p 1) 7 times, k 1, p 3 *; repeat from * to *, ending k 1, p 1, k 1, k 1 (selvage).

Row 2 and all even-numbered rows: Working selvage st at each end in garter st (k every row), work each remaining stitch as it appears on this side of work (k the k sts and p the p sts).

Row 3: K 1, * k st in row below next st and drop unworked st above (double st made), p 1, double st, p 2 sts together, p 1, work (double st, p 1) 3 times, with tip of left needle pick up connecting strand between last st worked and next st, k into back loop of this strand (1 increase k st made), double st, p 1, double st, increase 1 k st as before, p 1, work (double st, p 1) 3 times, p 2 sts together *; repeat from * to *; ending with double st, p 1, double st, k 1.

Row 5: K 1, * double st, p 1, double st, p 2 sts together, work (double st, p 1) 3 times, double st, with left needle pick up connecting strand between sts and p into back loop of strand (1 increase p st made); double st, p 1, double st, increase 1 p st as before, work (double st, p 1) 3 times, double st, p 2 sts together *; repeat from * to *; ending with double st, p 1, double st, k 1.

Repeat Rows 3 through 6 for pattern.

• = 1 selvage st
I = k 1
− = p 1
∨ = double st
⋎ = p 2 tog
+ = inc 1 k

∧ = inc 1 p

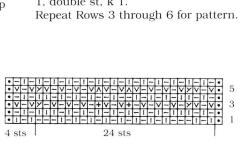

4 sts   24 sts

CLASSIC STITCHES

Crossover rib pattern

Work with a multiple of 14 sts, plus 1.

Note: To slip sts, carry yarn on wrong side of work.

Row 1 (right side): P 1, * k 3, slip 1, p 1, k 3, p 1, slip 1, k 3, p 1 *; repeat from * to *.

Row 2: K 1, * p 3, slip 1, work (k 2, slip 1) twice, p 3, k 1 *; repeat from * to *.

Row 3: P 1, * k 1, work right cross on sts as follows: slip 2 sts to dp needle and hold in back of work, k 1, k 2 sts from dp needle (right cross made); p 1, k 3, p 1, work left cross on 3 sts as follows: slip 1 st to dp needle and hold in front of work, k next 2 sts, k st from dp needle (left cross made); k 1, p 1 *; repeat from * to *.

Rows 4 and 8: K 1, * p 4, k 2, slip 1, k 2, p 4, k 1 *; repeat from * to *.

Row 5: P 1, * slip 1, work (k 3, p 1) twice, k 3, slip 1, p 1 *; repeat from * to *.

Row 6: K 1, * slip 1, p 3, k 2, slip 1, k 2, p 3, slip 1, k 1 *; repeat from * to *.

Row 7: P 1, * left cross, k 1, p 1, k 3, p 1, k 1, right cross, p 1 *; repeat from * to *.

Repeat Rows 1 through 8 for pattern.

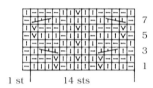

1 st   14 sts

| = k 1
− = p 1
∨ = slip st
= 3-st right cross
= 3-st left cross

Cableway

Work with a multiple of 12 stitches.

Note: To work moss st, always p over k st (as it faces you) and k over p st.

Rows 1, 3, 5, 7, and 9: K 1, p 1, k 1 (3 moss sts worked), * k 2, p 2, k 2, work (p 1, k 1) 3 times (6 moss sts) *; repeat from * to *, ending last repeat with p1, k 1, p 1 (3 moss sts).

Row 2 and all even-numbered rows: Working moss st over moss sts, work each remaining st as it appears on this side of work (k the k sts and p the p sts).

Rows 11, 13, 15, 17, and 19: P 1, * k 2, work (p 1, k 1) 3 times (6 moss sts), p 2, k 2 *; repeat from * to *, ending last repeat with k 1.

Repeat Rows 1 through 20 for pattern.

| = k 1
− = p 1
• = 1 moss st

□ = 1 st as shown

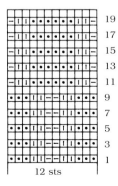

12 sts

CROSSOVER STITCHES

Braid

Work on 2 stitches. For pattern as shown, work 2-st braids evenly spaced on a background of reverse stockinette st.

Row 1 (right side): Work braid on 2 sts as follows: Skip first st, reaching behind work k second st through back loop, then k skipped st through front loop, drop original 2 sts from left needle (braid made).

Row 2: Purl.

Repeat these 2 rows for braid.

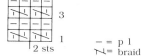

− = p 1
⅄ = braid

Continuous braid

Work on 2 sts. For pattern as shown, work 2-st braids evenly spaced on a background of reverse stockinette st.

Row 1 (right side): Work braid on 2 sts as follows: Skip first st, reaching behind work k 2nd st through back loop, then k skipped st, dropping original 2 sts from left needle (k 2 for braid made).

Row 2: Skip first st, reaching in front of work, p next st, then p skipped st, dropping original 2 sts from left needle (p 2 for braid made).

Repeat these 2 rows for braid.

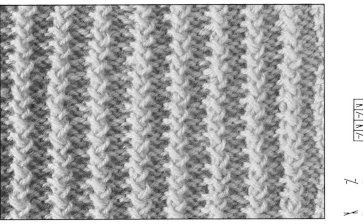

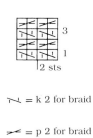

⅄ = k 2 for braid

⤢ = p 2 for braid

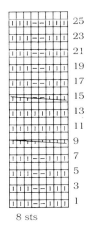

8 sts

ı = k 1
− = p 1
⊤⊤⊤⊤⊥⊥ = 8-st first twist
⊤⊤⊤⊥⊥⊥ = 8-st 2nd twist

☐ = 1 st as shown

Big cables, little cables

Work on 8 sts. For cable pattern as shown, work evenly-spaced cables on background of reverse stockinette st.

Rows 1, 3, 5, and 7: K 3, p 2, k 3.

Row 2 and all even-numbered rows: Work each stitch as it appears on this side of work (k the k sts, p the p sts).

Row 9 (first twist): Slip 4 sts to dp needle and hold in front of work, k next 4 sts, k 4 sts from dp needle.

Rows 11 and 13: Knit.

Row 15 (2nd twist): Slip 4 sts to dp needle and hold in front of work, k next 3 sts, p 1 st, then work (p 1, k 3) on sts from dp needle.

Rows 17, 19, 21, 23, and 25: K 3, p 2, k 3.

Repeat Rows 9 through 26 for cable.

CROSSOVER STITCHES

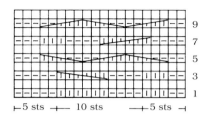

⊢5 sts⊣ 10 sts ⊢5 sts⊣

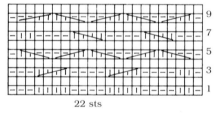

  − = p 1
  | = k 1
⊢┬┬┬┴┴ = 6-st left crossover
⊢┬┬┬< = 5-st left cross
=>┬┬┬ = 5-st right cross
┴┴┴┬┬┬ = 6-st right crossover
  □ = 1 st as shown

Wide lattice

Work with a multiple of 10 stitches.
Row 1: P 2, k 3, * p 4, k 6 * repeat from * to *; ending p 5.
Row 2 and all even-numbered rows: K the k sts as they face you and p the p sts.
Row 3: P 2, k 3, * p 4, work 6-st left crossover as follows: slip 3 sts to dp needle and hold in front of work, k 3, k 3 from dp needle *; repeat from * to *, p 5.

Row 5: P 2, * work 5-st left cross as follows: slip 3 sts to dp needle and hold in front, p 2, k 3 from dp needle, then work 5-st right cross as follows: slip 2 sts to dp needle and hold in back, k 3, p 2 from dp needle *; repeat from * to *, ending with 5-st left cross, p 3.
Row 7: P 4, * work 6-st right crossover as follows: slip 3 sts to dp needle and hold in back, k 3, k 3

from dp needle, p 4 *; repeat from * to *, ending k 3, p 3.
Row 9: P 2, * work 5-st right cross, then 5-st left cross *; repeat from * to *, ending with 5-st right cross, p 3. Repeat Rows 3 through 10 for pattern.

22 sts

  − = p 1
  | = k 1
└┴┬┬┘ = 4-st right crossover
┌┬┬< = 4-st left cross
=>┬┬ = 4-st right cross
┌┬┬┴┘ = 4-st left crossover
  □ = 1 st as shown

Lattice stripe

Work on 22 stitches. For pattern as shown, work evenly-spaced stripes on reverse stockinette st background.
Row 1: P 1, k 2, work (p 4, k 4) twice, p 3.
Row 2 and all even-numbered rows: K the k sts as they face you and p the p sts.
Row 3: P 1, k 2, p 4, work right cross on 4 sts as follows: slip 2 to dp nee-

dle and hold in back of work, k 2, then k 2 from dp needle; p 4, work another right crossover, p 3.
Row 5: P 1, * work left cross on 4 sts as follows: slip 2 to dp needle and hold in front, p 2, k 2 from dp needle; work right cross on 4 sts as follows: slip 2 to dp needle and hold in back, k 2, p 2 from dp needle *; repeat from * to * once, work left cross, p 1.
Row 7: P 3, * work left crossover on

4 sts as follows: slip 2 to dp needle and hold in front, k 2, k 2 from dp needle, p 4 *; repeat from * to * once, k 2, p 1.
Row 9: P 1, work (right cross, left cross) twice, right cross, p 1. Repeat Rows 3 through 10 for stripe.

CROSSOVER STITCHES

Convergence

Work with a multiple of 20 stitches.
Row 1: * Work left cross on 3 sts as follows: slip 2 to dp needle and hold in front of work, p 1, k 2 from dp needle; p 14, work right cross on 3 sts as follows: slip 1 to dp needle and hold in back of work, k 2, p 1 from dp needle *; repeat from * to *.
Row 2 and all even-numbered rows: K the k sts as they face you and p the p sts.
Row 3: P 1, * work left cross, p 12, right cross, p 2 *; repeat from * to *, ending last repeat with p 1.
Row 5: P 2, * left cross, p 10, right cross, p 4 *; repeat from * to *, ending p 2.
Row 7: P 3, * left cross, p 8, right cross, p 6 *; repeat from * to *, ending p 3.
Row 9: P 4, * left cross, p 6, right cross, p 8 *; repeat from * to *, ending p 4.
Row 11: P 5, * left cross, p 4, right

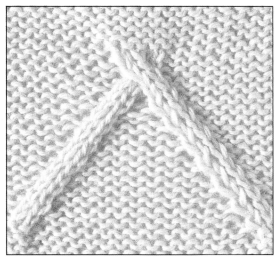

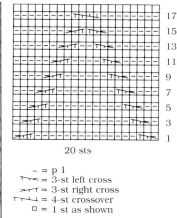

20 sts

– = p 1
⊤⊏ = 3-st left cross
⊐⊤ = 3-st right cross
⊤⊏⊥ = 4-st crossover
□ = 1 st as shown

cross, p 10 *; repeat from * to *, ending p 5.
Row 13: P 6, *left cross, p 2, right cross, p 12 *; repeat from * to *, ending p 6.
Row 15: P 7, * left cross, right cross,

p 14 *; repeat from * to *, ending p 7.
Row 17: P 8, * work crossover on 4 sts as follows: slip 2 to dp needle and hold in front, k 2, k 2 from dp needle, p 16 *; repeat from * to *, ending p 8.
Row 18: Knit.

Diamond with moss st

Work on 18 sts for single diamond.
Note: To work moss st, p over k st (as it faces you) and k over p st.
Row 1: P 6, work right cross on 3 sts as follows: slip 1 st to dp needle and hold in back of work, k 2, p 1 from dp needle; work left cross on 3 sts as follows: slip 2 sts to dp needle and hold in front of work, p 1, k 2 from dp needle, p 6.
Row 2: Work moss st over moss sts and work each remaining st as it appears on this side of work (k the k sts and p the p sts).
Row 3: P 5, right cross, k 1, p 1 (2 moss sts worked), left cross, p 5.
Row 5: P 4, right cross, 4 moss sts, left cross, p 4.
Row 7: P 3, right cross, 6 moss sts, left cross, p 3.
Row 9: P 2, right cross, 8 moss sts, left cross, p 2.
Row 11: P 1, right cross, 10 moss sts, left cross, p 1.
Row 13: Right cross, 12 moss sts, right cross.
Row 15: K 2, 14 moss sts, k 2.
Row 17: Left cross, 12 moss sts, right cross.
Row 19: P 1, left cross, 10 moss sts, right cross, p 1.
Row 21: P 2, left cross, 8 moss sts, right cross, p 2.

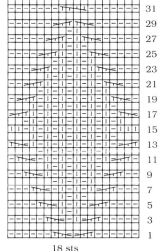

ı = k 1
– = p 1
⊐⊤ = 3-st right cross
⊤⊏ = 3-st left cross
⊤⊏⊥ = 4-st crossover
□ = 1 st as shown

18 sts

Row 23: P 3, left cross, 6 moss sts, right cross, p 3.
Row 25: P 4, left cross, 4 moss sts, right cross, p 4.
Row 27: P 5, left cross, 2 moss sts, right cross, p 5.
Row 29: P 6, left cross, right cross, p 6.

Row 31: P 7, work crossover on 4 sts as follows: slip 2 to dp needle and hold in front, k 2, k 2 from dp needle, p 7.
Repeat Rows 1 through 32 for pattern.

CROSSOVER STITCHES

Zigzags with bobbles

Work with a multiple of 14 stitches.

Row 1: P 3, * k 2, p 12 *; repeat from * to *, ending with p 9.

Row 2 and all even-numbered rows: K the k sts as they face you and p the p sts. K bobble sts on Rows 14 and 26.

Row 3: P 3, * work left cross on 3 sts as follows: slip 2 to dp needle and hold in front, p 1, k 2 from dp needle; p 11 *; repeat from * to *, ending p 8.

Row 5: P 4, left cross, p 11 *; repeat from * to *, ending p 7.

Row 7: P 5, left cross, p 11 *; repeat from * to *, ending p 6.

Row 9: P 6, left cross, p 11 *; repeat from * to *, ending p 5.

Row 11: P 7, left cross, p 11 *; repeat from * to *, ending p 4.

Row 13: P 5, work bobble in next st as follows: k in front loop, then back, front, back for 4 sts, turn, p 4, turn, k 4, turn, p 4, turn, k 4, then pass 3 sts one by one over 4th stitch to complete bobble, p 2, left cross, p 8 *; repeat from * to *, ending p 3.

Row 15: P 8, * work right cross on

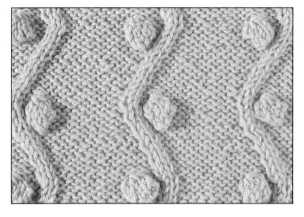

I = k 1
− = p 1
⊤⊤ = 3-st left cross
⊐ = 1 st as shown
⊤⊤ = 3-st right cross
• = 1 bobble

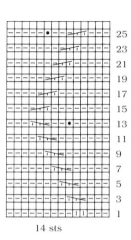

14 sts

3 sts as follows: slip 1 to dp needle and hold in back, k 2, p 1 from dp needle, p 11 *; repeat from * to *, ending p 3.

Row 17: P 7, * right cross, p 11 *; repeat from * to *, ending p 4.

Row 19: P 6, * right cross, p 11 *; repeat from * to *, ending p 5.

Row 21: P 5, * right cross, p 11 *; repeat from * to *, ending p 6.

Row 23: P 4, * right cross, p 11 *; repeat from * to *, ending p 7.

Row 25: P 3, * right cross, p 2, bobble, p 8 *; repeat from * to *, ending p 5.
Repeat Rows 3 through 26 for pattern.

Diamond pattern

Work with a multiple of 16 sts.

Row 1: P 5, * work right cross on 3 sts as follows: slip 1 to dp needle and hold in back of work, k 2, p 1 from dp needle, work left cross on 3 sts as follows: slip 2 to dp needle and hold in front, p 1, k 2 from dp needle, p 10 *; repeat from * to *, ending with p 5.

Row 2 and all even-numbered rows: K the k sts as they face you and p the p sts.

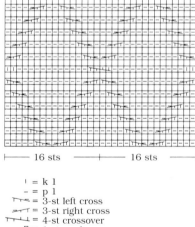

I = k 1
− = p 1
⊤⊤ = 3-st left cross
⊤⊤ = 3-st right cross
⊤⊤⊥ = 4-st crossover
⊐ = 1 st as shown

16 sts   16 sts

Row 3: P 4, * right cross, p 2, left cross, p 8 *; repeat from * to *, ending p 4.

Row 5: P 3, * right cross, p 4, left cross, p 6 *; repeat from * to *, ending p 3.

Row 7: P 2, * right cross, p 6, left cross, p 4 *; repeat from * to *, ending p 2.

Row 9: P 1, * right cross, p 8, left cross, p 2 *; repeat from * to *, ending p 1.

Row 11: * Right cross, p 10, left cross *; repeat from * to *.

Row 13: K 2, * p 12, work crossover on 4 sts as follows: slip 2 to dp needle and hold in front, k 2, k 2 from dp needle *; repeat from * to *, ending p 12, k 2.

Row 15: * Left cross, p 10, right cross *; repeat from * to *.

Row 17: P 1, * left cross, p 8, right cross, p 2 *; repeat from * to *, ending p 1.

Row 19: P 2, * left cross, p 6, right cross, p 4 *; repeat from * to *, ending p 2.

Row 21: P 3, * left cross, p 4, right cross, p 6 *; repeat from * to *, ending p 3.

Row 23: P 4, * left cross, p 2, right cross, p 8 *; repeat from * to *, ending p 4.

Row 25: P 5, * left cross, right cross, p 10 *; repeat from * to *, ending p 5.

Row 27: P 6, * crossover, p 12, *; repeat from * to *, ending p 6.
Repeat Rows 1 through 28 for pattern.

CROSSOVER STITCHES

Opulent cables

Work cable on 13 stitches. For chain pattern as shown, work evenly-spaced cables on background of reverse stockinette st.

Rows 1, 3, 5, 7, 9, 11, 15, and 17: K 6, p 1, k 6.

Row 2 and all even-numbered rows: Work each stitch as it appears on this side of work (k the k sts and p the p sts).

Rows 13 and 19: Work crossover on 13 sts as follows: slip 6 to dp needle and hold in front of work, k 6, p 1, k 6 from dp needle.

Repeat Rows 1 through 20 for cable.

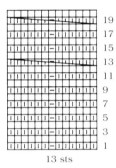

13 sts

Puckered pattern

Work with a multiple of 16.

Rows 1, 3, 5, and 7: * K 8, p 8 *; repeat from * to *.

Row 2 and all even-numbered rows: K the k sts as they face you and p the p sts.

Row 9: * Work crossover on 8 sts as follows: slip 4 to dp needle and hold in front of work, p 4, p 4 from dp needle, k 8 *; repeat from * to *.

Rows 11, 13, and 15: * P 8, k 8 *; repeat from * to *.

Row 17: * K 8, work crossover on next 8 sts *; repeat from * to *.

Repeat Rows 3 through 20 for pattern.

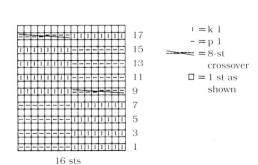

16 sts

57

CROSSOVER STITCHES

Set of diamonds

Work with a multiple of 18 sts.

Row 1: P 5, *work (right cross-p on 2 sts as follows: skip 1, k in next st, p skipped st, dropping both original sts from left needle) twice, work (left cross-p on 2 sts as follows: slip 1 to dp needle and hold in front, p 1, k 1 from dp needle) twice, p 10 *; repeat from * to *, ending with p 5.

Row 2 and all even-numbered rows: Work each stitch as it appears on this side of work (k the k sts and p the p sts).

Row 3: P 4, * work right cross-P, work right cross-K on 2 sts as follows: skip 1, k next st, k skipped st, p 2, work left-cross-K on 2 sts as follows: reaching behind, work k 1 in back loop of next st, k in front loop of skipped st and drop 2 original sts from left needle; work left cross-P, p 10 *; repeat from * to *, ending with p 4.

Row 5: P 3, work right cross-P twice, left cross-P, right cross P, left cross-P twice, p 6 *; repeat from * to *, ending with p 3.

Row 7: P 3, * k 1, p 1, k 1, p 2, k 2, p 2, k 1, p 1, k 1, p 6 *; repeat from * to *, ending with p 3.

Row 9: P 3, * work left cross-P twice, right cross-P, left cross-P, right cross-P twice, p 6 *; repeat from * to *, ending with p 3.

Row 11: P 4, * work left cross-P twice, p 2, right cross-P twice, p 8 *; repeat from * to *, ending with p 4.

Row 13: P 5, * work left cross-P

twice, right cross-P twice, p 10 *; repeat from * to *, ending with p 5.

Row 15: P 6, * k 1, p 1, k 2, p 1, k 1, p 12 *; repeat from * to *, ending with p 6.

Repeat Rows 1 through 16 for pattern.

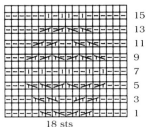

18 sts

	= k 1	⊁	= 2-st right cross-K
- = p 1	
⊁ = 2-st right cross-P	⊼ = 2-st left cross-K
⊼ = 2-st left cross-P	□ = 1 st as shown

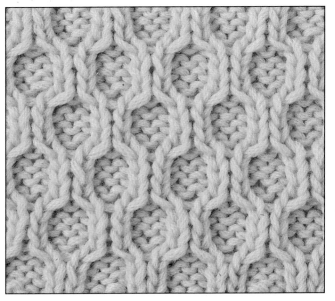

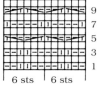

| = k 1
- = p 1
⊁⊤ = 3-st right cross
⊤⊼ = 3-st left cross
□ = 1 st as shown

Honeycomb

Work with a multiple of 6 sts.

Rows 1 and 3: P 2, * k 2, p 4 *; repeat from * to *, ending with p 2.

Row 2 and all even-numbered rows: K the k sts as they face you and p the p sts.

Row 5: * Work right cross on 3 sts as follows: slip 2 to dp needle and hold in back, k 1, p 2 from dp needle; work left cross on 3 sts as follows: slip 1 to dp needle and hold in front, p 2, k 1 from dp needle *; repeat from * to *.

Row 7: K 1, * p 4, k 2 *; repeat from * to *, ending with k 1.

Row 9: * Work left cross, then right cross *; repeat from * to *.

Repeat Rows 1 through 10 for pattern.

CROSSOVER STITCHES

Wavy braid

Work with a multiple of 12 stitches.

Row 1: * P 6, k 2, work 4-st right crossover as follows: slip 2 to dp needle and hold in back of work, k 2, k 2 from dp needle *; repeat from * to *.

Row 2 and all even-numbered rows: Work each stitch as it appears on this side of work (k the k sts and p the p sts).

Rows 3 and 15: * P 6, k 6 *; repeat from * to *.

Row 5: P 3, * work 6-st right cross as follows: slip 3 to dp needle and hold in back of work, k 3, k 3 from dp needle, p 6 *; repeat from * to *, ending with p 3.

Rows 7 and 11: P 3, * k 6, p 6 *; repeat from * to *, ending with p 3.

Row 9: P 3, * k 2, work 4-st left cross as follows: slip 2 to dp needle and hold in front, k 2, k 2 from dp needle, p 6 *; repeat from * to *, ending with p 3.

Row 13: P 6, work 6-st left cross as follows: slip 3 to dp needle and hold in front, k 3, k 3 from dp needle *; repeat from * to *.

Repeat Rows 1 through 16 for pattern.

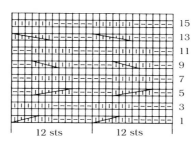

12 sts   12 sts

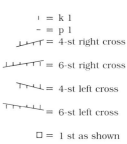

ı = k 1
− = p 1
= 4-st right cross
= 6-st right cross
= 4-st left cross
= 6-st left cross
□ = 1 st as shown

ı = k 1
− = p 1
= 6-st crossover
□ = 1 st as shown

2 sts   12 sts   12 sts

Wandering ribs

Work with a multiple of 12 stitches, plus 2.

Rows 1, 3, 7, 9, 13, and 15: P 2, * k 2, p 2 *; repeat from * to *.

Row 2 and all even-numbered rows: K the k sts as they face you and p the p sts.

Row 5: P 2, * k 2, p 2, work 6-st crossover as follows: slip 4 to dp needle and hold in back of work, k 2, move dp needle to front, return 2 p sts from dp needle to left needle and p them, then k 2 from dp needle, p 2 *; repeat from * to *.

Row 11: * P 2, * work crossover, p 2, k 2, p 2 *; repeat from * to *.

Row 17: P 2, work (k 2, p 2) twice, * work crossover, p 2, k 2, p 2 *; repeat from * to *, ending (k 2, p 2) in last 4 sts.

Repeat Rows 1 through 18 for pattern.

CROSSOVER STITCHES

Asymmetric diamonds

Work with a multiple of 22 stitches.

Row 1: P 3, * work right cross on 3 sts as follows: slip 1 to dp needle and hold in back of work, k 2, p 1 from dp needle, work left cross on 3 sts as follows: slip 2 to dp needle and hold in front, p 1, k 2 from dp needle, p 4, right cross, left cross, p 6 *; repeat from * to *, ending last repeat with p 3.

Row 2 and all even-numbered rows: K the k sts as they face you and p the p sts.

Row 3: P 2, * right cross, p 2, left cross, p 2, right cross, p 2, left cross, p 4 *; repeat from * to *, ending last repeat with p 2.

Row 5: P 1, * work (right cross, p 4, left cross) twice, p 2 *; repeat from * to *, ending last repeat with p 1.

Row 7: P 1, * left cross, p 4, work 6-st crossover as follow: slip 3 to dp needle and hold in back, k 3, k 3 from dp needle, p 4, right cross, p 2 *; repeat from * to *, ending last repeat with p 1.

Row 9: P 2, * left cross, p 2, right cross, p 2, left cross, p 2, right cross, p 4 *; repeat from * to *, ending last repeat with p 2.

Row 11: P 3, * left cross, right cross, p 4, left cross, right cross, p 6 *; repeat from * to *, ending last repeat with p 3.

Row 13: P 4, * work 4-st crossover as follows: slip 2 to dp needle and hold in back, k 2, k 2 from dp needle, p 6, work 4-st crossover, p 8 *; repeat from * to *, ending last repeat with p 4.

Row 15: P 4, *k 4, p 6, k 4, p 8 *; repeat from * to *, ending last repeat with p 4.

Repeat Rows 1 through 16 for pattern.

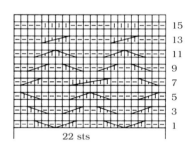

Ribbed cable

Work on 18 stitches.

Rows 1, 3, 5, 7, 9, and 11: P 2, * k 2, p 2 *; repeat from * to *.

Row 2 and all even-numbered rows: K the k sts as they face you and p the p sts.

Row 13: P 2, work knitted crossover as follows: slip 7 to dp needle and hold in front of work, k 7, k 7 from dp needle, p 2.

Rows 15, 17, 19, 21, and 23: P 2, k 14, p 2.

Row 25: P 2, work ribbed crossover as follows: slip 6 sts to dp needle and hold in front of work, work (k 2, p 2) twice on next 8 sts, then k 2, p 2, k 2 on sts from dp needle, p 2.

Uneven-numbered rows from 27 to 47: P 2, * k 2, p 2 *; repeat from * to *.

Repeat Rows 13 through 48 for pattern.

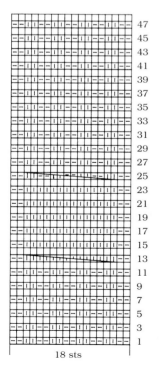

CROSSOVER STITCHES

Diamond with parallelograms

Work on 32 stitches. Diamond pattern is shown on a background of reverse stockinette st.

Row 1: P 12, k 8, p 12.

Row 2 and all even-numbered rows: Work each stitch as it appears on this side of work (k the k sts and p the p sts).

Row 3: P 11, work 5-st right cross as follows: slip 1 st to dp needle and hold in back of work, k 4, p 1 from dp needle; work 5-st left cross as follows: slip 4 to dp needle and hold in front of work, p 1, k 4 from dp needle, p 11.

Row 5: P 10, work 5-st right cross, p 2, work 5-st left cross, p 10.

Row 7: P 9, work 5-st right cross, p 4, work 5-st left cross, p 9.

Row 9: P 8, work 5-st right cross, p 6, work 5-st left cross, p 8.

Row 11: P 7, work 5-st right cross, work 2-st left cross as follows: slip 1 to dp needle and hold in front, p 1, k st from dp needle, p 4, work 2-st right cross-P as follows: skip 1, k next st, p skipped st and drop original sts from left needle, work 5-st left cross, p 7.

Row 13: P 6, work 5-st right cross, p 2, work 2-st left cross, p 2, work 2-st right cross-P, p 2, work 5-st left cross, p 6.

Row 15: P 5, work 5-st right cross, p 4, work 2-st left cross, 2-st right cross-P, p 4, work 5-st left cross, p 5.

Row 17: P 4, work 5-st right cross, p 6, work 2-st right cross-K as follows: skip 1, k next st, k skipped st, p 6, work 5-st left cross, p 4.

Row 19: P 3, work 5-st right cross, p 6, work 2-st right cross-P, 2-st left cross, p 6, work 5-st left cross, p 3.

Row 21: P 2, work 5-st right cross, 2-st left cross, p 4, work 2-st right cross-P, p 2, work 2-st left cross, p 4, work 2-st right cross-P, 5-st left cross, p 2.

Row 23: P 1, work 5-st right cross, p 2, work 2-st left cross, p 2, work 2-st right cross-P, p 4, work 2-st left cross, p 2, work 2-st right cross-P, p 2, 5-st left cross, p 1.

Row 25: Work 5-st right cross, p 4, work 2-st left cross, 2-st right cross-P, p 6, work 2-st left cross, 2-st right cross-P, p 4, work 5-st left cross.

Row 27: Work 5-st left cross, p 5, work 2-st right cross-K, p 8, work 2-st right cross-K, p 5, work 5-st right cross.

Row 29: P 1, work 5-st left cross, p 3, work 2-st right cross-P, 2-st left cross, p 6, work 2-st right cross-P, 2-st left cross, p 3, 5-st right cross, p 1.

Row 31: P 2, work 5-st left cross, p 1, work 2-st right cross-P, p 2, work 2-st left cross, p 4, work 2-st right cross-P, p 2, work 2-st left cross, p 1, work 5-st right cross, p 2.

Row 33: P 3, work 5-st left cross, p 5, work 2-st left cross, p 2, work 2-st right cross-P, p 5, work 5-st right cross, p 3.

Row 35: P 4, work 5-st left cross, p 5, work 2-st left cross, 2-st right cross-P, p 5, work 5-st right cross, p 4.

Row 37: P 5, work 5-st left cross, p 5, work 2-st right cross-K, p 5, work 5-st right cross, p 5.

Row 39: P 6, work 5-st left cross, p 3, work 2-st right cross-P, 2-st left cross, p 3, work 5-st right cross, p 6.

Row 41: P 7, work 5-st left cross, p 1, work 2-st right cross-P, p 2, work 2-st left cross, p 1, work 5-st right cross, p 7.

Row 43: P 8, work 5-st left cross, p 6, work 5-st right cross, p 8.

Row 45: P 9, work 5-st left cross, p 4, work 5-st right cross, p 9.

Row 47: P 10, work 5-st left cross, p 2, work 5-st right cross, p 10.

Row 49: P 11, work 5-st left cross, 5-st right cross, p 11.

Repeat Rows 3 through 50 for pattern.

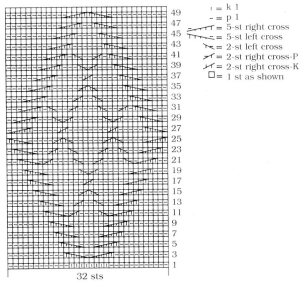

ı = k 1
− = p 1
= 5-st right cross
= 5-st left cross
= 2-st left cross
= 2-st right cross-P
= 2-st right cross-K
□ = 1 st as shown

32 sts

CROSSOVER STITCHES

Wavy ribs

Work with a multiple of 13 stitches, plus 12.

Row 1: K 5, p 7, * k 6, p 7 *; repeat from * to *.

Row 2 and all even-numbered rows: Work each stitch as it appears on this side of work (k the k sts and p the p sts).

Row 3: K 4, p 7, * work right cross on 7 stitches as follows: slip 1 to dp needle and hold in back of work, k 6, p 1 from dp needle, p 6 *; repeat from * to *, ending k 1.

Row 5: K 3, p 7, * right cross, p 6 *; repeat from * to *, ending k 2.

Row 7: K 2, p 7, * right cross, p 6 *; repeat from * to *, ending k 3.

Row 9: K 1, p 7, * right cross, p 6 *; repeat from * to *, ending k 4.

Row 11: P 7, * right cross, p 6 *; repeat from * to *, ending k 5.

Row 13: P 6, * right cross, p 6 *; repeat from * to *, ending k 6.

Row 15: P 5, * right cross, p 6 *; repeat from * to *, ending with right cross.

Row 17: P 4, * right cross, p 6 *; repeat from * to *, ending right cross, p 1.

Row 19: P 3, * right cross, p 6 *; repeat from * to *, ending right cross, p 2.

Row 21: P 2, * right cross, p 6 *; repeat from * to *, ending right cross, p 3.

Row 23: P 1, * right cross, p 6 *; repeat from * to *, ending right cross, p 4.

Row 25: * Right cross, p 6 *; repeat from * to *, ending right cross, p 5.

Row 27: * Work left cross on 7 sts as follows: slip 6 sts to dp needle and hold in front of work, p 1, k 6 from dp needle, p 6 * repeat from * to *, ending left cross, p 5.

Row 29: P 1, * left cross, p 6 *; repeat from * to *, ending left cross, p 4.

Row 31: P 2, * left cross, p 6 *; repeat from * to *, ending left cross, p 3.

Row 33: P 3, * left cross, p 6 *; repeat from * to *, ending left cross, p 2.

Row 35: P 4, * left cross, p 6 *; repeat from * to *, ending left cross, p 1.

Row 37: P 5, * left cross, p 6 *; repeat from * to *, ending with left cross.

Row 39: * P 6, left cross *; repeat from * to *, ending p 7, k 5.

Row 41: K 1, * p 6, left cross *; repeat from * to *, ending p 7, k 4.

Row 43: K 2, * p 6, left cross *; repeat from * to *, ending p7, k 3.

Row 45: K 3, * p 6, left cross *; repeat from * to *, ending p 7, k 2.

Row 47: K 4, * p 6, left cross *; repeat from * to *, ending p 7, k 1.

Row 49: K 5, * p 6, left cross *; repeat from * to *, ending p 7. Repeat Rows 3 through 50 for pattern.

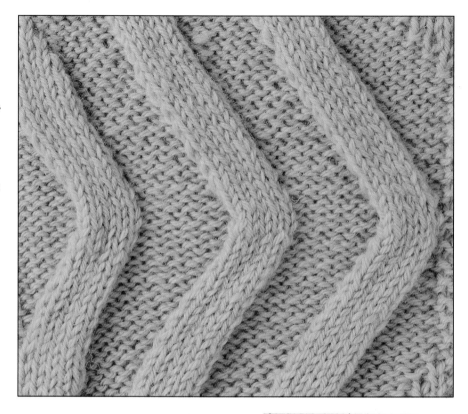

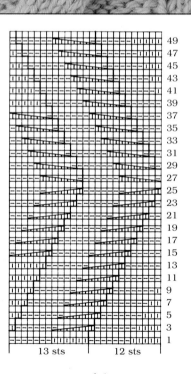

13 sts   12 sts

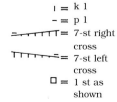

ı = k 1

− = p 1

= 7-st right cross

= 7-st left cross

□ = 1 st as shown

CROSSOVER STITCHES

Slanted double cable

Work center cable panel on 20 stitches.

Row 1: P 2, k 1 in back loop (twisted k st made), p 2, k 2, p 4, k 4, p 2, twisted k st, p 2.

Row 2 and all even-numbered rows: Work each stitch as it appears on this side of work (k the k sts and p the p sts); work twisted p st above twisted st.

Row 3: P 2, twisted k st, p 2, work left cross on 4 sts as follows: slip 2 to dp needle and hold in front of work, p 2, k 2 from dp needle, p 2, k 4, p 2, twisted k st, p 2.

Row 5: P 2, twisted k st, p 4, work crossover on 4 sts as follows: slip 2 to dp needle and hold in front, k 2, k 2 from dp needle, work left cross, p 2, twisted k st, p 2.

Row 7: P 2, twisted k st, p 2, work right cross on 4 sts as follows: slip 2 to dp needle and hold in back of work, k 2, p 2 from dp needle, work left cross-P, k 2, p 2, twisted k st, p 2.

Row 9: P 2, twisted k st, p 2, k 2, p 4, crossover, p 2, twisted k st, p 2. Repeat Rows 3 through 10 for pattern.

ı = k 1	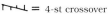 = 4-st crossover
− = p 1	= 4-st right cross
� = 1 twisted st	
= 4-st left cross	□ = 1 st as shown

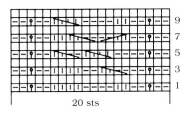

20 sts

Triple braids

Work triple braid on 10 sts. For pattern as shown, work triple braids evenly spaced on a background of reverse stockinette st.

Row 1: P 1, * work twist on 2 sts as follows: skip 1, k next st, k skipped st and drop original sts from left needle, work (twist, p 1) twice more, p 1.

Row 2: K 1, work (p 2, k 1) 3 times. Repeat these 2 rows for triple braids.

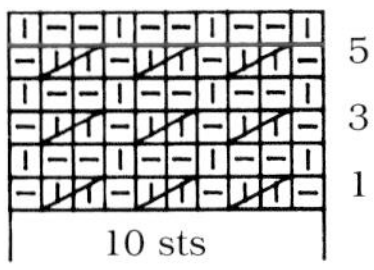

10 sts

ı = k 1	
− = p 1	
= 2-st twist	

CROSSOVER STITCHES

Interlocking diamonds

Work with a multiple of 10 sts, plus 2.

Row 1: Work left cross on 2 sts as follows: slip 1 to dp needle and hold in front of work, p 1, k 1 from dp needle, * p 8, work crossover on 2 sts as follows: slip 1 to dp needle, k 1, k 1 from dp needle *; repeat from * to *.

Row 2 and all even-numbered rows: Work each stitch as it appears on this side of work (k the k sts, p the p sts).

Row 3: P 1, * left cross, p 6, work right cross on 2 sts as follows: skip 1, k next st, then p skipped st and drop original sts from left needle *; repeat from * to *, ending p 1.

Row 5: P 2, * left cross, p 4, right cross, p 2 *; repeat from * to *.

Row 7: P 3, * left cross, p 2, right cross, p 4 *; repeat from * to *, ending last repeat with p 3.

Row 9: P 4, * left cross, right cross, p 6 *; repeat from * to *, ending with p 4.

Row 11: P 5, * crossover, p 8 *; repeat from * to *, ending with p 5.

Row 13: P 4, * right cross, left cross, p 6 *; repeat from * to *, ending with p 4.

Row 15: P 3, * right cross, p 2, left cross, p 4 *; repeat from * to *, ending with p 3.

Row 17: P 2, * right cross, p 4, left cross, p 2 *; repeat from * to *.

Row 19: P 1, * right cross, p 6, left cross *; repeat from * to *, ending p 1.
Repeat Rows 1 through 20 for pattern.

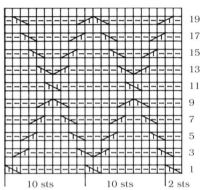

- = p 1
⋏ = 2-st left cross
⋏ = 2-st crossover
⋌ = 2-st right cross
□ = 1 st as shown

ı = k 1
- = p 1
⊢ = 2-st twist
□ = 1 st as shown

Infinite diagonals

Work with a multiple of 4 stitches, plus 2.

Row 1: P 2, * work twist on 2 sts as follows: skip 1, k next st, k skipped st and drop original sts from left needle, p 2 *; repeat from * to *.

Row 2 and all even-numbered rows: Work each st as it appears on this side of work (k the k sts and p the p sts).

Row 3: P 1, * twist, p 2 *; repeat from * to *, ending k 1.

Row 5: Twist, * p 2, twist *; repeat from * to *.

Row 7: K 1, * p 2, twist *; repeat from * to *, ending p 1.
Repeat Rows 1 through 8 for pattern.

CROSSOVER STITCHES

Flame cable

Work with a multiple of 10 stitches.

Row 1 (right side): * K 5, p 5 *; repeat from * to *.

Row 2: P 1, * k 5, p 5 *; repeat from * to *, ending with p 4.

Row 3: K 3, * p 5, k 5 *; repeat from * to *, ending with k 2.

Row 4: P 3, * k 5, p 5 *; repeat from * to *, ending with p 2.

Row 5: K 1, * p 5, k 5 *; repeat from * to *, ending with k 4.

Row 6: * P 5, k 5 *; repeat from * to *.

Row 7: P 4, * k 5, p 5 *; repeat from * to *, ending with p 1.

Row 8: K 2, * p 5, k 5 *; repeat from * to *, ending with k 3.

Row 9: P 2, * k 5, p 5 *; repeat from * to *, ending with p 3.

Row 10: K 4, * p 5, k 5 *; repeat from * to *, ending k 1.

Rows 11 and 12: * K 5, p 5 *; repeat from * to *.

Row 13: * Work left crossover on 5 sts as follows: slip 3 to dp needle and hold in front of work, k 2, k 3 from dp needle, p 5 *; repeat from * to *.

Rows 14 through 18: * K 5, p 5 *; repeat from * to *.

Row 19: * Work right crossover on 5 sts as follows: slip 2 to dp needle and hold in back of work, k 3, k 2 from dp needle, p 5 *; repeat from * to *.

Row 20: * K 5, p 5 *; repeat from * to *.

Row 21: K 4, * p 5, k 5 *; repeat from * to *, ending k 1.

Row 22: P 2, * k 5, p 5 *; repeat from * to *, ending p 3.

Row 23: K 2. * p 5, k 5 *; repeat from * to *, ending k 3.

Row 24: P 4, * k 5, p 5 *; repeat from * to *, ending p 1.

Row 25: * P 5, k 5; repeat from * to *.

Row 26: K 1, * p 5, k 5 *; repeat from * to *, ending k 4.

Row 27: P 3, * k 5, p 5 *; repeat from * to *, ending p 2.

Row 28: K 3, * p 5, k 5 *; repeat from * to *, ending k 2.

Row 29: P 1, * k 5, p 5 *; repeat from * to *, ending p 4.

Row 30: * K 5, p 5 *; repeat from * to *.

Row 31: Repeat Row 19.

Rows 32 through 36: * K 5, p 5 *; repeat from * to *.

Row 37: Repeat Row 13.

Rows 38 through 48: Repeat Rows 20 through 30.

Repeat Rows 13 through 48 for pattern.

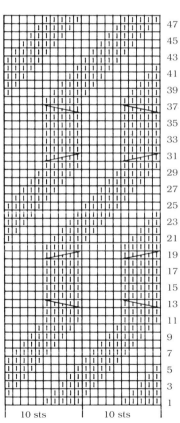

| =1 st in stockinette st

□ =1 st in reverse stockinette st

⊤⊤⊤⌐ =5-st left crossover

⌐⊤⊤⊤ =5-st right crossover

CROSSOVER STITCHES

Tepees

Work with a multiple of 20 stitches.
Row 1: * Work left cross on 4 sts as follows: slip 3 to dp needle and hold in front of work, p 1, k 3 from dp needle, p 12, work right cross on 4 sts as follows: slip 1 to dp needle and hold in back of work, k 3, p 1 from dp needle *; repeat from * to *.
Row 2 and all even-numbered rows: K the k sts (as they face you) and p the p sts.
Row 3: P 1, * left cross, p 10, right cross, p 2 *; repeat from * to *, ending p 1.
Row 5: P 2, * left cross, p 8, right cross, p 4 *; repeat from * to *, ending p 2.
Row 7: P 3, * left cross, p 6, right cross, p 6 *; repeat from * to *, ending p 3.
Row 9: P 4, * left cross, p 4, right cross, p 8 *; repeat from * to *, ending p 4.
Row 11: P 5, * left cross, p 2, right cross, p 10 *; repeat from * to *, ending p 5.
Row 13: P 6, * left cross, right cross, p 12 *; repeat from * to *, ending p 6.
Repeat Rows 1 through 14 for pattern.

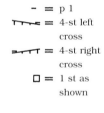

- = p 1
= 4-st left cross
= 4-st right cross
□ = 1 st as shown

20 sts

Ribs and cables

Work with a multiple of 12 stitches, plus 2.
Rows 1 and 3: K 2, * p 2, k 6, p 2, k 2 *; repeat from * to *.
Row 2 and all even-numbered rows: Work each stitch as it appears on this side of work (k the k sts and p the p sts).
Row 5: K 2, * p 2, work crossover on 6 sts as follows: slip 3 to dp needle and hold in back of work, k 3, k 3 from dp needle, p 2, k 2 *; repeat from * to *.
Repeat Rows 3 through 6 for pattern.

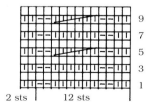

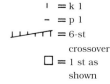

2 sts   12 sts

ı = k 1
- = p 1
= 6-st crossover
□ = 1 st as shown

66

CROSSOVER STITCHES

Winding cables

Work cable on 6 sts. For pattern as shown, work evenly-spaced cables on background of reverse stockinette st.
Rows 1 and 3: K 6.
Row 2 and all even-numbered rows: P 6.
Row 5: Work left cross on 6 sts as follows: slip 3 to dp needle and hold in front of work, k 3, k 3 from dp needle.
Rows 7, 9, and 11: K 6.
Row 13: Work right cross on 6 sts as follows: slip 3 sts to dp needle and hold in back of work, k 3, k 3 from dp needle.
Row 15: K 6.
Repeat Rows 1 through 16 for pattern.

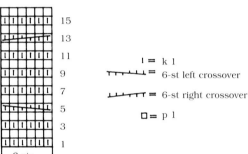

l = k 1

$\overline{\text{TTT}\llcorner\llcorner}$ = 6-st left crossover

$\llcorner\llcorner\text{TTT}$ = 6-st right crossover

□ = p 1

Serpentine cables

Work 2 cables on 19 sts or work with a multiple of 9 stitches, plus 1, for pattern as shown.
Rows 1 and 3: P 2, * k 6, p 3 *; repeat from * to *, ending with p 2.
Row 2 and all even-numbered rows: Work each stitch as it appears on this side of work (k the k sts, p the p sts).
Row 5: P 2, * work left crossover on 6 sts as follows: slip 3 to dp needle and hold in front of work, k 3, k 3 from dp needle, p 3 *; repeat from * to *, ending with p 2.
Rows 7 and 9: Repeat Rows 1 and 3.
Row 11: P 2, work right crossover on 6 sts as follows: slip 3 to dp needle and hold in back of work, k 3, k 3 from dp needle, p 3 *; repeat from * to *, ending p 2.
Repeat Rows 1 through 12 for pattern.

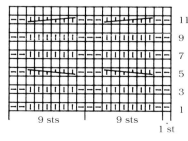

l = k 1

– = p 1

$\text{TTT}\llcorner\llcorner$ = 6-st left crossover

$\llcorner\llcorner\text{TTT}$ = 6-st right crossover

□ = 1 st as shown

CROSSOVER STITCHES

Diagonal bands

Work band on 10 stitches. For pattern as shown, work evenly-spaced bands on background of reverse stockinette st.

Row 1: * Work right cross on 2 sts as follows: skip 1, k next st, then k skipped st and drop original sts from left needle *; repeat from * to *.

Rows 2 and 4: Purl.

Row 3: K 1, * work right cross *; repeat from * to *, ending k 1.

Repeat Rows 1 through 4 for pattern.

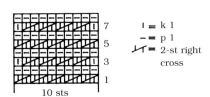

I = k 1
- = p 1
⤙⤚ = 2-st right cross

Oval cables

Work cable panel on 16 stitches.

Rows 1, 7, and 11: P 2, k 2, p 2, k 4, p 2, k 2, p 2.

Row 2 and all even-numbered rows: Work each stitch as it appears on this side of work (k the k sts and p the p sts).

Rows 3, 9, and 13: P 2, k 2, p 2, work 4-st crossover as follows: slip 2 to dp needle and hold in front of work, k 2, k 2 from dp needle, p 2, k 2, p 2.

Row 5: P 2, work 6-st right crossover as follows: slip 4 to dp needle and hold in back of work, k 2, bring dp needle to front of work, return 2 p sts from dp needle to left needle and p them, k last 2 from dp needle; work 6-st left crossover as follows: slip 2 to dp needle and hold in front, slip next 2 to another dp needle and hold in back, k next 2, p 2 from back dp needle, k 2 from front dp needle, p 2. Repeat from Rows 1 through 14 for cable.

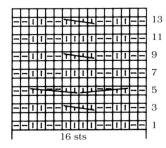

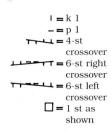

I = k 1
- = p 1
⊤⊤⤙⤚ = 4-st crossover
⤙⤙⤚⤚⊤⊤ = 6-st right crossover
⊤⊤⤙⤚⤚ = 6-st left crossover
☐ = 1 st as shown

CROSSOVER STITCHES

Interchanging cables

Work 2 cables on 15 stitches.

Rows 1, 3, and 7: K 2, p 2, k 2, p 3, k 2, p 2, k 2.

Row 2 and all even-numbered rows: P 2, k 2, p 2, k 3, p 2, k 2, p 2 (working each stitch as it appears).

Row 5: K 2, p 2, k 2, p 3, work crossover on next 6 sts as follows: slip 4 to dp needle and hold in back of work, k 2, bring dp needle to front of work, return 2 p sts from dp needle to left needle and p them, k 2 from dp needle.

Row 9: Work crossover, p 3, k 2, p 2, k 2.

Repeat Rows 3 through 10 for cables.

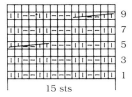

15 sts

ı = k 1
- = p 1
⌐⌐⌐⌐ = 6-st crossover

□ = 1 st as shown

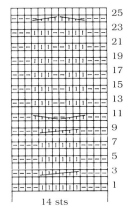

14 sts

ı = k 1
- = p 1
⌐⌐⌐⌐ = 6-st crossover
⌐⌐⌐ = 4-st right cross
⌐⌐⌐ = 4-st left cross
□ = 1 st as shown

Extended cable

Work cable panel on 14 stitches.

Rows 1, 5, and 7: P 4, k 6, p 4.

Row 2 and all even-numbered rows: Work each stitch as it appears on this side of work (k the k sts and p the p sts).

Rows 3 and 9: P4, work crossover on 6 sts as follows: slip 3 to dp needle and hold in back of work, k 3, k 3 from dp needles, p 4.

Row 11: P 3, work right cross on 4 sts as follows: slip 1 to dp needle and hold in back of work, k 3, p 1 from dp needle; work left cross on 4 sts as follows: slip 3 to dp needle and hold in front of work, p 1, k 3 from dp needle, p 3.

Rows 13, 15, 17, 19, 21, and 23: P 3, k 3, p 2, k 3, p 3.

Row 25: P 3, left cross, right cross, p 3.

Repeat Rows 3 through 26 for cable.

CROSSOVER STITCHES

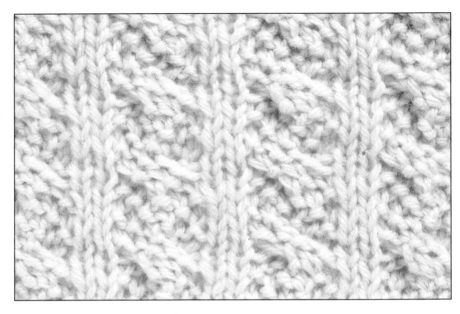

Textured rib stitch

Work with a multiple of 8 stitches. *Note*: To work moss st, always p above k st (as it faces you) and k above p st.

Rows 1 and 5: K 2, work (p 1, k 1) 3 times for 6 moss sts.

Row 2 and all even-numbered rows: Work moss st over moss sts and p 2 rib sts.

Row 3: K 2, work left cross on 6 moss sts as follows: slip 3 to dp needle and hold in front of work, work moss st on next 3 sts, work moss st on 3 sts from dp needle.

Repeat Rows 1 through 6 for pattern.

8 sts

| = k 1
− = p 1
• = 1 moss st

 = 6-st left cross

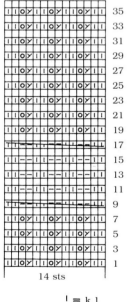

14 sts

| = k 1
− = p 1
o = yarn over
Y = p 2 tog

 = 14-st crossover
□ = 1 st as shown

Swirling cable

Work cable panel on 14 sts. For cable pattern as shown, work cable on background of reverse stockinette st.

Rows 1, 3, 5, and 7: K 2, * p 2 sts together, yarn over, k 2 *; repeat from * to *.

Row 2 and all even-numbered rows: P 2, * k 2, p 2 *; repeat from * to * (working each stitch as it appears).

Rows 9 and 17: Work crossover on 14 sts as follows: slip 6 to dp needle and hold in front of work, work (k 2, p 2) twice, then k 2, p 2, k 2 on 6 sts from dp needle.

Rows 11, 13, and 15: K 2, * p 2, k 2 *; repeat from * to *.

Rows 19, 21, 23, 25, 27, 29, 31, 33, and 35: K 2, * p 2 sts together, yarn over, k 2 *; repeat from * to *. Repeat Rows 1 through 36 for cable.

CROSSOVER STITCHES

Wrapped ribs

Work with a multiple of 7 sts.
Row 1: P 2, * yarn over, k 3, pass yarn-over loop over 3 k sts and drop it to wrap rib, p 4 *; repeat from * to *, ending with p 2.
Row 2: K 2, * p 3, k 4 *; repeat from * to *, ending with k 2.
Repeat these 2 rows for pattern.

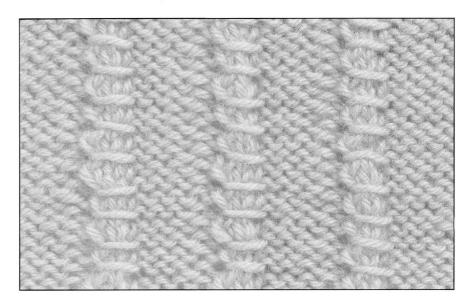

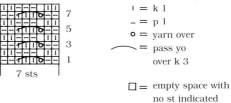

ı = k 1
− = p 1
o = yarn over
⌐ = pass yo over k 3
□ = empty space with no st indicated

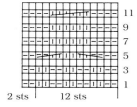

ı = k 1
− = p 1
⌐⌐⌐⌐ = 4-st left cross
⌐⌐⌐⌐ = 4-st right cross
⌐⌐⌐⌐⌐ = 6-st crossover
□ = 1 st as shown

Bells

Work with a multiple of 12 stitches, plus 2.
Rows 1 and 3: P 2, * k 2, p 2 *; repeat from * to *.
Row 2 and all even-numbered rows: Work each stitch as it appears on this side of work (k the k sts and p the p sts).
Row 5: P 2, * work left cross on 4 sts as follows: slip 2 to dp needle and hold in front of work, p 2, k 2 from dp needle, k 2, work right cross on 4 sts as follows: slip 2 to dp needle and hold in back of work, k 2, p 2 from dp needle, p 2 *; repeat from * to *.
Rows 7 and 9: P 4, * k 6, p 6 *; repeat from * to *, ending with k 4.
Row 11: P 4, * work crossover on 6 sts as follows: slip 3 to dp needle and hold in back of work, k 3, k 3 from dp needle, p 6 *; repeat from * to *, ending p 4.
Repeat Rows 1 through 12 for pattern.

CROSSOVER STITCHES

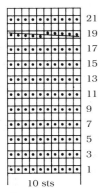

21
19
17
15
13
11
9
7
5
3
1

10 sts

• & □ = moss st

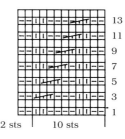

＝ 10-st crossover

Moss stitch cable

Work cable on 10 stitches. For pattern as shown, work cables set between 2-st stockinette st ribs.
Note: To work moss st, always work p over k st (as it faces you) and k over p st.
Row 1: Work (k 1, p 1) 5 times (10 sts in moss st).
Rows 2 through 18: Work in moss st.
Row 19: Work crossover on 10 sts as follows: slip 5 to dp needle and hold in front of work, work 5 moss sts, work 5 moss sts from dp needle.
Row 20: Work in moss st.
Repeat these 20 rows for pattern.

Columns and twists

Work with a multiple of 10 stitches, plus 2.
Row 1: P 2, * k 2, p 4, k 2, p 2 *; repeat from * to *.
Row 2 and all even-numbered rows: Work each stitch as it appears on this side of work (k the k sts and p the p sts).
Row 3: P 2, * k 2, p 3, work right cross-K on 3 sts as follows: slip 1 to dp needle and hold in back of work, k 2, k 1 from dp needle, p 2 * repeat from * to *.
Row 5: P 2, * k 2, p 2, right cross-K, k 1, p 2 *; repeat from * to *.
Row 7: P 2, * k 2, p 1, work right cross-P on 3 sts as follows: slip to dp needle and hold in back, k 2, p 1 from dp needle, k 2, p 2 *; repeat from * to *.
Row 9: P 2, * k 2, right cross-P, p 1, k 2, p 2 *; repeat from * to *.
Row 11: P 2, * k 1, right cross-P, p 2, k 2, p 2 *; repeat from * to *.
Row 13: P 2, * right cross-P, p 3, k 2, p 2 *; repeat from * to *.
Repeat Rows 3 through 14 for pattern.

13
11
9
7
5
3
1

2 sts | 10 sts

ı = k 1
– = p 1
＝ 3-st right cross-K
＝ 3-st right cross-P
□ = 1 st as shown

CROSSOVER STITCHES

Crossed braid

Work braid on 2 sts. For pattern as shown, work evenly-spaced braids on background of reverse stockinette st.
Row 1: Slip 1, k 1, yarn over, then pass slip st over k st and yarn-over and drop it.
Row 2: P 2.
Repeat these 2 rows for pattern.

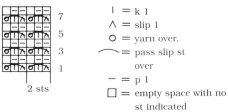

```
| = k 1
∧ = slip 1
○ = yarn over,
⌒ = pass slip st
     over
– = p 1
□ = empty space with no
     st indicated
```

Wavy stitches

Work with a multiple of 4 stitches.
Row 1: P 3, * work left cross on 2 sts as follows: skip 1, reach behind work to k in back loop of next st, then k in front loop of skipped st and drop original 2 sts from left needle, p 2 *; repeat from * to *, ending with p 3.
Row 2 and all even-numbered rows: Work each stitch as it appears on this side of work (k the k sts and p the p sts).
Row 3: K 3, * work right cross on 2 sts as follows: skip 1, k next st, k skipped st and drop original sts from left needle, k 2 *; repeat from * to *, ending with k 3.
Row 5: P 1, * left cross, p 2 *; repeat from * to *, ending with p 1.
Row 7: K 1, * right cross, k 2 *; repeat from * to *, ending with k 1.
Repeat Rows 1 through 8 for pattern.

```
| = k 1
– = p 1
⋌ = 2-st left
     cross
⋋ = 2-st right
     cross
□ = 1 st as
     shown
```

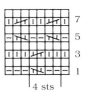

CROSSOVER STITCHES

Easy braid

Work braid on 2 stitches. For pattern as shown, work evenly-spaced braids on background of reverse stockinette st.

Row 1: Work right cross on 2 sts as follows: skip 1, k next st, then k skipped sts and drop the original 2 sts from left needle.

Row 2: P 2.

Repeat these 2 rows for braid.

= 2-st right cross

☐ = p 1

2 sts

Long and short cables

Work with a multiple of 12 stitches, plus 4.

Rows 1 and 3: P 5, * k 6, p 6 *; repeat from * to *, ending with p 5.

Row 2 and all even-numbered rows: Work each st as it appears on this side of work (k the k sts and p the p sts).

Rows 5 and 21: P 5, * work crossover on 6 sts as follows: slip 3 to dp needle and hold in front of work, k 3, k 3 from dp needle; p 6 *; repeat from * to *, ending p 5.

Rows 7 and 23: P 4, * work right cross on 4 sts as follows: slip 1 to dp needle and hold in back of work, k 3, p 1 from dp needle; work left cross on 4 sts as follows: slip 3 to dp needle and hold in front, p 1, k 3 from dp needle, p 4 *; repeat from * to *.

Rows 9, 11, 13, 15, 17, 25, and 27: P 4, * k 3, p 2, k 3, p 4 *; repeat from * to *.

Rows 19 and 29: P 4, * left cross, right cross, p 4 *; repeat from * to *. Repeat Rows 5 through 30 for pattern.

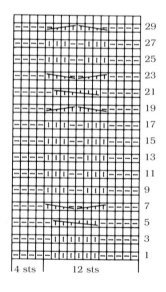

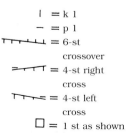

❙ = k 1

— = p 1

= 6-st crossover

= 4-st right cross

= 4-st left cross

☐ = 1 st as shown

CROSSOVER STITCHES

Continuous crossing

Work with a multiple of 7 stitches.
Rows 1 and 3: * P 2, k 5 *; repeat from * to *.
Row 2 (wrong side): * P 1, work left cross on 3 sts as follows: skip 1, p next st, then p following st, p skipped st and drop original 3 sts from left needle, p 1, k 2.
Row 4: * P 1, work right cross on 3 sts as follows: skip 2, reach from behind work to p in front loop of 3rd st, then p first skipped st, then p remaining skipped st and drop original sts from left needle, p 1, k 2 *; repeat from * to *.
Repeat these 4 rows for pattern.

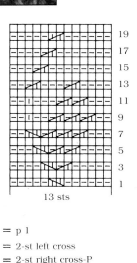

		= k 1
-	= p 1
⊼	= 3-st left cross
⊿	= 3-st right cross

Little branches with leaves

Work with a multiple of 13 stitches.
Row 1: P 6, * work left cross on 2 sts as follows: skip 1, reach behind work to k in back loop of next st, then k in front loop of skipped st and drop original sts from left needle, p 11 *; repeat from * to *, ending with p 5.
Row 2 and all even-numbered rows: K the k sts as they face you and p the p sts.
Row 3: P 5, * work right cross-P on 2 sts as follows: skip 1, k 1, p skipped st and drop original sts from left needle; left cross, p 9 *; repeat from * to *, ending with p 4.
Row 5: P 4, * work right cross-P twice, left cross, p 7 *; repeat from * to *, ending with p 3.
Row 7: P 3, * work right cross-P 3 times, left cross, p 5 *; repeat from * to *, ending with p 2.
Row 9: P 2, * work right cross-P 3 times, p 2, k 1, p 4 *; repeat from * to *, ending with p 2.
Row 11: P 3, * work right cross-P twice, p 3, k 1, p 5 *; repeat from * to *, ending with p 2.
Row 13: P 4, * right cross-P, p 3, right cross, p 6 *; repeat from * to *, ending with p 2.
Row 15: P 8, * right cross-P, p 11 *; repeat from * to *, ending p 3.
Row 17: P 7, * right cross-P, p 11 *; repeat from * to *, ending p 4.
Row 19: P 6, * work right cross-K on

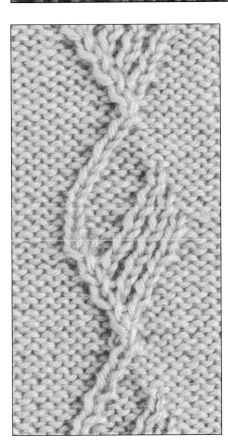

-	= p 1
⊼	= 2-st left cross
⊁	= 2-st right cross-P
⋌	= 2-st right cross-K
□	= 1 st as shown

2 sts as follows: skip 1, k 1, k skipped st, drop original sts, p 11 *; repeat from * to *, ending p 5.

Repeat Rows 1 through 20 for pattern.

CROSSOVER STITCHES

Headed left

Work with a multiple of 12 stitches, plus 6.

Rows 1, 3, 7, and 9 (right side): Knit.

Row 2: K 6 (garter st), * p 6 (stockinette st), k 6 (garter st) *; repeat from * to *.

Row 4: P 2, * k 6, p 6 *; repeat from * to *, ending with k 4.

Row 5: K 2, * work left cross on 6 sts as follows: slip 3 to dp needle and hold in front, k 3, k 3 from dp needle, k 6 *; repeat from * to *, ending with k 10.

Row 6: P 4, * k 6, p 6, * repeat from * to *, ending k 2.

Row 8: P 6, * k 6, p 6 * repeat from * to *.

Row 10: K 2, * p 6, k 6 *; repeat from * to *, ending p 4.

Row 11: K 8, * left cross, k 12 *; repeat from * to *, ending k 4.

Row 12: K 4, * p 6, k 6 *; repeat from * to *, ending p 2.

Repeat these 12 rows for pattern.

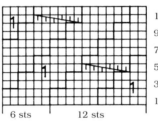

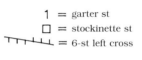

1 = garter st

□ = stockinette st

= 6-st left cross

Headed right

Work with a multiple of 12 stitches, plus 6.

Rows 1, 3, 7, and 9 (right side): Knit.

Row 2: K 6 (garter st), * p 6 (stockinette st), k 6 (garter st) *; repeat from * to *.

Row 4: K 4, * p 6, k 6 *; repeat from * to *, ending with p 2.

Row 5: K 10, * work right cross on 6 sts as follows: slip 3 to dp needle and hold in back of work, k 3, k 3 from dp needle, k 6 *; repeat from * to *, ending with k 2.

Row 6: K 2, * p 6, k 6 *; repeat from * to *, ending with p 4.

Row 8: P 6, * k 6, p 6 *; repeat from * to *.

Row 10: K 4, * p 6, k 6 *; repeat from * to *, ending with k 2.

Row 11: K 4, * right cross, k 6 *; repeat from * to *, ending with k 8.

Row 12: P 2, * k 6, p 6 *; repeat from * to *, ending with k 4.

Repeat these 12 rows for pattern.

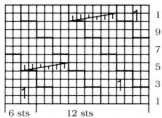

1 = garter st

□ = stockinette st

= 6-st right cross

CROSSOVER STITCHES

Crisscross

Work with multiple of 6 stitches.

Row 1: Knit.

Row 2 and all even-numbered rows: Purl.

Row 3: * Work right cross on 4 sts as follows: slip 2 to dp needle and hold in back of work, k 2, k 2 from dp needle, k 2 *; repeat from * to *.

Row 5: Knit.

Row 7: * K 2, work left cross on 4 sts as follows: slip 2 to dp needle and hold in front of work, k 2, k 2 from dp needle *; repeat from * to *.

Repeat Rows 1 through 8 for pattern.

$\mathbf{l}$	= k 1
$\square$	= p 1
	= 4-st right cross
	= 4-st left cross

Crossed rib stitch

Work with a multiple of 6 stitches, plus 2.

Rows 1 and 5: P 2, * k 4, p 2 *; repeat from * to *.

Row 2 and all even-numbered rows: Work each stitch as it appears on this side of work (k the k sts and p the p sts).

Row 3: P 2, * work crossover on 4 sts as follows: slip 2 to dp needle and hold in front of work, k 2, k 2 from dp needle, p 2 *; repeat from * to *.

Row 7: P 1, * work right cross on 3 sts as follows: slip 1 to dp needle and hold in back of work, k 2, p 1 from dp needle, work left cross on 3 sts as follows: slip 2 to dp needle and hold in front, p 1, k 2 from dp needle *; repeat from * to *, ending p 1.

Row 9: P 1, k 2, p 2, * crossover, p 2 *; repeat from * to *, ending k 2, p 1.

Row 11: P 1, k 2, p 2, * k 4, p 2 *; repeat from * to *, ending k 2, p 1.
Repeat Rows 1 through 12 for pattern.

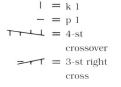

$\mathbf{l}$	= k 1
$-$	= p 1
	= 4-st crossover
	= 3-st right cross
	= 3-st left cross
$\square$	= 1 st as shown

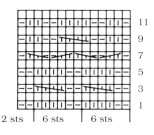

2 sts   6 sts   6 sts

CROSSOVER STITCHES

Split logs

Work with a multiple of 12 stitches, plus 2.

Rows 1, 3, 5, and 7: K 1, p 3, * k 6, p 6 *; repeat from * to *, ending with p 3, k 1.

Row 2 and all even-numbered rows: Work each stitch as it appears on this side of work (k the k sts and p the p sts).

Row 9: Knit.

Row 11: K 1, * work left cross on 6 sts as follows: slip 3 to dp needle and hold in front of work, k 3, k 3 from dp needle, work right cross on 6 sts as follows: slip 3 to dp needle and hold in back of work, k 3, k 3 from dp needle *; repeat from * to *, ending k 1.

Repeat Rows 1 through 12 for pattern.

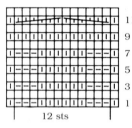

| = k 1
− = p 1
= 6-st left cross
= 6-st right cross
□ = 1 st as shown

12 sts

Little diagonals

Work with a multiple of 9 stitches, plus 3.

Row 1: K 3, * work 2-st cross as follows: skip 1, k 1, k skipped st and drop original 2 sts from left needle; work 2-st cross twice more, k 3 *; repeat from * to *.

Row 2 and all even-numbered rows: Purl.

Row 3: K 3, * work 3-st cross as follows: slip 1 to dp needle and hold in back of work, slip next st to second dp needle and hold in back of work, k next st, k 1 from second dp needle, k 1 from first dp needle; work 3-st cross once more, k 3 *; repeat from * to *.

Repeat Rows 1 through 4 for pattern.

| = k 1
□ = p 1
= 2-st cross
= 3-st cross

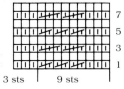

3 sts   9 sts

CROSSOVER STITCHES

Mated cables

Work with a multiple of 16 sts, plus 1.

Rows 1, 3, and 7: P 2, * k 6, p 1, k 6, p 3 *; repeat from * to *, ending with p 2.

Row 2 and all even-numbered rows: Work each stitch as it appears on this side of work (k the k sts and p the p sts).

Row 5: P 2, * work right cross on 6 sts as follows: slip 3 to dp needle and hold in back of work, k 3, k 3 from dp needle, p 1, work left cross on 6 sts as follows: slip 3 to dp needle and hold in front, k 3, k 3 from dp needle, p 3 *; repeat from * to *, ending with p 2.

Repeat Rows 1 through 8 for pattern.

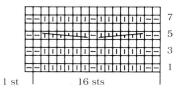

1 st   16 sts

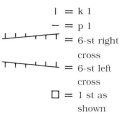

| = k 1
— = p 1
= 6-st right cross
= 6-st left cross
☐ = 1 st as shown

Artistic cables

Work with a multiple of 14 stitches, plus 8.

Row 1: P 1, * k 2, work left cross on 4 sts as follows: slip 2 sts to dp needle and hold in front of work, k 2, k 2 from dp needle, p 3, k 2, p 3 *; repeat from * to *, ending k 2, left cross, p 1.

Row 2 and all even-numbered rows: Work each stitch as it appears on this side of work (k the k sts and p the p sts).

Rows 3 and 13: P 1, * k 6, p 2, k 4, p 2 *; repeat from * to *, ending k 6, p 1.

Rows 5 and 11: P 2, * k 4, p 2, k 6, p 2 *; repeat from * to *, ending k 4, p 2.

Row 7: P 3, * k 2, p 3, work right cross on 4 sts as follows: slip 2 sts to dp needle and hold in back of work, k 2, k 2 from dp needle, k 2, p 3 *; repeat from * to *, ending with k 2, p 3.

Row 9: P 3, * k 2, p 3, k 2, left cross, p 3 *; repeat from * to *, ending with k 2, p 3.

Row 15: P 1, * right cross, k 2, p 3, k 2, p 3 *; repeat from * to *, ending right cross, k 2, p 1.

Repeat Rows 1 through 16 for pattern.

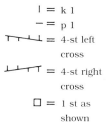

| = k 1
— = p 1
= 4-st left cross
= 4-st right cross
☐ = 1 st as shown

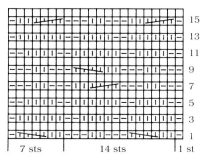

7 sts   14 sts   1 st

CROSSOVER STITCHES

Mirrored loops

Work with a multiple of 12 stitches, plus 2.

Note: Carry yarn on wrong side to work slip sts.

Row 1 (right side): P 4, * work 1 long st as follows: k st wrapping yarn twice around needle; work another long st, p 2, k 2 long sts, p 6 *; repeat from * to *, ending with p 4.

Rows 2 and 6: K 4, * with yarn forward, work (slip long st as if to p, letting extra yarn loop drop from needle) twice, k 2, slip 2 long sts as before, k 6 *; repeat from * to *, ending with k 4.

Row 3: P4, * slip 2, p 2, slip 2, p 6 *; repeat from * to *, ending p 4.

Row 4: K 4, * slip 2, k 2, slip 2, k 6 *; repeat from * to *, ending k 4.

Row 5: * P 2, work right cross on 4 sts as follows: slip 2 to dp needle and hold in back, k 2, k 2 from dp needle working them as long sts (wrapping yarn twice), p 2, work left cross on 4 sts as follows: slip 2 to dp needle and

hold in front, k 2 as long sts, k 2 from dp needle *; repeat from * to *, ending p 2.

Repeat Rows 3 through 6 for pattern.

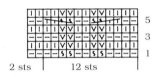

2 sts   12 sts

| = k 1
− = p 1
S = 1 long st

V = 1 slip st
= 4-st right cross
= 4-st left cross

Wavy moss stitch cables

Work on multiple of 15 sts, plus 3.

Note: To work moss st, always p the k st (as it faces you) and k the p st.

Rows 1, 3, 15, and 17: P 3 * k 3, work (k 1, p 1) 3 times for 6 moss sts, k 3, p 3 *; repeat from * to *.

Row 2 and all even-numbered rows: Work moss st over moss sts and work each remaining st as it appears (k the k sts and p the p sts).

Row 5: P 3, * work right cross-A on 6 sts as follows: slip 3 to dp needle and hold in back of work, work 3 moss sts, k 3 from dp needle; work right cross-B on 6 sts as follows: slip 3 to dp needle and hold in back, k 3, work 3 moss sts from dp needle, p 3 *; repeat from * to *.

Rows 7, 9, and 11: P 3, * work 3 moss sts, k 6, work 3 moss sts, p 3 *; repeat from * to *.

Row 13: P 3, * work left cross-A on 6 sts as follows: slip 3 to dp needle and hold in front, k 3, work 3 moss sts from dp needle; work left cross-B on 6 sts as follows: slip 3 to dp needle and hold in front, 3 moss sts, k 3 from dp needle, p 3 *; repeat from * to *.

Repeat Rows 3 through 18 for pattern.

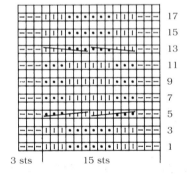

3 sts   15 sts

| = k 1
− = p 1
• = 1 moss st

= 6-st right cross-A
= 6-st right cross-B
= 6-st left cross-A
= 6-st left cross-B

□ = 1 st as shown

CROSSOVER STITCHES

Peanuts and hazelnuts

Work with a multiple of 8 stitches, plus 3.

Row 1: P 3, * work 5 sts in next st as follows: work (k 1, yarn over) twice, k 1, then p 7 *; repeat from * to *.

Row 2 and all even-numbered rows: Work each stitch as it appears on this side of work (k the k sts and p the p sts). Purl any yarn-overs.

Row 3: P 3, * k 2, work right cross on 3 sts as follows: slip 1 to dp needle and hold in back of work, k 2, k 1 from dp needle, p 7 *; repeat from * to *.

Row 5: P 3, * work left cross on 3 sts as follows: slip 2 to dp needle and hold in front, k 1, k 2 from dp needle, k 2, p 7 *; repeat from * to *.

Row 7: P 3, * k 5 sts together, p 3, work 5 sts in 1 st as before, p 3 *; repeat from * to *.

Row 9: * P 7, k in back loop, then front loop of next st, k 3, k in front, then back loop of next st *; repeat from * to *, ending p 3.

Rows 11 and 15: * P 7, k 7 *; repeat from * to *, ending p 3.

Row 13: * P 7, left cross, k 1, right cross *; repeat from * to *, ending p 3.

Row 17: * P 7, slip 1, k 1, pass slipped st over k st and drop it, k 3,

k 2 sts together *; repeat from * to *, ending p 3.

Row 19: P 3, * work 5 sts in 1 st, p 3, k 5 sts together, p 3 *; repeat from * to *.

Repeat Rows 3 through 20 for pattern.

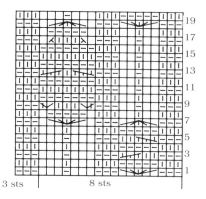

3 sts   8 sts

| = k 1

— = p 1

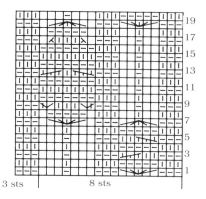 = 5 sts in 1 st

= 5 sts tog

⊥⊤⊤ = 3-st right cross

⊤⊤⊥ = 3-st left cross

= k in back + front

= k in front + back

λ = slip 1, k 1, psso

⋏ = k 2 tog

□ = empty space with no st indicated

Twisted bands

Work with a multiple of 12 stitches, plus 1.

Row 1: P 1 * work (k 1 in back loop to make twisted st, p 1) 3 times, work left cross on 2 sts as follows: slip 1 to dp needle and hold in front of work, p 1, k 1 twisted st from dp needle, k 1 twisted st, work right cross on 2 sts as follows: slip 1 to dp needle and hold in back of work, k 1 twisted st, p 1 from dp needle, p 1 * repeat from * to *.

Row 2 and all even-numbered rows: Working twisted p st over twisted st below, work each stitch as it appears on this side of work (k the k sts and p the p sts).

Row 3: P 1, * k 1 twisted st, work (p 1, k 1 twisted st) twice, p 2, work crossover on 3 sts as follows: slip 2 to dp needle and hold in back of work, k 1 twisted st, k 2 twisted sts from dp needle, p 2 *; repeat from * to *.

Row 5: P 1, * work (k 1 twisted st, p 1) 3 times, right cross, k 1 twisted st, left cross, p 1 *; repeat from * to *.

Rows 7 and 15: P 1, * k 1 twisted st, p 1 *; repeat from * to *.

Row 9: P 1, * left cross, k 1 twisted st, right cross, p 1, work (k 1 twisted st, p 1) 3 times *; repeat from * to *.

Row 11: * P 2, crossover, p 2, k 1 twisted st, work (p 1, k 1 twisted st)

twice *; repeat from * to *, ending p 1.

Row 13: P 1, * right cross, k 1 twisted st, left cross, work (p 1, k 1 twisted st) 3 times, p 1 *; repeat from * to *.

Repeat Rows 1 through 16 for pattern.

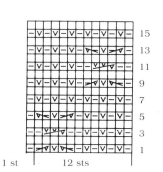

1 st   12 sts

— = p 1

V = k 1 twisted st

▽⋖ = 2-st left cross

⋗▽ = 2-st right cross

V⋎▽ = 3-st crossover

□ = 1 st as shown

CROSSOVER STITCHES

Chutes

Work with a multiple of 14 stitches, plus 2.

Rows 1, 3, 5, 7, and 9: P 2, * yarn over, k 4, slip 1, k 1, pass slip st over k st and drop it, k 2 sts together, k 4, yarn over, p 2 *; repeat from * to *.

Row 2 and all even-numbered rows: Work each stitch as it appears on this side of work (k the k sts and p the p sts). Purl yarn-overs.

Row 11: P 2, * work left cross on 6 sts as follows: slip 3 to dp needle and hold in front of work, k 3, k 3 from dp needle, work right cross on 6 sts as follows: slip 3 to dp needle and hold in back of work, k 3, k 3 from dp needle, p 2 *; repeat from * to *.

Row 13: P 2, * right cross, left cross, p 2 *; repeat from * to *.

Repeat Rows 1 through 14 for pattern.

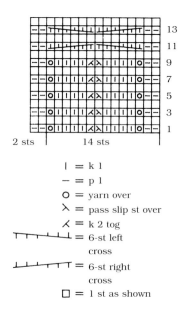

2 sts | 14 sts | 13 11 9 7 5 3 1

| = k 1
— = p 1
O = yarn over
⅄ = pass slip st over
⅄ = k 2 tog
⊤⊤⊤⊥⊥⊥ = 6-st left cross
⊥⊥⊥⊤⊤⊤ = 6-st right cross
☐ = 1 st as shown

Divided diamonds

Work with a multiple of 11 stitches, plus 5.

Row 1: K 7, * k 1 in back loop for twisted st, k another twisted st, p 9 *; repeat from * to *, ending with k 7.

Row 2 and all even-numbered rows: Working twisted p st over twisted st below, work each stitch as it appears on this side of work (k the k sts and p the p sts).

Row 3: P 6, * work right cross-K on 2 sts as follows: slip 1 to dp needle and hold in back, k 1 twisted st, k 1 twisted st from dp needle, work left cross-K on 2 sts as follows: slip 1 to dp needle and hold in front, k 1 twisted st, k 1 twisted st from dp needle, p 7 *; repeat from * to *, ending with p 6.

Row 5: P 5, * work right cross-P on 2 sts as follows: slip 1 to dp needle and hold in back, k 1 twisted st, p 1 from dp needle, k 2 twisted sts, work left cross-P on 2 sts as follows: slip 1 to dp needle and hold in front, p 1, k 1 twisted st from dp needle, p 5 *; repeat from * to *.

Row 7: P 4, * right cross-P, p 1, k 2 twisted sts, p 1, left cross-P, p 3 *; repeat from * to *, ending with p 4.

Row 9: P 3, * right cross-P, p 2, k 2 twisted sts, p 2, right cross-P, p 1 *; repeat from * to *, ending with p 3.

Row 11: P 1, * work knot on 3 sts as follows: k 3 sts together, keeping

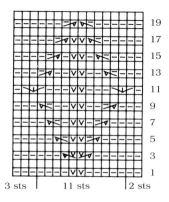

3 sts | 11 sts | 2 sts | 19 17 15 13 11 9 7 5 3 1

— = p 1
∨ = k 1 twisted st
⋎⋌ = 2-st right cross-K
⋏⋎ = 2-st left cross-K
⋝⋎ = 2-st right cross-P
⋎⋜ = 2-st left cross-P
⋎ = 3-st knot
☐ = 1 st as shown

them on left needle, p same sts together, then k them together again, drop original sts from left needle, p 3, k 2 twisted sts, p 3 *; repeat from * to *, ending with knot, p 1.

Row 13: P 3, * left cross-P, p 2, k 2 twisted sts, p 2, right cross-P, p 1 *; repeat from * to *, ending with p 3.

Row 15: P 4, * left cross-P, p 1, k 2 twisted sts, p 1, right cross-P, p 3 *;

repeat from * to *, ending with p 4.

Row 17: P 5, * left cross-P, k 2 twisted sts, right cross-P, p 5 *; repeat from * to *.

Row 19: P 6, * left cross-P, right cross-P, p 7 *; repeat from * to *, ending p 6.

Repeat Rows 1 through 20 for pattern.

CROSSOVER STITCHES

Rockets

Work with a multiple of 15 stitches, plus 7.

Row 1: P 3, * k 1, p 14 *; repeat from * to *, ending k 1, p 3.

Row 2 and all even-numbered rows: K the k sts (as they face you) and p the p sts).

Row 3: P 2, * k 3, p 12 *; repeat from * to *, ending k 3, p 2.

Row 5: P 2, * work 2 k-increases by knitting into front, then back loop of each st, k 1, p 12 *; repeat from * to *, ending with 2 k-increases, k 1, p 2.

Row 7: P 2, * work left cross + on 5 sts as follows: slip 3 to dp needle and hold in front, k-increase, k 1, k 3 from dp needle, p 12 *; repeat from * to *, ending left cross +, p 2.

Rows 9 and 13: P 2, * k 6, p 12 *; repeat from * to *; ending k 6, p 2.

Rows 11 and 15: P 2, * work 6-st left cross as follows: slip 3 to dp needle and hold in front, k 3, k 3 from dp needle, p 12 *; repeat from * to *, ending 6-st left cross, p 2.

Row 17: P 2, * work (k 2 sts together) 3 times, p 12 *; repeat from * to *, ending with p 2.

Row 19: P 11, * k 1, p 14 *; repeat from * to *, ending with p 10.

Row 21: P 10, * k 3, p 12 *; repeat from * to *, ending with p 9.

Row 23: P 10 * work 2 k-increases, k 1, p 12 *; repeat from * to *, ending p 9.

Row 25: P 10, * work left cross +, p 12 *; repeat from * to *, ending p 9.

Rows 27 and 31: P 10, * k 6, p 12 *; repeat from * to *, ending p 9.

Rows 29 and 33: P 10, work 6-st left cross, p 12 *; repeat from * to *, ending p 9.

Row 35: P 10, * work (k 2 sts together) 3 times, p 12 *; repeat from * to *, ending p 9.

Repeat Rows 1 through 36 for pattern.

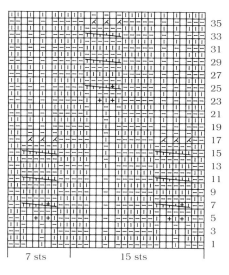

```
35
33
31
29
27
25
23
21
19
17
15
13
11
9
7
5
3
1
```

7 sts   15 sts

| = k 1

— = p 1

+ = 1 k-increase

⊤⊤⊤⊥⊥ = 5-st left cross +

⊤⊤⊤⊥⊥ = 6-st left cross

ⳤ = k 2 tog

□ = empty space with no st indicated

Wicker stitch

Work with a multiple of 13 stitches, plus 4.

Row 1: P 4, * k 1, work left cross on 2 sts as follows: slip 1 to dp needle and hold in front of work, k 1, k 1 from dp needle, work 3 more left crosses, p 4 *; repeat from * to *.

Row 2: K 4, * p 1, work right cross on 2 sts as follows: skip 1, p next st, p skipped st, drop original sts from left needle, work 3 more right crosses, p 4 *; repeat from * to *.

Repeat these 2 rows for pattern.

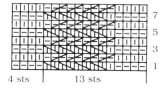

```
7
5
3
1
```

4 sts   13 sts

| = k 1

— = p 1

N = 2-st left cross

⤬ = 2-st right cross

CROSSOVER STITCHES

Sailboats

Work with a multiple of 11 stitches, plus 3.

Row 1: P 3, * k 8, p 3 *; repeat from * to *.

Row 2 and all even-numbered rows: Work each stitch as it appears on this side of work (k the k sts and p the p sts).

Row 3: P 3, * work right cross-K on 2 sts as follows: skip 1, k 1, k skipped st and drop original sts from left needle, work 2 more right cross-K, work right cross-P on 2 sts as follows: skip 1, k 1, p skipped st and drop original sts from left needle, p 3 *; repeat from * to *.

Row 5: P 3, * k 1, work 2 right cross-K, 1 right cross-P, p 4 *; repeat from * to *.

Row 7: P 3, * work 2 right cross-K, 1 right cross-P, p 5 *; repeat from * to *.

Row 9: P 3, * k 1, right cross-K, right cross-P, p 6 *; repeat from * to *.

Row 11: P 3, * right cross-K, right cross-P, p 7 *; repeat from * to *.

Row 13: P 3, * k 1, right cross-P, p 8 *; repeat from * to *.

Row 15: P 3, * right cross-P, p 9 *; repeat from * to *.

Repeat Rows 3 through 16 for pattern.

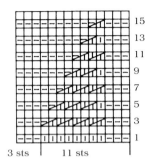

3 sts   11 sts

| = k 1
— = p 1
⊐⊤ = 2-st right cross-K
⊐⊤ = 2-st right cross-P
□ = 1 st as shown

Fountains

Work with a multiple of 10 stitches.

Row 1: K 2, * work crossover on 6 sts as follows: slip 3 to dp needle and hold in back of work, k 3, k 3 from dp needle, k 4 *; repeat from * to *, ending with k 2.

Row 2 and all even-numbered rows: Purl.

Row 3: * Work right cross on 3 sts as follows: slip 2 to dp needle and hold in back, k 1, k 2 from dp needle, yarn over, slip 1, k 1, pass slip st over k st and drop (psso), k 2 sts together, yarn over, work left cross on 3 sts as follows: slip 1 to dp needle and hold in front, k 2, k 1 from dp needle *; repeat from * to *.

Rows 5 and 9: K 3, * yarn over, slip 1, k 1, psso, k 2 sts together, yarn over, k 6 *; repeat from * to *, ending with k 3.

Row 7: K 3, * yarn over, slip 1, k 1, psso, k 2 sts together, yarn over, crossover *; repeat from * to *, ending with k 3.

Row 11: * Left cross, yarn over, slip 1,

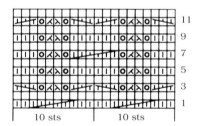

10 sts   10 sts

| = k 1
□ = p 1
O = yarn over
⋋ = pass slip st over
⋌ = k 2 tog
⊥⊥⊤⊤ = 6-st crossover
⊥⊤ = 3-st right cross
⊤⊥ = 3-st left cross

k 1, psso, k 2 sts together, yarn over, right cross *; repeat from * to *.
Repeat Rows 1 through 13 for pattern.

84

CROSSOVER STITCHES

Compound cable

Work cable on 19 stitches.

Rows 1, 3, 13, 15, 17, 19, 21, 23, and 25: P 2, k 3, p 1, work (k 1 in back loop for twisted k st, p 1) 4 times, k 3, p 2.

Row 2 and all even-numbered rows: Work each st as it appears on this side of work (k the k sts and p the p sts) and work twisted p st (p in back loop) above each twisted st.

Row 5: P 2, work right cross A on 7 sts as follows: slip 4 to dp needle and hold in back of work, k 1 twisted st, p 1, k 1 twisted st, return p st from dp needle to left needle and p 1, then k 3 from dp needle, p 1, work left cross A on 7 sts as follows: slip 4 to dp needle and hold in front, k 3, return p st from dp needle to left needle and p 1, then k 1 twisted st, p 1, k 1 twisted st from dp needle, p 2.

Rows 7 and 9: P 2, work (twisted k st, p 1) twice, k 3, p 1, k 3, work (p 1, twisted k st) twice, p 2.

Row 11: P 2, work right cross B on 7 sts as follows: slip 4 to dp needle and hold in back, k 3, return last p st from dp needle to left needle and p 1, then work (k 1 twisted st, p 1, k 1 twisted st) from dp needle, p 1, work left cross B on 7 sts as follows: slip 3 to dp needle and hold in front, work (k 1 twisted st, p 1) twice, then k 3 from dp needle, p 2.

Repeat Rows 1 through 16 for pattern.

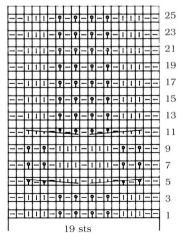

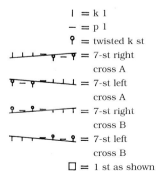

19 sts

I = k 1

— = p 1

φ = twisted k st

⌐⌐⌐⌐φ = 7-st right cross A

φ—⌐⌐⌐ = 7-st left cross A

φ—φ⌐⌐ = 7-st right cross B

⌐⌐—φ—φ = 7-st left cross B

□ = 1 st as shown

CROSSOVER STITCHES

Fastened diamonds

Work panel on 32 sts.

Row 1: K 9, p 14, k 9.

Row 2 and all even-numbered rows: Work each stitch as it appears on this side of work (k the k sts and p the p sts).

Row 3: K 6, work left cross on 4 sts as follows: slip 3 to dp needle and hold in front of work, p 1, k 3 from dp needle, p 12, work right cross on 4 sts as follows: slip 1 to dp needle and hold in back of work, k 3, p 1 from dp needle, k 6.

Row 5: K 6, p 1, left cross, p 10, right cross, p 1, k 6.

Row 7: K 6, p 2, left cross, p 8, right cross, p 2, k 6.

Row 9: K 6, p 3, left cross, p 6, right cross, p 3, k 6.

Row 11: K 6, p 4, left cross, p 4, right cross, p 4, k 6.

Row 13: K 6, p 5, left cross, p 2, right cross, p 5, k 6.

Row 15: K 6, p 6, left cross, right cross, p 6, k 6.

Rows 17 and 21: K 6, p 7, work left crossover on 6 sts as follows: slip 3 to dp needle and hold in front of work, k 3, k 3 from dp needle, p 7, k 6.

Row 19: K 6, p 7, k 6, p 7, k 6.

Row 23: K 6, p 6, right cross, left cross, p 6, k 6.

Row 25: K 6, p 5, right cross, p 2, left cross, p 5, k 6.

Row 27: K 6, p 4, right cross, p 4, left cross, p 4, k 6.

Row 29: K 6, p 3, right cross, p 6, left cross, p 3, k 6

Row 31: K 6, p 2, right cross, p 8, left cross, p 2, k 6.

Row 33: K 6, p 1, right cross, p 10, left cross, p 1, k 6.

Row 35: K 6, right cross, p 12, left cross, k 6.

Rows 37 and 41: K 3, work right crossover on 6 sts as follows: slip 3 to dp needle and hold in back of work, k 3, k 3 from dp needle, p 14, left crossover, k 3.

Row 39: K 9, p 14, k 9.

Repeat Rows 3 through 42 for panel.

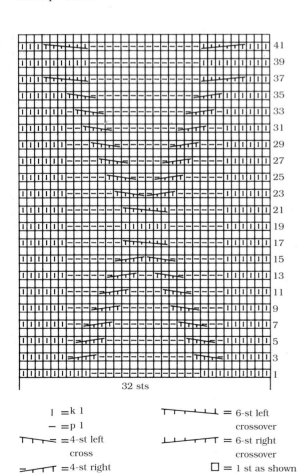

32 sts

| = k 1
− = p 1

⊤⊤⊤⊥⊐ = 4-st left cross
⊐⊤⊤⊤ = 4-st right cross

⊤⊤⊤⊥⊥⊥ = 6-st left crossover
⊥⊥⊥⊤⊤⊤ = 6-st right crossover
□ = 1 st as shown

CROSSOVER STITCHES

Swallow nests

Work with a multiple of 6 stitches.
Rows 1 and 3: P 1, * work right cross on 2 sts as follows: skip 1, k 1, k skipped st and drop original sts from left needle; work 2-st left cross as follows: slip 1 to dp needle and hold in front of work, k 1, k st from dp needle, p 2 *; repeat from * to *, ending last repeat with p 1.
Row 2 and all even-numbered rows: Work each stitch as it appears on this side of work (k the k sts and p the p sts).
Rows 5 and 7: * Left cross, p 2, right cross *; repeat from * to *.
Repeat Rows 1 through 8 for pattern.

− = p 1
⟋ = 2-st right cross
⟍ = 2-st left cross
□ = 1 st as shown

6 sts

7
5
3
1

Alternating wedges

Work on a multiple of 8 stitches.
Rows 1 and 3: * K 4, p 4 *; repeat from * to *.
Row 2 and all even-numbered rows: Work each stitch as it appears on this side of work (k the k sts and p the p sts).
Row 5: * P 4, work left cross on 4 sts as follows: slip 2 to dp needle and hold in front of work, k 2, k 2 from dp needle *; repeat from * to *.
Rows 7 and 9: * P 4, k 4 *; repeat from * to *.
Row 11: * Work right cross on 4 sts as follows: slip 2 to dp needle and hold in back of work, k 2, k 2 from dp needle, p 4 *; repeat from * to *.
Repeat Rows 1 through 12 for pattern.

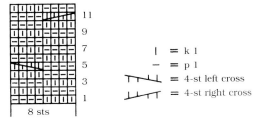

| = k 1
− = p 1
⊤⊤⊤⊤ = 4-st left cross
⊥⊥⊤⊤ = 4-st right cross

8 sts

11
9
7
5
3
1

CROSSOVER STITCHES

Little roofs

Work with a multiple of 10 stitches.
Rows 1 and 3: K 1, * work (p 2, k 1) twice, p 2, k 2 *; repeat from * to *, ending last repeat with k 1.
Row 2 and all even-numbered rows: Work each stitch as it appears on this side of work (k the k sts and p the p sts).
Row 5: * Work left cross on 2 sts as follows: slip 1 to dp needle and hold in front of work, p 1, k 1 from dp needle, p 1, k 1, p 2, k 1, p 1, work right cross on 2 sts as follows: skip 1, k 1, p skipped st, drop original sts from left needle *; repeat from * to *.
Row 7: P 1, * work left cross twice, work right cross twice, p 2 *; repeat from * to *, ending last repeat with p 1.
Row 9: P 2, * left cross, work left crossover on 2 sts as follows: slip 1 to dp needle and hold in front, k 1, k 1 from dp needle, right cross, p 4 *; repeat from * to *, ending last repeat with p 2.
Row 11: P 3, * left cross, right cross, p 6 *; repeat from * to *, ending last repeat with p 3.

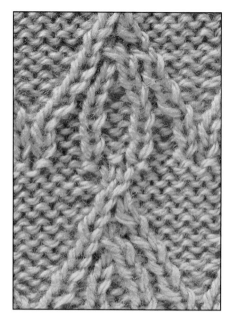

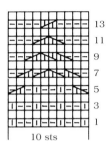

	= k 1
-	= p 1
⌐	= 2-st left cross
⌐	= 2-st right cross
⌐	= 2-st right crossover
⌐	= 2-st left crossover
□	= 1 st as shown

Row 13: P 4, * work right crossover on 2 sts as follows: skip 1, k 1, k skipped st, drop original sts, p 8 * repeat from * to *, ending last repeat with p 4.

Repeat Rows 1 through 14 for pattern.

Chain links

Work with a multiple of 8 stitches, plus 2.
Rows 1, 3, 9, and 11: P 2, * k 2, p 2 *; repeat from * to *.
Row 2 and all even-numbered rows except Row 8: Work each stitch as it appears on this side of work (k the k sts and p the p sts).
Row 5: P 2, * work decreasing crossover on 6 sts as follows: slip 2 to dp needle and hold in back of work, slip 2 to another dp needle and hold in front, k 2 sts together, k 2 from front dp needle, k 2 sts from back dp needle together, p 2 *; repeat from * to *.
Row 7: P 2, * k 4, p 4 * repeat from * to *, ending last repeat with p 2.
Row 8: K 2, * work increasing crossover on 4 sts as follows: slip 1 to dp needle and hold in front, slip 2 to another dp needle and hold in back, p in front and in back loop of next st, k 2 from back dp needle, p in front and in back loop of st on front dp needle, k 2 * repeat from * to *.
Repeat Rows 1 through 12 for pattern.

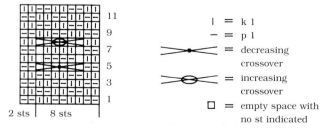

	= k 1
-	= p 1
⤬	= decreasing crossover
⤬	= increasing crossover
□	= empty space with no st indicated

CROSSOVER STITCHES

Repeated diamonds

Work with a multiple of 8 stitches, plus 2.

Row 1: P 4, * work crossover on 2 sts as follows: skip 1, k 1, k skipped st, drop original sts from left needle, p 6 *; repeat from * to *, ending last repeat with p 4.

Row 2 and all even-numbered rows: Work each stitch as it appears on this side of work (k the k sts and p the p sts).

Row 3: P 3, * work right cross on 2 sts as follows: skip 1, k 1, p skipped st, drop original sts from left needle, work left cross on 2 sts as follows: slip 1 to dp needle and hold in front of work, p 1, k 1 from dp needle, p 4

*; repeat from * to *, ending last repeat with p 3.

Row 5: P 2, * right cross, p 2, left cross, p 2 *; repeat from * to *.

Row 7: P 1, * right cross, p 4, left cross *; repeat from * to *, ending p 1.

Row 9: P 1, k 1, * p 6, crossover *; repeat from * to *, ending with k 1, p 1.

Row 11: P 1, * left cross, p 4, right cross *; repeat from * to *, ending p 1.

Row 13: P 2, * left cross, p 2, right cross, p 2 *; repeat from * to *.

Row 15: P 3, * left cross, right cross, p 4 *; repeat from * to *, ending with p 3.

Repeat Rows 1 through 16 for pattern.

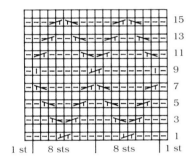

| = k 1

− = p 1

⊥⊤ = 2-st crossover

⇗⊤ = 2-st right cross

⊤⇖ = 2-st left cross

□ = 1 st as shown

CROSSOVER STITCHES

Switching tracks

Work with a multiple of 16 stitches.

Row 1: P 2, * work 4-st left crossover as follows: slip 2 to dp needle and hold in front of work, k 2, k 2 from dp needle, p 4, work 4-st right crossover as follows: slip 2 to dp needle and hold in back of work, k 2, k 2 from dp needle, p 4 *; repeat from * to *, ending last repeat with p 2.

Row 2 and all even-numbered rows: Work each stitch as it appears on this side of work (k the k sts and p the p sts).

Row 3: P 1, * work 2-st right crossover as follows: skip 1, k 1, then k skipped st, drop original 2 sts from left needle, k 1, work left cross on 3 sts as follows: slip 2 to dp needle and

hold in front, p 1, k 2 from dp needle, p 2, work right cross on 3 sts as follows: slip 1 to dp needle and hold in back, k 2, p 1 from dp needle, k 1, work 2-st left crossover as follows: slip 1 to dp needle and hold in front, k 1, k 1 from dp needle, p 2 *; repeat from * to *, ending last repeat with p 1.

Row 5: P 2, * k 2, p 1, left cross, right cross, p 1, k 2, p 4 *; repeat from * to *, ending last repeat with p 2.

Row 7: P 1, * work 2-st right crossover, k 1, p 2, work 4-st right crossover, p 2, k 1, work 2-st left crossover, p 2 *; repeat from * to *, ending last repeat with p 1.

Row 9: * Work 2-st right crossover,

k 2, p 1, right cross, left cross, p 1, k 2, 2-st left crossover *; repeat from * to *.

Row 11: P 1, * work 2-st right crossover, k 1, right cross, p 2, left cross, k 1, work 2-st left crossover, p 2 *; repeat from * to *, ending last repeat with p 1.

Repeat Rows 1 through 12 for pattern.

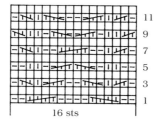

16 sts

| = k 1
− = p 1
⊤⊤⌐⌐ = 4-st left crossover
⌐⌐⊤⊤ = 4-st right crossover
⌐⊤ = 2-st right crossover
⊤⊤⊏ = 3-st left cross
⊐⊤⊤ = 3-st right cross
⊤⌐ = 2-st left crossover
□ = 1 st as shown

CROSSOVER STITCHES

Compact chevrons

Work with a multiple of 28 stitches.
Note: To work moss st, p above k st (as it faces you) and k above p st.
Row 1: K 1, p 1 (2 moss sts), * k 6, work right crossover on 6 sts as follows: slip 3 to dp needle and hold in back of work, k 3, k 3 from dp needle; work left crossover on 6 sts as follows: slip 3 to dp needle and hold in front of work, k 3, k 3 from dp needle, k 6, work (k 1, p 1) twice for 4 moss sts *; repeat from * to *, ending with k 1, p 1 (2 moss sts).
Row 2 and all even-numbered rows: Working moss st over moss sts, work each remaining st as it appears on this side of work (k the k sts and p the p sts).
Row 3: Work 2 moss sts, * k 3, right crossover, k 6, left crossover, k 3, work 4 moss sts *; repeat from * to *, ending last repeat with 2 moss sts.
Row 5: Work 2 moss sts, * right crossover, k 12, left crossover, 4 moss sts *; repeat from * to *, ending with 2 moss sts.
Repeat Rows 1 through 6 for pattern.

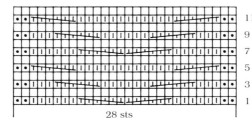

28 sts

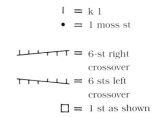

| = k 1
• = 1 moss st
⊥⊥⊤⊤ = 6-st right crossover
⊤⊤⊥⊥ = 6 sts left crossover
□ = 1 st as shown

Sliding boards

Work with a multiple of 6 stitches, plus 1.
Rows 1, 3, 7, and 9: P 1, * k 2, p 1 *; repeat from * to *.
Row 2 and all even-numbered rows: Work each stitch as it appears on this side of work (k the k sts and p the p sts).
Row 5: P 1, k 2, p 1, * work crossover of 5 sts as follows: slip 3 to dp needle and hold in back of work, k 2, then return p st from dp needle to left needle and p 1, k 2 from dp needle, p 1 *; repeat from * to *, ending with k 2, p 1.
Row 11: P 1, * crossover, p 1 *; repeat from * to *.
Repeat Rows 1 through 12 for pattern.

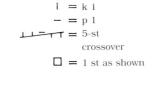

6 sts

| = k 1
– = p 1
⊥⊥⊤⊤ = 5-st crossover
□ = 1 st as shown

CROSSOVER STITCHES

Mini and maxi ovals

Work on a multiple of 8 sts, plus 3.

Row 1: K 1, p 3, * work crossover on 3 sts as follows: slip 2 to dp needle and hold in back of work, k 1, return 2nd st from dp needle to left needle and p1, k remaining st from dp needle, p 5 *; repeat from * to *, ending crossover, p 3, k 1.

Row 2 and all even-numbered rows: Work each stitch as it appears on this side of work (k the k sts and p the p sts).

Row 3: K 1, p 2, * work right cross on 2 sts as follows: skip 1, k 1, p skipped st, drop original 2 sts from left needle, p 1, work left cross on 2 sts as follows: slip 1 to dp needle and hold in front of work, p 1, k 1 from dp needle, p 3 *; repeat from * to *, ending last repeat with p 2, k 1.

Row 5: K 1, p 1, * right cross, p 3, left cross, p 1 *; repeat from * to * ending with k 1.

Rows 7 and 11: Work crossover, * p 5, crossover *; repeat from * to *.

Row 9: K 1, p 1, k 1, * p 5, k 1, p 1, k 1 *; repeat from * to *.

Row 13: K 1, p 1, * left cross, p 3, right cross, p 1 *; repeat from * to *, ending k 1.

Row 15: K 1, p 2, * left cross, p 1,

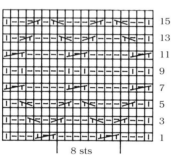

8 sts

| | = k 1
– = p 1
3-st crossover
2-st right cross
2-st left cross
□ = 1 st as shown

right cross, p 3 *; repeat from * to *, ending last repeat with p 2, k 1.

Repeat Rows 1 through 16 for pattern.

Harmony

Work with a multiple of 8 stitches, plus 4.

Rows 1, 3, and 9: Knit.

Row 2 and all even-numbered rows: Purl.

Row 5: K 2, * work crossover on 8 sts as follows: slip 4 to dp needle and hold in back of work, k 4, k 4 from dp needle *; repeat from * to *, ending k 2.

Row 7: K 2, * work bobble on next st as follows: work (k 1, yarn over) twice, k 1, turn work, p 5, turn, slip 4 to right needle, k 1, then pass the 4 slip sts one by one over k st and drop, k 7 *; repeat from * to *, k last 2 sts.

Row 11: K 6, * crossover *; repeat from * to *, ending with k 6.

Row 13: K 6, * bobble, k 7 *; repeat from * to *, ending k last 13 sts.

Repeat Rows 3 through 14 for pattern.

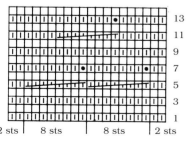

2 sts | 8 sts | 8 sts | 2 sts

| = k 1
8-st crossover
● = bobble
□ = p 1

CROSSOVER STITCHES

Roof tiles

Work with a multiple of 6 stitches.

Row 1: * K 4, p 2 *; repeat from * to *.

Rows 2, 6, and 14: * K 2, p 4 *; repeat from * to *.

Row 3: * Slip 1 as if to purl, k 2, k 1 double stitch by inserting needle into st in row below next st on left needle, k 1, slip unworked st from left to right needle and pass k st (worked from below) over this slipped st and drop it to complete double st, p 2 *; repeat from * to *.

Row 4: * K 2, p 3, with yarn in front of work, slip 1 *; repeat from * to *.

Row 5: * Work crossover on 3 sts as follows: slip 1 to dp needle and hold in front of work, k 2, k 1 from dp needle, k 1 double st, p 2 *; repeat from * to *.

Row 7: * K 1 double st, p 2 *; repeat from * to *.

Rows 8 and 12: * P 3, k 2, p 1 *; repeat from * to *.

Row 9: * K 1 double st, p 2, with yarn in back slip 1, k 2 *; repeat from * to *.

Row 10: * P 2, with yarn in front skip 1, k 2, p 1 *; repeat from * to *.

Row 11: * K 1 double st, p 2, work crossover as before *; repeat from * to *.

Row 13: * K 1 double st, k 2, k 1 double st, p 2 *; repeat from * to *. Repeat Rows 3 through 14 for pattern.

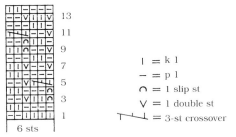

I = k 1
− = p 1
∩ = 1 slip st
V = 1 double st
⊤⊥ = 3-st crossover

CROSSOVER STITCHES

Pagoda

Work with a multiple of 18 stitches.

Row 1, 35, and 37: P 6, * k 6, p 12 *; repeat from * to *, ending last repeat with p 6.

Row 2 and all even-numbered rows: Work each stitch as it appears on this side of work (k the k sts and p the p sts).

Row 3: P 3, * k 3, work left crossover on 6 sts as follows: slip 3 to dp needle and hold in front of work, k 3, k 3 from dp needle, k 3, p 6 * repeat from * to *, ending last repeat with p 3.

Rows 5, 7, 29, and 31: P 3, * k 12, p 6 *; repeat from * to *, ending last repeat with p 3.

Row 9: K 3, * work right cross on 6 sts as follows: slip 3 to dp needle and hold in back of work, k 3, p 3 from dp needle, work left cross on 6 sts as follows: slip 3 to dp needle and hold in front of work, p 3, k 3 from dp needle, k 6 *; repeat from * to *, ending last repeat with k 3.

Rows 11, 13, 23, and 25: K 6, * p 6, k 12 *; repeat from * to *, ending last repeat with k 6.

Row 15: * Right cross, p 6, left cross *; repeat from * to *.

Rows 17 and 19: K 3, * p 3, k 6 *; repeat from * to *, ending last repeat with k 3.

Row 21: * Left crossover, p 6, work right crossover on 6 sts as follows: slip 3 to dp needle and hold in back of work, k 3, k 3 from dp needle *; repeat from * to *.

Row 27: P 3, * left crossover, right crossover, p 6 *; repeat from * to *, ending last repeat with p 3.

Row 33: P 6, * left crossover, k 12 *; repeat from * to *, ending last repeat with p 6.

Repeat Rows 1 through 38 for pattern.

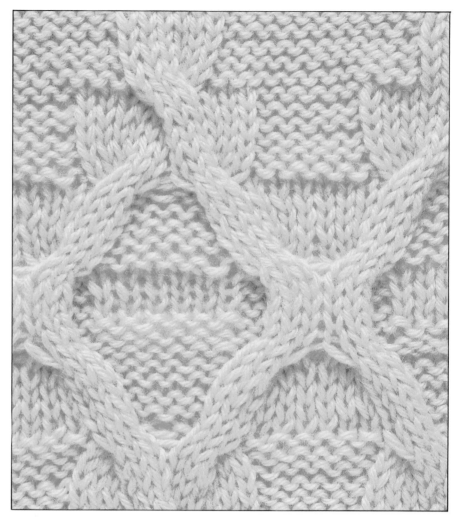

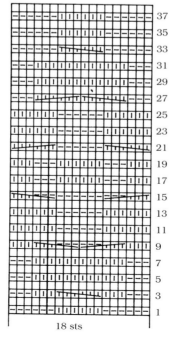

l =	k 1
− =	p 1
(6-st symbol) =	6-st left crossover
(6-st symbol) =	6-st right cross
(6-st symbol) =	6-st left cross
(6-st symbol) =	6-st right crossover
□ =	1 st as shown

18 sts

CROSSOVER STITCHES

Honeycomb cable

Work with a multiple of 12 stitches.
Rows 1 and 5: P 2, * k 8, p 4 *;
repeat from * to *, ending last repeat
with p 2.
Row 2 and all even-numbered rows:
Work each stitch as it appears on this
side of work (k the k sts and p the p
sts).
Row 3: P 2, * work left crossover on
4 sts as follows: slip 2 to dp needle
and hold in front of work, k 2, k 2
from dp needle; work right crossover
on 4 sts as follows: slip 2 to dp needle and hold in back of work, k 2, k 2
from dp needle, p 4 *; repeat from *
to *, ending last repeat with p 2.
Row 7: P 2, * right crossover, left
crossover, p 4 *; repeat from * to *,
ending last repeat with p 2.
Repeat Rows 1 through 8 for pattern.

- = p 1
| = k 1
= 4-st right crossover
= 4-st left crossover
□ = 1 st as shown

Tight braid

Work braid on 2 stitches. For pattern
as shown, work evenly-spaced braids
on a background of reverse stockinette st.
Row 1 (right side): Work K crossover
on 2 sts as follows: skip 1, k 1, k
skipped st and drop original 2 sts
from left needle.
Row 2: Work P crossover on 2 sts as
follows: skip 1, p 1, p skipped st and
drop original sts.
Repeat these 2 rows for pattern.

= 2-st K crossover
= 2-st P crossover

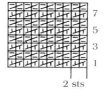

2 sts

CROSSOVER STITCHES

Trace

Work panel in 22 stitches.
Note: To work moss st, p over k st (as it faces you) and k over p st.
Row 1: P 9, k 4, p 9.
Row 2 and all even-numbered rows: Work moss st over moss sts, maintaining alternating k and p sts, and work each remaining stitch as it appears on this side of work (k the k sts and p the p sts).
Row 3: P 8, work right cross-P on 3 sts as follows: slip 1 to dp needle and hold in back of work, k 2, p 1 from dp needle; work left cross-K on 3 sts as follows: slip 2 to dp needle and hold in front of work, k 1, k 2 from dp needle, p 8.
Row 5: P 7, work right cross-K on 3 sts as follows: slip 1 to dp needle and hold in back of work, k 2, k 1 from dp needle; work 2 moss sts, work left cross-P on 3 sts as follows: slip 2 to dp needle and hold in front of work, p 1, k 2 from dp needle, p 7.
Row 7: P 6, right cross-P, 4 moss sts, left cross-K, p 6.
Row 9: P 5, right cross-K, 6 moss sts, left cross-P, p 5.
Row 11: P 4, right cross-P, 8 moss sts, left cross-K, p 4.

Row 13: P 3, right cross-K, 10 moss sts, left cross-P, p 3.
Row 15: P 3, left cross-P, 10 moss sts, right cross-P, p 3.
Row 17: P 4, left cross-P, 8 moss sts, right cross-P, p 4.
Row 19: P 5, left cross-P, 6 moss sts, right cross-P, p 5.
Row 21: P 6, left cross-P, 4 moss sts, right cross-P, p 6.
Row 23: P 7, left cross-P, 2 moss sts, right cross-P, p 7.
Row 25: P 8, left cross-P, right cross-P, p 8.
Repeat Rows 3 through 26 for pattern.

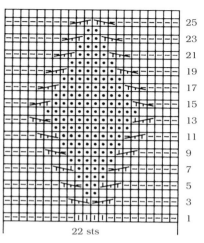

22 sts

| = k 1
− = p 1
• = 1 moss st
⇀⊤⊤ = 3-st right cross-P
⊤⊤⇁ = 3-st left cross-K
⌐⊤⊤ = 3-st right cross-K
⊤⊤◄ = 3-st left cross-P
□ = 1 st as shown

Intertwined cables

Work cable panel on 22 stitches.
Row 1: P 3, k 2, p 4, k 4, p 4, k 2, p 3.
Row 2 and all even-numbered rows: Work each stitch as it appears on this side of work (k the k sts and p the p sts).
Rows 3 and 19: P 3, k 2, p 4, work crossover on 4 sts as follows: slip 2 to dp needle and hold in back of work, k 2, k 2 from dp needle, p 4, k 2, p 3.
Row 5: P 3, work left cross on 3 sts as follows: slip 2 to dp needle and hold in front of work, p 1, k 2 from dp needle, p 2, work right cross on 3 sts as follows: slip 1 to dp needle and hold in back of work, k 2, p 1 from dp needle, left cross, p 2, right cross, p 3.
Row 7: P 4, left cross, right cross, p 2, left cross, right cross, p 4.
Rows 9 and 13: P 5, crossover, p 4, crossover, p 5.
Row 11: P 5, k 4, p 4, k 4, p 5.
Row 15: P 4, right cross, left cross, p 2, right cross, left cross, p 4.

Row 17: P 3, right cross, p 2, left cross, right cross, p 2, left cross, p 3.
Repeat Rows 1 through 20 for pattern.

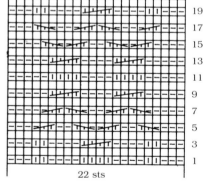

22 sts

| = k 1
− = p 1
⌐⊤⊤ = 4-st crossover
⊤⊤◄ = 3-st left cross
⇀⊤⊤ = 3-st right cross
□ = 1 st as shown

CROSSOVER STITCHES

Flat cables

Work cable on 10 stitches. For pattern as shown, work cables on a background of reverse stockinette st.

Row 1: Work left crossover on 4 sts as follows: slip 2 to dp needle and hold in front of work, k 2, k 2 from dp needle, k 2, work right crossover on 4 sts as follows: slip 2 to dp needle and hold in back of work, k 2, k 2 from dp needles.

Row 2 and all even-numbered rows: Purl.

Rows 3, 5, 7, 9, 11, and 13: Knit. Repeat Rows 1 through 14 for pattern.

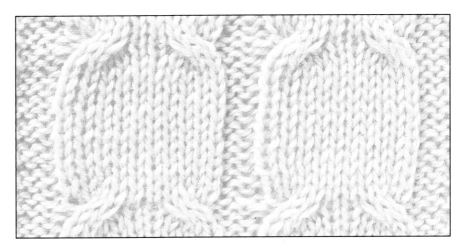

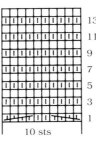

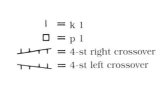

I = k 1
□ = p 1
⌐┬┐ = 4-st right crossover
┌┬⌐ = 4-st left crossover

10 sts

Waves

Work with a multiple of 4 stitches, plus 1.

Rows 1 and 5: K 2, * slip 1 as if to p, k 3 *; repeat from * to *, ending with k 2.

Rows 2 and 6: P 2, * with yarn in front slip 1, p 3 *; repeat from * to *, ending slip 1, p 2.

Row 3: * Work right cross on 3 sts as follows: slip 2 to dp needle and hold in back of work, p 1, k 2 from dp needle, k 1 *; repeat from * to *, ending last repeat with k 2.

Rows 4 and 8: K 1, * p 3, k 1; repeat from * to *.

Row 7: K 2, * work left cross on 3 sts as follows: slip 1 to dp needle (this st is the slipped st on previous rows) and hold in front of work, k 2, k 1 from dp needle, k 1 *; repeat from * to *, ending with left cross.
Repeat Rows 1 through 8 for pattern.

I = k 1
− = p 1
∧ = 1 slip st
⌐┬┐ = 3-st right cross
┌┬⌐ = 3-st left cross

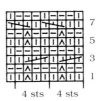

4 sts   4 sts

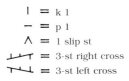

CROSSOVER STITCHES

Staircase cables

Work with a multiple of 11 stitches, plus 2.

Row 1: P 2, * k 4, k 1 in back loop for twisted k st, work right crossover on 4 sts as follows: slip 2 to dp needle and hold in back of work, k 2, k 2 from dp needle, p 2 *; repeat from * to *.

Row 2 and all even-numbered rows: Work each stitch as it appears on this side of work (k the k sts and p the p sts). Work in back loop to p twisted st over twisted st below.

Row 3: P 2, * work left crossover on 4 sts as follows: slip 2 to dp needle and hold in front of work, k 2, k 2 from dp needle, k 1 twisted st, k 4, p 2 *; repeat from * to *.

Repeat Rows 1 through 4 for pattern.

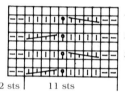

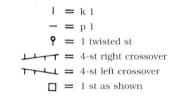

| | = k 1
| — = p 1
| ? = 1 twisted st
| = 4-st right crossover
| = 4-st left crossover
| □ = 1 st as shown

2 sts | 11 sts

| = k 1
□ = p 1
= 4-st right crossover
= 2-st left crossover

Paving

Work with a multiple of 6 stitches, plus 4.

Row 1: * Work left crossover on 4 sts as follows: slip 2 to dp needle and hold in front of work, k 2, k 2 from dp needle; work right crossover as follows: skip 1 st, k 1, k skipped st and drop both original sts from left needle *; repeat from * to *, ending with 4-st left crossover.

Row 2 and all even-numbered rows: Purl.

Row 3: * Work 2-st right crossover, k 6 *; repeat from * to *, ending last repeat with k 2.

Row 5: K 2, * work 2-st right crossover, 4-st left crossover *; repeat from * to *, ending with 2-st right crossover.

Repeat Rows 1 through 6 for pattern.

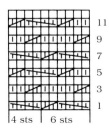

4 sts | 6 sts

CROSSOVER STITCHES

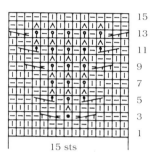

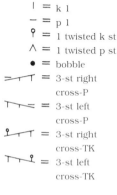

| = k 1
− = p 1
� = 1 twisted k st
∧ = 1 twisted p st
● = bobble
= 3-st right cross-P
= 3-st left cross-P
= 3-st right cross-TK
= 3-st left cross-TK

Coconut palm

Work design panel on 15 sts. For pattern as shown, work evenly-spaced designs on background of reverse stockinette st.

Row 1: Knit.

Row 2: K 5, p 2, k 1, p 2, k 5.

Row 3: P 4, work right cross-P on 3 sts as follows: slip to dp needle and hold in back of work, k 2, p 1 from dp needle, work bobble on next st as follows: knit, purl, knit, purl and knit all in same st (5 sts in 1 st), turn work, k 5, turn, slip first 4 to right needle, k 1, then pass the 4 slip sts one by one over k st and drop (bobble made); work left cross-P on 3 sts as follows: slip 2 to dp needle and hold in front of work, p 1, k 2 from dp needle, p 4.

Row 4: K 4, p 2, k 1, p in back loop for twisted p st (made over bobble), k 1, p 2, k 4.

Row 5: P 3, work right cross-TK on 3 sts as follows: slip 1 to dp needle and hold in back, k 2, k 1 twisted st from dp needle, p 1, k 1 twisted st, p 1, work left cross-TK on 3 sts as follows: slip 2 to dp needle and hold in front, k 1 twisted st, k 2 from dp needle, p 3.

Row 6 and all following even-numbered rows: K the k sts (as they face you) and p the p sts, working twisted st above each twisted st.

Row 7: P 3, k 2, k 1 twisted st, work (p 1, k 1 twisted st) twice, k 2, p 3.

Row 9: P 2, right cross-P, work (k 1 twisted st, p 1) twice, 1 twisted k st, left cross-P, p 2.

Row 11: P 1, right cross-TK, p 1, work (k 1 twisted st, p 1) 3 times, left cross-TK, p 1.

Row 13: Right cross-P, k 1 twisted st, work (p 1, k 1 twisted st) 4 times, left cross-P.

Row 15: P 5, k 2, p 1, k 2, p 5. Repeat Rows 2 through 15 for design panel.

CROSSOVER STITCHES

Diamonds and cables

Work design panel on 19 stitches.
Note: To work moss st, always p over k sts (as they face you) and k over p sts, maintaining alternating k and p sts.

Row 1: Knit.

Row 2: K 7, p 2, k 1(moss st), p 2, k 7.

Row 3: P 6, work right cross-M on 3 sts as follows: slip 1 to dp needle and hold in back of work, k 2, work 1 moss st (in this case, p 1) on st from dp needle, k 1 for center moss st, work left cross-M on 3 sts as follows: slip 2 to dp needle and hold in front of work, 1 moss st (in this case, p 1), k 2 from dp needle, p 6.

Row 4 and all following even-numbered rows: Working moss st over moss sts, work each remaining stitch as it appears on this side of work (k the k sts and p the p sts).

Row 5: P 5, right cross-M, 3 moss sts, left cross-M, p 5.

Row 7: P 4, right cross-M, 5 moss sts, left cross-M, p 4.

Row 9: P 3, right cross-M, 7 moss sts, left cross-M, p 3.

Row 11: P 2, right cross-M, 9 moss sts, left cross-M, p 2.

Row 13: P 1, right cross-M, 11 moss sts, left cross-M, p 1.

Row 15: P 1, work left cross-P on 3 sts as follows: slip 2 to dp needle and hold in front of work, p 1, k 2 from dp needle, 11 moss sts, work right cross-P on 3 sts as follows: slip 1 to dp needle and hold in back of work, k 2, p 1 from dp needle, p 1.

Row 17: P 2, left cross-P, work 9 moss sts, right cross-P, p 2.

Row 19: P 3, left cross-P, work 7 moss sts, right cross-P, p 3.

Row 21: P 4, left cross-P, work 5 moss sts, right cross-P, p 4.

Row 23: P 5, work right crossover on 4 sts as follows: slip 2 to dp needle and hold in back of work, k 2, k 2 from dp needle, p 1, work left

crossover on 4 sts as follows: slip 2 to dp needle and hold in front of work, k 2, k 2 from dp needle, p 5.

Rows 25, 27, 31, and 33: P 5, k 4, p 1, k 4, p 5.

Rows 29 and 35: P 5, right crossover, p 1, left crossover, p 5.

Row 36: K 5, p 2, work (k 1, p 1) twice and k 1 for 5 moss sts, p 2, k 5. Repeat Rows 7 through 36 for pattern.

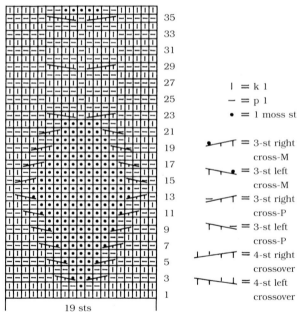

| = k 1

— = p 1

• = 1 moss st

= 3-st right cross-M

= 3-st left cross-M

= 3-st right cross-P

= 3-st left cross-P

= 4-st right crossover

= 4-st left crossover

19 sts

CROSSOVER STITCHES

Claw cable

Work cable on 9 stitches. For pattern as shown, work evenly-spaced cables on background of reverse stockinette st.

Row 1: Knit.

Row 2: Purl.

Row 3: Work right cross on 4 sts as follows: slip 3 to dp needle and hold in back of work, k 1, k 3 from dp needle, k 1, work left cross on 4 sts as follows: slip 1 to dp needle and hold in front of work, k 3, k 1 from dp needle.

Row 4: Purl.

Repeat these 4 rows for cable.

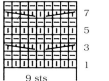

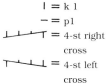

| = k 1
− = p 1

⌐ = 4-st right cross

⌐ = 4-st left cross

Cables and ribs

Work with a multiple of 9 stitches, plus 6.

Row 1: * P 1, k 4, work (p 1, k 1) twice *; repeat from * to *, ending p 1, k 4, p 1.

Rows 2 and 4: Work each stitch as it appears on this side of work (k the k sts and p the p sts).

Row 3: * P 1, work right crossover on 4 sts as follows: slip 2 to dp needle and hold in back of work, k 2, k 2 from dp needle, work (p 1, k 1) twice *; repeat from * to *, ending p 1, right crossover, p 1.

Repeat Rows 1 through 4 for pattern.

| = k 1
− = p 1

⌐ = 4-st right crossover

⌐ = 4-sts left crossover

□ = 1 st as shown

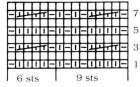

CROSSOVER STITCHES

Wide cables

Work cable on 20 stitches. For pattern, work cable on background of reverse stockinette st.

Rows 1, 3, 5 and 7: Knit.

Row 2 and all even-numbered rows: Purl.

Row 9 (crossover row): Work right crossover on 10 sts as follows: slip 5 to dp needle and hold in back of work, k 5, k 5 from dp needle, work left crossover on 10 sts as follows: slip 5 to dp needle and hold in front of work, k 5, k 5 from dp needle.

Rows 11 through 30: Repeat Rows 1 through 10 twice.

Rows 31 through 58: Work in stockinette st (k 1 row, p 1 row).

Row 59: Repeat Row 9.

Repeat Rows 1 through 60 for cable.

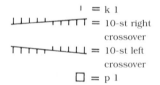

| = k 1

⊥⊥⊥⊥⊥⊤⊤⊤⊤⊤ = 10-st right crossover

⊤⊤⊤⊤⊤⊥⊥⊥⊥⊥ = 10-st left crossover

□ = p 1

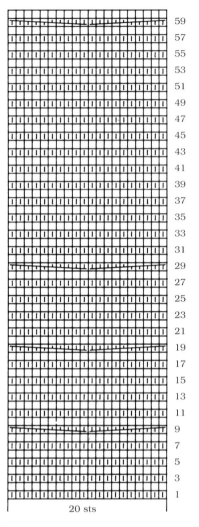

20 sts

Greek key diamonds

Work diamond on 6 sts. For pattern as shown, work evenly-spaced diamonds on background of reverse stockinette st.

Row 1: P 2, work crossover on 2 sts as follows: sl 1 to dp needle and hold in front of work, k 1, k 1 from dp needle, p 2.

Row 2 and all even-numbered rows: Work each stitch as it appears on this side of work (k the k sts and p the p sts).

Row 3: P 1, work right cross on 2 sts as follows: skip 1, k 1, p skipped st, drop original 2 sts from left needle, work left cross on 2 sts as follows: slip 1 to dp needle and hold in front of work, p 1, k 1 from dp needle, p 1.

Row 5: Right cross, p 2, left cross.

Row 7: Left cross, p 2, right cross.

Row 9: P 1, left cross, right cross, p 1.

Repeat Rows 1 through 10 for diamond pattern.

6 sts

– = p 1

⊤⊾ = 2-st crossover

⌐⊤ = 2-st right cross

⊤⌐ = 2-st left cross

□ = 1 st as shown

CROSSOVER STITCHES

Cable motif

Work with a multiple of 18 stitches.

Row 1: Purl.

Row 2 and all even-numbered rows: Work each stitch as it appears on this side of work (k the k sts and p the p sts).

Row 3: P 12, * k 3, p 15 *; repeat from * to *, ending k 3, p 3.

Row 5: P 6, * k 9, p 9 *; repeat from * to *, ending last repeat with p 3.

Row 7: P 3, * k 3, work left crossover on 6 sts as follows: slip 3 to dp needle and hold in front, k 3, k 3 from dp needle, k 3, p 6 *; repeat from * to *, ending with p 3.

Row 9: P 3, * k 12, p 6 *; repeat from * to *, ending with p 3.

Row 11: P 3, * work right crossover on 6 sts as follows: slip 3 to dp needle and hold in back of work, k 3, k 3 from dp needle, repeat right crossover, p 6 *; repeat from * to *; ending with p 3.

Row 13: P 3, * k 9, p 9 *; repeat from * to *, ending with p 6.

Row 15: P 3, * k 3, left crossover, p 9 *; repeat from * to *, ending with p 6.

Row 17: P 3, * k 3, p 3, k 3, p 9 *; repeat from * to *, ending with p 6.

Row 19: P 3, * k 3, p 15 *; repeat from * to *, ending with p 12.

Row 21: Purl.

Repeat Rows 1 through 22 for pattern.

Ribbed diamond

Work with a multiple of 17 stitches, plus 1.

Row 1: K 1, * p 1, work left cross on 2 sts as follows: slip 1 to dp needle and hold in front of work, p 1, k 1 from dp needle, 2 more left crosses, p 1, k 1, work right cross on 2 sts as follows: skip 1, k 1, p skipped st, drop original 2 sts from left needle, 2 more right crosses, p 1, k 1 *; repeat from * to *.

Row 2 and all even-numbered rows: Work each stitch as it appears on this side of work (k the k sts and p the p sts).

Row 3: K 1, p 1, * k 1, 3 left crosses, 3 right crosses, work (k 1, p 1) twice *; repeat from * to *, ending with k 1, p 1, k 1.

Row 5: * Work (k 1, p 1) twice, * 2 left crosses, 3 right crosses, (p 1, k 1) 3 times, p 1 *; repeat from * to *, ending with (p 1, k 1) twice.

Row 7: Work (k 1, p 1) twice, * k 1, left cross, 3 right crosses, (k 1, p 1) 4 times *; repeat from * to *, ending with (k 1, p 1) twice, k 1.

Row 9: Work (k 1, p 1) 3 times, * 3 right crosses, p 1, (k 1, p 1) 5 times *; repeat from * to *, ending with (p 1, k 1) 3 times.

Row 11: K 1, (p 1, k 1) twice, * 3 right crosses, left cross, (k 1, p 1) 4 times, k 1 *; repeat from * to *, ending with (k 1, p 1) twice, k 1.

Row 13: Work (k 1, p 1) twice, * 3 right crosses, 2 left crosses, (p 1, k 1) 3 times, p 1 *; repeat from * to *, ending with (p 1, k 1) twice.

Row 15: K 1, p 1, * k 1, 3 left crosses, 3 right crosses, (k 1, p 1) twice *; repeat from * to *, ending k 1, p 1, k 1.

Row 17: K 1, * p 1, 3 right crosses, p 1, k 1, 3 left crosses, p 1, k 1 *; repeat from * to *.

Repeat Rows 1 through 18 for pattern.

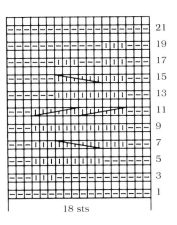

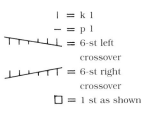

18 sts

| = k 1

− = p 1

⊤⊤⊤⊥⊥⊥ = 6-st left crossover

⊥⊥⊥⊤⊤⊤ = 6-st right crossover

☐ = 1 st as shown

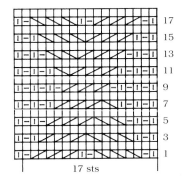

17 sts

| = k 1   ╱ = 2-st right cross

− = p 1

╲ = 2-st left cross   ☐ = 1 st as shown

CROSSOVER STITCHES

Fancy diamond

Work with a multiple of 19 stitches.
Row 1: P 3, * k 2 sts together (k 2 tog), k 4, yarn over (yo), p 1, yo, k 4, slip 1, k 1, pass slip st over k st (psso), p 6 *; repeat from * to *, ending with p 3.
Row 2 and all even-numbered rows: K the k sts as they face you and p the p sts. K any yarn-overs.
Row 3: P 2, * k 2 tog, work right cross on 4 sts as follows: slip 2 to dp needle and hold in back, k 2, k 2 from dp needle, yo, p 3, yo, work left cross on 4 sts as follows: slip 2 to dp needle and hold in front, k 2, k 2 from dp needle, slip 1, k 1, psso, p 4 *; repeat from * to *, ending p 2.
Row 5: P 1, * k 2 tog, k 4, yo, p 5, yo, k 4, slip 1, k 1, psso, p 2 *; repeat from * to *, ending with p 1.
Row 7: P 2, * right cross, p 7, left cross, p 4 *; repeat from * to *, ending p 2.
Row 9: P 2, * k 4, p 7, k 4, p 4 *; repeat from * to *, ending with p 2.
Row 11: P 2, * left cross, p 7, right cross, p 4 *; repeat * to *, ending p 2.
Row 13: P 2, * yo, k 4, slip 1, k 1, psso, p 3, k 2 tog, k 4, yo, p 4 *; repeat from * to *, ending with p 2.

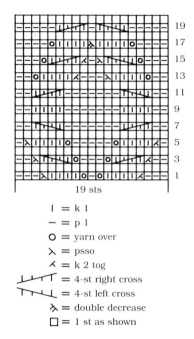

| | = k 1
— = p 1
O = yarn over
⟍ = psso
⟋ = k 2 tog
4-st right cross
4-st left cross
⟋ = double decrease
□ = 1 st as shown

19 sts

Row 15: P 3, * yo, left cross, slip 1, k 1, psso, p 1, k 2 tog, right cross, yo, p 6 *; repeat from * to *, ending p 3.
Row 17: P 4, * yo, k 4, slip 1, k 2 tog, psso (double decrease made), k 4, yo, p 8 *; repeat * to *, ending p 4.
Row 19: P 5, * left cross, p 1, right cross, p 10 *; repeat * to *, ending p 5.
Repeat Rows 1 through 20 for pattern.

Complementary diamonds

Work with a multiple of 20 stitches.
Row 1: P 2, * work right cross on 2 sts as follows: skip 1, k 1, p skipped st, drop original 2 sts from left needle, p 2, 2 right crosses, work left cross on 2 sts as follows: slip 1 to dp needle and hold in front of work, p 1, k 1 from dp needle, another left cross, p 2, left cross, p 4 *; repeat from * to *, ending last repeat with p 2.
Row 2 and all even-numbered rows: K the k sts as they face you and p the p sts.
Row 3: P 1, * right cross, p 2, 2 right crosses, p 2, 2 left crosses, p 2, left cross, p 2 *; repeat from * to *, ending last repeat with p 1.
Row 5: * Right cross, p 2, 2 right crosses, p 4, 2 left crosses, p 2, left cross *; repeat from * to *.
Row 7: * Left cross, p 2, 2 left crosses, p 4, 2 right crosses, p 2, right cross *; repeat from * to *.
Row 9: P 1, * left cross, p 2, 2 left crosses, p 2, 2 right crosses, p 2, right cross, p 2 *; repeat from * to *,
Row 11: P 2, * left cross, p 2, 2 left crosses, 2 right crosses, p 2, right cross, p 4 *; repeat from * to *, ending with p 1.
Repeat Rows 1 through 12 for pattern.

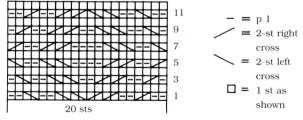

— = p 1
╱ = 2-st right cross
╲ = 2-st left cross
□ = 1 st as shown

20 sts

CROSSOVER STITCHES

Palm fronds

Work with a multiple of 18 sts.

Rows 1 and 21: P 5, * work right cross on 2 sts as follows: skip 1, k 1, k skipped st and drop original 2 sts from left needle, p 1, right cross, p 1, work left cross on 2 sts as follows: slip 1 to dp needle and hold in front of work, k 1, k 1 from dp needle, p 10 *; repeat from * to *, ending last repeat with p 5.

Row 2 and all even-numbered rows: Work each stitch as it appears on this side of work (k the k sts and p the p sts).

Rows 3 and 19: P 4, * right cross, k 1, p 1, right cross, p 1, k 1, left cross, p 8 *; repeat from * to *, ending last repeat with p 4.

Rows 5 and 17: P 3, * 2 right crosses, p 1, right cross, p 1, 2 left crosses, p 6 *; repeat from * to *, ending last repeat with p 3.

Rows 7 and 15: P 2, * 2 right crosses, k 1, p 1, right cross, p 1, k 1, 2 left crosses, p 4 *; repeat from * to *, ending last repeat with p 2.

Rows 9 and 13: P 1, * 3 right crosses, p 1, right cross, p 1, 3 left crosses, p 2 *; repeat from * to *, ending last repeat with p 1.

Row 11: * Work 3 right crosses, k 1, p 1, right cross, p 1, k 1, 3 left crosses *; repeat from * to *.

Row 23: P 6, * k 1, p 1, right cross, p 1, k 1, p 12 *; repeat from * to *, ending last repeat with p 6.

Row 25: Purl.

Repeat Rows 1 through 26 for pattern.

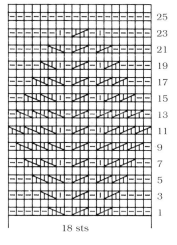

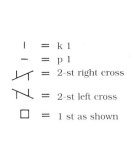

| | = k 1

— = p 1

⋊ = 2-st right cross

⋉ = 2-st left cross

□ = 1 st as shown

18 sts

CROSSOVER STITCHES

Reeds to the left

Work with a multiple of 4 stitches, plus 3.

Row 1: P 3, * k 1, k 1 and p 1 in next st (increase), p 2 *; repeat from * to *.

Row 2 and all even-numbered rows: Work each stitch as it appears on this row (k the k sts and p the p sts).

Rows 3 and 13: K 1, p 2, * work left cross-P on 3 sts as follows: slip 2 to dp needle and hold in front, p 1, k 2 from dp needle, p 2 *; repeat from * to *.

Rows 5 and 15: K 2, * p 2, left cross-P *; repeat from * to *, ending with p 1.

Row 7: Left cross-P, * p 2, left cross-P *; repeat from * to *.

Row 9: P 1, * left cross-P, p 2 *; repeat from * to *, ending with p 3, k 1.

Row 11: * P 2, left cross-P *; repeat from * to *, ending p 3.

Row 17: * Work 3-st left cross-dec as follows: slip 1 to dp needle and hold in front, p 1, k 2 sts together from dp needle, p 2 *; repeat * to *, ending with left cross-P.

Repeat Rows 1 through 18 for pattern.

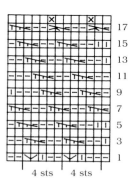

| = k 1
− = p 1
∨ = increase

= left cross-P

= left cross-dec

✕ = 1 st decreased below
☐ = 1 st as shown

Reeds to the right

Work with a multiple of 4 stitches, plus 3.

Row 1: P 3, * k 1, k 1 and p 1 in next st (increase), p 2 *; repeat from * to *.

Row 2 and all even-numbered rows: Work each stitch as it appears on this row (k the k sts and p the p sts).

Rows 3 and 13: * P 2, work 3-st right cross-P as follows: slip to dp needle, hold in back, k 2, p 1 from dp needle *; repeat from * to *, ending p 2, k 1.

Rows 5 and 15: P 1, * right cross-P, p 2 *; repeat from * to *, ending k 2.

Row 7: Right cross-P, * p 2, right cross-P *; repeat from * to *.

Row 9: K 1, p 3, * right cross-P, p 2 *; repeat from * to *, ending with p 1.

Row 11: P 3, * right cross-P, p 2 *; repeat from * to *.

Row 17: Right cross-P, * p 2, work right cross-dec on 3 sts as follows: slip 1 to dp needle, hold in back, k 2 sts together, p 1 from dp needle *; repeat from * to *.

Repeat Rows 1 through 18 for pattern.

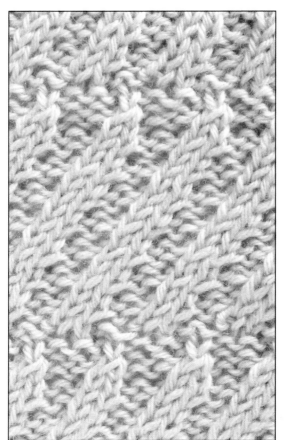

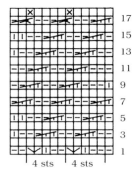

| = k 1
− = p 1
∨ = increase st

= right cross-P

= right cross-dec

✕ = 1 st decreased below
☐ = 1 st as shown

CROSSOVER STITCHES

Dual cable

Work cable panel on 22 stitches.

Rows 1, 3, and 5: P 4, work 7 moss sts (see page 5), k 7, p 4.

Row 2 and all even-numbered rows: Work moss st over moss sts and work each remaining st as it appears on this row (k the k sts and p the p sts).

Row 7: P 4, to work 14-st crossover-A: slip 7 to dp needle, hold in front, k 7, work moss st on 7 sts from dp needle, p 4.

Rows 9, 11, 13, 15, 17, 19, and 21: P 4, k 7, work 7 moss sts, p 4.

Row 23: P 4, to work 14-st crossover-B: slip 7 to dp needle, hold in front, 7 moss sts, k 7 from dp needle, p 4.

Rows 25, 27, and 29: P 4, 7 moss sts, k 7, p 4.

Repeat Rows 1 through 30 for pattern.

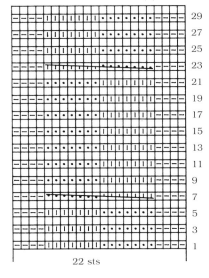

22 sts

| | = k 1

— = p 1

• = 1 moss st

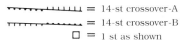 = 14-st crossover-A

= 14-st crossover-B

□ = 1 st as shown

Double-patterned cables

Work with a multiple of 22 stitches, plus 12.

Rows 1, 3, 5, and 7: P 2, * work 8 moss sts (see page 5), p 3, k 8, p 3 *; repeat from * to *, ending with p 2.

Row 2 and all even-numbered rows: Work moss st over moss sts and work each remaining st as it appears on this row (k the k sts and p the p sts).

Row 9: P 2, * k 8, p 3, work crossover on 3 sts as follows: slip 4 to dp needle and hold in front of work, k 4, k 4 from dp needle, p 3 *; repeat from * to *, ending k 8, p 2.

Rows 11, 13, 15, and 17: P 2, * k 8, p 3 *; repeat from * to *, ending p 2.

Row 19: P 2, * crossover, p 3, work 8 moss sts, p 3 *; repeat from * to *, ending crossover, p 2.

Rows 21, 23, 25, 27, and 29: P 2, * k 8, p 3, work 8 moss sts, p 3 *; repeat from * to *, ending with k 8, p 2.

Repeat Rows 1 through 30 for pattern.

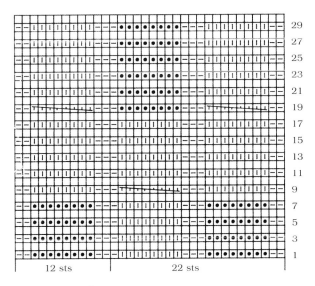

12 sts   22 sts

| | = k 1

— = p 1

• = 1 moss st

= 8-st crossover

□ = 1 st as shown

CROSSOVER STITCHES

Elegant diamonds

Work diamond on 16 stitches.
Row 1: K 6, to work 4-st right crossover: slip 2 to dp needle, hold in back, k 2, k 2 from dp needle, k 6.
Row 2 and all even-numbered rows: K the k sts as they face you and p the p sts.
Rows 3 and 29: P 5, to work 3-st right cross-P: slip 1 to dp needle, hold in back, k 2, p 1 from dp needle, to work left cross-P: slip 2 to dp needle, hold in front, p 1, k 2 from dp needle, k 5.
Rows 5 and 31: P 4, right cross-P, p 2, left cross-P, k 4.
Rows 7 and 33: P 3, right cross-P, p 4, left cross-P, p 3.
Rows 9 and 35: P 2, right cross-P, p 6, left cross-P, p 2.
Rows 11 and 37: P 1, right cross-p, p 8, left cross-P, p 1.
Rows 13 and 39: Right cross-P, p 10, left cross-P.
Rows 15 and 41: To work left cross-K: slip 2 to dp needle, hold in front, k 1, k 2 from dp needle, p 10, to work right cross-K: slip 1 to dp needle, hold in back, k 2, k 1 from dp needle.
Rows 17 and 43: K 1, left cross-K, p 8, right cross-K, k 1.
Rows 19 and 45: K 2, left cross-K, p 6, right cross-K, k 2.
Rows 21 and 47: K 3, left cross-K, p 4, right cross-K, k 3.
Rows 23 and 49: K 4, left cross-K, p 2, right cross-K, k 4.

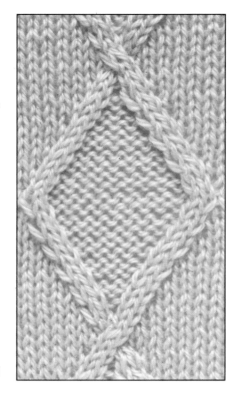

Rows 25 and 51: K 5, left cross-K, right cross-K, k 5.
Row 27: K 6, to work 4-st left crossover: slip 2 to dp needle, hold in front, k 2, k 2 from dp needle, k 6.
Repeat Rows 1 through 52 for pattern.

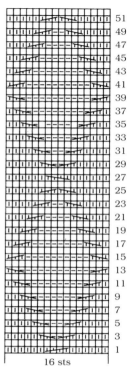

16 sts

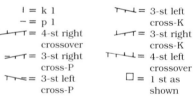

| = k 1
- = p 1
= 4-st right crossover
= 3-st right cross-P
= 3-st left cross-P
= 3-st left cross-K
= 3-st right cross-K
= 4-st left crossover
□ = 1 st as shown

Teardrops

Work with a multiple of 8 stitches, plus 4.
Row 1: P1, k 2, * p 6, k 2 *; repeat from * to *, ending p 1.
Row 2 and all even-numbered rows: Work each stitch as it appears on this side of work (k the k sts and p the p sts).
Rows 3 and 9: P 1, work crossover on 2 sts as follows: skip 1, k 1, k skipped st, drop original 2 sts from left needle, * p 6, crossover, *; repeat from * to *, ending p 1.
Rows 5 and 11: Work right cross on 2 sts as follows: skip 1, k 1, p skipped st, drop original sts from left needle, work left cross on 2 sts as follows: slip 1 to dp needle and hold in front of work, p 1, k 1 from dp needle, * p 4, right cross, left cross *; repeat from * to *.
Row 7: Left cross, right cross, * p 4,

left cross, right cross *; repeat from * to *.
Row 13: K 1, p 2, * left cross, p 2, right cross, p 2, *; repeat from * to *, ending k 1.
Row 15: K 1, p 3, * left cross, right cross, p 4 *; repeat from * to *, ending last repeat with p 3, k 1.
Repeat Rows 3 through 16 for pattern.

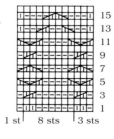

1 st 8 sts 3 sts

| = k 1
- = p 1
= 2-st crossover
= 2-st right cross
= 2-st left cross
□ = 1 st as shown

CROSSOVER STITCHES

Cables and lace

Work with a multiple of 11 stitches, plus 7.

Rows 1 and 5: K 1, * yarn over, slip 1, k 1, pass slip st over k st (psso), k 1, k 2 sts together, yarn over, k 6 *; repeat from * to *, ending last repeat with k 1.

Row 2 and all even-numbered rows: Purl.

Row 3: K 2, * yarn over, slip 1, k 2 sts together, psso (double decrease made), yarn over, k 1, work crossover on 6 sts as follows: slip 3 to dp needle and hold in back of work, k 3, k 3 from dp needle, k 1 *; repeat from * to *, ending last repeat with k 2.

Row 7: K 2, * yarn over, slip 1, k 2 sts together, psso, yarn over, k 8 *; repeat from * to *, ending last repeat with k 2.

Repeat Rows 1 through 8 for pattern.

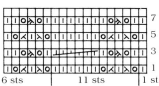

| | = k 1
□ = p 1
O = yarn over
⋋ = psso
⋌ = k 2 tog
⋌ = double dec
= 6-st crossover

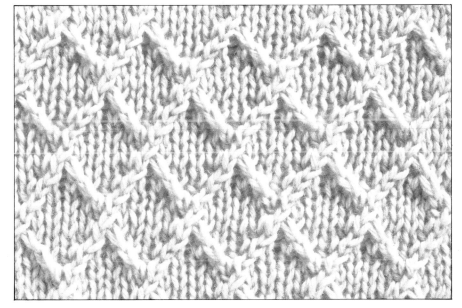

| = k 1
□ = p 1
⊢ = 2-st right cross
⊣ = 2-st left cross

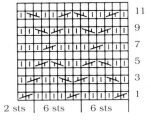

Dainty diamonds

Work with a multiple of 6 sts, plus 2.

Row 1: Work right cross on first 2 sts as follows: skip 1, k 1, k skipped st and drop original 2 sts, * k 4, right cross *; repeat from * to *.

Row 2 and all even-numbered rows: Purl.

Row 3: K 1, * work left cross on 2 sts as follows: slip 1 to dp needle and hold in front of work, k 1, slip st from dp needle to right needle without working it, k 2, right cross *; repeat from * to *, ending k 1.

Row 5: K 2, * left cross, right cross, k 2 *; repeat from * to *.

Row 7: K 3, * right cross, k 4 *; repeat from * to *, ending last repeat with k 3.

Row 9: K 2, * right cross, left cross, k 2 *; repeat from * to *.

Row 11: K 1, * right cross, k 2, left cross *; repeat from * to *, ending k 1.

Repeat Rows 1 through 12 for pattern.

CROSSOVER STITCHES

Thick and thin cables

Work with a multiple of 10 stitches, plus 5.

Row 1: * P 1, work (k 1 in back loop for twisted k st, p 1) twice, work 2-st right cross as follows: skip 1, k 1, k skipped st, drop original sts from left needle, k 1, to work 2-st left cross: slip 1 to dp needle, hold in front, k 1, k 1 from dp needle *; repeat from * to *, ending p 1, (twisted k st, p 1) twice.

Row 2 and all even-numbered rows: Working twisted p sts (p in back loop) over twisted sts of row below, work each stitch as it appears on this side of work (k the k sts and p the p sts.

Row 3: P 1, (k 1 twisted st, p 1) twice, * 2-st left cross, k 1, 2-st right cross, p 1, (k 1 twisted st, p 1) twice *; repeat from * to *.

Row 5: P 1, * work right cross-T as follows: slip 1 to dp needle, hold in back, slip next st to 2nd dp needle, hold in back, k 1 twisted st, p 1 from 2nd dp needle, k 1 twisted st from remaining dp needle, p 2, work right cross-K as follows: slip 2 to dp needle, hold in back, k 1, k 2 from dp needle, p 2 *; repeat from * to *, ending right cross-T, p 1.

Repeat Rows 1 through 6 for pattern.

5 sts | 10 sts

| = k 1
— = p 1
φ = 1 twisted k st
⌐⌐ = 2-st right cross
⌐⌐ = 2-st left cross
⌐⌐ = 3-st right cross-T
⌐⌐ = 3-st right cross-K
☐ = 1 st as shown

Wishbones

Work with a multiple of 18 stitches, plus 1.

Rows 1 and 5: P 1, * k 2, p 4, k 2, p 1 *; repeat from * to *.

Row 2 and all even-numbered rows: Work each stitch as it appears on this side of work (k the k sts and p the p sts). K any yarn overs in back loop.

Row 3: P 1, * work left cross on 4 sts as follows: slip 2 to dp needle and hold in front, p 2, yarn over, from dp needle k 2 sts together through back loops, work right cross on 4 sts as follows: slip 2 to dp needle and hold in back, k 2 sts together, yarn over, p 2 from dp needle, p 1, k 2, p 4, k 2, p 1 *; repeat from * to *.

Row 7: P 1, * k 2, p 4, k 2, p 1, left cross, right cross, p 1 *; repeat from * to *.

Repeat Rows 1 though 8 for pattern.

| = k 1
— = p 1
⌐⌐ = 4-st left cross
⌐⌐ = 4-st right cross
☐ = 1 st as shown

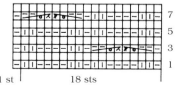

1 st | 18 sts

CROSSOVER STITCHES

Long, lean cables

Work cable pair on 9 stitches. For pattern as shown, work evenly-spaced pairs on background of reverse stockinette st.

Rows 1 and 9: Work right crossover on 4 sts as follows: slip 2 to dp needle and hold in back of work, k 2, k 2 from dp needle, p 1, work left crossover on 4 sts as follows: slip 2 to dp needle and hold in front of work, k 2, k 2 from dp needle.

Row 2 and all even-numbered rows: Work each stitch as it appears on this side of work (k the k sts and p the p sts).

Rows 3, 7, 11, 13, 15, 17, 19, 21, 23, and 27: K 4, p 1, k 4.

Rows 5 and 25: Left crossover, p 1, right crossover.

Repeat Rows 1 through 28 for cables.

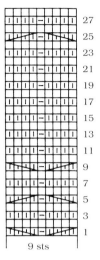

9 sts

| = k 1
− = p 1
⌐┴┬┐ = 4-st right crossover
┌┬┴¬ = 4-st left crossover
☐ = 1 st as shown

Cables in boxes

Work cable panel on 14 stitches.

Rows 1 and 5: K 3, p 2, work left crossover on 4 sts as follows: slip 4 to dp needle and hold in front of work, k 2, k 2 from dp needle, p 2, k 3.

Row 2 and all even-numbered rows: K the k sts (as they face you) and p the p sts.

Row 3: K 3, p 2, k 4, p 2, k 3.

Row 7: K 3, work right cross-P on 4 sts as follows: slip 2 to dp needle and hold in back of work, k 2, p 2 from dp needle, work left cross-P on 4 sts as follows: slip 2 to dp needle and hold in front of work, p 2, k 2 from dp needle, k 3.

Row 9: K 1, work right crossover on 4 sts as follows: slip 2 to dp needle and hold in back of work, k 2, k 2 from dp needle, p 4, work left crossover, k 1.

Row 11: K 2, work left cross-KP on 4 sts as follows: slip 2 to dp needle and hold in front of work, k 1, p 1, k 2 from dp needle, p 2, work right cross-PK on 4 sts as follows: slip 2 to dp needle and hold in back of work, k 2, then (p 1, k 1) from dp needle, k 2.

Row 13: P 3, left cross-P, right cross-P, k 3.

Repeat Rows 1 through 14 for cable.

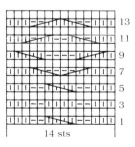

14 sts

| = k 1
− = p 1
┌┬┴┐ = 4-st left crossover
⌐┴┬┐ = 4-st right crossover
┌┬== = 4-st left cross-P
==┬┐ = 4-st right cross-P
┌┬┴┐ = 4 st left cross-KP
⌐┴┬┐ = 4-st right cross-PK
☐ = 1 st as shown

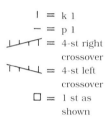

CROSSOVER STITCHES

Plain and fancy stripes

Work with a multiple of 10 stitches, plus 4.

Row 1: K 5, * work right cross on 2 sts as follows: skip 1, k 1, k skipped st, drop original 2 sts from left needle, work left cross on 2 sts as follows: slip 1 to dp needle and hold in front of work, k 1, k 1 from dp needle, k 6 *; repeat from * to *, ending last repeat with k 5.

Row 2 and all even-numbered rows: Purl.

Row 3: K 4, * right cross, k 2, left cross, p 4 *; repeat from * to *.

Repeat Rows 1 through 4 for pattern.

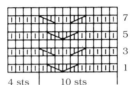

4 sts	10 sts

| = k 1
⟋⟍ = 2-st right cross
⟍⟋ = 2-st left cross
□ = p 1

| = k 1
− = p 1
⟍⟋ = 4-st right cross-PKKP
⟋⟍ = 4-st right cross-KPPK
□ = 1 st as shown

Alternating loops

Work on a multiple of 6 stitches, plus 4.

Row 1: P 1, * k 2, p 1 *; repeat from * to *.

Row 2 and all even-numbered rows: Work each stitch as it appears on this side of work (k the k sts and p the p sts).

Row 3: Work right cross-PKKP on 4 sts as follows: slip 1 to dp needle and hold in back of work, slip next 2 sts to 2nd dp needle and hold in back, p 1, k 2 from 2nd dp needle, p 1 from remaining dp needle, * k 2, right cross-PKKP *; repeat from * to *.

Row 5: K 1, * p 2, k 1 *; repeat from * to *.

Row 7: K 1, p 2, * work right cross-KPPK on 4 sts as follows: slip 1 to dp needle and hold in back, slip 2 to 2nd dp needle and hold in back, k 1, p 2 from 2nd dp needle, k 1 from remaining dp needle, p 2 *; repeat from * to *, ending k 1.

Repeat Rows 1 through 8 for pattern.

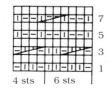

4 sts	6 sts

CROSSOVER STITCHES

Cable's out of the bag

Work with a multiple of 12 stitches.

Row 1: P 4, * work 4-st left crossover as follows: slip 1 to dp needle and hold in front of work, slip next 2 sts to 2nd dp needle and hold in back of work, k 1, p 2 from back dp needle, k 1 from front dp needle, p 8 *; repeat from * to *, ending last repeat with p 4.

Row 2 and all even-numbered rows: Work each stitch as it appears on this side of work (k the k sts and p the p sts).

Rows 3, 5, and 7: P 4, * k 1, p 2, k 1, p 8 *; repeat from * to *, ending last repeat with p 4.

Row 9: P 4, * work right crossover on 4 sts as follows: slip 1 to dp needle and hold in back of work, slip next 2 to 2nd dp needle and hold in back of work, k 1, k 2 from 2nd dp needle, k 1 from remaining dp needle, p 8 *; repeat from * to *, ending last repeat with p 4.

Rows 11, 13, 15, and 17: P 4, * k 4, p 8 *; repeat from * to *, ending last repeat with p 4.

Row 19: P 3, * work right cross on 2 sts as follows: skip 1, k 1, p skipped st and drop original 2 sts from left needle, work 2-st crossover as follows: slip 1 to dp needle and hold in front of work, k 1, k 1 from dp needle, work left cross on 2 sts as follows: slip 1 to dp needle and hold in front of work, p 1, k 1 from dp needle, p 6 *; repeat from * to *, ending last repeat with p 3.

Row 21: P 2, * work 2 right crosses, then 2 left crosses, p 4 *; repeat from * to *, ending last repeat with p 2.

Row 23: Repeat Row 3.

Repeat Rows 1 through 24 for pattern.

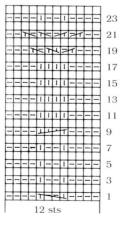

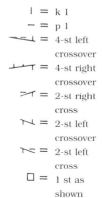

												23
												21
												19
												17
												15
												13
												11
												9
												7
												5
												3
												1

12 sts

| = k 1

− = p 1

= 4-st left crossover

= 4-st right crossover

= 2-st right cross

= 2-st left crossover

= 2-st left cross

□ = 1 st as shown

113

CROSSOVER STITCHES

Trevi fountain

Work with a multiple of 30 stitches, plus 2.

Row 1: P 2, * k 2, p 24, k 2, p 2 *; repeat from * to *.

Rows 2, 4, and 6: K 2, * p 2, k 9, p 6, k 9 p 2, k 2 *; repeat from * to *.

Rows 3 and 5: P 2, * k 2, p 9, k 6, p 9, k 2, p 2 *; repeat from * to *.

Row 7: P 2, * work left cross-A on 3 sts as follows: slip 2 to dp needle and hold in front of work, p 1, k 2 from dp needle, p 7; work right cross-A on 3 sts as follows: slip 1 to dp needle and hold in back of work, k 2, p 1 from dp needle, k 2 *, left cross-A, p 7, right cross-A, p 2 *; repeat from * to *.

Row 8: K 3, * work right cross-B on 3 sts as follows: slip 2 to dp needle and hold in back of work, k 1, p 2 from dp needle, k 5; work left cross-B on 3 sts as follows: slip 1 to dp needle and hold in front of work, p 2, k 1 from dp needle, k 1, p 2, k 1, right cross-B, k 5, left cross-B, k 4 *; repeat from * to *, ending last repeat with k 3.

Row 9: P 4, * work 4-st left cross as follows: slip 2 to dp needle and hold in front of work, p 2, k 2 from dp needle, p 1; work 4-st right cross as follows: slip 2 to dp needle and hold in back of work, k 2, p 2 from dp needle, p 2, k 2, p 2, 4-st left cross, p 1, 4-st right cross, p 6 *; repeat from * to *, ending last repeat with p 4.

Row 10: K 2, * p 2, k 24, p 2, k 2 *; repeat from * to *.

Repeat these 10 rows for pattern.

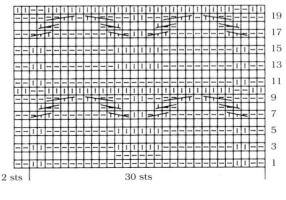

2 sts   30 sts

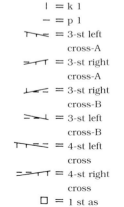

| = k 1

− = p 1

⊤⤙ = 3-st left cross-A

⤚⊤ = 3-st right cross-A

⤝ = 3-st right cross-B

⤞ = 3-st left cross-B

⊤⊤⤙ = 4-st left cross

⤚⤚⊤⊤ = 4-st right cross

☐ = 1 st as shown

114

CROSSOVER STITCHES

Intersections

Work with a multiple of 6 stitches.

Row 1: * Work left cross on 2 sts as follows: slip 1 to dp needle and hold in front of work, k 1, k 1 from dp needle; work right cross on 2 sts as follows: skip 1, k 1, k skipped st, drop original 2 sts from left needle; work another right cross *; repeat from * to *.

Row 2 and all even-numbered rows: Purl.

Row 3: K 1, left cross, * right cross, work left cross twice *; repeat from * to *, ending with right cross, k 1.

Row 5: * Work left cross twice, k 2 *; repeat from * to *.

Row 7: K 1, * left cross twice, right cross *; repeat from * to *, ending left cross twice, k 1.

Row 9: Right cross, * left cross, right cross twice *; repeat from * to *, ending with left cross, right cross.

Row 11: K 3, * right cross twice, k 2 *; repeat from * to *, ending with right cross, k 1.

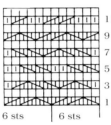

| = k 1
⅃ = 2-st left crossover
⅃⌐ = 2-st right crossover
□ = p 1

Pretty little cables

Work on a multiple of 6 stitches, plus 3.

Row 1: K 3, * p 1, with yarn in back slip 1 as if to p, p 1, k 3 *; repeat from * to *.

Row 2 and all even-numbered rows: P 3, * k 3, p 3 *; repeat from * to *.

Row 3: Work crossover on 3 sts as follows: slip 1 to dp needle and hold in front of work, k 2, k 1 from dp needle, * p 1, slip 1, p 1, crossover *; repeat from * to *.

Repeat Rows 1 through 4 for pattern.

| = k 1
− = p 1
V = slip st
⊤⅃ = 3-st crossover

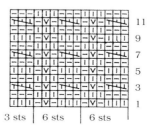

6 sts | 6 sts

3 sts | 6 sts | 6 sts

CROSSOVER STITCHES

Easy cables
Work with a multiple of 8, plus 2.
Row 1: P 2, * k 2, p 1, work crossover on 2 sts as follows: skip 1, k next st retaining original st on left needle, k skipped st and drop 2 original sts from left needle, p 2 *; repeat from * to *.
Row 2 and all even-numbered rows: Work each stitch as it appears on this side of work (k the k sts and p the p sts).
Row 3: P 2, * crossover, p 2, k 2, p 2 *; repeat from * to *.
Repeat Rows 1 through 4 for pattern.

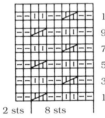

| = k 1
− = p 1
⤸⊤ = 2-st crossover
□ = 1 st as shown

2 sts | 8 sts

Single and double claw pattern
Work with a multiple of 17, plus 2.
Row 1: P 2, * work 2-st left crossover as follows: slip 1 to dp needle and hold in front of work, k 1, k 1 from dp needle, p 2, k 7, p 2, work 2-st right crossover as follows: skip 1, k 1, k skipped st and drop original sts from left needle, p 2 *; repeat from * to *.
Row 2 and all even-numbered rows: Work each stitch as it appears on this side of work (k the k sts and p the p sts).
Row 3: P 2, * 2-st left crossover, p 2; work 3-st right crossover as follows: slip 2 to dp needle and hold in back of work, k 1, k 2 from dp needle, k 1; work 3-st left crossover as follows: slip 1 to dp needle and hold in front of work, k 2, k 1 from dp needle, p 2, 2-st right crossover, p 2 *; repeat from * to *.
Repeat Rows 1 through 4 for pattern.

| = k 1
− = p 1
⤹ = 2-st left crossover
⤸⊤ = 2-st right crossover
⤸⊤ = 3-st right crossover
⤹⊤ = 3-st left crossover
□ = 1 st as shown

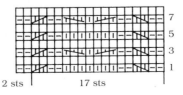

2 sts | 17 sts

116

CROSSOVER STITCHES

Medallion cable

Work with a multiple of 20 stitches.

Rows 1, 3, and 5: P 7, * k 6, p 14 *; repeat from * to *, ending with p 7.

Row 2 and all even-numbered rows: Work each stitch as it appears on this side of work (k the k sts and p the p sts).

Row 7: P 4, * k 3, work left crossover-K on 6 sts as follows: slip 3 to dp needle and hold in front of work, k 3, k 3 from dp needle, k 3, p 8 *; repeat from * to *, ending last repeat with p 4.

Rows 9 and 11: P 4, * k 12, p 8 *; repeat from * to *, ending with p 4.

Row 13: P 1, * k 3, work 6-st right crossover-P as follows: slip 3 to dp needle, hold in back, k 3, p 3 from dp needle, work 6-st left crossover-P as follows: slip 3 to dp needle, hold in front, p 3, k 3 from dp needle, k 3, p 2 *; repeat from * to *, ending with p 1.

Rows 15 and 17: P 1, * k 6, p 6, k 6, p 2 *; repeat from * to *, ending last repeat with p 1.

Row 19: P 1, * right cross-P, p 6, left cross-P, p 2 *; repeat from * to *, ending last repeat with p 1.

Rows 21 and 23: P 1, * k 3, p 12, k 3, p 2 * repeat from * to *, ending last repeat with p 1.

Row 25: P 1, * work left crossover-K, p 6, work right crossover-K on 6 sts as follows: slip 3 to dp needle, hold in back, k 3, k 3 from dp needle, p 2 *;

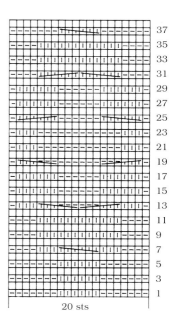

repeat from * to *, ending with p 1.

Rows 27 and 29: Repeat Rows 15 and 17.

Row 31: P 4, * left crossover-K, right crossover-K, p 8 *; repeat from * to *, ending last repeat with p 4.

Rows 33 and 35: Repeat Rows 9 and 11.

Row 37: P 7, * left crossover-K, p 14 *; repeat from * to *, ending with p 7.
Repeat Rows 3 through 38 for pattern.

20 sts

− = p 1
| = k 1
= 6-st left crossover-K
= 6-st right crossover-P
= 6-st left crossover-P
= 6-st right crossover-K
□ = 1 st as shown

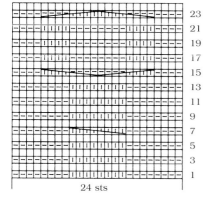

24 sts

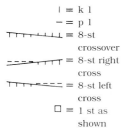

| = k 1
− = p 1
= 8-st crossover
= 8-st right cross
= 8-st left cross
□ = 1 st as shown

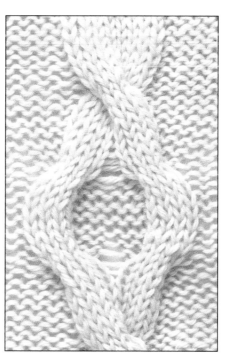

Single medallion cable

Work cable panel on 24 stitches.

Rows 1, 3, 5, 9, and 11: P 8, k 8, p 8.

Row 2 and all even-numbered rows: Work each stitch as it appears on this side of work (k the k sts and p the p sts).

Row 7: P 8, to work 8-st crossover: slip 4 to dp needle, hold in front, k 4, k 4 from dp needle, p 8.

Row 15: P 4, to work 8-st right cross: slip 4 to dp needle, hold in back, k 4, p 4 from dp needle; to work 8-st left cross: slip 4 to dp needle, hold in front, p 4, k 4 from dp needle, p 4.

Rows 17, 19, and 21: P 4, k 4, p 8, k 4, p 4.

Row 23: P 4, left cross, right cross, p 4.
Repeat Rows 1 through 24 for pattern.

CROSSOVER STITCHES

Parquet

Work with a multiple of 16 sts, plus 4.

Row 1: P 1, work 2-st crossover as follows: skip 1, k 1, k skipped st and drop original sts from left needle, p 1, * work left cross on 4 sts as follows: slip 2 to dp needle, hold in front, k 2, k 2 from dp needle, k 4, work right crossover on 4 sts as follows: slip 2 to dp needle, hold in back, k 2, k 2 from dp needle, p 1, 2-st crossover, p 1 *; repeat from * to *.

Row 2 and all even-numbered rows: Work each stitch as it appears on this side of work (k the k sts and p the p sts).

Row 3: P 1, 2-st crossover, p 1, * k 2, left crossover, k 6, p 1, 2-st crossover, p 1 *; repeat from * to *.

Row 5: P 1, 2-st crossover, p 1, * k 4, left crossover, right crossover, p 1, 2-st crossover, p 1 *; repeat from * to *.

Row 7: P 1, 2-st crossover, p 1, * k 6, left crossover, k 2, p 1, 2-st crossover, p 1 *; repeat from * to *.

Row 9: P 1, 2-st crossover, p 1, * k 8, right crossover, p 1, 2-st crossover, p 1 *; repeat from * to *.

Row 11: P 1, 2-st crossover, p 1, * k 12, p 1, 2-st crossover, p 1 *; repeat from * to *.
Repeat Rows 1 through 12 for pattern.

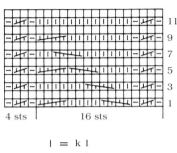

| = k 1

− = p 1

⌐⊤ = 2-st crossover

⌐⌐⊤ = 4-st right crossover

⊤⌐⌐ = 4-st left crossover

☐ = 1 st as shown

Commanding zigzags

Work with a multiple of 6.

Row 1: * Work 1 moss st (see page 5), work left cross on 3 sts as follows: slip 2 to dp needle and hold in front, work 1 more moss st, k 2 from dp needle, k 2 *; repeat from * to *.

Row 2 and all even-numbered rows: Work moss st over moss sts and work each remaining stitch as it appears on this row (k the k sts and p the p sts).

Row 3: * Work 2 moss sts, left cross, k 1 *; repeat from * to *.

Row 5: * Work 3 moss sts, left cross *; repeat from * to *.

Row 7: * Work 3 moss sts, work right cross on 3 sts as follows: slip 1 to dp needle and hold in back, k 2, k 1 from dp needle *; repeat from * to *.

Row 9: * Work 2 moss sts, right crossover, k 1 *; repeat from * to *.

Row 11: * Work 1 moss st, right cross, k 2 *; repeat from * to *.

Row 13: * Right cross, k 3 *; repeat from * to *.

Row 15: * Left cross, k 3 *; repeat from * to *.
Repeat Rows 1 through 16 for pattern.

| = k 1

• = 1 moss st

⊤⌐ = 3-st left cross

⌐⊤ = 3-st right cross

☐ = 1 st as shown

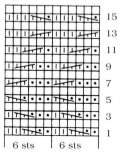

CROSSOVER STITCHES

Double hourglass

Work with a multiple of 14 stitches.
Row 1: K 1, * p 2, k 1, work 6 moss sts (see page 5), k 1, p 2, k 2 *; repeat from * to *, ending last repeat with k 1.
Row 2 and all even-numbered rows: Work moss st over moss sts and work each remaining stitch as it appears on this row (k the k and p the p sts).
Row 3: * Work left cross on 2 sts as follows: slip 1 to dp needle and hold in front of work, p 1, k 1 from dp needle, p 1, left cross, 4 moss sts, work right cross on 2 sts as follows: skip 1, k 1, p skipped st and drop original 2 sts from left needle, p 1, right cross *; repeat from * to *.
Row 5: Work 1 moss st, * left cross, p 1, left cross, 2 moss sts, right cross, p 1, right cross, 2 moss sts *; repeat from * to *, ending last repeat with 1 moss st.
Row 7: Work 2 moss sts, * left cross, p 1, left cross, right cross, p 1, right cross, 4 moss sts *; repeat from * to *, ending last repeat with 2 moss sts.
Row 9: Work 3 moss sts, * k 1, p 2, k 2, p 2, k 1, 6 moss sts *; repeat

from * to *, ending last repeat with 3 moss sts.
Row 11: Work 2 moss sts, * right cross, p 1, right cross, left cross, p 1, left cross, 4 moss sts *; repeat from * to *, ending last repeat with 2 moss sts.
Row 13: Work 1 moss st, * right cross, p 1, right cross, 2 moss sts, left cross, p 1, left cross, p 2 *; repeat from * to *, ending last repeat with 1 moss st.
Row 15: * Right cross, p 1, right cross, 4 moss sts, left cross, p 1, left cross *; repeat from * to *.
Repeat Rows 1 through 16 for pattern.

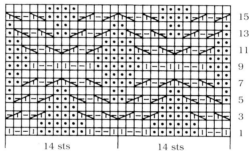

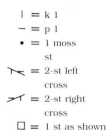

	= k 1
– = p 1
• = 1 moss st
⅄ = 2-st left cross
⅄ = 2-st right cross
☐ = 1 st as shown

14 sts   14 sts

Blossoms

Work with a multiple of 13 stitches, plus 2.
Rows 1 and 5: P 5, * k 2, work bobble in next st as follows: knit, purl, knit, purl, knit all in same st (5 sts in 1 st), turn work, k 5, turn, p 5, turn, k 5, turn, k 5, then pass first 4 sts, one by one, over 5th st and drop (bobble made), k 2, p 8 *; repeat from * to *, ending last repeat with p 5.
Row 2 and all even-numbered rows: Work each stitch as it appears on this side of work (k the k sts and p the p sts).
Row 3: P 5, * bobble, k 3, bobble, p 8 *; repeat from * to *, ending last repeat with p 5.
Row 7: P 4, * work right cross on 3 sts as follows: slip 1 to dp needle and hold in back of work, k 2, p 1 from dp needle, p 1; work left cross on 3 sts as follows: slip 2 to dp needle and hold in front of work, p 1, k 2 from dp needle, p 6 *; repeat from * to *, ending last repeat with p 4.
Row 9: P 3, * right cross, p 3, left cross, p 4 *; repeat from * to *, ending last repeat with p 3.
Row 11: P 2, * right cross, p 5, left

cross, p 2 *; repeat from * to *.
Row 13: P 2, * k 2, p 3, bobble, p 3, k 2, p 2 *; repeat from * to *.
Row 15: P 2, * left cross, p 5, right cross, p 2 *; repeat from * to *.
Row 17: P 3, * left cross, p 3, right cross, p 4 *; repeat from * to *, ending last repeat with p 3.
Row 19: P 4, * left cross, p 1, right cross, p 6 *; repeat from * to *, ending last repeat with p 4.
Repeat Rows 1 through 20 for pattern.

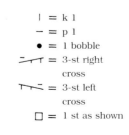

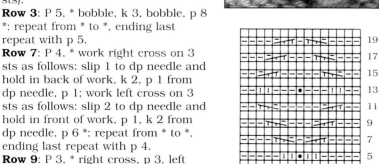

	= k 1
– = p 1
• = 1 bobble
⊤⅂ = 3-st right cross
⊤⅂ = 3-st left cross
☐ = 1 st as shown

2 sts   13 sts

CROSSOVER STITCHES

Split image

Work with a multiple of 16 stitches.
Rows 1, 3, 5, 9, and 11: P 2, * k 2, p 2, k 4, p 2, k 2, p 4 *; repeat from * to *, ending last repeat with p 2.
Rows 2, 4, 6, 8, and 10: K the k sts (as they face you) and p the p sts.
Row 7: P 2, * work right cross on 6 sts as follows: slip 4 to dp needle and hold it in back of work, k 2, return 2 p sts from dp needle to left needle and p 2, k last 2 from dp needle; work left cross on 6 sts as follows: slip 2 to dp needle and hold in front of work, slip next 2 to 2nd dp needle and hold in back of work, k 2, p 2 from back dp needle, k 2 from front dp needle, p 4 *; repeat from * to *, ending last repeat with p 2.
Rows 12 through 16: Knit.
Repeat these 16 rows for pattern.

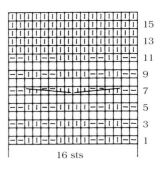

16 sts

| = k 1
− = p 1
⌐⊥⊥—⊤⊤ = 6-st right cross
⊤⊤—⊥⊥⌐ = 6-st left cross
☐ = 1 st as shown

Shooting stars

Work with a multiple of 14 stitches, plus 9.
Row 1: P 2, * work right cross on 2 sts as follows: skip 1, k 1, p skipped st and drop original 2 sts from left needle, k 1; work left cross on 2 sts as follows: slip 1 to dp needle and hold in front of work, p 1, k 1 from dp needle, p 3, k 1; work right crossover on 2 sts as follows: skip 1, k 1, k skipped st and drop original 2 sts from left needle, p 3 *; repeat from * to *, ending right cross, k 1, left cross, p 2.
Row 2 and all even-numbered rows: Work each stitch as it appears on this side of work (k the k sts and p the p sts).
Row 3: P 1, * right cross, p 1, k 1, p 1, left cross, p 2, work left crossover on 2 sts as follows: slip 1 to dp needle and hold in front of work, k 1, k 1 from dp needle, k 1, p 2 *; repeat from * to *, ending last repeat with left cross, p 1.
Row 5: P 1, * left cross, p 1, k 1, p 1, right cross, p 2, k 1, right crossover, p 2 *; repeat from * to *, ending last repeat with right cross, p 1.
Row 7: P 2, * left cross, k 1, right cross, p 3, left crossover, k 1, p 3 *; repeat from * to *, ending last repeat with right cross, p 2.
Row 9: * P 3, k 1, right crossover, p 3, right cross, k 1, left cross *; repeat from * to *, ending last repeat with right crossover, p 3.
Row 11: P 3, * left crossover, k 1, p 2, right cross, p 1, k 1, p 1, left cross, p 2 *; repeat from * to *, ending left crossover, k 1, p 3.
Row 13: P 3, * k 1, right crossover, p 2, left cross, p 1, k 1, p 1, right cross, p 2 *; repeat from * to *, ending k 1, right crossover, p 3.
Row 15: * P 3, left crossover, k 1, p 3, left cross, k 1, right cross *; repeat from * to *, ending last repeat with p 3.
Repeat Rows 1 through 16 for pattern.

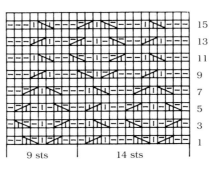

9 sts   14 sts

| = k 1
− = p 1
⌐⊤ = 2-st right cross
⊤⌐ = 2-st left cross
⌐⊤ = 2-st right crossover
⊤⌐ = 2-st left crossover
☐ = 1 st as shown

CROSSOVER STITCHES

Four-stranded cable

Work with a multiple of 17 stitches, plus 3.

Row 1: P 3, * k 6, p 2, k 6, p 3 *; repeat from * to *.

Row 2 and all even-numbered rows: Work each stitch as it appears on this side of work (k the k sts and p the p sts).

Row 3: P 3, * work 6-st right crossover as follows: slip 4 to dp needle and hold in back of work, k 2, k 4 from dp needle, p 2; work 6-st left crossover as follows: slip 2 to dp needle and hold in front, k 4, k 2 from dp needle, p 3 *; repeat from * to *.

Row 5: P 3, * k 4, work left cross on 3 sts as follows: slip 2 to dp needle and hold in front, p 1, k 2 from dp needle; work right cross on 3 sts as follows: slip 1 to dp needle and hold in back, k 2, p 1 from dp needle, k 4, p 3 *; repeat from * to *.

Row 7: P 3, * k 4, p 1, work 4-st crossover as follows: slip 2 to dp needle and hold in front, k 2, k 2 from dp needle, p 1, k 4, p 3 *; repeat from * to *.

Row 9: P 3, * k 4, right cross, left cross, k 4, p 3 *; repeat from * to *. Repeat Rows 3 through 10 for pattern.

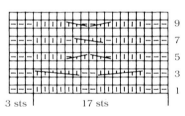

| = k 1
− = p 1
⊥⊥⊥⊥⊤ = 6-st right crossover
⊤⊥⊥⊥⊥ = 6-st left crossover
⊤⊏ = 3-st left cross
⊐⊤ = 3-st right cross
⊤⊤⊥⊥ = 4-st crossover
□ = 1 st as shown

3 sts | 17 sts

Superimposed cables

Work with a multiple of 16 sts, plus 3.

Rows 1, 3, 7, 11, and 15: P 3, * k 6, p 1, k 6, p 3 *; repeat from * to *.

Row 2 and all even-numbered rows: Work each stitch as it appears on this side of work (k the k sts and p the p sts).

Row 5: P 3, * work left crossover on 6 sts as follows: slip 3 to dp needle and hold in front of work, k 3, k 3 from dp needle, p 1; work right crossover on 6 sts as follows: slip 3 to dp needle and hold in back, k 3, k 3 from dp needle, p 3 *; repeat from * to *.

Row 9: P 3, * k 3, work 7-st crossover as follows: slip 3 to dp needle, hold in front, slip next st to 2nd dp needle, hold in back, k 3, p 1 from back dp needle, k 3 from front dp needle, k 3, p 3 *; repeat from * to *.

Row 13: P 3, right crossover, p 1, left crossover, p 3 * repeat from * to *. Repeat Rows 1 through 16 for pattern.

| = k 1
− = p 1
⊤⊤⊤⊥⊥⊥ = 6-st left crossover
⊥⊥⊥⊤⊤⊤ = 6-st right crossover
⊤⊤⊤⊥⊥⊥ = 7-st crossover
□ = 1 st as shown

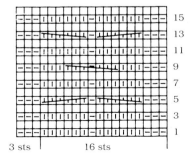

3 sts | 16 sts

CROSSOVER STITCHES

Elongated cables

Work with a multiple of 15 sts, plus 3.

Rows 1, 3, 11, and 13: P 3, * k 4, p 1, k 2, p 1, k 4, p 3 *; repeat from * to *.

Row 2 and all even-numbered rows: Work each stitch as it appears on this side of work (k the k sts and p the p sts).

Rows 5, 7, and 9: P 3, * k 4, p 1, work right crossover on 2 sts as follows: skip 1, k 1, k skipped st and drop both original sts from left needle, p 1, k 4, p 3 *; repeat from * to *.

Row 15: P 3, * work left crossover on 4 sts as follows: slip 2 to dp needle and hold in front of work, k 2, k 2 from dp needle, p 1, k 2, p 1, left crossover, p 3 *; repeat from * to *. Repeat Rows 1 through 16 for pattern.

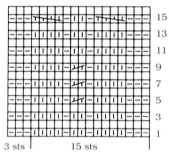

```
| = k 1
− = p 1
⊢⊤ = 2-st right crossover
⊤⊤⊥⊥ = 4-st left crossover
□ = 1 st as shown
```

3 sts   15 sts

Woven cable

Work with a multiple of 21 stitches, plus 3.

Rows 1 and 5: P 3, * k 18, p 3 *; repeat from * to *.

Row 2 and all even-numbered rows: Work each stitch as it appears on this side of row (k the k sts and p the p sts).

Row 3: P 3, * work right crossover on 6 sts as follows: slip 3 to dp needle and hold in back of work, k 3, k 3 from dp needle; work 2 more right crossovers, p 3 *; repeat from * to *.

Row 7: P 3, * k 3, work left crossover on 6 sts as follows: slip 3 to dp needle and hold in front, k 3, k 3 from dp needle; work another left crossover, k 3, p 3 *; repeat from * to *.

Repeat Rows 1 through 8 for pattern.

```
| = k 1
− = p 1
⊤⊤⊤⊥⊥⊥ = 6-st left crossover
⊥⊥⊥⊤⊤⊤ = 6-st right crossover
□ = 1 st as shown
```

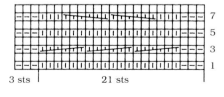

3 sts   21 sts

CROSSOVER STITCHES

Spiral cables

Work cable on 10 stitches. For pattern as shown, work evenly-spaced cables on background of reverse stockinette st.

Row 1: Knit.

Row 2 and all even-numbered rows: Purl.

Row 3: K 4, work 4-st crossover as follows: slip 2 to dp needle and hold in back of work, k 2, k 2 from dp needle; work 2-st crossover as follows: skip 1 st, k 1, k skipped st and drop both original sts from left needle.

Row 5: K 2, 4-st crossover, 2-st crossover, k 2.

Row 7: Work 4-st crossover, 2-st crossover, k 4.

Repeat Rows 1 through 8 for pattern.

| | = k 1
⌐┬⊤ = 4-st crossover
⌐ = 2-st crossover
□ = p 1

10 sts

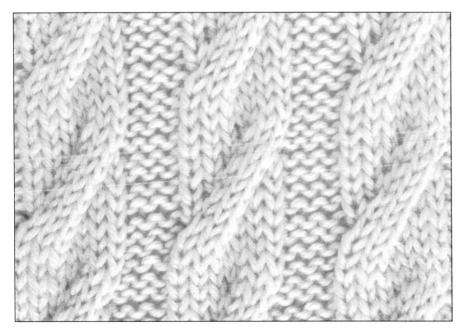

| | = k 1
— = 4-st crossover
⌐┬⊤ = 2-st crossover
□ = p 1

Slow and easy cable

Work with a multiple of 11 stitches.

Row 1: P 2, * k 7, p 4 *; repeat from * to *, ending with p 2.

Row 2 and all even-numbered rows: Work each stitch as it appears on this side of work (k the k sts and p the p sts).

Row 3: P 2, * k 3, work crossover on 4 sts as follows: slip 1 to dp needle and hold in back of work, k 3, k 1 from dp needle, p 4 *; repeat from * to *, ending last repeat with p 2.

Row 5: P 2, * k 2, crossover, k 1, p 4 *; repeat from * to *, ending with p 2.

Row 7: P 2, * k 1, crossover, k 2, p 4 *; repeat from * to *, ending with p 2.

Row 9: P 2, * crossover, k 3, p 4 *; repeat from * to *, ending with p 2.

Repeat Rows 1 through 10 for pattern.

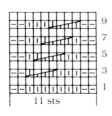

11 sts

CROSSOVER STITCHES

Slalom

Work with a multiple of 3 stitches.
Row 1: * P 1, work right cross on 2 sts as follows: skip 1, k 1, p skipped st and drop both original sts from left needle *; repeat from * to *.
Row 2 and all even-numbered rows: Work each stitch as it appears on this side of work (k the k sts and p the p sts).
Row 3: * Right cross, p 1 *; repeat from * to *.
Row 5: * K 1, p 2 *; repeat from * to *.
Row 7: * Work left cross on 2 sts as follows: slip 1 to dp needle and hold in front of work, p 1, k 1 from dp needle, p 1 *; repeat from * to *.
Row 9: * P 1, left cross *; repeat from * to *.
Row 11: * P 2, k 1 *; repeat from * to *.
Repeat Rows 1 through 12 for pattern.

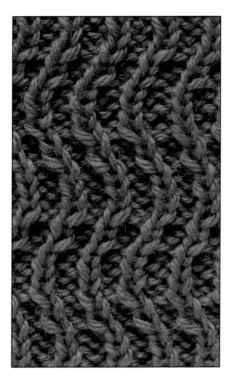

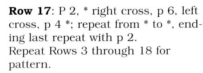

- = p 1
- = 2-st left cross
- = 2-st right cross
- = 1 st as shown

Somersault cable

Work with a multiple of 16 stitches.
Row 1: K 4, * p 2, k 4, p 2, k 8 *; repeat from * to *, ending last repeat with k 4.
Row 2 and all even-numbered rows: Work each stitch as it appears on this side of work (k the k sts and p the p sts).
Row 3: * Work left cross on 3 sts as follows: slip 2 to dp needle and hold in front of work, p 1, k 2 from dp needle, k 1, p 2, k 4, p 2, k 1, work right cross on 3 sts as follows: slip 1 to dp needle and hold in back, k 2, p 1 from dp needle *; repeat from * to *.
Row 5: P 1, * left cross, p 2, k 4, p 2, right cross, p 2 *; repeat from * to *, ending last repeat with p 1.
Row 7: P 2, * left cross, p 1, k 4, p 1, right cross, p 4 *; repeat from * to *, ending last repeat with p 2.
Row 9: P 3, * left cross, k 4, right cross, p 6 *; repeat from * to *, ending last repeat with p 3.
Row 11: P 4, * k 1, right cross, left cross, k 1, p 8 *; repeat from * to *, ending last repeat with p 4.
Row 13: P 4, * right cross, p 2, left cross, p 8 * repeat from * to *, ending last repeat with p 4.
Row 15: P 3, * right cross, p 4, left cross, p 6 *; repeat from * to *, ending last repeat with p 3.

Row 17: P 2, * right cross, p 6, left cross, p 4 *; repeat from * to *, ending last repeat with p 2.
Repeat Rows 3 through 18 for pattern.

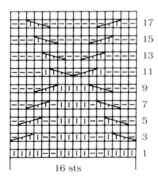

- = k 1
- = p 1
- = 3-st right cross
- = 3-st left cross
- = 1 st as shown

CROSSOVER STITCHES

Outlines

Work with a multiple of 14 stitches, plus 4.

Row 1: K 4, * p 1, work crossover on 2 sts as follows: slip 1 to dp needle and hold in front of work, k 1, k 1 from dp needle, k 6, p 1, k 4 *; repeat from * to *.

Row 2 and all even-numbered rows: Slip first st above crossover as if to purl, carrying yarn in front of work, and work each remaining stitch as it appears on this side of work (k the k sts and p the p sts).

Row 3: K 4, * p 1, k 1, crossover, k 5, p 1, k 4 *; repeat from * to *.

Row 5: K 4, * p 1, k 2, crossover, k 4, p 1, k 4 *; repeat from * to *.

Row 7: K 4, * p 1, k 3, crossover, k 3, p 1, k 4 *; repeat from * to *.

Row 9: K 4, * p 1, k 4, crossover, k 2, p 1, k 4 *; repeat from * to *.

Row 11: K 4, * p 1, k 5, crossover, k 1, p 1, k 4 *; repeat from * to *.

Row 13: K 4, * p 1, k 6, crossover, p 1, k 4 *; repeat from * to *.

Repeat Rows 1 through 14 for pattern.

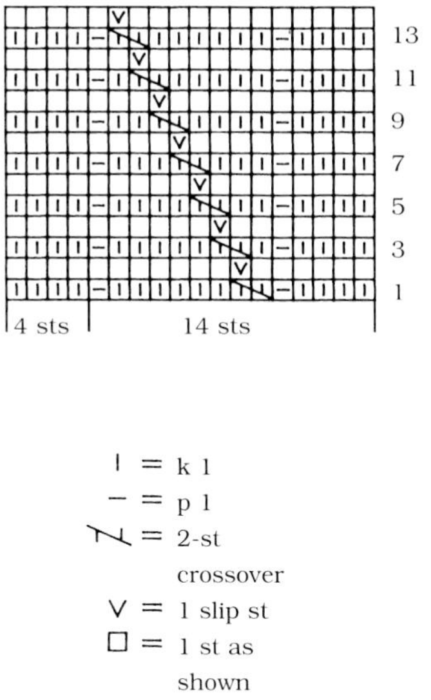
13
11
9
7
5
3
1
4 sts
14 sts
= k 1
= p 1
= 2-st crossover
= 1 slip st
= 1 st as shown

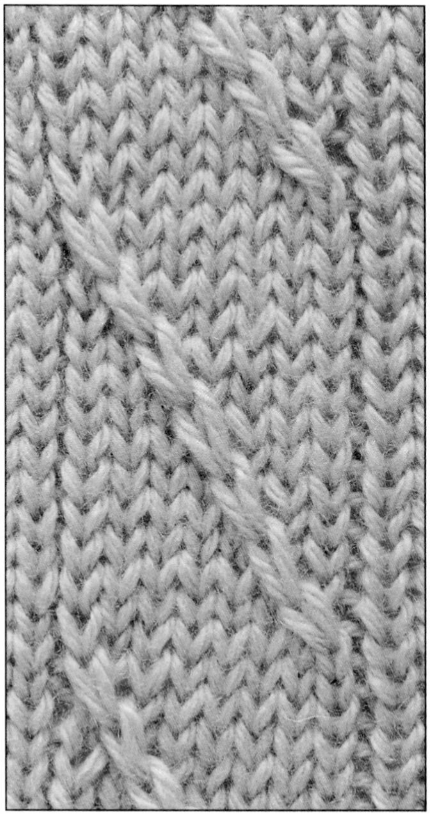

Double wicker

Work with a multiple of 6 stitches, plus 4.

Row 1: * Work left cross on 2 sts as follows: slip 1 to dp needle and hold in front of work, p 1, k 1 from dp needle; work right cross on 2 sts as follows: skip 1, k 1, p skipped st and drop both original sts from left needle; work right crossover on 2 sts as follows: skip 1, k 1, k skipped st and drop original sts from left needle *; repeat from * to *, ending last repeat with 1 right cross.

Row 2 and all even-numbered rows: Work each stitch as it appears on this side of work (k the k sts and p the p sts).

Row 3: K 1, left cross, * right cross, 2 left crosses *; repeat from * to *, ending p last st.

Row 5: * Work left crossover on 2 sts as follows: slip 1 to dp needle and hold in front, k 1, k 1 from dp needle, left cross, p 2 *; repeat from * to *, ending last repeat with left cross.

Row 7: P 1, * left crossover, left cross, right cross *; repeat from * to *, ending with left crossover, p 1.

Row 9: Right cross, * left cross, 2 right crosses *; repeat from * to *, ending with left cross.

Row 11: K 1, * p 2, right cross, right crossover *; repeat from * to *, ending with p 2, k last st.

Repeat Rows 1 through 12 for pattern.

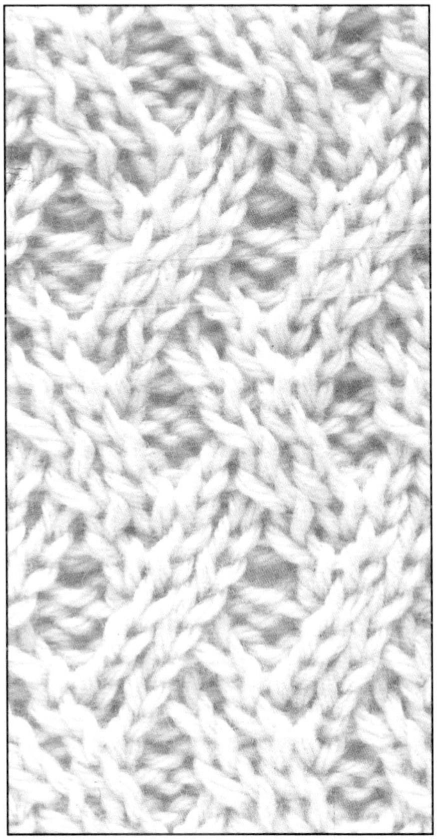

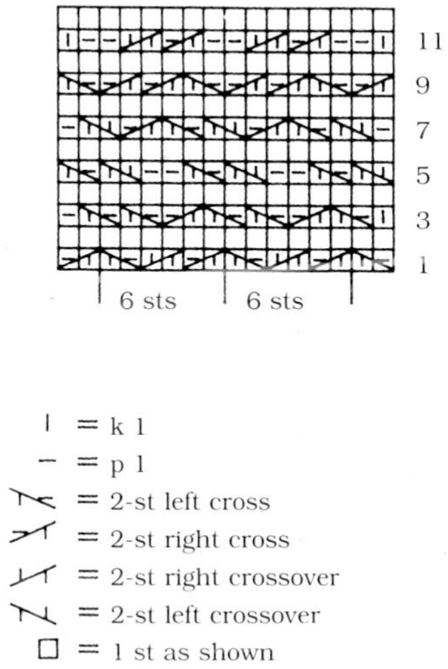
11
9
7
5
3
1
6 sts
6 sts
= k 1
= p 1
= 2-st left cross
= 2-st right cross
= 2-st right crossover
= 2-st left crossover
= 1 st as shown

CROSSOVER STITCHES

Leaves on branches

Work with a multiple of 20 sts.

Row 1: P 4, * work right crossover-K on 2 sts as follows: skip 1, k 1, k skipped st and drop both original sts from left needle, k 1; work right cross on 2 sts as follows: skip 1, k 1, p skipped st, k 2, p 3; work left cross on 2 sts as follows: slip 1 to dp needle and hold in front of work, p 1, k 1 from dp needle, k 1, p 7 * repeat from * to *, ending last repeat with p 3.

Row 2: K 3, * p 2, k 4, p 2, k 1, p 3, work right crossover-P on 2 sts as follows: skip 1, p 1, p skipped st and drop original sts from left needle, k 6 *; repeat from * to *, ending last repeat with p 3.

Row 3: P 3, * k 3, right cross, p 1, k 1, work left crossover-K on 2 sts as follows: slip 1 to dp needle and hold in front of work, k 1, k 1 from dp needle, p 3, left cross, p 6 *; repeat from * to *, ending with p 3.

Row 4: K 3, * p 1, k 3, work left crossover-P on 2 sts as follows: slip 1 to dp needle and hold in front of work, p 1, p 1 from dp needle, p 2, k 2, p 4, k 6 *; repeat from * to *, ending with k 3.

Row 5: P 3, * k 2, right cross, p 2, k 1, work left crossover-K twice, p 9 *; repeat from * to *, ending with p 6.

Row 6: K 5, * left crossover-P, p 4, k 3, p 3, k 8 *; repeat from * to *, ending with k 3.

Row 7: P 3, * k 1, right cross, p 3, k 2, left cross, k 1, left crossover-K, p 7 *; repeat from * to *, ending with p 4.

Row 8: K 3, * left crossover-P, p 3, k 1, p 2, k 4, p 2, k 6 *; repeat from *

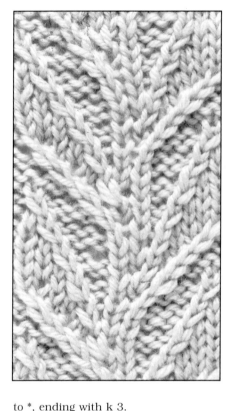

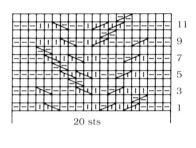

20 sts

Repeat these 12 rows for pattern.

to *, ending with k 3.

Row 9: P 3, * right cross, p 3, right crossover-K, k 1, p 1, left cross, k 3, p 6 *; repeat from * to *, ending with p 3.

Row 10: K 3, * p 4, k 2, p 2, right crossover-P, k 3, p 1, k 6 *; repeat from * to *, ending with k 3.

Row 11: P 6, * work right crossover-K twice, k 1, p 2, left cross, k 2, p 9 *; repeat from * to *, ending with p 3.

Row 12: K 3, * p 3, k 3, p 4, right crossover-P, k 8 *; repeat from * to *, ending with k 5.

| = k 1
− = p 1
⊬ = 2-st right crossover-K
⊁ = 2-st right cross
⊼ = 2-st left cross
⊤⌐ = 2-st left crossover-K
⊁ = 2-st right crossover-P
⊰ = 2-st left crossover-P
□ = 1 st as shown

Simplicity

Work with a multiple of 4 stitches, plus 2.

Row 1: K 1, * p 2, k 2 *; repeat from * to *, ending last repeat with k 3.

Row 2: P 3, * k 2, p 2 *; repeat from * to *, ending last repeat with p 1.

Row 3: K 1, * work crossover on 4 sts as follows: slip 2 to dp needle, hold in back of work, k 2, k 2 from dp needle *; repeat from * to *, ending k 1.

Row 4: Knit.

Repeat these 4 rows for pattern.

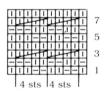

4 sts 4 sts

| = k 1
− = p 1
⌐┬⌐ = 4-st crossover

CROSSOVER STITCHES

Interlaced columns

Work double-column panel on 23 stitches.

Rows 1, 3, 5, 7, 9, 13, 15, 17, and 19: P 6, k 3, p 5, k 3, p 6.

Row 2 and all even-numbered rows: Work each stitch as it appears on this side of row (k the k sts and p the p sts).

Row 11: P 6, work right crossover on 6 sts as follows: slip 3 to dp needle and hold in back of work, k 3, k 3 from dp needle, p 2, right crossover, p 3.

Row 21: P 3, work left crossover on 6 sts as follows: slip 3 to dp needle and hold in front of work, k 3, k 3 from dp needle, p 2, left crossover, p 6. Repeat Rows 3 through 22 for pattern.

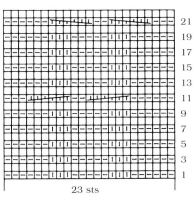

	= k 1
−	= p 1
⊤⊤⊤⊥⊥⊥	= 6-st left crossover
⊥⊥⊥⊤⊤⊤	= 6-st right crossover
□	= 1 st as shown

23 sts

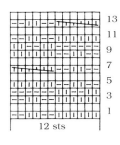

	= k 1
−	= p 1
⊤⊤⊤⊥⊥⊥	= crossover
□	= 1 st as shown

12 sts

Staggering cables

Work with a multiple of 12 stitches.

Rows 1, 3, and 11: * K 6, p 2, k 2, p 2 *; repeat from * to *.

Rows 2, 6, 8, 12, and 14: Work each stitch as it appears on this side of work (k the k sts and p the p sts).

Row 4: * P 6, k 2, p 2, k 2 *; repeat from * to *.

Rows 5 and 9: * P 2, k 2, p 2, k 6 *; repeat from * to *.

Row 7: * P 2, k 2, p 2, work crossover on 6 sts as follows: slip 3 to dp needle and hold in front of work, k 3, k 3 from dp needle *; repeat from * to *.

Row 10: * K 2, p 2, k 2, p 6 *; repeat from * to *.

Row 13: * Crossover, p 2, k 2, p 2 *; repeat from * to *.
Repeat Rows 3 through 14 for pattern.

CROSSOVER STITCHES

Slip stitch cable

Work with a multiple of 13 stitches.

Rows 1, 3, 5, 7, 9, 11, 15, 17, and 19: P 3, * k 7, p 6 *; repeat from * to *, ending last repeat with p 3.

Row 2 and all even-numbered rows: K 3, * p 1, work double st as follows: insert needle into st below next st and k 1, drop unworked st above from left needle, work (p 1, double st) twice more, p 1, k 6 *; repeat from * to *, ending last repeat with p 3.

Row 13: P 3, * work crossover on 7 sts as follows: slip 4 to dp needle and hold in back of work, k 3, k 4 from dp needle, p 6 *; repeat from * to *, ending last repeat with p 3.

Repeat Rows 1 through 20 for pattern.

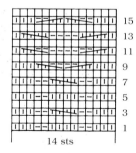

| = k 1
− = p 1
∨ = double stitch
⊥⊥⊥⊥⊤⊤ = 7-st crossover
□ = 1 st as shown

Joined cables

Work with a multiple of 14 stitches.

Rows 1 and 5: K 3, * p 2, k 4, p 2, k 6 *; repeat from * to *, ending last repeat with k 3.

Row 2 and all even-numbered rows: Work each stitch as it appears on this side of work (k the k sts and p the p sts).

Rows 3 and 7: K 3, * p 2, work left crossover on 4 sts as follows: slip 2 to dp needle and hold in front of work, k 2, k 2 from dp needle, p 2, k 6 *; repeat from * to *, ending with k 3.

Row 9: K 3, * work right cross on 4 sts as follows: slip 2 to dp needle and hold in back, k 2, p 2 from dp needle; work left cross on 4 sts as follows: slip 2 to dp needle and hold in front, p 2, k 2 from dp needle, k 6 *; repeat from * to *, ending with k 3.

Row 11: K 1, * right cross, p 4, left cross, k 2 *; repeat from * to *, ending with k 1.

Row 13: K 1, * work right crossover on 4 sts as follows: slip 2 to dp needle and hold in back, k 2, k 2 from dp needle, p 4, left crossover, k 2 *;

repeat from * to *, ending with k 1.

Row 15: K 3, * left cross, right cross, k 6 *; repeat from * to *, ending with k 3.

Repeat Rows 3 through 16 for pattern.

| = k 1
− = p 1
⊤⊤⊥⊥ = 4-st left crossover
⊐⊐⊤⊤ = 4-st right cross
⊥⊥⊤⊤ = 4-st right crossover
⊤⊤⊐⊐ = 4-st left cross
□ = 1 st as shown

CROSSOVER STITCHES

Diverging diagonals

Work with a multiple of 16 sts, plus 1.

Row 1: K 1, * work right crossover on 2 sts as follows: skip 1, k 1, k skipped st and drop both original sts from left needle, k 5, right crossover, work left crossover on 2 sts as follows, slip 1 to dp needle and hold in front of work, k 1, k 1 from dp needle, k 2, right cross, k 1 *; repeat from * to *.

Row 2 and all even-numbered rows: Work each stitch as it appears on this side of work (k the k sts and p the p sts).

Row 3: K 1, * right crossover, k 4, right crossover, k 2, left crossover, k 1, right crossover, k 1 *; repeat from * to *.

Row 5: K 1, * right crossover, k 3, right crossover, k 4, left crossover, right crossover, k 1 *; repeat from * to *.

Row 7: K 1, * right crossover, k 2, right crossover, left crossover, k 5, right crossover, k 1 *; repeat from * to *.

Row 9: K 1, * right crossover, k 1, right crossover, k 2, left crossover, k 4, right crossover, k 1 *; repeat from * to *.

Row 11: K 1, * work 2 right crossovers, k 4, left crossover, k 3, right crossover, k 1 *; repeat from * to *.

Repeat Rows 1 through 12 for pattern.

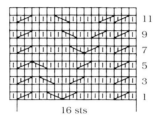

| = k 1
∕⊺ = 2-st right cross
⊺∖ = 2-st left cross
□ = p 1

Knotted cable

Work with a multiple of 20 stitches, plus 4.

Rows 1, 3, 5, 7, 9, 13, 15, 17, 19, and 21: P 4, * k 6, p 4 *; repeat from * to *.

Row 2 and all even-numbered rows: Work each stitch as it appears on this side of work (k the k sts and p the p sts).

Row 11: P 4, * work crossover on 16 sts as follows: slip 6 to dp needle and hold in back of work, slip 4 to 2nd dp needle and hold in front, k 6, p 4 from front dp needle, k 6 from back dp needle, p 4 *; repeat from * to *.

Row 23: P 4, k 6, * p 4, work crossover *; repeat from * to *, ending with p 4, k 6, p 4.

Repeat Rows 1 through 24 for pattern.

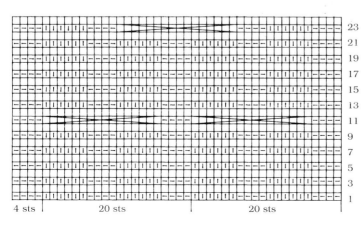

| = k 1
— = p 1
✕ = 16-st crossover
□ = 1 st as shown

CROSSOVER STITCHES

Lacy strips

Work with a multiple of 9 stitches, plus 1.

Row 1: P 1, * work right cross on 3 sts as follows: slip 2 to dp needle and hold in back of work, k 1, k 2 from dp needle, work (k 2 sts together, yarn over) twice, k 1, p 1 *; repeat from * to *.

Row 2 and all even-numbered rows: K 1, * p 8, k 1 *; repeat from * to *.

Row 3: P 1, * k 1, work (yarn over, k 2 sts together) twice, work left cross on 3 sts as follows: slip 1 to dp needle and hold in front, k 2, k 1 from dp needle, p 1 *; repeat from * to *.

Row 5: P 1, * left cross, work (k 2 sts together, yarn over) twice, k 1, p 1 *; repeat from * to *.

Row 7: P 1, * k 1, work (yarn over, k 2 sts together) twice, right cross, p 1 *; repeat from * to *.

Repeat Rows 1 through 8 for pattern.

- = p 1
| = k 1
⊢⊤ = 3-st right cross
O = yarn over
⋋ = k 2 tog
⊤⊣ = 3-st left cross
□ = 1 st as shown

| = k 1
− = p 1
ᶦ = 1 loop st
∪ = p 1 dropping extra yo

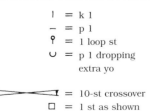

▷—◁ = 10-st crossover
□ = 1 st as shown

Loop-stitch cables

Work with a multiple of 12 stitches, plus 2.

Row 1: P 2, * k 1 wrapping yarn 3 times around needle (loop st made), k 8, 1 loop st, p 2 *; repeat from * to *.

Rows 2 and 4: Work each stitch as it appears on this side of work (k the k sts and p the p sts) and as you purl each loop st, drop the extra wraps from needle.

Row 3: P 2, * work crossover on 10 sts as follows: slip 1 to dp needle and hold in front of work, work loop st in next st, k 3, slip next 4 sts to 2nd dp needle and hold in back of work, k 1, k 1 from front dp needle, then work k 3 and 1 loop st on 4 sts from back dp needle, p 2 *; repeat from * to *.

Repeat Rows 1 through 4 for pattern.

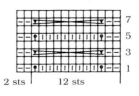

2 sts   12 sts

CROSSOVER STITCHES

Interrupted diamonds

Work with a multiple of 15 stitches.

Row 1: Purl.

Row 2 and all even-numbered rows: K the k sts (as they face you) and p the p sts.

Row 3: P 5, * k 4, p 11 *; repeat from * to *, ending with p 6.

Row 5: P 4, * work right cross on 3 sts as follows: slip 1 to dp needle and hold in back of work, k 2, p 1; work left cross on 3 sts as follows: slip 2 to dp needle and hold in front of work, p 1, k 2 from dp needle, p 9 *; repeat from * to *, ending with p 5.

Row 7: P 3, * right cross, p 2, left cross, p 7 *; repeat from * to *, ending p 4.

Row 9: P 2, * right cross, p 4, left cross, p 5 *; repeat from * to *, ending p 3.

Row 11: P 2, * left cross, p 4, right cross, p 5 *; repeat from * to *, ending p 3.

Row 13: P 3, * left cross, p 2, right cross, p 7 *; repeat from * to *, ending p 4.

Row 15: P 4, * left cross, right cross, p 9 *; repeat from * to *, ending p 5.

Row 17: Purl.

Repeat Rows 1 through 18 for pattern.

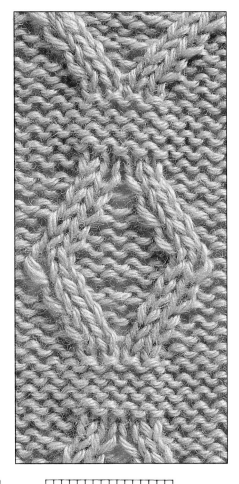

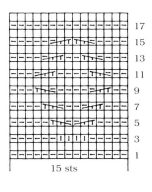

15 sts

| = k 1
— = p 1
= 3-st right cross
= 3-st left cross
□ = 1 st as shown

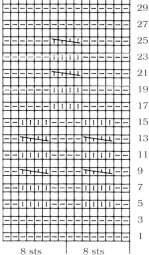

8 sts | 8 sts

| = k 1
— = p 1
= 4-st crossover
□ = 1 st as shown

Short cables

Work with a multiple of 8 stitches.

Rows 1, 3, 27, and 29: Purl.

Row 2 and all even-numbered rows: Work each stitch as it appears on this side of work (k the k sts and p the p sts).

Rows 5, 7, 11, and 15: P 2, * k 4, p 4 *; repeat from * to *, ending with p 2.

Rows 9 and 13: P 2, * work crossover on 4 sts as follows: slip 2 to dp needle and hold in front of work, k 2, k 2 from dp needle, p 4 *; repeat from * to *, ending with p 2.

Rows 17, 19, and 23: P 6, * k 4, p 4 *; repeat from * to *, ending with p last 6.

Rows 21 and 25: P 6, * crossover, p 4 *; repeat from * to *, ending with p 6.

Repeat Rows 1 through 30 for pattern.

CROSSOVER STITCHES

Three-strand cable

Work cable on 9 stitches. For pattern as shown, work evenly-spaced cables on background of reverse stockinette st.

Rows 1, 3, 5, and 9: Knit.

Row 2 and all even-numbered rows: Purl.

Row 7: Work right crossover on 6 sts as follows: slip 3 to dp needle and hold in back of work, k 3, k 3 from dp needle, k 3.

Row 11: K 3, work left crossover on 6 sts as follows: slip 3 to dp needle and hold in front of work, k 3, k 3 from dp needle.

Repeat Rows 5 through 12 for pattern.

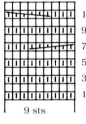

| = k 1

⊥⊥⊤⊤⊤⊤ = 6-st right crossover

⊤⊤⊤⊤⊥⊥ = 6-st left crossover

☐ = p 1

Cable twist motif

Work motif on 7 stitches. For pattern as shown, work evenly-spaced motifs on a background of reverse stock-inette st and stagger vertical place-ment of motifs.

Rows 1 and 19: P 3, k 1, p 3.

Row 2 and all even-numbered rows: Work each stitch as it appears on this side of work (k the k sts and p the p sts).

Rows 3 and 17: P 2, k 3, p 2.

Rows 5 and 15: P 1, k 5, p 1.

Rows 7, 9 and 13: Knit.

Row 11: Work crossover on 7 sts as follows: slip 3 to dp needle and hold in front of work, k 4, k 3 from dp needle.

Repeat Rows 1 through 20 for motif.

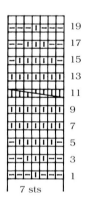

| = k 1

– = p 1

⊤⊤⊤⊤⊥⊥⊥ = 7-st crossover

☐ = 1 st as shown

CREATIVE STITCHES

Leaf for appliqué

Start work with 1 stitch.

Row 1: In single st knit, then purl, knit, purl, and knit (5 sts made in 1 st).

Row 2 and all even-numbered rows: Purl.

Row 3: K 1, increase 1 st by picking up and knitting connecting strand between last st worked and next one, k 3, increase 1 st as before, k 1.

Row 5: K 1, increase, k 5, increase, k 1.

Row 7: K 1, increase, k 7, increase, k 1.

Row 9: K 3, slip 1, k 1, pass slip st over k st and drop it (psso), k 1, k 2 sts together, k 3.

Row 11: K 2, slip 1, k 1, psso, k 1, k 2 sts together, k 2.

Row 13: K 1, slip 1, k 1, psso, k 1, k 2 sts together, k 1.

Row 15: K 1, k 3 sts together, k 1.

Row 17: K 3 sts together. Fasten off.

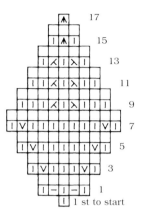

1 st to start

| = k 1
− = p 1
V = 1 increase
⅄ = slip 1, k 1, psso
⅄ = k 2 tog
⋀ = k 3 tog
● = 1 bobble

Side edging

Start work with 3 stitches. This edging can be worked separately or worked at edge of piece as you knit it (as shown).

Row 1: K 1, increase 1 st by picking up and knitting connecting strand between last st and next st, k 2.

Rows 2 and 18: K 2, p 2.

Row 3: K 1, increase 1 st, k 3.

Rows 4 and 16: K 2, p 3.

Row 5: K 1, increase 1 st, k 4.

Rows 6 and 14: K 2, p 4.

Row 7: K 1, increase 1 st, k 5.

Rows 8 and 12: K 2, p 5.

Row 9: K 1, increase 1 st, k 2, work bobble in next st as follows: knit in front, then back, front, and back loop of st, turn work, p 4, turn, k 4, then pass 3 sts, one at a time, over the 4th st to complete bobble, k 3.

Row 10: K 2, p 6.

Row 11: K 1, k 2 sts together, k 5.

Row 13: K 1, k 2 sts together, k 4.

Row 15: K 1, k 2 sts together, k 3.

Row 17: K 1, k 2 sts together, k 2.

Row 19: K 1, k 2 sts together, k 1.

Row 20: K 2, p 1.

Repeat these 20 rows for pattern.

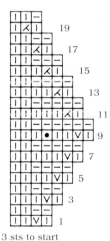

3 sts to start

See above key for chart.

CREATIVE STITCHES

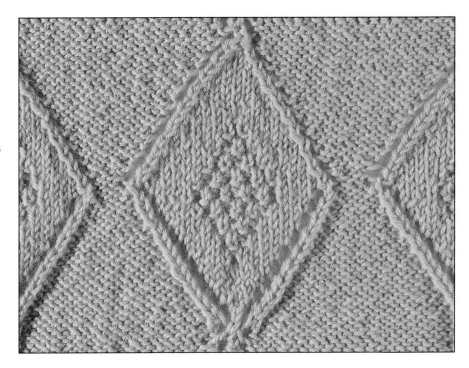

Large lace diamond

Work diamond on 21 stitches. For pattern as shown, work evenly-spaced diamonds on a background of reverse stockinette st.

Row 1: P 8, k 2 sts together (k 2 tog), yarn over (yo), k 1, yo, slip 1, k 1, pass slip st over k st (psso), p 8.

Row 2 and all even-numbered rows: Work each stitch as it appears on this side of work (k the k sts and p the p sts), and purl each yarn-over loop.

Row 3: P 7, k 2 tog, yo, k 3, yo, slip 1, k 1, psso, p 7.

Row 5: P 6, k 2 tog, yo, k 5, yo, slip 1, k 1, psso, p 6.

Row 7: P 5, k 2 tog, yo, k 7, yo, slip 1, k 1, psso, p 5.

Row 9: P 4, k 2 tog, yo, k 4, p 1, k 4, yo, slip 1, k 1, psso, p 4.

Row 11: P 3, k 2 tog, yo, k 4, p 1, k 1, p 1, k 4, yo, slip 1, k 1, psso, p 3.

Row 13: P 2, k 2 tog, yo, k 4, p 1, work (k 1, p 1) twice, k 4, yo, slip 1, k 1, psso, p 2.

Row 15: P 1, k 2 tog, yo, k 4, p 1, work (k 1, p 1) 3 times, k 4, yo, slip 1, k 1, psso, p 1.

Row 17: K 2 tog, yo, k 4, p 1, work (k 1, p 1) 4 times, k 4, yo, slip 1, k 1, psso.

Row 19: Yo, slip 1, k 1, psso, k 5, p 1, work (k 1, p 1) 3 times, k 5, k 2 tog, yo.

Row 21: P 1, yo, slip 1, k 1, psso, k 5, p 1, work (k 1, p 1) twice, k 5, k 2 tog, yo, p 1.

Row 23: P 2, yo, slip 1, k 1, psso, k 5, p 1, k 1, p 1, k 5, k 2 tog, yo, p 2.

Row 25: P 3, yo, slip 1, k 1, psso, k 5, p 1, k 5, k 2 tog, yo, p 3.

Row 27: P 4, yo, slip 1, k 1, psso, k 9, k 2 tog, yo, p 4.

Row 29: P 5, yo, slip 1, k 1, psso, k 7, k 2 tog, yo, p 5.

Row 31: P 6, yo, slip 1, k 1, psso, k 5, k 2 tog, yo, p 6.

Row 33: P 7, yo, slip 1, k 1, psso, k 3, k 2 tog, yo, p 7.

Row 35: P 8, yo, slip 1, k 1, psso, k 1, k 2 tog, yo, p 8.

Row 37: P 9, yo, slip 2, k 1, pass each slip st over k st, yo, p 9.

Row 39: P 8, k 1, yo, k 3 sts together, yo, k 1, p 8.

Repeat Rows 3 through 40 for pattern.

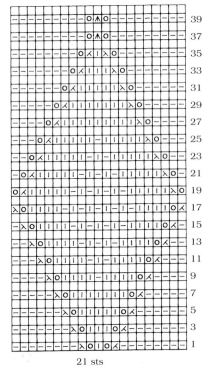

21 sts

| = k 1
− = p 1
O = yarn over
⋌ = k 2 tog
⋋ = slip 1, k 1, psso
⋀ = 1 double dec
□ = 1 st as shown

CREATIVE STITCHES

Snowflakes

Work on a multiple of 18 stitches, plus 20.

Rows 1 and 3: Knit.

Row 2 and all even-numbered rows: Purl.

Rows 5 and 9: K 9, * work snowflake on 3 sts as follows: p next 3 sts together and retain original sts on left needle, k same 3 sts together and then p them together again, drop original sts from left needle, k 15 *; repeat from * to *, ending last repeat with k 8.

Row 7: K 6, * snowflake, k 3, snowflake, k 9 *; repeat from * to *, ending last repeat with k 5.

Rows 11, 13, and 15: Knit.

Rows 17 and 21: K 18, * snowflake, k 15 *; repeat from * to *, ending last repeat with k 17.

Row 19: K 15, * snowflake, k 3, snowflake, k 9 *; repeat from * to *, ending last repeat with k 14.

Rows 23, 25, and 27: Knit.

Repeat Rows 5 through 28 for pattern.

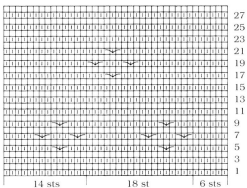

14 sts   18 st   6 sts

ı = k 1
ʌ = snowflake
□ = p 1

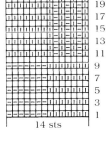

14 sts

ı = k 1
– = p 1
□ = 1 st as shown

Creative checkerboard

Work with a multiple of 14 sts.

Rows 1 through 10: * K 7, p 7 *; repeat from * to *.

Rows 11, 13, 15, 17, and 19: * K 1, work (p 1, k 1) 3 times for 7 moss sts, k 7 *; repeat from * to *.

Rows 12, 14, 16, 18, and 20: * P 7, work 7 moss sts as before *; repeat from * to *.

Repeat Rows 1 through 20 for pattern.

CREATIVE STITCHES

Windows of moss stitch

Work with a multiple of 10 stitches.
Rows 1, 3, 5, and 7: Work (k 1, p 1) 4 times for 8 moss sts, * k 5, p 1, work (k 1, p 1) twice *; repeat from * to *, ending last repeat with p 1, (k 1, p 1) 3 times.
Rows 2, 4, 6, and 8: Work (p 1, k 1) 4 times, * p 4, work (p 1, k 1) 3 times *; repeat from * to *, ending with p 1, k 1.
Row 9 (moss st): * K 1, p 1 *; repeat from * to *.
Row 10 (moss st): * P 1, k 1 *; repeat from * to *.
Rows 11, 13, 15, and 17: K 1, p 1, * k 5, work (p 1, k 1) twice, p 1 *; repeat from * to *, ending last repeat with p 1, k 1, p 1.
Rows 12, 14, 16, and 18: P 1, k 1, * p 5, k 1, work (p 1, k 1) twice *; repeat from * to *, ending last repeat with k 1, p 1, k 1.
Rows 19 and 20: Repeat Rows 9 and 10.
Repeat these 20 rows for pattern.

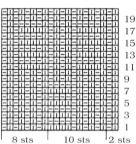

ˡ = k 1
⁻ = p 1

Dots and dashes

Work with a multiple of 30 stitches.
Row 1: * P 15, k 7, work 1 dot in next st as follows: knit, then purl, then knit in back loop of st, pass first 2 sts over 3rd st and drop to complete dot, k 7 *; repeat from * to *.
Row 2 and all even-numbered rows: Work each stitch as it appears on this side of row (k the k sts and p the p sts), purling any dot stitch.
Row 3: * P 15, k 5, 1 dot, k 3, 1 dot, k 5 *; repeat from * to *.
Row 5: * K 7, 1 dot, k 7, p 15 *; repeat from * to *.
Row 7: * K 5, 1 dot, k 3, 1 dot, k 5, p 15 *; repeat from * to *.
Repeat Rows 1 through 8 for pattern.

ˡ = k 1
⁻ = p 1
• = 1 dot
□ = 1 st as shown

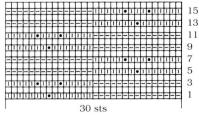

CREATIVE STITCHES

Creative embossing

Work with a multiple of 24 stitches, plus 5.

Row 1: * K 4, yarn over (yo), k 2 sts together (k 2 tog) *; repeat from * to *, ending with k in last 5 sts.

Rows 2, 4, and 6: Purl.

Row 3: K 2, * k 2 tog, yo, k 1, yo, slip 1, k 1, pass slip st over k st and drop it (psso), k 1 *; repeat from * to *, ending last repeat with k 4.

Row 5: K 3, * k 2 tog, yo, k 4 *; repeat from * to *, ending last repeat with k 6.

Rows 7 and 9: * K 5, p 3 *; repeat from * to *, ending with k 5.

Row 8: P 5, * k 3, p 5 *; repeat from * to *.

Row 10: Work 5 embossed sts as follows: work (p 5, turn work, k 5, turn) 3 times, then purl each st together with corresponding st 6 rows below, inserting needle through top st and back loop of st below, * p 3, work 5 embossed sts as before *; repeat from * to *.

Repeat these 10 rows for pattern.

I = k 1
– = p 1
O = yarn over
⋌ = k 2 tog
⋋ = slip 1, k 1, psso
V = 1 embossed st
□ = 1 st as shown

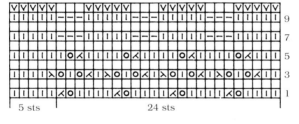

5 sts   24 sts

Embossed stripes

Work stripe on 5 stitches. For pattern as shown, work evenly-spaced stripes on a background of reverse stockinette st.

Rows 1 through 5: Work in stockinette st (k 1 row, p 1 row) for 5 rows.

Row 6 (wrong side): Work 5 embossed sts as follows: work (p 5, turn work, k 5, turn) 3 times, then purl each st together with the corresponding st 6 rows below, inserting needle through top st and back loop of st below.

Repeat these 6 rows for stripe.

5 sts

I = k 1
– = p 1
V = 1 embossed st

CREATIVE STITCHES

Aligned parentheses

Work with a multiple of 3 stitches, plus 2 for selvages.

Row 1: K 1 (selvage), * work left cross on 3 sts as follows: slip 1 to dp needle and hold in front of work, k 2, k 1 from dp needle *; repeat from * to *, ending with k 1 (selvage).

Rows 2, 4, and 6: Purl.

Row 3: K 1, * work right cross on 3 sts as follows: slip 2 to dp needle and hold in back of work, k 1, k 2 from dp needle *; repeat from * to *, ending with k 1.

Row 5: Knit.

Repeat Rows 1 through 6 for pattern.

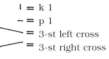

l = k 1
- = p 1
\ = 3-st left cross
/ = 3-st right cross

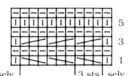

selv. 3 sts selv.

Half-opened seeds

Work with a multiple of 3 stitches, plus 2 for selvages.

Row 1 (wrong side): Knit.

Row 2: K 1 (selvage), * work seed on 3 sts as follows: k 3 sts together and retain on left needle, k first st again, knit remaining 2 sts together, and drop original sts from left needle *; repeat from * to *, ending k 1 (selvage).

Row 3: Purl.

Row 4: Knit.

Repeat these 4 rows for pattern.

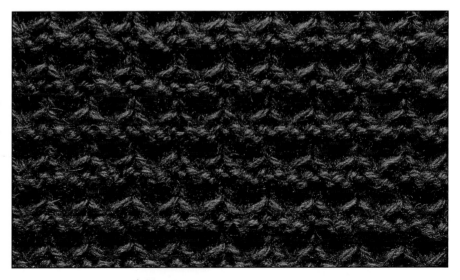

l = k 1
- = p 1
⌄ = 3-st seed

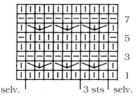

selv. 3 sts selv.

CREATIVE STITCHES

Dewdrops

Work with a multiple of 6 sts, plus 2.

Rows 1 and 3: * P 5, k 1 in back loop for twisted k st *; repeat from * to *, ending p 2.

Row 2 and all even-numbered rows: Work each stitch as it appears on this side of work (k the k sts and p the p sts) and purl twisted st (p in back loop) over twisted st.

Row 5: * P 5, work 5 sts in next st as follows: knit, purl, knit, purl, and knit all in same st *; repeat from * to *, ending p 2.

Row 7: * P 2, k 1 twisted st, p 2, k 5 *; repeat from * to *, ending p 2.

Row 9: * P 2, k 1 twisted st, p 2, work 4-st decrease on 5 sts as follows: slip 2, k 3 sts together, pass each slip st over k st and drop *; repeat from * to *, ending p 2.

Row 11: P 2, * k 1 twisted st, p 5 *; repeat from * to *.

Row 13: P 2, * work 5 sts in 1 st, p 5 *; repeat from * to *.

Row 15: P 2, * k 5, p 2, k 1 twisted st, p 2 *; repeat from * to *.

Row 17: P 2, * work 4-st decrease on 5 sts, p 2, k 1 twisted st, p 2 *; repeat from * to *.

Repeat Rows 3 through 18 for pattern.

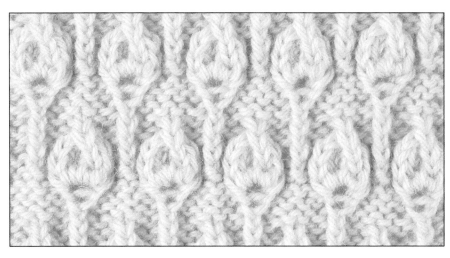

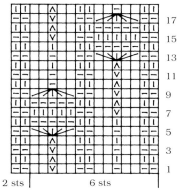

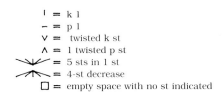

| = k 1
− = p 1
V = twisted k st
∧ = 1 twisted p st
⥿ = 5 sts in 1 st
⤬ = 4-st decrease
☐ = empty space with no st indicated

2 sts | 6 sts

Closely-wrapped stitch

Work with a multiple of 4 stitches, plus 2.

Row 1 and all odd-numbered rows: Knit.

Row 2: K 1, * yarn over (yo), p 2, pass yo over 2 p sts just worked and drop, p 2 *; repeat from * to *, ending k in last st.

Row 4: K 1, * p 2, yo, p 2, pass yo over 2 p sts just worked and drop *; repeat from * to *, ending k in last st.

Repeat Rows 2 through 5 for pattern.

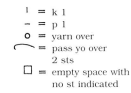

| = k 1
− = p 1
o = yarn over
⌒ = pass yo over 2 sts
☐ = empty space with no st indicated

2 sts | 4 sts

CREATIVE STITCHES

Flight of the bumblebee

Work with a multiple of 4 stitches, plus 3.
Rows 1 and 5: Purl.
Row 2 and all even-numbered rows: Knit.
Row 3: P 3, * work long st, inserting needle into st 2 rows below next st and k 1, drop unworked st above, k 3 *; repeat from * to *.
Row 7: P 1, * work long st, p 3 *; repeat from * to *, ending long st, p 1.
Repeat Rows 1 through 8 for pattern.

I = k 1
— = p 1
V = 1 long st

3 sts | 4 sts

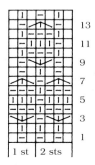

1 st | 2 sts

I = k 1
— = p 1
⋎ = 3 sts in 1 st
⋏ = k 3 tog
□ = empty space with no st indicated

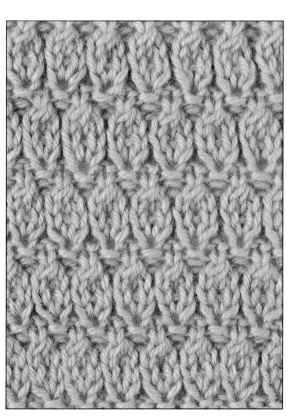

Little flakes

Work on an uneven number of stitches.
Row 1: Purl.
Rows 2, 6, 8, 12, and 14: Work each stitch as it appears on this side of work (k the k sts and p the p sts).
Row 3: * Work 3 sts in 1 st as follows: in next st, knit, then purl and knit all in same st, p 1 *; repeat from * to *, ending with work 3 sts in last st.
Row 4: P 3, * k 1, p 3 *; repeat from * to *.
Row 5: K 3, * p 1, k 3 *; repeat from * to *.
Row 7: K 3 sts together, * p 1, k 3 together *; repeat from * to *.
Row 9: P 1, * work 3 sts in 1 st, p 1 *; repeat from * to *.
Row 10: K 1, * p 3, k 1 *; repeat from * to *.
Row 11: P 1, * k 3, p 1 *; repeat from * to *.
Row 13: P 1, * k 3 sts together, p 1 *; repeat from * to *.
Repeat Rows 3 through 14 for pattern.

140

CREATIVE STITCHES

Split granite

Work on an uneven number of stitches.

Rows 1, 3, and 5 (right side): P 1, * slip 1 as if to p and with yarn in back of work, p 1 *; repeat from * to *.

Row 2 and all even-numbered rows: Purl.

Rows 7, 9, and 11: P 2, * slip 1 as before, p 1 *; repeat from * to *, ending slip 1, p 2.

Repeat Rows 1 through 12 for pattern.

− = p 1
∧ = slip 1

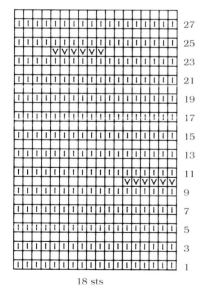

ı = k 1
□ = p 1
v = 1 embossed st

Alternating embossed stitches

Work with a multiple of 18 stitches.

Rows 1 through 9: Work in stockinette st (k 1 row, p 1 row).

Row 10: * P 12, work 6 embossed sts as follows: purl each st together with corresponding st 4 rows below, inserting needle through top st and back loop of st below *; repeat from * to *.

Rows 11 through 23: Work in stockinette st.

Row 24: P 4, * work 6 embossed sts as before, p 12 *; repeat from * to *, ending last repeat with p 8.

Rows 25 through 28: Work in stockinette st.

Repeat Rows 1 through 28 for pattern.

CREATIVE STITCHES

Waves

Work with a multiple of 14 stitches, plus 3.

Row 1: K 3, * increase 1 st by picking up and knitting connecting strand between last st worked and next one, slip 1, k 1, pass slip st over k st and drop it (psso), k 4, k 2 sts together (k 2 tog), k 3, increase 1 st, k 3 *; repeat from * to *.

Row 2 and all even-numbered rows: Purl.

Row 3: K 3, * increase 1 st, k 1, slip 1, k 1, psso, k 2, k 2 tog, k 4, increase 1 st, k 3 *; repeat from * to *.

Row 5: K 3, * increase 1 st, k 2, slip 1, k 1, psso, k 2 tog, k 5, increase 1 st, k 3 *; repeat from * to *.

Row 7: K 3, * increase 1 st, k 3, slip 1, k 1, psso, k 4, k 2 tog, increase 1 st, k 3 *; repeat from * to *.

Row 9: K 3, * increase 1 st, k 4, slip 1, k 1, psso, k 2, k 2 tog, k 1, increase 1 st, k 3 *; repeat from * to *.

Row 11: K 3, * increase 1 st, k 5, slip 1, k 1, psso, k 2 tog, k 2, increase 1 st, k 3 *; repeat from * to *.

Repeat Rows 1 through 12 for pattern.

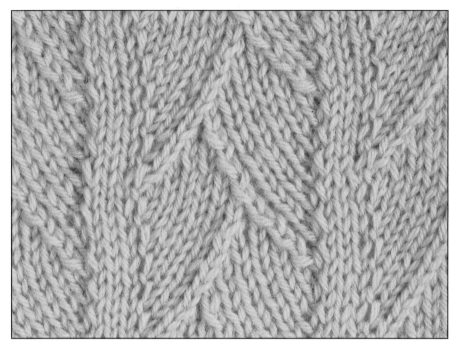

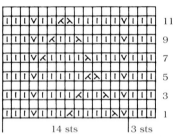

I = k 1
□ = p 1
λ = slip 1, k 1, psso
入 = k 2 tog
V = 1 increase

14 sts   3 sts

I = k 1
− = p 1
○ = yarn over
λ = slip 1, k 1, psso
□ = 1 st as shown

1 st   6 sts   6 sts   1 st

Oblique pattern

Work with a multiple of 6 stitches, plus 2.

Row 1: K 1, * p 1, k 5 * repeat from * to *, ending last repeat with k 6.

Row 2 and all even-numbered rows: Work each stitch as it appears on this side of work (k the k sts and p the p sts) and k any yarn overs.

Row 3: K 1, * yarn over (yo), p 1, k 1, slip 1, k 1, pass slip st over k st and drop it (psso), k 2 *; repeat from * to *, ending last repeat with k 3.

Row 5: K 1, * yo, p 2, k 1, slip 1, k 1, psso, k 1 *; repeat from * to *, ending last repeat with k 2.

Row 7: K 1, * yo, p 3, k 1, slip 1, k 1, psso *; repeat from * to *, ending k 1.

Repeat Rows 1 through 8 for pattern.

142

CREATIVE STITCHES

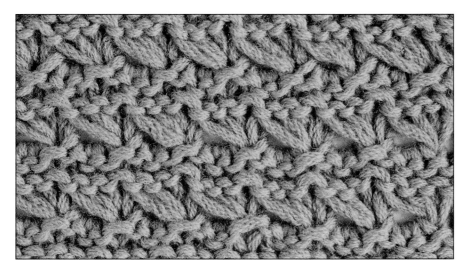

Eyelets

Work with a multiple of 3 stitches, plus 2.

Row 1: Knit.

Row 2: K 1, * yarn over (yo) twice, k 1 *; repeat from * to *, ending last repeat with k 2.

Row 3: K 1, * (make long st by slipping next st and dropping both yo's that follow it) 3 times, return 3 long sts to left needle and k them together through back loops, then p them and k them again through back loops before dropping original sts from left needle *; repeat from * to *, ending with k 1.

Row 4: Purl.

Repeat these 4 rows for pattern.

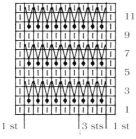

$\imath$ = k 1

ϕ = 2 yo + k 1

V = 1 long st

Triple-wrapped stitches

Work with a multiple of 6 stitches, plus 2.

Row 1: Knit.

Row 2: K 1, * k 1, yarn over (yo) twice *; repeat from * to *, ending with k 1.

Row 3: K 1, * work triple wrap on 6 sts as follows: dropping both yo's in front of each st, slip each st to right needle drawing up excess yarn to lengthen st, pass the first 3 long sts over the last 3 long sts and drop them, return the 3 wrapped sts to left needle, k in front, then back loop of each wrapped st *; repeat from * to *, ending k 1.

Repeat these 3 rows for pattern.

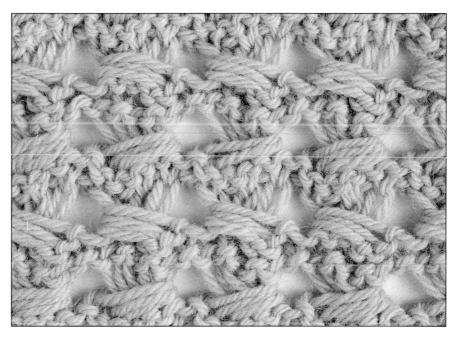

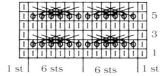

$\imath$ = k 1

ϕ = k 1 + 2 yo

$\Join$ = 6 wrapped sts

CREATIVE STITCHES

Easy ripple pattern

Work with a multiple of 8 stitches, plus 2.

Row 1: K 2, * increase 1 st by picking up and knitting connecting strand between last st worked and next st, k 2, work reverse psso as follows: k 2 sts together and return resulting st to left needle, with tip of right needle lift the following st and pass it over the returned st and drop it, slip remaining st back to right needle, k 2, increase 1 st, k 1 *; repeat from * to *.

Row 2: Purl.

Repeat these 2 rows for pattern.

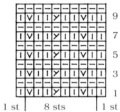

```
I = k 1
− = p 1
V = 1 increase
⅄ = reverse psso
```

Creative zigzag

Work with a multiple of 10 stitches, plus 1.

Row 1: K 1, * yarn over, k 3, k 3 sts together, k 3, yarn over, k 1 *; repeat from * to *.

Row 2: Purl.

Repeat these 2 rows for pattern.

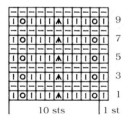

```
I = k 1
− = p 1
o = yarn over
⋏ = k 3 tog
```

144

CREATIVE STITCHES

Bundles

Work with a multiple of 16 stitches, plus 14.

Rows 1, 3, and 5: P 2, * k 2, p 6, work (k 2, p 2) twice *; repeat from * to *, ending last repeat with k 2, p 2.

Row 2 and all even-numbered rows: Work each st as it appears on this side of work (k the k sts and p the p sts).

Row 7: P 2, * work wrap on 10 sts as follows: slip 10 sts to dp needle, wrap the yarn from front to back 3 times around base of sts (just below dp needle) drawing sts gently together as shown, then k 2 and work (p 2, k 2) twice on 10 sts from dp needle, p 6 *; repeat from * to *, ending with wrap, p 2.

Rows 9, 11, and 13: P 2, * k 2, work (p 2, k 2) twice, p 6 *; repeat from * to *, ending (k 2, p 2) 3 times.

Row 15: P 2, k 2, * p 6, work wrap as before *; repeat from * to *, ending p 6, k 2, p 2.

Repeat Rows 1 through 16 for pattern.

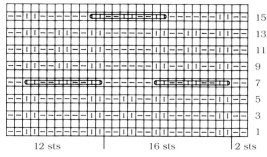

| = k 1
− = p 1
⊏▭▭⊐ = 10-st wrap
□ = 1 st as shown

12 sts   16 sts   2 sts

Little cascades

Start work with a multiple of 6 stitches, plus 5.

Row 1: P 5, * yarn over (yo), k 1, p 5 *; repeat from * to *.

Rows 2, 4, 6, and 8: Work each stitch as it appears on this side of work (k the k sts and p the p sts) and k the yarn over loop.

Row 3: P 5, * yo, k 1, p 1, k 1, p 5 *; repeat from * to *.

Row 5: P 5, * yo, k 1, work (p 1, k 1) twice, p 5 *; repeat from * to *.

Row 7: P 5, * work k 1, (p 1, k 1) 3 times, p 5 *; repeat from * to *.

Row 9: P 5, * work decrease on 7 sts as follows: slip 6 sts to right needle, k 1, then pass each slip st over the k st and drop it (6 sts decreased), p 5 *; repeat from * to *.

Rows 10 and 12: Knit.

Row 11: Purl.

Repeat Rows 1 through 12 for pattern.

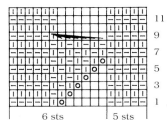

| = k 1
− = p 1
o = yarn over
= 6-st decrease
□ = empty space with no st indicated

6 sts   5 sts

CREATIVE STITCHES

Hairpin curves

Work with a multiple of 11 stitches, plus 3.

Row 1: P 3, * yarn over (yo), k 4, slip 1, k 1, pass slip st over k st and drop it (psso), k 2, p 3 *; repeat from * to *.

Rows 2, 4, 6, 7, 8, 9, 10, 14, 15, and 16: Work each stitch as it appears on this side of work (k the k sts and p the p sts) and purl any yarn-over loops.

Row 3: P 3, * k 1, yo, k 4, slip 1, k 1, psso, k 1, p 3 *; repeat from * to *.

Row 5: P 3, * k 2, yo, k 4, slip 1, k 1, psso, p 3 *; repeat from * to *.

Row 11: P 3, * k 2, k 2 sts together (k 2 tog), k 4, yo, p 3 *; repeat from * to *.

Row 12: K 3, * p 1, yo, p 4, p 2 sts together, p 1, k 3 *; repeat from * to *.

Row 13: P 3, * k 2 tog, k 4, yo, k 2, p 3 *; repeat from * to *.

Repeat Rows 1 through 16 for pattern.

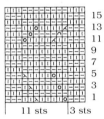

| = k 1
− = p 1
o = yarn over
λ = slip 1, k 1, psso
⋋ = k 2 tog
∩ = p 2 tog

11 sts   3 sts

Plain and textured diamonds

Work with a multiple of 15 stitches, plus 2.

Rows 1 and 9 (wrong side): P 5, * to work bobble: knit, purl, and knit all in next st, pass p st over last k st worked and drop it, then pass first k st over st to complete bobble, p 5, yarn over (yo) k 2 sts together (k 2 tog), p 7 *; repeat from * to *, ending with p 4.

Row 2 and all even-numbered rows: Knit.

Rows 3 and 7: P 4, * bobble, p 1, bobble, p 3, work (yo, k 2 tog) twice, p 5 *; repeat from * to *, ending with p 3.

Row 5: P 3, * bobble, p 3, bobble, p 1, work (yo, k 2 tog) 3 times, p 3 *; repeat from * to *, ending with p 2.

Rows 11 and 19: P 4, * yo, k 2 tog, p 6, bobble, p 6 *; repeat from * to *, ending with p 4.

Rows 13 and 17: P 3, * work (yo, k 2 tog) twice, p 4, bobble, p 1, bobble, p 4 *; repeat from * to *, ending with p 3.

Row 15: P 2, * work (yo, k 2 tog) 3 times, p 2, bobble, p 3, bobble, p 2 *; repeat from * to *.

Repeat Rows 1 through 20 for pattern.

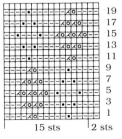

− = p 1
o = yarn over
⋋ = k 2 tog
• = 1 bobble
□ = k 1

15 sts   2 sts

146

CREATIVE STITCHES

Wrapped ribs

Work with a multiple of 18 stitches, plus 4.

Rows 1, 3, 5, 7, 9, 11, 13, and 15: K 4, * p 5, k 4 *; repeat from * to *.

Row 2 and all even-numbered rows: P 4, * k 5, p 4 *; repeat from * to *.

Rows 17 and 19: * With yarn forward, slip 4 to right needle, wrap yarn across front of these sts and return it to back, return the 4 sts to left needle and knit them, p 5, k 4, p 5 *; repeat from * to *, ending with 4 wrapped sts.

Rows 21, 23, 25, 27, 29, 31, and 33: Work ribs as established on Row 1.

Rows 33 and 35: K 4, * p 5, wrap and k next 4 sts as before, p 5, k 4 *; repeat from * to *.

Repeat Rows 5 through 38 for pattern.

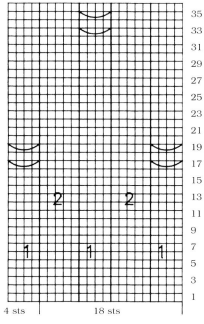

1 = stockinette st rib
2 = reverse stockinette rib
⌣ = 4-st wrap

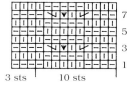

l = k 1
— = p 1
↙ = p and k in back loop of 1 st

Ⅴ = p 3 tog
↘ = k in front and back loop of 1 st

False knots

Work with a multiple of 10 stitches, plus 3.

Row 1: P 4, * k 5, p 5 *; repeat from * to *, ending last repeat with p 4.

Row 2: K 4, * p 5, k 5 *; repeat from * to *, ending with k 4.

Row 3: P 3, * p next st and k in back loop of same st, k 1, p 3 sts together, k next st in front and then back loop, p 4 *; repeat from * to *.

Row 4: Repeat Row 2.

Repeat these 4 rows for pattern.

CREATIVE STITCHES

Swirling pattern

Work with a multiple of 16 sts, plus 1.

Rows 1, 5, 9,13, 17, 21, 25, and 29: Knit.

Row 2 and all even-numbered rows: Purl.

Rows 3, 7, 11, and 15: Work (k 1, yarn over) 3 times, * work (slip 1, k 1, pass slip st over k st) twice, work double decrease on 3 sts as follows: slip 2 sts together as if to k, k 1, then lifting them together, pass slip sts over the k st and drop them, (k 2 sts together) twice, yarn over (yo), work (k 1, yo) 5 times *; repeat from * to *, ending last repeat with (yo, k 1) 3 times.

Rows 19, 23, 27 and 31: (K 2 sts together) 3 times, * (yo, k 1) 5 times, yo, (slip 1, k 1, pass slip st over k st) twice, double decrease, (k 2 sts together) twice *; repeat from * to *, ending with (slip 1, k 1, pass slip st over k st) 3 times.

Repeat Rows 1 through 32 for pattern.

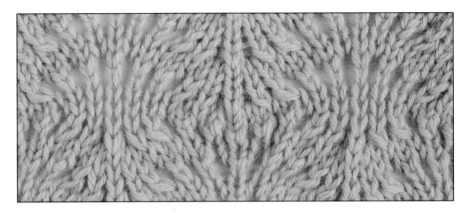

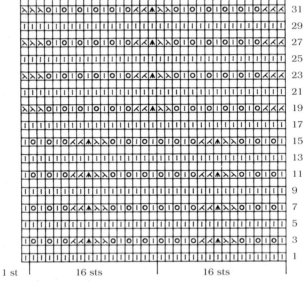

| = k 1
□ = p 1
O = yarn over
λ = slip 1, k 1, psso
Λ = double dec
⋌ = k 2 tog

Palmetto

Work with a multiple of 7 stitches.

Row 1: P 3, * yarn over (yo), k 1, yo, p 6 *; repeat from * to *, ending last repeat with p 3.

Row 2 and all even-numbered rows: Work each stitch as it appears on this side of work (k the k sts and p the p sts). Purl any yarn-overs.

Row 3: P 3, * yo, p 3, yo, p 6 *; repeat from * to *, ending with p 3.

Rows 5 and 7: P 3, * yo, k 1, to work double decrease on 3 sts: slip 1, k 2 sts together, pass slip st over k st and drop it, k 1, yo, p 6 *; repeat from * to *, ending with p 3.

Row 9: P 3, * k 1, double decrease, k 1, p 6 *; repeat from * to *, ending with p 3.

Row 11: P 3, * double decrease, p 6 *; repeat from * to *, ending with p 3.

Rows 13 and 15: Purl.

Repeat Rows 1 through 16 for pattern.

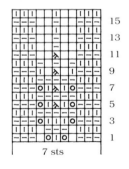

| = k 1
− = p 1
O = yarn over
⋋ = double dec
□ = empty space with no st indicated

148

CREATIVE STITCHES

Chinese fans

Work fan on 5 sts. For pattern as shown, work evenly-spaced fans on a background of stockinette st, alternating positions for each row of fans. Work several rows of stockinette st.

Row 1: Insert needle into st 3 rows below center st (center st of 5 fan sts), yarn over and draw up a long loop, place loop on right needle, k 1 from left needle, * draw up another long loop from same st below, place it on right needle, k 1 from left needle *; repeat from * to * 3 more times (10 sts on needle).

Row 2: Work (k 2 sts together through back loops) 5 times.

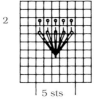

I = k 1

= 1 long loop

♀ = k 2 tog in back loop

□ = 1 background st in stockinette st

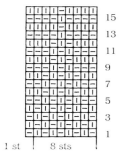

I = k 1
— = p 1

Alternating triangles

Work with a multiple of 8 stitches, plus 1.

Rows 1 and 3: P 1, * k 1, p 1 *; repeat from * to *.

Row 2 and all even-numbered rows: Work each stitch as it appears on this side of work (k the k sts and p the p sts).

Rows 5 and 7: P 2, * work (k 1, p 1) twice, k 1, p 3 *; repeat from * to *, ending last repeat with p 2.

Rows 9 and 11: P 3, * k 1, p 1, k 1, p 5 *; repeat from * to *, ending with p 3.

Rows 13 and 15: P 4, * k 1, p 7 *; repeat from * to *, ending with p 4. Repeat Rows 1 through 16 for pattern.

CREATIVE STITCHES

Mock moss stitch

Work with an even number of stitches.

Note: For slip stitches, always carry yarn on wrong side of work.

Row 1 (right side): K 1, * p 1, then with yarn in back, slip 1 as if to p *; repeat from * to *, ending k last st.

Row 2: P 2, * with yarn in front, slip 1, p 1 *; repeat from * to *.

Row 3: K 1, * slip 1, p 1 *; repeat from * to *, ending k last st.

Row 4: P 1, * slip 1, p 1 *; repeat from * to *, ending p last st.

Repeat these 4 rows for pattern.

| = k 1

− = p 1

V = 1 slip st

2 sts

Framed diamonds

Work with a multiple of 14 stitches.

Row 1: * P 1, work (k 1, p 1) 3 times, k 7 *; repeat from * to *.

Row 2 and all even-numbered rows: Work each stitch as it appears on this side of work (k the k sts and p the p sts).

Rows 3 and 15: K 1, * work (p 1, k 1) twice, p 1, k 4, p 1, k 4 *; repeat from * to *, ending last repeat with p 3.

Rows 5 and 13: K 2, * p 1, k 1, p 1, k 4 *; repeat from * to *, ending last repeat with k 2.

Rows 7 and 11: K 3, * p 1, k 4, p 1, work (k 1, p 1) twice, k 4 *; repeat from * to *, ending last repeat with k 1.

Row 9: * K 7, p 1, (work k 1, p 1) 3 times *; repeat from * to *.

Repeat Rows 1 through 16 for pattern.

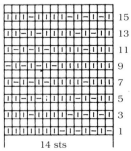

| = k 1

− = p 1

☐ = 1 st as shown

14 sts

150

CREATIVE STITCHES

Clams

Start work with a multiple of 6 stitches.

Row 1: * P 2, k 1 *; repeat from * to *.

Row 2: *P 1, k 2 *; repeat from * to *.

Row 3: * P 2, k 1, work 3-st increase as follows: with tip of left needle, pick up connecting strand between last st worked and next st on left needle, then k 1, p 1, and k 1 into this loop, p 2, k 1 *; repeat from * to *.

Rows 4 and 6: * P 1, k 8 *; repeat from * to *.

Rows 5 and 7: * P 2, k 4, p 2, k 1 *; repeat from * to *.

Row 8: * P 1, k 2, p 4 sts together, k 2 *; repeat from * to *.

Row 9: * Work (p 2, k 1) twice, work 3-st increase *; repeat from * to *.

Rows 10 and 12: K 6, * p 1, k 8 *; repeat from * to *, ending with k 2.

Rows 11 and 13: * P 2, k 1, p 2, k 4 *; repeat from * to *.

Row 14: * P 4 sts together, k 2, p 1, k 2 *; repeat from * to *.

Repeat Rows 3 through 14 for pattern.

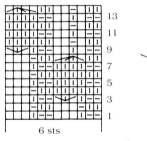

| = k 1
− = p 1
= 3-st increase between 2 sts
= p 4 tog
□ = empty space with no st indicated

6 sts

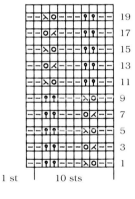

1 st   10 sts

− = p 1
O = yarn over
⅄ = slip 1, k 1, psso
∕ = k 2 tog

♀ = 1 twisted k st
□ = 1 st as shown

Lacy ribs

Work with a multiple of 10 stitches, plus 1.

Rows 1, 5, and 9: P 2, * yarn over (yo), slip 1, k 1, pass slip st over k st and drop (psso), p 3, k 2 twisted sts by working in back loop for each st, p 3 *; repeat from * to *, ending last repeat with p 2.

Row 2 and all even-numbered rows: Work each stitch as it appears on this side of work (k the k sts and p the p sts). K yarn-overs and p twisted st (p in back loop) over each twisted st.

Rows 3 and 7: P 2, * k 2 sts together (k 2 tog), yo, p 3, k 2 twisted sts, p 3 *; repeat from * to *, ending with p 2.

Rows 11, 15, and 19: P 2, * k 2 twisted sts, p 3, yo, slip 1, k 1, psso, p 3 *; repeat from * to *, ending with p 2.

Rows 13 and 17: P 2, * k 2 twisted sts, p 3, k 2 tog, yo, p 3 *; repeat from * to *, ending with p 2.

Repeat Rows 1 through 20 for pattern.

CREATIVE STITCHES

Spun leaves

Work with a multiple of 12 stitches, plus 1.

Row 1: P 2, * slip 1, k 1, pass slip st over k st and drop it (psso), k 2, yarn over (yo), k 1, yo, k 2, k 2 sts together (k 2 tog), p 3 *; repeat from * to *, ending last repeat with p 2.

Row 2 and all even-numbered rows: Work each stitch as it appears on this side of work (k the k sts and p the p sts) and p the yarn-overs.

Row 3: P 2, * slip 1, k 1, psso, k 1, yo, k 3, yo, k 1, k 2 tog, p 3 *; repeat from * to *, ending last repeat with p 2.

Row 5: P 2, * slip 1, k 1, psso, yo, k 5, yo, k 2 tog, p 3 *; repeat from * to *, ending last repeat with p 2.

Row 7: K 1, yo, * k 2, k 2 tog, p 3, slip 1, k 1, psso, k 2, yo, k 1, yo *; repeat from * to *, ending last repeat with yo, k 1.

Row 9: K 2, * yo, k 1, k 2 tog, p 3, slip 1, k 1, psso, k 1, yo, k 3 *; repeat from * to *, ending last repeat with k 2.

Row 11: K 3, * yo, k 2 tog, p 3, slip 1, k 1, psso, yo, k 5 *; repeat from * to *, ending last repeat with p 3.

Repeat Rows 1 through 12 for pattern.

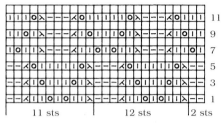

11 sts | 12 sts | 2 sts

| = k 1
− = p 1
O = yarn over
λ = slip 1, k 1, psso
⋌ = k 2 tog
□ = 1 st as shown

Poufs

Work with a multiple of 4 stitches, plus 2.

Row 1: P 2, * work knit, purl and knit all in next st (3 sts worked in 1 st), work 3 sts in following st, p 2 *; repeat from * to *.

Row 2: P 2, * work long st by wrapping yarn twice around needle to knit next st, work 5 more long sts, k 2 *; repeat from * to *.

Row 3: P 2, * one by one, slip 3 long sts to right needle, dropping extra loop for each st, then return the 3 sts to left needle and k them together through back loops, slip next 3 long sts to right needle, dropping extra loop from each, return 3 sts to left needle and k 3 together through front loops, p 2 *; repeat from * to *.

Row 4: K 2, * p 2, k 2; repeat from * to *.

Repeat these 4 rows for pattern.

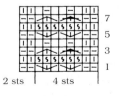

2 sts | 4 sts

| = k 1
− = p 1
⌄ = 3 sts worked in 1 st
ς = 1 long k st
⌃ = slip 3 and k 3 tog in back loop
⌃ = slip 3 and k 3 tog
□ = empty space with no st indicated

CREATIVE STITCHES

Stockade

Work with a multiple of 4 stitches, plus 3.

Rows 1, 3, 5, 9, 11, and 13: P 3, * k 1, p 3 *; repeat from * to *.

Row 2 and all even-numbered rows: K 3, * p 1, k 3 *; repeat from * to *.

Row 7: * P 2, yarn over, p 2 sts together *; repeat from * to *, ending with p 3.

Row 15: P 3, * p 2 tog, yarn over, p 2 *; repeat from * to *.

Repeat Rows 1 through 16 for pattern.

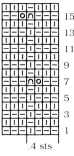

```
   15
   13
   11
    9
    7
    5
    3
    1
4 sts
```

− = p 1
| = k 1
o = yarn over
∩ = p 2 tog

Peepholes in ribs

Work with a multiple of 12 stitches, plus 1.

Rows 1 and 5: K 3, * p 2, k 3, p 2, k 5 *; repeat from * to *, ending last repeat with k 3.

Row 2 and all even-numbered rows: P 3, * k 2, p 3, k 2, p 5 *; repeat from * to *, ending last repeat with p 3.

Row 3: K 3, * p 2, k 1, yarn over, slip 1, k 1, pass slip st over k st and drop it, p 2, k 5 *; repeat from * to *, ending last repeat with k 3.

Row 7: K 3, * p 2, k 2 tog, yarn over, k 1, p 2, k 5 * repeat from * to *, ending last repeat with k 3.

Repeat Rows 1 through 8 for pattern.

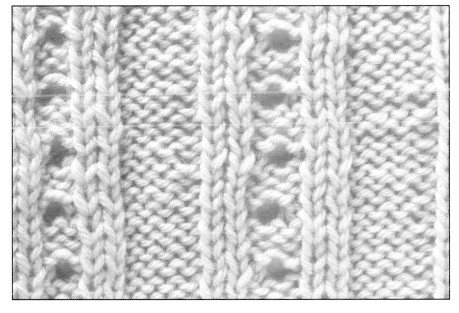

| = k 1
− = p 1
o = yarn over
λ = slip 1, k 1, psso
⋏ = k 2 tog

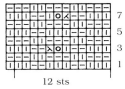

```
   7
   5
   3
   1
12 sts
```

153

CREATIVE STITCHES

Lacy cables

Work with a multiple of 11 stitches, plus 6.

Rows 1 and 5: K 6, * yarn over (yo), slip 1, k 1, pass slip st over k st and drop it (psso), k 1, k 2 sts together (k 2 tog), yo, k 6 *; repeat from * to *.

Row 2 and all even-numbered rows: Purl.

Row 3: * Work crossover on 6 sts as follows: slip 3 to dp needle and hold in back of work, k 3, k 3 from dp needle, k 1, yo, work double decrease on 3 sts as follows: slip 2 sts (as if to k) to right needle, k 1, pass both slip sts over k st and drop them, yo, k 1 *; repeat from * to *, ending last repeat with k 7.

Row 7: * K 7, yo, double decrease, yo, k 1 *; repeat from * to *, ending with crossover on last 6 sts.

Repeat Rows 1 through 8 for pattern.

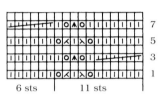

6 sts   11 sts

I	=	k 1
□	=	p 1
O	=	yarn over
⋋	=	slip 1, k 1, psso
⋌	=	k 2 tog
⋏	=	double dec
	=	6 sts crossover

Cluster stitch

Work with a multiple of 6 stitches, plus 5.

Rows 1 and 5: Knit.

Rows 2 and 6: Purl,

Row 3: K 3, * work 4-st decrease on 5 sts as follows: slip 4 sts (as if to k) onto right needle, k 1, then one by one, pass each slip st over k st and drop it, k 1 *; repeat from * to *, ending last repeat with k 3.

Row 4: P 3, * purl, knit, purl, knit and purl all in next st (5 sts worked in 1 st), p 1 *; repeat from * to *, ending last repeat with p 3.

Row 7: Work 4-st decrease as before, * k 1, work 4 st-decrease *; repeat from * to *.

Row 8: Work 5 sts in 1 st, * p 1, work 5 sts in 1 st *; repeat from * to *.

Repeat these 8 rows for pattern.

I	=	k 1
−	=	p 1
⋏	=	4-st decrease
⋎	=	5 sts worked in 1 st

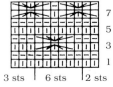

3 sts   6 sts   2 sts

CREATIVE STITCHES

Two-rib pattern

Work with a multiple of 10 stitches, plus 3.

Row 1: P 3, * work long st by wrapping yarn twice around needle to knit next st, p 3, k 3, p 3 *; repeat from * to *.

Row 2: K 3, * work double st by inserting needle into corresponding st 1 row below next st to knit it, drop unworked st above from left needle, k 1, double st, k 3, then with yarn forward, slip long st, dropping extra yarn loop from st, k 3 *; repeat from * to *.

Row 3: P 3, * with yarn at back, slip 1, p 3, k 1, double st, k 1, p 3 *; repeat from * to *.

Row 4: K 3, * double st, k 1, double st, k 3, with yarn forward, slip 1, k 3 *; repeat from * to *.

Rows 5 and 7: P 3, * k 1, p 3, k 1, double st, k 1, p 3 *; repeat from * to *.

Rows 6 and 8: K 3, * double st, k 1, double st, k 3, p 1, k 3 *; repeat from * to *.

Row 9: P 3, *work long st as before, p 3, k 1, double st, k 1, p 3 *; repeat from * to *.

Row 10: Repeat Row 2.

Repeat these 10 rows for pattern.

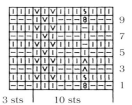

3 sts | 10 sts

I = k 1

− = p 1

8 = 1 long st

V = 1 double st

S = slip 1 long st

∧ = slip st

Seeds and squares

Work with a multiple of 12 sts, plus 2.

Row 1: Knit.

Row 2: K 4, * p 6, k 6 *; repeat from * to *, ending last repeat with k 4.

Rows 3, 5, and 13: P 4, * k 6, p 6 *; repeat from * to *, ending last repeat with p 4.

Row 4 and all following even-numbered rows: Work each stitch as it appears on this side of work (k the k sts and p the p sts).

Rows 7 and 11: K 4, * p 2, k 2, p 2, k 6 *; repeat from * to *, ending last repeat with k 4.

Row 9: K 6, * p 2, k 10 *; repeat from * to *, ending last repeat with k 6.

Repeat Rows 3 through 14 for pattern.

I = k 1
− = p 1

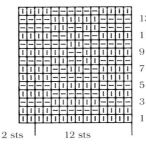

2 sts | 12 sts

CREATIVE STITCHES

Cables and lace pattern

Work with a multiple of 14 stitches, plus 3.

Row 1 (wrong side): K 3, * yarn over (yo), slip 1, k 1, pass slip st over k st and drop it (psso), k 2, p 3, k 2, k 2 sts together (k 2 tog), yo, p 3 *; repeat from * to *.

Row 2 and all even-numbered rows: Work each stitch as it appears on this side of work (k the k sts and p the p sts), and purl each yarn-over.

Row 3: K 3, * p 1, yo, slip 1, k 1, psso, k 1, work knot on 3 sts as follows: p 3 sts together, retaining them on left needle, then k them again through back loops and purl through back loops, dropping original sts from left needle; k 1, k 2 tog, yo, p 1, k 3 *; repeat from * to *.

Row 5: K 3, * p 2, yo, slip 1, k 1, psso, p 3, k 2 tog, yo, p 2, k 3 *; repeat from * to *.

Row 7: K 3, * p 2, yo, k 2 tog, work knot, slip 1, k 1, psso, yo, p 2, k 3 *; repeat from * to *.

Row 9: K 3, * p 1, yo, k 2 tog, k 1, p 3, k 1, slip 1, k 1, psso, yo, p 1, k 3 *; repeat from * to *.

Row 11: K 3, * yo, k 2 tog, k 2, work knot, k 2, slip 1, k 1, psso, yo, k 3 *; repeat from * to *.

Repeat Rows 1 through 12 for pattern.

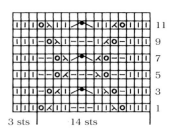

3 sts   14 sts

| = k 1
O = yarn over
⅄ = slip 1, k 1, psso
⋏ = k 2 tog
– = p 1
⬩ = 1 knot
□ = 1 st as shown

Bobble pattern

Start work with a multiple of 14 stitches, plus 3.

Row 1: P 3, * k 1, work increase by picking up connecting strand between last st worked and next st on left needle and knitting it, work (k 1, increase) twice more, k 5, work (increase, k 1) 3 times, p 3 *; repeat from * to *.

Row 2 and all even-numbered rows: Work each stitch as it appears on this side of work (k the k sts and p the p sts). On Row 6, p bobble st.

Row 3: P 3, * k 4, k 2 sts together (k 2 tog), p 2, k 1, p 2, slip 1, k 1, pass slip st over k st and drop it (psso), k 4, p 3 *; repeat from * to *.

Row 5: P 3, * k 3, k 2 tog, p 2, work bobble as follows: knit, purl, knit, purl, and knit all in next st, then, one at a time, pass first 4 sts over 5th bobble st, dropping each, to complete bobble; p 2, skip 1, k 1, psso, k 3, p 3 *; repeat from * to *.

Row 7: P 3, * k 2, k 2 tog, p 2, k 1, p 2, slip 1, k 1, psso, k 2, p 3 *; repeat from * to *.

Repeat Rows 1 through 8 for pattern.

| = k 1
– = p 1
+ = 1 increase

⬤ = 1 bobble
⋏ = k 2 tog
⅄ = slip 1, k 1, psso
□ = empty space with no st indicated

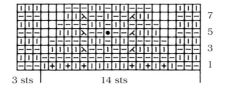

3 sts   14 sts

CREATIVE STITCHES

Open mock cable

Start work with a multiple of 4 stitches, plus 2.

Row 1: P 2, * k 2, p 2 *; repeat from * to *.

Rows 2, 4, and 8: K 2, * p 2, k 2 *; repeat from * to *.

Row 3: P 2, * yarn over, k 2, pass yarn-over loop over the 2 k sts and drop it, p 2 *; repeat from * to *.

Row 5: P 2, * k 1, yarn over, k 1, p 2 *; repeat from * to *.

Row 6: K 2, * p 3, k 2 *: repeat from * to *.

Row 7: P 2, * slip 1, k 2, pass slip st over the 2 k sts and drop it, p 2 *; repeat from * to *.

Repeat Rows 5 through 8 for pattern.

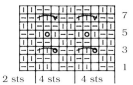

I = k 1
− = p 1
O = yarn over
V = slip st
⌣ = pass st over k 2

☐ = empty square with no st indicated

Moss stitch dots

Work with a multiple of 6 stitches, plus 5.

Rows 1 and 3: K 4, * p 1, k 1, p 1, k 3 *; repeat from * to *, ending last repeat with k 4.

Rows 2 and 4: P 5, * k 1, p 5 *; repeat from * to *.

Rows 5 and 11: Knit.

Rows 6 and 12: Purl.

Rows 7 and 9: K 1, * p 1, k 1, p 1, k 3 *; repeat from * to *, ending with (p 1, k 1) twice.

Rows 8 and 10: P 2, * k 1, p 5 *; repeat from * to *, ending with k 1, p 2.

Repeat Rows 1 through 12 for pattern.

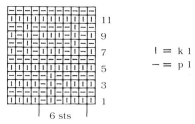

I = k 1
− = p 1

CREATIVE STITCHES

Knotted rib

Work with an uneven number of stitches.

Row 1: K in back loop of st for twisted st, * p 1, k 1 twisted st *; repeat from * to *.

Row 2: P 1, * k 1 twisted st, p 1 *; repeat from * to *.

Row 3: K 1 twisted st, * p 1, k in front and then in back loop of next st * repeat from * to *, ending with p 1, k 1 twisted st.

Row 4: P 1, k 1 twisted st, * p 2 sts together, k 1 twisted st *; repeat from * to *, ending p 1.

Repeat Rows 1 through 4 for pattern.

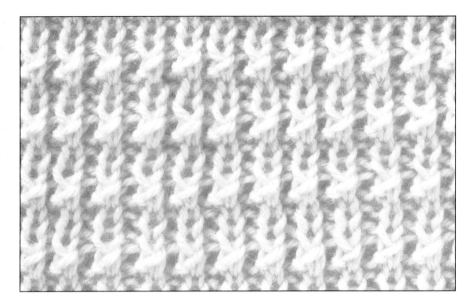

2 sts

$\upharpoonleft$ = 1 twisted k st

− = p 1

$\perp$ = k in front and back of st

$\cap$ = p 2 tog

Zigzag wraps

Work with a multiple of 6 stitches, plus 4.

Row 1 and all odd-numbered rows: Purl.

Rows 2 and 10 (right side): K 4, * work wrap on 2 sts as follows: yarn over, k 2, pass yarn-over loop over the 2 k sts and drop it, k 4 *; repeat from * to *.

Rows 4 and 8: K 5, * work wrap as before, k 4 *; repeat from * to *, ending last repeat with k 3.

Row 6: K 6, * work wrap, k 4 *; repeat from * to *, ending last repeat with k 2.

Rows 12 and 16: K 3, * work wrap, p 4 *; repeat from * to *, ending last repeat with k 5.

Row 14: K 2, * work wrap, p 4 *; repeat from * to *, ending last repeat with k 6.

Repeat Rows 1 through 16 for pattern.

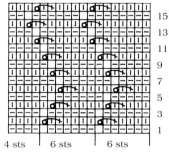

4 sts   6 sts   6 sts

l = k 1

− = p 1

= wrap on 2 sts

□ = empty space with no st indicated

CREATIVE STITCHES

Cords

Work set of cords on 19 stitches. For pattern, repeat set of cords on background of reverse stockinette st.

Row 1: K 4, work (p 2, k 1 in back loop for twisted k st) 3 times, p 2, k 4.

Rows 2 and 4: P 4, work (k 2, p 1) 3 times, k 2, p 4.

Row 3: Work wrap on 4 sts as follows: slip 1 as if to k, k 3, yarn over, pass the slip st over the 3 k sts and yarn-over and drop it, work (p 2, k 1 twisted st) 3 times, p 2, work wrap on last 4 sts.

Repeat Rows 1 through 4 for pattern.

19 sts

| = k 1
− = p 1
φ = 1 twisted k st
⌣ = wrap on 4 sts

Eyelet cables

Work with a multiple of 7 stitches, plus 1.

Row 1: P 1, * work wrap on 3 sts as follows: with yarn in back slip 1, k 2, pass slip st over the 2 k sts and drop it, k 3, p 1 *; repeat from * to *.

Row 2: K 1, * p 4, yarn over, p 1, k 1 *; repeat from * to *.

Row 3: P 1, * k 3, work wrap as before, p 1 *; repeat from * to *.

Row 4: K 1, * p 1, yarn over, p 4, k 1 *; repeat from * to *.

Repeat these 4 rows for pattern.

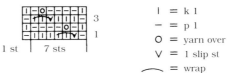

1 st   7 sts

| = k 1
− = p 1
O = yarn over
V = 1 slip st
⌣ = wrap

CREATIVE STITCHES

Mesh

Work with a multiple of 4 stitches, plus 2.

Row 1: K 1, yarn over, * slip 1, k 1, pass slip st over k st and drop it, k 2 sts together, yarn over twice *; repeat from * to *, ending last repeat with yarn over, k 1.

Row 2: P 1, k 1, p 2, * k 1, p 1 in back loop of yarn-over for twisted st, p 2 *; repeat from * to *, ending k 1, p 1.

Row 3: K 1, p 1, * work crossover on 2 sts as follows: skip 1, k 1, k skipped st, p 2 *; repeat from * to *, ending with p 1, k 1.

Row 4: P 1, k 1, p 2, * k 2, p 2 *; repeat from * to *, ending k 1, p 1.

Repeat these 4 rows for pattern.

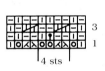

| = k 1
− = p 1
O = yarn over
⋋ = slip 1, k 1, psso
⋌ = k 2 tog
φ = 1 twisted st
⋌⊤ = 2-st crossover

Raspberries

Start work with a multiple of 5 stitches, plus 1.

Row 1: P 1, * work k 1, yarn over, and k 1 all in next st (3 sts worked in 1 st), p 4 *; repeat from * to *.

Row 2: K 1, * p 3 sts together, k 4 *; repeat from * to *.

Row 3: *P 4, work (k 1, yarn over, k 1) in next st *; repeat from * to *, ending p 1.

Row 4: * K 4, p 3 sts together *; repeat from * to *, ending k 1.

Repeat these 4 rows for pattern.

| = k 1
− = p 1
⋋O⊤ = k 1, yo, k 1 worked in 1 st
⊤ = p 3 tog

160

CREATIVE STITCHES

Chevrons

Work with a multiple of 14 stitches, plus 13, plus 6 for selvage sts.

Row 1 and all odd-numbered rows: K 3 (selvage), * yarn over (yo), k 5, slip 1, k 2 tog, pass slip st over k st (double decrease made), k 5, yo, k 1 *; repeat from * to *, ending last repeat with yo, k 3 (selvage).

Rows 2, 4, 6, 8, and 10: K 3, purl to last 3 sts, k 3.

Rows 12 and 14: Knit.

Rows 16, 18, 20, 22, 24, 26, and 28: K 3, purl to last 3 sts, k 3.

Rows 30 and 32: Knit.

Repeat these 32 rows for pattern.

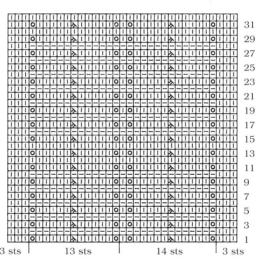

ǀ = k 1
‒ = p 1
o = yarn over
⅄ = double dec

3 sts · 13 sts · 14 sts · 3 sts

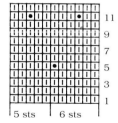

5 sts · 6 sts

ǀ = k 1
● = 1 bobble

Bobbles on garter stitch

Work with a multiple of 6 stitches, plus 5.

Rows 1 through 4: Knit.

Row 5: K 5, * work bobble on 1 st as follows: knit, purl, knit, purl, and knit all in next st, turn work, p 5, turn, k 5, turn, p 5, turn, slip 4 to right needle, k last st, then, one at a time, pass slipped sts over k st to complete bobble, k 5 *; repeat from * to *.

Rows 6 through 10: Knit.

Row 11: K 2, * bobble, k 5 *; repeat from * to *, ending last repeat with k 2.

Row 12: Knit.

Repeat these 12 rows for pattern.

CREATIVE STITCHES

Bobbles on the bias

Work with a multiple of 5 stitches, plus 2.

Row 1: P 3, * k 2, work bobble on 1 st as follows: knit, purl, knit, purl, and knit all in the next st, turn work, k 5, turn, slip 4 to right needle, k last st, then, one at a time, pass slipped sts over k st to complete bobble, p 2 *; repeat from * to *, ending last repeat with p 1.

Row 2 and all even-numbered rows: Work each stitch as it appears on this side of work (k the k sts and p the p sts) and purl bobble st.

Row 3: P 2, * k 2, bobble, p 2 *; repeat from * to *.

Row 5: P 1, * k 2, bobble, p 2 *; repeat from * to *, ending last repeat with p 3.

Row 7: P 1, k 1, * bobble, p 2, k 2 *; repeat from * to *.

Row 9: P 1, * bobble, p 2, k 2 * repeat from * to *, ending p 1.
Repeat Rows 1 through 10 for pattern.

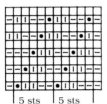

| = k 1
− = p 1
● = bobble
□ = 1 st as shown

5 sts | 5 sts

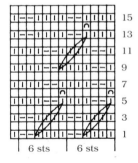

6 sts | 6 sts

| = k 1
− = p 1
/ = 1 loop
∩ = p 2 tog
□ = 1 st as shown

Diagonal loops

Work with a multiple of 6 stitches, plus 1.

Rows 1, 3 and 15: * K 4, p 2 *; repeat from * to *, ending with k 1.

Rows 2, 4, 8, 10, 12, and 16: Work each stitch as it appears on this side of work (k the k sts and p the p sts).

Row 5: * Work loop as follows: skip 4 stitches and insert needle between 4th and 5th sts 4 rows below the corresponding sts on left needle and k 1 st drawing up long loop, then starting with skipped sts on left needle, k 1, p 2, k 3 *; repeat from * to *, ending last repeat with k 4.

Row 6: P 4, * k 2, p 2 sts together (long loop is one of these sts), p 3 *; repeat from * to *, ending with p 2 sts together.

Rows 7, 9, and 11: K 1, * p 2, k 4 *; repeat from * to *.

Row 13: K 3, * work loop as before, k 1, p 2, k 3 *; repeat from * to *, ending last repeat with k 4, p 2, k 1.

Row 14: P 1, k 2, p 4, * k 2, p 2 sts together, p 3 *; repeat from * to *.
Repeat Rows 1 through 16 for pattern.

CREATIVE STITCHES

Flowers in squares

Work with a multiple of 16 stitches, plus 2.

Note: See page 5 for how to work moss st.

Row 1: Work 2 moss sts, * k 6, work 10 moss sts *; repeat from * to *.

Row 2: * Work 10 moss sts, p 6 *; repeat from * to *, ending 2 moss sts.

Row 3: Work 2 moss sts, * k 1, work 4 long sts by wrapping yarn twice around needle to p each one, k 1, work 2 moss sts, k 6, work 2 moss sts *; repeat from * to *.

Row 4: Work 2 moss sts, * p 6, work 2 moss sts, p 1, work flower on 4 long sts as follows: with yarn in front, slip 4 sts, one by one, dropping extra loop for each st, return the 4 sts to left needle and k 4 together, retaining them on left needle, purl them together again, then knit and purl them together once more, drop original sts from left needle, p 1, work 2 moss sts *; repeat from * to *.

Row 5: * Work 10 moss sts, k 1, work 4 long sts, k 1 *; repeat from * to *,

ending with 2 moss sts.

Row 6: Work 2 moss sts, * p 1, work flower, p 1, work 10 moss sts *; repeat from * to *.

Repeat these 6 rows for pattern.

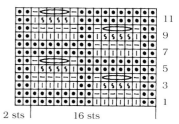

2 sts   16 sts

| = k 1
− = p 1
• = 1 moss st
ς = 1 p long st
⬯ = 1 flower

Textured diagonals

Work with a multiple of 6 stitches, plus 2.

Note: See page 5 for how to work moss stitch.

Row 1: K 2, * work textured st as follows: k 1, retaining original st on left needle, slip st just made to left needle and k it, retaining it on left needle, slip latest st made to left needle, pass second st on left needle over first and drop it, then pass following st over first st and drop it, knit remaining st to complete textured st; k 1, work (p 1, k 1, p 1) for 3 moss sts, k 1 * repeat from * to *.

Row 2: P 2, * work 3 moss sts, p 3 *; repeat from * to *.

Row 3: K 2, * work 3 moss sts, k 1, textured st, k 1 *; repeat from * to *.

Row 4: P 4, * work 3 moss sts, p 3 *; repeat from * to *, ending with p 1.

Row 5: K 1, work 2 moss sts, * k 1, textured st, k 1, work 3 moss sts *; repeat from * to *, ending with 1 moss st, k 1.

Row 6: P 1, work 2 moss sts, * p 3, work 3 moss sts *; repeat from * to *, ending with 1 moss st, p 1.

Repeat Rows 1 through 6 for pattern.

| = k 1
− = p 1
• = 1 moss st
ᴠ = textured st

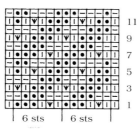

6 sts   6 sts

CREATIVE STITCHES

Long stitch pattern

Work with a multiple of 6 stitches, plus 5.

Rows 1, 4, 5, 8, 9, and 12: Purl.
Rows 2, 3, 6, and 10: Knit.
Row 7: K 2, * work long st as follows: insert needle in corresponding st 6 rows below next st and k 1, drawing up long loop to place st on left needle, k long st together with next st on left needle, k 5 *; repeat from * to *, ending last repeat with k 2.
Row 11: * K 5, work long st *; repeat from * to *, ending with k 5.
Repeat Rows 5 through 12 for pattern.

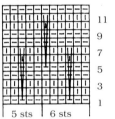

```
11
 9
 7
 5
 3
 1
```
| 5 sts | 6 sts |

- = p 1
| = k 1
= long st

Little leaves

Work with a multiple of 5 stitches, plus 2.

Rows 1 and 3: Knit.
Row 2 and all even-numbered rows: Purl.
Row 5: K 2, * work leaf as follows: insert needle 4 rows below in st corresponding to 3rd st on left needle and k 1, drawing up loop, place loop on left needle, make yarn-over on right needle, then, in same manner, work 2 more long sts from same st below, omitting yarn-over after last st, then k these 3 long sts and next st (on left needle) together through back loops, pass both yarn-over loops (on right needle) over st just worked to complete top, k 4 *; repeat from * to *.
Repeat Rows 1 through 6 for pattern.

| = k 1
□ = p 1
⁄ = 1 leaf

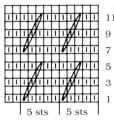

```
11
 9
 7
 5
 3
 1
```
| 5 sts | 5 sts |

CREATIVE STITCHES

Cord with knots

Work with a multiple of 7 stitches.
Row 1: P 2, * k 1, p 1, k 1, p 4 *; repeat from * to *, ending last repeat with p 2.
Row 2: K 2, * p 1, k 1, p 1, k 4 *; repeat from * to *, ending with k 2.
Row 3: P 2, * k in front, then back, and front loop of next st (3 sts worked in 1 st), p 1, work 3 sts in next st, p 4 *; repeat from * to *, ending with p 2.
Row 4: K 2, * p 3 sts together, k 1, p 3 sts together, k 4 *; repeat from * to *, ending with k 2.
Repeat these 4 rows for pattern.

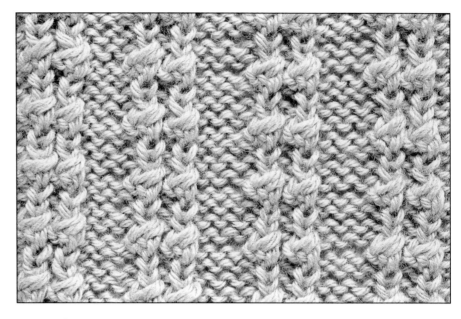

I = k 1

− = p 1

Ψ = 3 sts worked in 1 st

Λ = p 3 together

7 sts

Creative cord

Work single cord on 2 stitches. For pattern as shown, work evenly-spaced cords on background of reverse stockinette st. Cords can also be worked side by side for a solid pattern as shown in chart.
Row 1: Knit.
Row 2: With yarn in front (on wrong side of work), use tip of right needle to lift second st on left needle over the first, slipping it onto right needle, then purl the remaining st on left needle.
Repeat these 2 rows for cord.

I = k 1

⌒ = slip st

2 sts

CREATIVE STITCHES

Openwork checkerboard

Work with a multiple of 6 stitches.
Row 1: * K 3, p 3 *; repeat from * to *.

Row 2 and all even-numbered rows: Work each stitch as it appears on this side of work (k the k sts and p the p sts). Purl the yarn-overs.
Row 3: * K 1, yarn over, k 2 sts together, p 3 *, repeat from * to *.
Row 5: * P 3, k 3 *; repeat from * to *.
Row 7: * P 3, k 1, yarn over, k 2 sts together *; repeat from * to *.
Repeat Rows 1 through 8 for pattern.

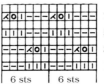

6 sts	6 sts

| = k 1
− = p 1
O = yarn over
⋀ = k 2 tog

☐ = 1 st as shown

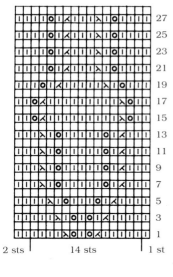

2 sts | 14 sts | 1 st

| = k 1
O = yarn over
⋏ = k 2 tog

⋋ = slip 1, k 1, psso
☐ = p 1

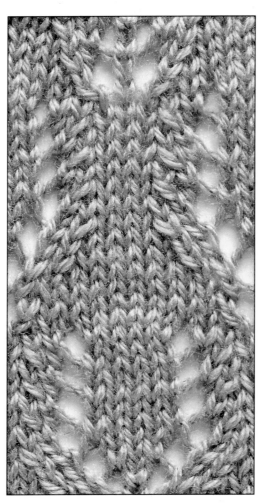

Low relief

Work with a multiple of 14 stitches, plus 3.
Row 1: K 6, * k 2 sts together (k 2 tog), yarn over (yo), k 1, yo, slip 1, k 1, pass slip st over k st and drop it (psso), k 9 *; repeat from * to *, ending last repeat with k 6.
Row 2 and all even-numbered rows: Purl.
Row 3: K 5, * k 2 tog, k 1, work (yo, k 1) twice, slip 1, k 1, psso, k 7 *; repeat from * to *, ending with k 5.
Row 5: K 4, * k 2 tog, k 1, yo, k 3, yo, k 1, slip 1, k 1, psso, k 5 *; repeat from * to *, ending with k 4.
Rows 7, 9, 11, and 13: K 3, * k 2 tog, k 1, yo, k 5, yo, k 1, slip 1, k 1, psso, k 3 *; repeat from * to *.
Rows 15 and 17: K 2, * yo, slip 1, k 1, psso, k 9, k 2 tog, yo, k 1 *; repeat from * to *, ending with k 2.
Row 19: K 3, * yo, k 1, slip 1, k 1, psso, k 5, k 2 tog, k 1, yo, k 3 *; repeat from * to *.
Rows 21, 23, 25, and 27: K 4, * yo, k 1, slip 1, k 1, psso, k 3, k 2 tog, k 1, yo, k 5 *; repeat from * to *, ending with k 4.
Repeat Rows 1 through 28 for pattern.

CREATIVE STITCHES

Lace in a frame

Work with a multiple of 22 stitches, plus 5.

Row 1: P 1, * work right crossover on 3 sts as follows: slip 1 to dp needle and hold in back of work, k 2, k 1 from dp needle; p 3, work triple slip st on 4 sts as follows: slip 3, k 1, then one at a time, pass each slip st over k st and drop, yarn over (yo), work (k 1, yo) 5 times, k 4 sts together (k 4 tog), p 3 *; repeat from * to *, ending right crossover, p 1.

Row 2 and all even-numbered rows: Work each stitch as it appears on this side of work (k the k sts and p the p sts). Purl each yarn-over loop.

Rows 3 and 7: P 1, * k 3, p 3, triple slip st, yo, work (k 1, yo) 5 times, k 4 tog, p 3 *; repeat from * to *, ending with k 3, p 1.

Row 5: P 1, * work left crossover on 3 sts as follows: slip 2 to dp needle and hold in front of work, k 1, k 2 from dp needle; p 3, triple slip st, yo, work (k 1, yo) 5 times, k 4 tog, p 3 *; repeat from * to *, ending with left crossover, p 1.

Repeat Rows 1 through 8 for pattern.

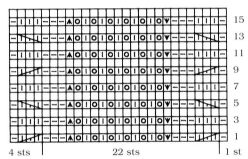

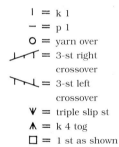

	= k 1
−	= p 1
O	= yarn over
⌁	= 3-st right crossover
⌁	= 3-st left crossover
V	= triple slip st
Λ	= k 4 tog
□	= 1 st as shown

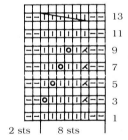

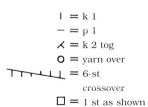

	= k 1
−	= p 1
⋌	= k 2 tog
O	= yarn over
⊤⊤⊤⊥⊥	= 6-st crossover
□	= 1 st as shown

Vertical scallops

Work with a multiple of 8 stitches, plus 2.

Rows 1 and 11: P 2, * k 6, p 2 *; repeat from * to *.

Row 2 and all even-numbered rows: Work each stitch as it appears on this side of work (k the k sts and p the p sts). Purl yarn-over loops.

Row 3: P 2, * k 2 sts together (k 2 tog), k 4, yarn over (yo), p 2 *; repeat from * to *.

Row 5: P 2, * k 2 tog, k 3, yo, k 1, p 2 *; repeat from * to *.

Row 7: P 2, * k 2 tog, k 2, yo, k 2, p 2 *; repeat from * to *.

Row 9: P 2, * k 2 tog, k 1, yo, k 3, p 2 *; repeat from * to *.

Row 13: P 2, * work crossover on 6 sts as follows: slip 3 to dp needle and hold in front of work, k 3, k 3 from dp needle, p 2 *; repeat from * to *. Repeat Rows 1 through 14 for pattern.

CREATIVE STITCHES

Matched ribs and lace

Work with a multiple of 12 stitches, plus 1.

Row 1: P 1, * work group cross on 4 sts as follows: slip 1 to dp needle and hold in front of work, k 1, k 1 from dp needle, skip 1 on left needle, k next st, k skipped st, dropping both original sts from left needle, p 1, k 1, p 6 *; repeat from * to *.

Row 2 and all even-numbered rows: Work each stitch as it appears on this side of work (k the k sts and p the p sts). Purl yarn-over loop on Row 10.

Row 3: P 1, * group cross, p 1, work left cross on 2 sts as follows: slip 1 to dp needle, p 1, k 1 from dp needle, p 5 *; repeat from * to *.

Row 5: P 1, * group cross, p 2, left cross, p 4 *; repeat from * to *.

Row 7: P 1, * group cross, p 1, k 1, p 1, left cross, p 3 *; repeat from * to *.

Row 9: P 1, * group cross, p 1, left cross, p 2, yarn over, p 2 sts together, p 1 *; repeat from * to *.

Repeat Rows 5 through 10 for pattern.

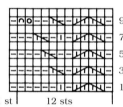

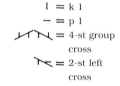

| = k 1
− = p 1
⌐⌐⌐ = 4-st group cross
⟍ = 2-st left cross
o = yarn over
∩ = p 2 tog
□ = 1 st as shown

Paired columns

Work with a multiple of 12 stitches, plus 3.

Rows 1 and 5: P 3, * k 4, p 1, k 4, p 3 *; repeat from * to *.

Row 2 and all even-numbered rows: Work each stitch as it appears on this side of work (k the k sts and p the p sts).

Row 3: P 3, * knit, purl, and knit all in the next st (3 sts in 1 st), work double dec on 3 sts as follows: slip 1, k 2 sts together, pass slip st over k st and drop it; p 1, k 3 sts together, work 3 sts in 1 st as before, p 3 *; repeat from * to *.

Repeat Rows 1 through 6 for pattern.

| = k 1
− = p 1
Ⅴ = 3 sts worked in 1 st
⟍ = double dec
⟋ = k 3 tog
□ = 1 st as shown

CREATIVE STITCHES

Bobble fantasy

Work with a multiple of 8 sts, plus 4.
Rows 1, 3, 7, and 9: Knit.
Row 2 and all even-numbered rows: Purl.
Row 5: * K 7, work bobble on next st as follows: knit, purl, knit, purl, and knit all in next st, turn work, k 5, turn, p 5 sts together to complete bobble *; repeat from * to *, ending with k last 4 sts.
Row 11: K 3, * bobble, k 7 *; repeat from * to *, ending last repeat with k 8.

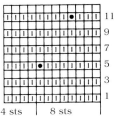

4 sts | 8 sts

| | = k 1
☐ = p 1
● = 1 bobble

Textured panels

Work with a multiple of 9 stitches, plus 4.
Row 1: K 4, * p 2, work (purl, knit in front loop, purl and knit in back loop) all in next st (4 sts worked in 1 st), p 2, k 4 *; repeat from * to *.
Row 2 and all even-numbered rows: Work each stitch as it appears on this side of work (k the k sts and p the p sts) and knit all 4 sts worked in each one st.
Row 3: K 4, * p 2, p 4 sts together, p 2, k 4 *; repeat from * to *.
Row 5: P 1, k 2, p 1, * work 4 sts in 1 st as before, p 3, work 4 sts in 1 st, p 1, k 2, p 1 *; repeat from * to *.
Row 7: P 1, k 2, p 1, * p 4 sts together, p 3, p 4 sts together, p 1, k 2, p 1 *; repeat from * to *.
Repeat Rows 1 through 8 for pattern.

4 sts | 9 sts

| | = k 1
— = p 1
Ψ = 4 sts worked in 1 st
|||| = k 4
⋀ = p 4 tog
☐ = 1 st as shown

CREATIVE STITCHES

Lacy leaves

Work with a multiple of 33 stitches, plus 2.

Row 1: * Work right cross on 2 sts as follows: skip 1, k 1, k skipped st and drop both original sts from left needle, yarn over (yo), k 2 sts together (k 2 tog), yo, k 1, yo, k 4, work double decrease on 3 sts as follows: slip 2 sts together as if to k onto right needle, k 1, then pass both slip sts over k and drop them; k 4, yo, double decrease, yo, k 4, double decrease, k 4, yo, k 1, yo, slip 1, k 1, pass slip st over k st and drop it (psso), yo * repeat from * to *, ending right cross on last 2 sts.

Row 2 and all even-numbered rows: Purl.

Row 3: * Work left cross on 2 sts as follows: slip 1 to dp needle and hold in front of work, k 1, k 1 from dp needle; yo, k 2 tog, yo, k 3, yo, k 3, double decrease, k 3, yo, double decrease, yo, k 3, double decrease, k 3, yo, k 3, yo, slip 1, k 1, psso, yo *; repeat from * to *, ending with left cross.

Row 5: * Right cross, yo, k 2 tog, yo, k 5, yo, k 2, double decrease, k 2, yo, double decrease, yo, k 2, double decrease, k 2, yo, k 5, yo, slip 1, k 1, psso, yo *; repeat from * to *, ending with right cross.

Row 7: * Left cross, yo, k 2 tog, yo, k 7, yo, k 1, double decrease, k 1, yo, double decrease, yo, k 1, double decrease, k 1, yo, k 7, yo, slip 1, k 1, yo *; repeat from * to *, ending with left cross.

Row 9: * Right cross, yo, k 2 tog, yo, k 9, yo, work (double decrease, yo) 3 times, k 9, yo, slip 1, k 1, psso, yo *; repeat from * to *, ending with right cross.

Row 11: * Left cross, yo, k 2 tog, yo, k 10, k 2 tog, yo, double decrease, yo, slip 1, k 1, psso, k 10, yo, slip 1, k 1, psso, yo *; repeat from * to *, ending with left cross.

Repeat Rows 1 through 12 for pattern.

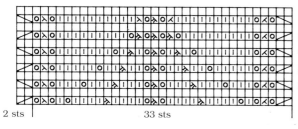

I	=	k 1
/	=	2-st right cross
\	=	2-st left cross
O	=	yarn over
⋏	=	k 2 tog
λ	=	slip 1, k 1, psso
⋋	=	double dec
□	=	p 1

CREATIVE STITCHES

Spiral columns

Work single column on 6 sts. For pattern as shown, work evenly-spaced columns on a background of reverse stockinette st.

Rows 1 and 3: Knit.
Rows 2 and 4: Purl.
Row 5: K 2, k 2 sts together, k 2, yarn over.
Row 6: P 1 in back loop of yarn-over, p 5.
Row 7: K 1, k 2 sts together, k 2, yarn over, k 1.
Row 8: P 1, p 1 in back loop of yarn-over, p 4.
Row 9: K 2 sts together, k 2, yarn over, k 2.
Row 10: P 2, p 1 in back loop of yarn-over, p 3.
Repeat these 10 rows for pattern.

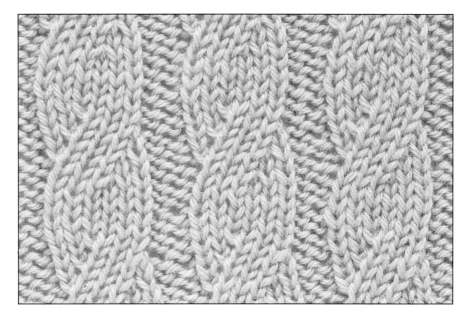

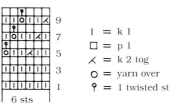

```
| = k 1
□ = p 1
⟍ = k 2 tog
O = yarn over
ᶈ = 1 twisted st
```

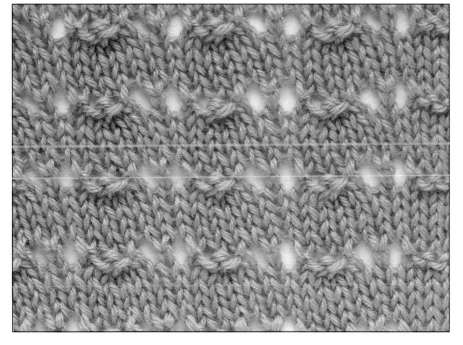

Groups with eyelets

Work with a multiple of 6 stitches, plus 4.

Rows 1 and 5: Knit.
Rows 2, 4, and 6: Purl.
Row 3: P 3, * work (yarn over, p 1) twice, p 3 sts together, p 1 *; repeat from * to *, ending last repeat with p 2.
Repeat Rows 1 through 6 for pattern.

```
| = k 1
□ or − = p 1
O = yarn over
ᴧ = p 3 tog
```

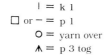

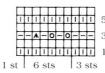

CREATIVE STITCHES

Empty seashells

Work with a multiple of 14 stitches, plus 2.

Row 1: P 2, * k 4, k 2 sts together (k 2 tog), slip 1, k 1, pass slip st over k st and drop it (psso), k 4, p 2 *; repeat from * to *.

Row 2: K 2, * p 3, p 2 sts together in back loops, p 2 sts together (p 2 tog), p 3, k 2 *; repeat from * to *.

Row 3: P 2, * k 2, k 2 tog, slip 1, k 1, psso, k 2, p 2 *; repeat from * to *.

Row 4: K 2, * p 1, p 2 tog in back loops, p 2 tog, p 1, k 2 *; repeat from * to *.

Row 5: P 2, * k 2 tog, cast on 4 sts, work 3 long sts as follows: insert needle into space between k 2 tog and psso 4 rows below to k 1, drawing up long st and yarn over after each long st, cast on 3 sts, slip 1, k 1, psso, p 2 *; repeat from * to *.

Row 6: K 2, * p 4, (p yo and long st tog) 3 times, p 5, k 2 *; repeat from * to *.

Repeat these 6 rows for pattern.

2 sts   14 sts

| = k 1
— = p 1

⋏ = k 2 tog
⋋ = slip, k 1, psso
~ = 1 st cast on
| = 1 long st
□ = empty space with no st indicated
∩ = p 2 tog
∪ = p 2 tog in back loops

| = k 1
O = yarn over
⋏ = k 2 tog

⊤⊤⊥⊥ = 4-st left crossover

⊥⊥⊤⊤ = 4-st right crossover

□ = p 1

Seahorses

Work with a multiple of 8 stitches, plus 2.

Rows 1, 3, and 7: K 5, * yarn over (yo), k 2 sts together (k 2 tog), yo, k 2 tog, k 4 *; repeat from * to *, ending last repeat with k 1.

Row 2 and all even-numbered rows: Purl.

Row 5: K 1, * work left crossover on 4 sts as follows: slip 2 to dp needle and hold in front of work, k 2, k 2 from dp needle, work (yo, k 2 tog) twice *; repeat from * to *, ending with k 1.

Rows 9, 11, and 15: K 1, * work (yo, k 2 tog) twice, k 4 *; repeat from * to *, ending with k 1.

Row 13: K 1, * work (yo, k 2 tog) twice, work right cross on 4 sts as follows: slip 2 to dp needle and hold in back of work, k 2, k 2 from dp needle *; repeat from * to *, ending with k 1.

Repeat Rows 1 through 16 for pattern.

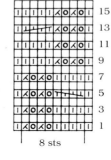

8 sts

CREATIVE STITCHES

Ribs and dots

Work with a multiple of 24 stitches.
Rows 1, 5, and 9: * K 2, p 2 *; repeat from * to *.
Row 2 and all even-numbered rows: Work each stitch as it appears on this side of work (k the k sts and p the p sts).
Rows 3, 7, 13, and 17: * Work (k 2, p 2) twice, * k 4, work (p 2, k 2) 3 times *; repeat from * to *.
Rows 11, 15, and 19: * P 2, k 2 *; repeat from * to *.
Repeat Rows 1 through 20 for pattern.

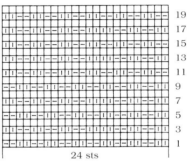

| = k 1
− = p 1
□ = 1 st as shown

| = k 1
− = p 1
⌐⊥⊤ = 4-st right crossover
⊤⌐⊥ = 4-st left crossover
● = bobble
□ = 1 st as shown

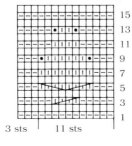

3 sts | 11 sts

Flowering bush

Work with a multiple of 11 stitches, plus 3.
Rows 1 and 15: Purl.
Row 2 and all even-numbered rows: Work each stitch as it appears on this side of work (k the k sts and p the p sts). K any bobble sts.
Row 3: P 5, * work right crossover on 4 sts as follows: slip 2 to dp needle and hold in back of work, k 2, k 2 from dp needle, p 7 *; repeat from * to *, ending last repeat with k 5.
Row 5: P 3, * right crossover, work left crossover on 4 sts as follows: slip 2 to dp needle and hold in front of work, k 2, k 2 from dp needle, p 3 *; repeat from * to *.
Row 7: P 3, * k 8, p 3 *; repeat from * to *.
Row 9: P 3, * work bobble on 1 st as follows: knit, yarn over, knit, yarn over, and knit in back loop all in next st, turn work, k 5, turn, p 5, then one by one, pass first 4 sts over last one to complete bobble; k 6, bobble, p 3 *; repeat from * to *.
Row 11: P 5, * k 4, p 7 *; repeat from * to *, ending with p 5.
Row 13: P 5, * bobble, k 2, bobble, p 7 *; repeat from * to *, ending p 5.
Repeat Rows 1 through 16 for pattern.

CREATIVE STITCHES

Wave on wave

Work with a multiple of 12 stitches, plus 7.

Rows 1 and 5: K 2, * p 3, k 3, yarn over (yo), work double decrease on 3 sts as follows: slip 2 sts together as if to k, k 1, pass both slip sts over the k st and drop them; yo, k 3 * repeat from * to *, ending p 3, k 2.

Row 2 and all even-numbered rows: Work each stitch as it appears on this side of work (k the k sts and p the p sts). Purl yarn-over loops.

Row 3: K 2, * p 3, k 1, k 2 sts together (k 2 tog), yo, k 3, yo, slip 1, k 1, pass slip st over k st and drop it (psso), k 1 *; repeat from * to *, ending p 3, k 2.

Rows 7 and 15: Knit.

Rows 9 and 13: K 2, * yo, double decrease, yo, k 3, p 3, k 3 *; repeat from * to *, ending last repeat with k 2.

Row 11: * K 2 tog, yo, k 3, yo, slip 1, k 1, psso, k 1, p 3, k 1 *; repeat from * to *, ending last repeat with slip 1, k 1, psso.

Repeat Rows 1 through 16 for pattern.

```
I = k 1
− = p 1
O = yarn over
⅄ = double dec
⋋ = k 2 tog
⋌ = slip 1, k 1, psso
□ = 1 st as shown
```

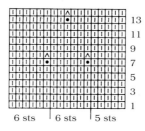

Hatchery

Work with a multiple of 6 stitches, plus 5.

Rows 1 through 6: Knit.

Row 7: K 5, * work bobble on 1 st as follows: work (yarn over and knit) 3 times all in next st, turn work, slip 1, p 5, turn, slip 1, k 5, turn, p 2 sts together 3 times, turn, slip 2, k 1, pass slip sts over k st to complete bobble, k 5 *; repeat from * to *.

Row 8: K 5, * p 1 in back loop, k 5 *; repeat from * to *.

Rows 9 through 12: Knit.

Row 13: K 8, * bobble, p 5 *; repeat from * to *, ending last repeat with k 8.

Row 14: K 8, * p 1 in back loop, k 5 *; repeat from * to *, ending with k 8.

Repeat Rows 3 through 14 for pattern.

```
I = k 1
• = 1 bobble
∧ = p 1 in back loop
```

CREATIVE STITCHES

Cornice

Work with a multiple of 14 sts.

Row 1: K 5, * k 3 in back loop for twisted k sts, k 11 *; repeat from * to *, ending last repeat with k 6.

Rows 2, 22, and 24: P 5, * k 1, p 3 in back loop for twisted p sts, k 1, p 9 *; repeat from * to *, ending last repeat with p 4.

Rows 3 and 21: K 3, * p 2, work crossover on 3 sts as follows: slip 2 to dp needle and hold in back of work, k 1, k 2 from dp needle, p 2, k 7 *; repeat from * to *, ending with k 4.

Rows 4 and 20: P 3, * k 3, p 3 twisted sts, k 3, p 5 *; repeat from * to *, ending with p 3.

Rows 5 and 19: K 1, * p 4, crossover, p 4, k 3 *; repeat from * to *, ending with k 2.

Row 6: * P 1, k 5, p 3 sts together, k 5 *; repeat from * to *.

Row 7: * P 5, k 1, p 5, k in back, then front and back loop of next st (3 sts in 1 st) *; repeat from * to *.

Rows 8 and 16: * P 3 twisted sts, k 4, p 3, k 4 *; repeat from * to *.

Rows 9 and 15: * P 3, k 5, p 3, crossover *; repeat from * to *.

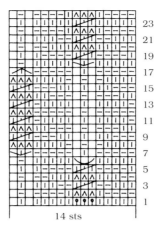

14 sts

| | = k 1
− = p 1
ᵠ = 1 twisted k st
∧ = 1 twisted p st
⌐/ = 3-st crossover

⌣ = p 3 tog
⌄ = 3 sts worked in 1 st
⌃ = k 3 tog
□ = empty space with no st indicated

Rows 10 and 14: * P 3 twisted sts, k 2, p 7, k 2 *; repeat from * to *.

Rows 11 and 13: * P 1, k 9, p 1, crossover *; repeat from * to *.

Row 12: * P 3 twisted sts, p 11 *; repeat from * to *.

Row 17: * P 5, k 1, p 5, k 3 sts together *; repeat from * to *.

Row 18: * P 1, k 5, work 3 sts in 1 st as before, k 5 *; repeat from * to *.

Row 23: K 5, * crossover, k 11 *; repeat from * to *, ending with k 6.
Repeat Rows 3 through 24 for pattern.

Carpet

Work with a multiple of 16 stitches.

Rows 1 and 9: * K 5, p 1, k 5, p 5 *; repeat from * to *.

Rows 2 and 8: * K 5, p 4, k 1, p 1, k 1, p 4 *; repeat from * to *.

Rows 3 and 7: * K 3, p 1, work (k 1, p 1) twice, k 3, p 5 *; repeat from * to *.

Rows 4 and 6: * K 5, p 2, work (k 1, p 1) 3 times, k 1, p 2 *; repeat from * to *.

Row 5: * Work (k 1, p 1) 5 times, k 1, p 5 *; repeat from * to *.

Rows 10 and 24: * P 5, k 1, p 9, k 1 *; repeat from * to *.

Rows 11 and 23: K 1, * p 1, k 7 *; repeat from * to *, ending last repeat with p 6.

Rows 12 and 22: P 7, * k 1, p 5, k 1, p 9 *; repeat from * to *, ending last repeat with p 2.

Rows 13 and 21: K 3, * p 5, k 5, p 1, k 5 *; repeat from * to *, ending with k 2.

Rows 14 and 20: P 1, * k 1, p 1, k 1, p 4, k 5, p 4 *; repeat from * to *, ending with p 3.

Rows 15 and 19: * K 3, p 5, k 3, p 1, (k 1, p 1) twice *; repeat from * to *.

Rows 16 and 18: * Work (p 1, k 1) 3 times, p 2, k 5, p 2, k 1 *; repeat from * to *.

Row 17: * K 1, p 1, k 1, p 5, work (k 1, p 1) 4 times *; repeat from * to *.
Repeat Rows 1 through 24 for pattern.

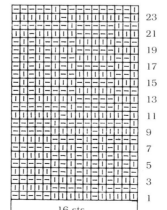

16 sts

| | = k 1
− = p 1

CREATIVE STITCHES

Sailor's knots

Work with a multiple of 9 stitches, plus 2.

Row 1: P 2, * work group on 3 sts as follows: slip 1 as if to k, k 2, pass slip st over both k sts (psso), yarn over to complete group, work (p 1, k 1) twice, p 2 *; repeat from * to *.

Row 2 and all even-numbered rows: K 2, * work (p 1, k 1) 3 times, p 1, k 2 *; repeat from * to *.

Row 3: P 2, * k 1, p 1, work group as before, p 1, k 1, p 2 *; repeat from * to *.

Row 5: P 2, * work (k 1, p 1) twice, work group, p 2 *; repeat from * to *.

Repeat Rows 1 through 6 for pattern.

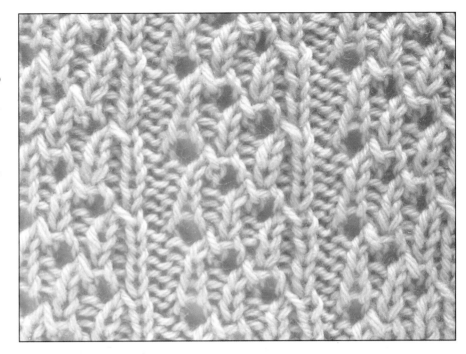

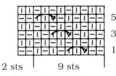

2 sts | 9 sts

| = k 1
− = p 1
∨ = 1 slip st
⌢ = psso + yarn over group

Bow ties

Work with a multiple of 10 stitches.
Note: Carry yarn on wrong side of work when slipping stitches. Slip as if p unless otherwise noted.

Rows 1, 3, 5, 11, 17, 19, and 21 (right side): * Slip 1, work (k 1, slip 1) twice, k 5 *; repeat from * to *.

Rows 2, 4, 6, 10, 12, 16, 18, 20, and 22: * P 5, k 1, work (slip 1, k 1) twice *; repeat from * to *.

Rows 7 and 13: * Slip 1, (k 1, slip 1) twice, slip 1 as if to k, k 3, slip 1 as if to k *; repeat from * to *.

Rows 8 and 14: * Slip 1 as if to k, p 3, slip 1 as if to k, work (k 1, slip 1) twice, k 1 *; repeat from * to *.

Rows 9 and 15: * Slip 1, work (k 1, slip 1) twice, work crossover on 5 sts as follows: slip 1 to dp needle and hold in back of work, slip 3 to 2nd dp needle and hold in back, k 1, bring first dp needle to front, k 3 from 2nd dp needle, k 1 from front dp needle *; repeat from * to *.

Repeat Rows 1 through 22 for pattern.

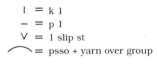

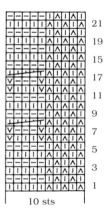

10 sts

| = k 1
− = p 1
∨ = slip 1 as if to k
∧ = slip 1 as if to p
⌐ = 5-st crossover

176

CREATIVE STITCHES

Buttercups

Work with a multiple of 16 stitches.

Row 1: P 6, * work right crossover on 2 sts as follows: skip 1, k 1, k skipped st and drop both original sts from left needle; work left crossover on 2 sts as follows: slip 1 to dp needle and hold in front of work, k 1, k 1 from dp needle, p 12 *; repeat from * to *, ending with p 6.

Row 2: P 5, * work left cross-K on 2 sts as follows: slip 1 to dp needle and hold in back, k 1, p 1 from dp needle, p 2, work right cross-K on 2 sts as follows: skip 1, p 1, k skipped st, drop original sts from left needle, k 10 *; repeat from * to *, ending with k 5.

Row 3: P 4, * work right cross-P on 2 sts as follows: skip 1, k 1, p skipped st, drop original sts, right crossover, left crossover, work left cross-P on 2 sts as follows: slip 1 to dp needle and hold in front, p 1, k 1 from dp needle, p 8 *; repeat from * to *, ending with p 4.

Row 4: K 3, * left cross-K, k 1, p 4, k 1, right cross-k, p 6 *; repeat from * to *, ending with p 3.

Row 5: P 2, * right cross-P, p 1, right cross-P, k 2, left cross-P, p 1, left cross-P, p 4 *; repeat from * to *, ending with p 2.

Row 6: K 2, * p 1, k 2, p 1, k 1, p 2, k 1, p 1, k 2, p 1, k 4 *; repeat from * to *, ending with k 2.

Row 7: P 2, * work bobble in 1 st as follows: knit, purl, knit and purl all in next st, turn work, p 4, turn, k 4, turn, p 2 sts together twice, turn, k 2 sts together to complete bobble; p 1, right cross-P, p 1, k 2, p 1, left cross-P, p 1, bobble, p 4 *; repeat from * to *, ending with p 2.

Row 8: K 4, * p 1, k 2, p 2, k 2, p 1, k 8 *; repeat from * to *, ending with k 4.

Row 9: P 4, * bobble, p 6, bobble, p 8 *; repeat from * to *, ending with p 4.

Row 10: Knit.

Repeat Rows 1 through 10 for pattern.

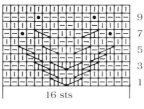

| = k 1
− = p 1
= 2-st right crossover
= 2-st left crossover
= 2-st left cross-K
= 2-st right cross-K
= 2-st right cross-P
= 2-st left cross-P
• = 1 bobble

16 sts

CREATIVE STITCHES

Holly berries

Work with a multiple of 10 stitches.
Rows 1 and 3 (right side): * K 1, p 3, k 3, p 3 *; repeat from * to *.
Rows 2 and 10: * K 3, p 3, k 3, p 1 *; repeat from * to *.
Row 4: * K 2, work left cross on 2 sts as follows: slip 1 to dp needle and hold in front of work, p 1, k 1 from dp needle; p 1, work right cross on 2 sts as follows: skip 1, k 1, p skipped st and drop both original sts from left needle, k 2, p 1 *; repeat from * to *.
Row 5: * K 1, p 2, work (k 1, p 1) twice, k 1, p 2 *; repeat from * to *.
Row 6: * K 1, left cross, k 1, p 1, k 1, right cross, k 1, p 1 *; repeat from * to *.
Row 7: * K 1, p 1, work (k 1, p 2) twice, k 1, p 1 *; repeat from * to *.
Row 8: * Left cross, k 2, p 1, k 2, right cross, p 1 *; repeat from * to *.
Row 9: * K 1, work bobble on 1 st as follows: knit, purl, knit, purl, knit, and purl all in next st, turn work, p 6, turn, k 6, turn, p 3 sts together twice, turn, k 2 sts together to complete bobble, p 2, k 3, p 2, bobble *; repeat from * to *.
Repeat Rows 1 through 10 for pattern.

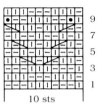

| | = k 1 |
| − = p 1 |
| = 2-st right cross |
| = 2-st left cross |
| ● = 1 bobble |

Falling leaves

Work with a multiple of 14 stitches.
Row 1: * Work crossover on 2 sts as follows: skip 1, k 1, k skipped st, drop both original sts from left needle; p 2, yarn over (yo), k 5, yo, slip 1, k 1, pass slip st over k st and drop it (psso), k 1 in back loop for twisted k st, p 2 *; repeat from * to *.
Row 2 and all even-numbered rows: Work each stitch as it appears on this side of work (k the k sts and p the p sts). Purl yarn-over loops.
Row 3: * Crossover, p 2, yo, k 1, slip 1, k 1, psso, p 1, k 2 sts together (k 2 tog), k 1, yo, p 1, k 1 twisted st, p 2 *; repeat from * to *.
Row 5: * Crossover, p 2, yo, k 1, slip 1, k 1, psso, p 1, k 2 tog, k 1, p 1, k 1 twisted st, p 2 *; repeat from * to *.
Row 7: * Crossover, p 2, yo, k 1, yo, slip 1, k 1, psso, p 1, k 2 tog, p 1, k 1 twisted st, p 2 *; repeat from * to *.
Row 9: * Crossover, p 2, yo, k 3, yo, to work double decrease: slip 2 sts together as if to k, k 1, pass both slip sts over k st and drop them, p 1, k 1 twisted st, p 2 *; repeat from * to *.
Repeat Rows 1 through 10 for pattern.

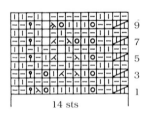

| | = k 1 |
| − = p 1 |
| O = yarn over |
| ⅄ = slip 1, k 1, psso |
| ⋋ = k 2 tog |
| = 2-st crossover |
| ⸸ = 1 twisted k st |
| = double dec |
| □ = empty space with no st indicated |

CREATIVE STITCHES

Droplets

Work with a multiple of 10 stitches, plus 2.

Row 1: K 1, * yarn over (yo), slip 1, k 1, pass slip st over k st and drop it (psso), k 8 *; repeat from * to *, ending last repeat with k 9.

Row 2 and all even-numbered rows: Purl.

Row 3: K 2, * yo, slip 1, k 1, psso, k 5, k 2 sts together (k 2 tog), yo, k 1 *; repeat from * to *.

Row 7: K 6, * yo, slip 1, k 1, psso, k 8 *; repeat from * to *, ending with k 4.

Row 9: K 4, * k 2 tog, yo, p 1, yo, slip 1, k 1, psso, k 5 *; repeat from * to *, ending with k 3.

Row 11: K 3, * k 2 tog, yo, p 3, yo, slip 1, k 1, psso, k 3 *; repeat from * to *, ending with k 2.

Repeat Rows 1 through 12 for pattern.

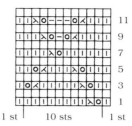

1 st | 10 sts | 1 st

| = k 1
□ or — = p 1
O = yarn over
⋋ = slip 1, k 1, psso
⋌ = k 2 tog

Agapanthus

Work with a multiple of 24 stitches.

Row 1: * P 1, K 1 in back loop for twisted st, p 8, work crossover on 3 sts as follows: slip 1 to dp needle and hold in front of work, k 2, k 1 from dp needle; p 8, k 1 twisted st, p 1, k 1 twisted st *; repeat from * to *.

Row 2 and all even-numbered rows: Work each stitch as it appears on this side of work (k the k sts and p the p sts). Work twisted p st (p in back loop) over twisted st on row below. On Row 10, purl 5 sts of bobble.

Row 3: * P 1, k 1 twisted st, p 7, work right cross on 2 sts as follows: slip 1 to dp needle and hold in back of work, k 1 twisted st, p 1 from dp needle; p 1, work left cross on 2 sts as follows: slip 1 to dp needle and hold in front of work, p 1, k 1 twisted st from dp needle; p 7, k 1 twisted st, p 1, k 1 twisted st *; repeat from * to *.

Row 5: * P 1, k 1 twisted st, p 6, right cross, p 3, left cross, p 6, k 1 twisted st, p 1, k 1 twisted st *; repeat from * to *.

Row 7: * P1, k 1 twisted st, p 5, right cross, p 5, left cross, p 5, k 1 twisted st, p 1, k 1 twisted st *; repeat from * to *.

Row 9: * P 1, k 1 twisted st, p 4, right cross, p 3, work bobble on 1 st as follows: knit, purl, knit, purl, and knit in back loop all in next st, then continuing on row, p 3, left cross,

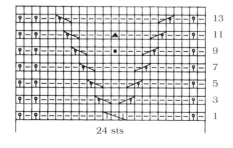

24 sts

p 4, k 1 twisted st, p 1, k 1 twisted st *; repeat from * to *.

Row 11: * P 1, k 1 twisted st, p 3, right cross, p 4, work 4-st decrease on 5 sts as follows: slip 3 sts together as if to k, k 2 sts together, pass all 3 slip sts over k st and drop them to complete bobble; p 4, left cross, p 3, k 1 twisted st, p 1, k 1 twisted st *; repeat from * to *.

Row 13: * P 1, k 1 twisted st, p 2, right cross, p 11, left cross, p 2, k 1 twisted st, p 1, k 1 twisted st *; repeat from * to *.

Repeat Rows 1 through 14 for pattern.

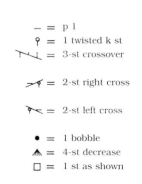

— = p 1
⃗ = 1 twisted k st
⋏ = 3-st crossover
⟋ = 2-st right cross
⟍ = 2-st left cross
● = 1 bobble
⋏ = 4-st decrease
□ = 1 st as shown

CREATIVE STITCHES

Diamonds in diamonds

Work with a multiple of 13 stitches, plus 2.

Row 1: K 2, * yarn over (yo), k 2, slip 1, k 1, pass slip st over k st and drop it (psso), k 3, k 2 sts together (k 2 tog), k 2, yo, k 2 *; repeat from * to *.

Row 2 and all even-numbered rows: Purl, except on Rows 10, 12, 22, and 24, work (p 1, k 1) over double yarn-overs of row below.

Row 3: K 3, * yo, k 2, slip 1, k 1, psso, k 1, k 2 tog, k 2, yo, k 4 *; repeat from * to *, ending last repeat with k 3.

Row 5: K 4, * yo, k 2, work double decrease on 3 sts as follows: slip 2 sts together as if to k, k 1, pass both slip sts over k st and drop them; k 2, yo, p 6 *; repeat from * to *, ending with k 4.

Row 7: K 5, * yo, k 2, double decrease, yo, k 2, k 2 tog, yo, p 4 *; repeat from * to *, ending with k 1.

Row 9: K 4, * k 2 tog, yo twice, k 2, slip 1, k 1, psso, k 1, k 2 tog, yo twice, slip 1, k 1, psso, k 2 *; repeat from * to *, ending with slip 1, k 1, psso.

Rows 10 and 12: See Row 2 for exception.

Row 11: K 3, * k 2 tog, k 2, yo twice, k 2, slip 1, k 1, psso, k 5 *; repeat from * to *, ending with k 4.

Row 13: K 2, * k 2 tog, work (k 2, yo) twice, k 2, slip 1, k 1, psso, k 3 *; repeat from * to *.

Row 15: K 1, * k 2 tog, k 2, yo, k 4, yo, k 2, slip 1, k 1, psso, k 1 *; repeat from * to *, ending with k 2.

Row 17: K 2 tog, * k 2, yo, k 6, yo, k 2, k 3 tog *; repeat from * to *, ending last repeat with k 2 tog, k 1.

Row 19: K 7, * yo, slip 1, k 1, psso, k 2, yo, k 3 tog, k 2, yo, k 4 *; repeat from * to *, ending with k 2 tog, k 2.

Row 21: K 6, * k 2 tog, yo twice, slip 1, k 1, psso, k 1, k 2 tog, k 2, yo twice, slip 1, k 1, psso, k 2 *; repeat from * to *, ending with k 5.

Rows 22 and 24: See Row 2 for exception.

Row 23: K 1, yo, * k 2, slip 1, k 1, psso, k 5, k 2 tog, k 2, yo twice *; repeat from * to *, ending with k 2 tog, yo, k 3.

Repeat Rows 1 through 24 for pattern.

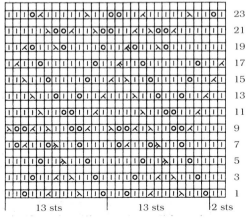

13 sts   13 sts   2 sts

| = k 1
O = yarn over
⅄ = slip 1, k 1, psso
⋌ = k 2 tog
⅄ = double dec
⋋ = k 3 tog
☐ = p 1

180

CREATIVE STITCHES

Triangular edging

Start work with 4 stitches. Edging can be made separately or on stitches added to edge of piece and worked as you work rows of main piece.

Rows 1 and 2: Knit. (To make attached edging, work both rows for right edge, as on chart, and knit only 1 row for left edge, so shaping occurs at outer edge, as in photograph.)

Row 3: Starting at outer edge, k in front and back loop of first st (increase made), k 3.

Row 4: K 4, increase in last st as before.

Row 5: Increase in first st, k 5.

Row 6: K 6, increase in last st.

Rows 7 and 8: K 8.

Row 9: Bind off first 4 sts, k remaining sts.

Row 10: K 4.

Repeat Rows 3 through 10 for pattern.

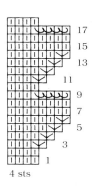

4 sts

$|$ = k 1

$\vee$ = k in front and
back of st

$\smile$ = 1 st bound off

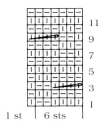

1 st   6 sts

$|$ = k 1
$-$ = p 1
⌐⌐⌐P = 4-st wrap

Sheaves of wheat

Work with a multiple of 6 stitches, plus 1.

Row 1: * k 4, p 2 *; repeat from * to *, ending k 1.

Rows 2 and 4: P 1, * k 2, p 4 *; repeat from * to *.

Row 3: * Work wrap on 4 sts as follows: insert right needle between 4th and 5th sts on left needle and k 1, drawing up a longer st than usual, k 4, slip one loop of long st over the 4 sts to wrap them, p 2 *; repeat from * to *, ending k 1.

Rows 5 and 11: Knit.

Rows 6 and 12: Purl.

Row 7: K 1, * p 2, k 4 *; repeat from * to *.

Rows 8 and 10: * P 4, k 2 *; repeat from * to *, ending p 1.

Row 9: K 1, * p 2, work wrap as before *; repeat from * to *.

Repeat Rows 1 through 12 for pattern.

CREATIVE STITCHES

Loops and blocks

Start work with a multiple of 12 stitches.

Row 1 (wrong side): * Work wrap on 3 sts as follows: yarn over (yo), k 3, pass yo loop over 3 k sts, then with yarn forward, slip 3 sts as if to p *; repeat from * to *.

Rows 2, 5, 6, 8, 11, and 12: Knit.

Row 3: * Work wrap as before, p 3 *; repeat from * to *.

Row 4: K 1, * work long loop as follows: with right needle, lift loop of next wrap (below and to the left) onto left needle, k loop together with next st, k 5 *; repeat from * to *, ending with k 4.

Row 7: * With yarn forward, slip 3 as if to p, work wrap *; repeat from * to *.

Row 9: * P 3, work wrap *; repeat from * to *.

Row 10: K 4, * work long loop as before, k 5 *; repeat from * to *, ending with k 7.

Repeat Rows 1 through 12 for pattern.

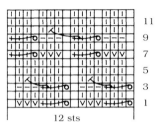

12 sts

| = k 1
− = p 1
V = 1 slip st
O = yarn over
⌣ = wrap

⌣ = 1 long loop
□ = empty space with no st indicated

Eyelet diamonds

Work with a multiple of 15 stitches.

Row 1: K 2, * p 2 sts together (p 2 tog), p 3, yarn over (yo), p 1, yo, p 3, p 2 tog, k 4 *; repeat from * to *, ending last repeat with k 2.

Row 2 and all even-numbered rows: Work each st as it appears on this side of work (k the k sts and p the p sts). Knit yarn-over loops.

Row 3: K 2, *, p 2 tog, p 2, yo, p 3, yo, p 2, p 2 tog, k 4 *; repeat from * to *, ending with k 2.

Row 5: K 2, * p 2 tog, p 1, yo, p 5, yo, p 1, p 2 tog, k 4 *; repeat from * to *, ending with k 2.

Row 7: K 2, * p 2 tog, yo, p 7, yo, p 2 tog, k 4 *; repeat from * to *, ending with k 2.

Row 9: P 1, * yo, p 3, p 2 tog, k 3, p 2 tog, p 3, yo, p 2 *; repeat from * to *, ending with p 1.

Row 11: P 2, * yo, p 2, p 2 tog, k 3, p 2 tog, p 2, yo, p 4 *; repeat from * to *, ending with p 2.

Row 13: P 3, * yo, p 1, p 2 tog, k 3, p 2 tog, p 1, yo , p 6 *; repeat from * to *, ending with p 3.

Row 15: P 4, * yo, p 2 tog, k 3, p 2 tog, yo, p 8 *; repeat from * to *, ending with p 4.

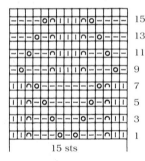

15 sts

| = k 1
− = p 1
O = yarn over
⌒ = p 2 tog
□ = 1 st as shown

Repeat Rows 1 through 16 for pattern.

CREATIVE STITCHES

Pairs of leaves

Work with a multiple of 15 stitches.

Row 1: K 1, * yarn over (yo), k 5, yo, k 3 sts together (k 3 tog), yo, k 5, yo, k 2 *; repeat from * to *, ending last repeat with k 1.

Row 2 and all even-numbered rows: Work each stitch as it appears on this side of work (k the k sts and p the p sts). Purl the yarn-over loops.

Row 3: K 1, * yo, k 1, k 2 tog, p 1, slip 1, k 1, pass slip st over k st and drop it (psso), k 1, yo, p 1, yo, k 1, slip 1, k 1, psso, p 1, k 2 tog, k 1, yo, k 2 *; repeat from * to *, ending with k 1.

Row 5: K 1, * yo, k 1, k 2 tog, p 1, slip 1, k 1, psso, k 1, p 1, k 1, slip 1, k 1, psso, p 1, k 2 tog, k 1, yo, k 2 *; repeat from * to *, ending with k 1.

Row 7: K 1, * yo, k 1, yo, k 2 tog, p 1, slip 1, k 1, psso, p 1, slip 1, k 1, psso, p 1, k 2 tog, yo, k 1, yo, k 2 *; repeat from * to *, ending with k 1.

Row 9: K 1, * yo, k 3, yo, slip 1, k 2 tog, psso (double decrease made), p 1, p 3 tog, yo, k 3, yo, k 2 *; repeat from * to *, ending k 1.
Repeat Rows 1 through 10 for pattern.

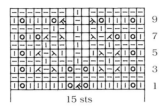

15 sts

| = k 1
− = p 1
O = yarn over
⼂ = k 2 tog
⼃ = slip 1, k 1, psso
⼅ = k 3 tog
⼇ = double dec
□ = empty space with no st indicated

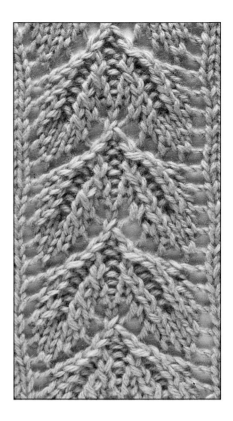

□ or | = k 1
O = yarn over
⼃ = slip 1, k 1, psso
⼂ = k 2 tog
⼇ = double dec

Garter stitch lace

Work with a multiple of 8 stitches, plus 1.

Row 1: K 1, * yarn over (yo), slip 1, k 1, pass slip st over k st and drop (psso), k 3, k 2 sts together (k 2 tog), yo, k 1 *; repeat from * to *.

Row 2 and all even-numbered rows: Knit.

Row 3: K 2, * yo, slip 1, k 1, psso, k 1, k 2 tog, yo, k 3 *; repeat from * to *, ending last repeat with k 2.

Row 5: K 3, * yo, work double decrease on 3 sts as follows: slip 2 sts together as if to k, k 1, pass both slip sts over k st and drop them, yo, k 5 *; repeat from * to *, ending with k 3.

Row 7: K 2, * k 2 tog, yo, k 1, yo, k 2 tog, p 3 *; repeat from * to *, ending with k 2.

Row 9: K 1, * k 2 tog, yo, k 3, yo, k 2 tog, k 1 *; repeat from * to *.

Row 11: K 2 tog, * yo, k 5, yo, double decrease *; repeat from * to *, ending with yo, k 2 tog.
Repeat Rows 1 through 12 for pattern.

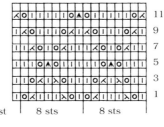

1 st   8 sts   8 sts

183

CREATIVE STITCHES

Gothic arches

Work with a multiple of 11 stitches, plus 3.

Row 1: K 4, * k 2 sts together (k 2 tog), yarn over (yo), p 2, yo, slip 1, k 1, pass slip st over k st and drop it (psso), k 5 *; repeat from * to *, ending last repeat with k 4.

Row 2 and all even-numbered rows: Work each stitch as it appears on this side of work (k the k sts and p the p sts). Purl yarn-over loops.

Row 3: K 3, * k 2 tog, yo, k 1, p 2, k 1, yo, slip 1, k 1, psso, k 3 *; repeat from * to *.

Row 5: K 2, * k 2 tog, yo, k 2, p 2, k 2, yo, slip 1, k 1, psso, k 1 *; repeat from * to *, ending with k 2.

Row 7: K 1, k 2 tog, * yo, k 3, p 2, k 3, yo, k 3 tog *; repeat from * to *, ending with slip 1, k 1, psso, k 1.

Rows 9 and 11: K 2, * yo, k 2, k 2 tog, p 2, slip 1, k 1, psso, k 2, yo, k 1 *; repeat from * to *, ending with k 2. Repeat Rows 1 through 12 for pattern.

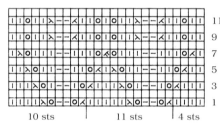

10 sts | 11 sts | 4 sts

| | = k 1
| − | = p 1
| O | = yarn over
| ⟨ | = k 2 tog
| ⟩ | = slip 1, k 1, psso
| ⟨⟩ | = k 3 tog
| □ | = 1 st as shown

Openwork diamonds

Work with a multiple of 8, plus 2.

Row 1: P 3, * k 2 sts together (k 2 tog), yarn over twice, slip 1, k 1, pass slip st over k st and drop it (psso), p 4 *; repeat from * to *, ending last repeat with p 3.

Row 2: K 3, * p 2, p 1 in back loop for twisted p st, p 1, k 4 *; repeat from * to *, ending with k 3.

Row 3: P 2, * k 2 tog, yarn over (yo), k 2, yo, slip 1, k 1, psso, p 2 *; repeat from * to *.

Rows 4, 6, 10, 12, and 14: Work each stitch as it appears on this side of work (k the k sts and p the p sts). Purl yarn-over loops.

Row 5: K 1, * work (k 2 tog, yo) 3 times, slip 1, k 1, psso *; repeat from * to *, ending with p 1.

Row 7: K 1, yo, * slip 1, k 1, psso, yo, k 2 tog, k 1, yo, k 2 tog, yo twice *; repeat from * to *, ending with k 2 tog, yo, p 1.

Row 8: * K 1, k 1 twisted st, p 6 *; repeat from * to *, ending k 2.

Row 9: P 2, * yo, slip 1, k 1, psso, k 2, k 2 tog, yo, p 2 *; repeat from * to *.

Row 11: P 3, * yo, slip 1, k 1, psso, k 2 tog, yo, p 4 *; repeat from * to *, ending with p 3.

Row 13: P 4, * k 2, p 6 *; repeat from * to *, ending with p 4. Repeat Rows 1 through 14 for pattern.

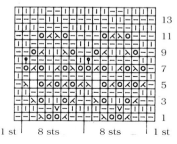

1 st | 8 sts | 8 sts | 1 st

| | = k 1
| − | = p 1
| O | = yarn over
| ⟨ | = k 2 tog
| ⟩ | = slip 1, k 1, psso
| V | = 1 twisted p st
| ᧐ | = 1 twisted k st
| □ | = empty space with no st indicated

CREATIVE STITCHES

Cluster motifs

Work with a multiple of 4 stitches.

Row 1: * K 3 sts together, purl, knit and purl all in next st (3 sts worked in 1 st) *; repeat from * to *.

Row 2: * K 3, p 1 *; repeat from * to *.

Row 3: * K 1, p 3 *; repeat from * to *.

Row 4: Knit.

Row 5: * Work 3 sts in 1 st , k 3 sts together *; repeat from * to *.

Row 6: * P 1, k 3 *; repeat from * to *.

Row 7: * P 3, k 1 *; repeat from * to *.

Row 8: Knit.

Repeat these 8 rows for pattern.

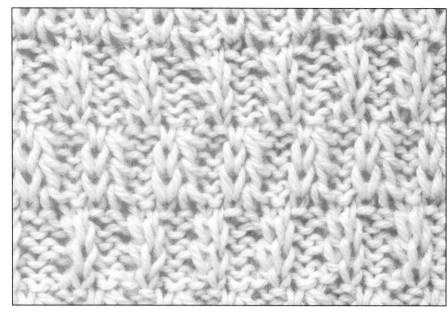

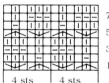

= k 3 tog
= 3 sts worked in 1 st
| = k 1
− = p 1
□ = empty space with no st indicated

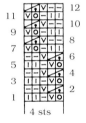

| = k 1
− = p 1
V = 1 slip st
O = yarn over
= k 2 tog in back loops

Little slip stitch pattern

Work with a multiple of 4 stitches.

Rows 1, 3, and 5 (wrong side):
* K 2, p 1, slip 1 with yarn in front, yarn over * ; repeat from * to *.

Rows 2, 4, and 6: * K the yarn-over and slip st together through back loops, slip 1, p 2 *; repeat from * to *.

Rows 7, 9, and 11: * Slip 1 with yarn in front, yarn over, p 1, k 2 *; repeat from * to *.

Rows 8, 10, and 12: * P 2, slip 1, k yarn-over and slip st together through back loops *; repeat from * to *.

Repeat Rows 1 through 12 for pattern.

CREATIVE STITCHES

Comets

Work with a multiple of 10 stitches, plus 9.

Row 1: * P 4, k 1, p 4, yarn over (yo), k 1, yo *; repeat from * to *, ending p 4, k 1, p 4.

Row 2: K 4, p 1, k 4, * yo, p 3, yo, k 4, p 1, k 4 *; repeat from * to *.

Row 3: * P 4, k 1, p 4, yo, k 5, yo *; repeat from * to *, ending last repeat with p 4.

Row 4: * K 4, p 1, k 4, yo, p 7, yo *; repeat from * to *, ending last repeat with k 4.

Row 5: * P 4, k 1, p 4, k 9 *; repeat from * to *, ending last repeat with p 4.

Row 6: * K 4, p 1, k 4, p 9 * repeat from * to *, ending with k 4.

Row 7: * P 4, k 1, p 4, slip 1, k 1, pass slip st over k st and drop it (psso), k 5, k 2 sts together (k 2 tog) *; repeat from * to *, ending with p 4.

Row 8: * K 4, p 1, k 4, p 2 tog, p 3, p 2 tog through back loops *; repeat from * to *, ending with k 4.

Row 9: * P 4, k 1, p 4, slip 1, k 1, psso, k 1, k 2 tog *; repeat from * to *, ending with p 4.

Row 10: * K 4, p 1, k 4, p 3 tog *; repeat from * to *, ending with k 4.

Row 11: * P 4, yo, k 1, yo , p 4, k 1 *; repeat from * to *, ending p 4, yo, k 1, yo, p 4.

Row 12: * K 4, yo, p 3, yo, k 4, p 1 *; repeat from * to *, ending last repeat with k 4.

Row 13: * P 4, yo, k 5, yo, p 4, k 1 *; repeat from * to *, ending with p 4.

Row 14: * K 4, yo, p 7, yo, k 4, p 1 *; repeat from * to *, ending with k 4.

Row 15: * P 4, k 9, p 4, k 1 *; repeat from * to *, ending with p 4.

Row 16: * K 4, p 9, k 4, p 1 *; repeat from * to *, ending with k 4.

Row 17: * P 4, slip 1, k 1, psso, k 5, k 2 tog, p 4, k 1 *; repeat from * to *, ending with p 4.

Row 18: * K 4, p 2 tog, p 3, p 2 tog through back loops, k 4, p 1 *; repeat from * to *, ending with k 4.

Row 19: * P 4, slip 1, k 1, psso, k 1, k 2 tog, p 4, k 1 *; repeat from * to *, ending with p 4.

Row 20: * K 4, p 3 tog, k 4, p 1 *; repeat from * to *, ending with k 4. Repeat these 20 rows for pattern.

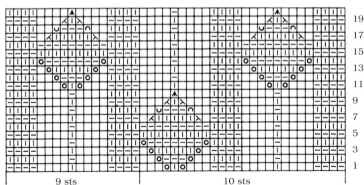

9 sts   10 sts

− = p 1

| = k 1

O = yarn over

⋋ = slip 1, k 1, psso

⋌ = k 2 tog

∪ = p 2 to

∩ = p 2 tog in back loops

⋀ = p 3 tog

□ = empty space with no st indicated

186

CREATIVE STITCHES

Framed bobbles

Work with a multiple of 13 stitches.
Row 1: P 2, * work right cross on 2 sts as follows: skip 1, k 1, p skipped st and drop both original sts from left needle; work right cross again, p 1, work left cross on 2 sts as follows: slip 1 to dp needle and hold in front of work, p 1, k 1 from dp needle; work left cross again, p 4 *; repeat from * to *, ending last repeat with p 2.
Row 2 and all even-numbered rows: Work each stitch as it appears on this side of work (k the k sts and p the p sts). On Row 6, knit bobble st.
Row 3: P 1, * work right cross twice, p 3, work left cross twice, p 2 *; repeat from * to *, ending with p 1.
Row 5: Work (p 1, k 1) twice, * p 2, work bobble on 1 st as follows: knit, yarn over and knit all in next st, turn work, k 3 sts, turn, p 3 sts together to complete bobble; p 2, k 1, p 1, k 1, p 2 *; repeat from * to *, ending with p 1.
Row 7: P 1, * left cross twice, p 3,

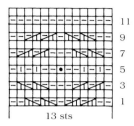

13 sts

| = k 1
− = p 1
⊐⫨ = 2-st right cross
⫪⊏ = 2-st left cross
● = bobble
□ = 1 st as shown

right cross twice, p 2 *; repeat from * to *, ending with p 1.
Row 9: P 2, * left cross twice, p 1, right cross twice, p 4 *; repeat from * to *, ending with p 2.
Row 11: Purl.
Repeat Rows 1 through 12 for pattern.

Lovely lace

Work with a multiple of 9 stitches.
Row 1: K 1, * k 2 sts together (k 2 tog), k 1 in back loop for twisted k st, work (yarn over, k 1 twisted st) twice, slip 1, k 1, pass slip st over k st and drop it (psso), k 2 *; repeat from * to *, ending last repeat with k 1.
Row 2 and all even-numbered rows: Purl, working twisted p st (p in back loop) above twisted sts of previous row.
Row 3: * K 2 tog, k 1 twisted st, yarn over (yo), k 1, k 1 twisted st, k 1, yo, k 1 twisted st, slip 1, k 1, psso *; repeat from * to *.
Row 5: * Slip 1, k 1, psso, k 1 twisted st, yo, k 1, k 1 twisted st, k 1, yo, k 1 twisted st, k 2 tog *; repeat from * to *.
Row 7: K 1, * slip 1, k 1, psso, work (k 1 twisted st, yo) twice, k 1 twisted st, k 2 tog, k 2 *; repeat from * to *, ending with k 1.
Repeat Rows 1 through 8 for pattern.

| = k 1
∧ = k 2 tog
ᖾ = 1 twisted k st
○ = yarn over
⋋ = slip 1, k 1, psso
□ = 1 st as shown

9 sts

CREATIVE STITCHES

Portcullis

Work with a multiple of 13 stitches, plus 5.

Row 1: K 2 sts together (k 2 tog), yarn over (yo), k 1, yo, * slip 1, k 1, pass slip st over k st and drop it (psso), work left cross on 2 sts as follows: slip 1 to dp needle and hold in front of work, k 1, k 1 from dp needle; k 4, work right cross on 2 sts as follows: skip 1, k 1, k skipped st and drop both original sts from left needle, k 2 tog, yo, k 1, yo *; repeat from * to *, ending slip 1, k 1, psso.

Row 2 and all even-numbered rows: Purl.

Row 3: K 2 tog, yo, k 1, yo, * slip 1, k 1, psso, k 1, left cross, k 2, right cross, k 1, k 2 tog, yo, k 1, yo *; repeat from * to *, ending slip 1, k 1, psso.

Row 5: K 2 tog, yo, k 1, yo, * slip 1, k 1, psso, k 2, left cross, right cross, k 2, k 2 tog, yo, k 1, yo *; repeat from * to *, ending slip 1, k 1, psso.

Row 7: Work (k 2 tog, yo) 8 times, * k 1, work (k 2 tog, yo) 6 times *; repeat from * to *, ending k 2.

Repeat Rows 1 through 8 for pattern.

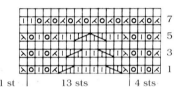

1 st   13 sts   4 sts

| = k 1
O = yarn over
⋌ = k 2 tog
⅂ = 2-st left cross
⅃ = 2-st right cross
⋋ = slip 1, k 1, psso
□ = p 1

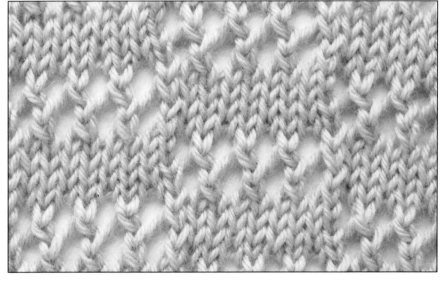

Faggoting pattern

Work with a multiple of 16 sts, plus 2.

Rows 1 and 3: K 1, * slip 1, k 1, pass slip st over k st and drop it (psso), yarn over (yo), work (slip 1, k 1, psso, yo) 3 times more, k 8 *; repeat from * to *, ending last repeat with k 9.

Row 2 and all even-numbered rows: Purl.

Rows 5 and 7: K 9, * work (slip 1, k 1, psso) 4 times, k 8 *; repeat from * to *, ending k 1.

Repeat Rows 1 through 8 for pattern.

| = k 1
⋋ = slip 1, k 1, psso
O = yarn over
□ = p 1

1 st   16 sts   1 st

CREATIVE STITCHES

Arrowheads

Work with a multiple of 12 stitches, plus 1.

Row 1: P 1, * k 11, p 1 *; repeat from * to *.

Row 2 and all even-numbered rows: Work each stitch as it appears on this side of work (k the k sts and p the p sts). Purl yarn-over loops.

Row 3: P 1, * yarn over (yo), slip 1, k 1, pass slip st over k st and drop it (psso), k 2, yo, work double decrease on 3 sts as follows: slip 2 sts together as if to k, k 1, pass both slip sts over k st and drop them; yo, k 2, k 2 sts together (k 2 tog), yo, p 1 *; repeat from * to *.

Row 5: P 2, * yo, slip 1, k 1, psso, k 1, yo, double decrease, yo, k 1, k 2 tog, yo, p 3 *; repeat from * to *, ending last repeat with p 2.

Row 7: P 3, * yo, slip 1, k 1, psso, yo, double decrease, yo, k 2 tog, yo, p 5 *; repeat from * to *, ending with p 3.

Row 9: P 4, * yo, slip 1, k 1, psso, k 1, k 2 tog, yo, p 7 *; repeat from * to *, ending with p 4.

Row 11: P 5, * yo, double decrease, yo, p 9 *; repeat from * to *, ending with p 5.
Repeat Rows 1 through 12 for pattern.

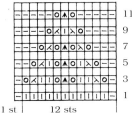

| = k 1
− = p 1
O = yarn over
⅄ = slip 1, k 1, psso
⋏ = k 2 tog
⋀ = double dec
□ = 1 st as shown

Undulating horseshoes

Start work with multiple of 11 stitches, plus 1.

Row 1: Slip 1, k 1, pass slip st over k st and drop it (psso), * k 2, increase between sts by picking up connecting strand between last st worked and next st and placing loop on left needle, then k 1 through back of this loop, k 1, increase as before, k 5, work double decrease on 3 sts as follows: slip 2 sts together as if to k, k 1, pass both slip sts over k st and drop them *; repeat from * to *, ending last repeat with k 2 sts together (k 2 tog).

Row 2 and all even-numbered rows: Purl.

Row 3: Slip 1, k 1, psso, * k 1, increase (inc), k 3, inc, k 4, double decrease (dec) *; repeat from * to *, ending last repeat with k 2 tog.

Row 5: Slip 1, k 1, psso, * inc, k 5, inc, k 3, double dec *; repeat from * to *, ending with k 2 tog.

Row 7: Slip 1, k 1, psso, * k 5, inc, k 1, inc, k 2, double dec *; repeat from * to *, ending with k 2 tog.

Row 9: Slip 1, k 1, psso, * k 4, inc, k 3, inc, k 1, double dec *; repeat from * to *, ending with k 2 tog.

Row 11: Slip 1, k 1, psso, * k 3, inc, k 5, inc, double dec *; repeat from * to *, ending with k 2 tog.
Repeat Rows 1 through 12 for pattern.

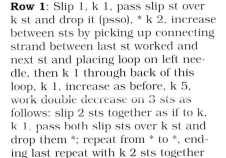

| = k 1
∨ = increase
⅄ = slip 1, k 1, psso
⋏ = k 2 tog
⋀ = double decrease
□ = p 1

CREATIVE STITCHES

Soft curves

Work with a multiple of 10 stitches.
Row 1: P 1, * k 1, slip 1, k 1, pass slip st over k st and drop it (psso), yarn over (yo), work (slip 1, k 1, psso, yo) twice more, k 1, p 2 *; repeat from * to *, ending last repeat with p 1.
Row 2 and all even-numbered rows: Work each stitch as it appears on this side of work (k the k sts and p the p sts). Purl yarn-over loops.
Row 3: P 1, * work (slip 1, k 1, psso, yo) 3 times, k 2, p 2 *; repeat from * to *, ending with p 1.
Row 5: P 1, * k 1, work (slip 1, k 1, psso, yo) twice, k 3, p 2 *; repeat from * to *, ending with p 1.
Row 7: P 1, * work crossover on 4 sts as follows: slip 2 to dp needle and hold in back of work, k 2, k 2 from dp needle, k 4, p 2 *; repeat from * to *, ending p 1.
Row 9: P 1, * k 8, p 2 *; repeat from * to *, ending with p 1.
Repeat Rows 1 through 10 for pattern.

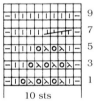

| | = k 1
— | = p 1
⅄ | = slip 1, k 1, psso
O | = yarn over
⊥⊥⊤⊤ | = 4-st crossover

□ | = 1 st as shown

Roman arches

Work with a multiple of 10 stitches, plus 1.
Row 1: K 1, * yarn over (yo), slip 1, k 1, pass slip st over k st and drop it (psso), k 5, k 2 sts together (k 2 tog), yo, k 1 *; repeat from * to *.
Row 2: P 2, * yo, p 2 tog, p 3, p 2 tog through back loops, yo, p 3 *; repeat from * to *, ending last repeat with p 2.
Row 3: P 3, * yo, slip 1, k 1, psso, k 1, k 2 tog, yo, k 5 *; repeat from * to *, ending last repeat with k 3.
Row 4: P 4, * yo, slip 1, p 2 tog, psso, yo, p 7 *; repeat from * to *, ending with p 4.
Row 5: K 4, * yo, work double decrease on 3 sts as follows: slip 2 sts together as if to k, k 1, pass both slip sts over k st and drop them, yo, k 7 *; repeat from * to *, ending with k 4.
Row 6: P 4, * yo, slip 1, p 2 tog, psso, yo, p 7 *; repeat from * to *, ending with p 4.
Repeat these 6 rows for pattern.

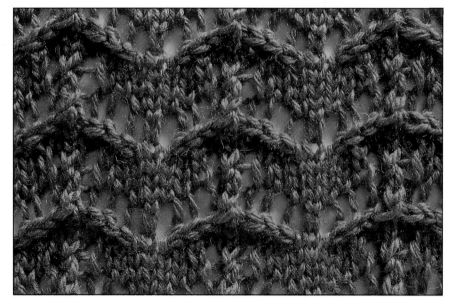

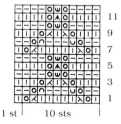

| | = k 1
— | = p 1
O | = yarn over
⅄ | = slip 1, k 1, psso
⅄ | = k 2 tog
∩ | = p 2 tog
∪ | = p 2 tog in back loop
ⴑ | = slip 1, p 2, psso
Λ | = double dec

190

CREATIVE STITCHES

Checkers

Work with a multiple of 18 stitches, plus 9.

Rows 1, 3, 11, and 13: P 9, * k 9, p 9 *; repeat from * to *.

Rows 2, 4, 12, and 14: K 9, * p 9, k 9 *; repeat from * to *.

Row 5: * P 4, k 1, p 4, k 4, yarn over (yo), k 2 sts together (k 2 tog), k 3 *; repeat from * to *, ending p 4, k 1, p 4.

Rows 6, 8, and 10: * K 4, slip 1 with yarn in front, k 4, p 9 *; repeat from * to *, ending k 4, slip 1 with yarn in front, k 4.

Row 7: * P 4, k 1, p 4, k 2, k 2 tog, yo, k 1, yo, slip 1, k 1, pass slip st over k st and drop it (psso), k 2 *; repeat from * to *, ending p 4, k 1, p 4.

Row 9: * P 4, k 1, p 4, k 4, yo, slip 1, k 1, psso, k 3 *; repeat from * to *, ending p 4, k 1, p 4.

Rows 15, 17, 25, and 27: K 9, * p 9, k 9 *; repeat from * to *.

Rows 16, 18, 26, and 28: P 9, * k 9, p 9 *; repeat from * to *.

Row 19: * K 4, yo, k 2 tog, k 3, p 4, k 1, p 4 * repeat from * to *, ending k 4, yo, k 2 tog, k 3.

Rows 20, 22, and 24: P 9, * k 4, slip 1 with yarn in front, k 4, p 9 *; repeat from * to *.

Row 21: * K 2, k 2 tog, yo, k 1, yo, slip 1, k 1, psso, k 2, p 4, k 1, p 4 *; repeat from * to *, ending k 2, k 2 tog, yo, k 1, yo, slip 1, k 1, psso, k 2.

Row 23: K 4, * yo, slip 1, k 1, psso, k 3, p 4, k 1, p 4 *; repeat from * to *, ending k 4, yo, slip 1, k 1, psso, k 3. Repeat Rows 1 through 28 for pattern.

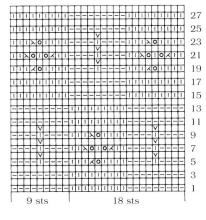

```
| = k 1
− = p 1
V = slip st
O = yarn over
⋋ = k 2 tog

⋌ = slip 1, k 1, psso
□ = 1 st as shown
```

Lacy mock cables

Start work with a multiple of 4 stitches, plus 2.

Row 1: P 2, * k 2, p 2 *; repeat from * to *.

Row 2: K 2, * p 1, yarn over (yo), p 1, k 2 *; repeat from * to *.

Row 3: P 2, * k 3, p 2 *; repeat from * to *.

Row 4: K 2, * p 3, k 2 *; repeat from * to *.

Row 5: P 2, * k 3, then pass the first of these k sts over the last 2 and drop it, p 2 *; repeat from * to *. Repeat Rows 2 through 5 rows for pattern.

```
| = k 1
− = p 1
O = yarn over
⌒ = pass 1 st over
      2 sts
□ = empty space with
      no st indicated
```

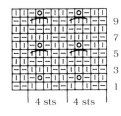

CREATIVE STITCHES

Alternating leaf pattern

Work with a multiple of 11 stitches, plus 1.

Row 1: K 2 sts together (k 2 tog), * k 5, yarn over (yo), k 1, yo, k 2, work double dec on 3 sts as follows: slip 2 sts together as if to k, k 1, pass both slip sts over k st and drop them *; repeat from * to *, ending last repeat with slip 1, k 1, pass slip st over k 1 and drop it (psso).

Row 2 and all even-numbered rows: Purl.

Row 3: K 2 tog, * k 4, yo, k 3, yo, k 1, double decrease *; repeat from * to *, ending last repeat with slip 1, k 1, psso.

Row 5: K 2 tog, * k 3, yo, k 5, yo, double decrease *; repeat from * to *, ending last repeat with slip 1, k 1, psso.

Row 7: K 2 tog, * k 2, yo, k 1, yo, k 5, double decrease *; repeat from * to *; ending last repeat with slip 1, k 1, psso.

Row 9: K 2 tog, * k 1, yo, k 3, yo, k 4, double decrease *; repeat from *

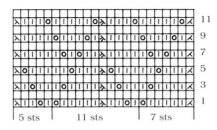

5 sts   11 sts   7 sts

	= k 1
O	= yarn over
⋀	= k 2 tog
⋋	= slip 1, k 1, psso
⋏	= double dec
□	= p 1

to *, ending last repeat with slip 1, k 1, psso.

Row 11: K 2 tog, * yo, k 5, yo, k 3, double decrease *; repeat from * to *, ending last repeat with slip 1, k 1, psso.

Repeat Rows 1 through 12 for pattern.

Lace wedges

Work with a multiple of 13 stitches, plus 2.

Row 1: K 1, * yarn over (yo), k 2, slip 1, k 1, pass slip st over k st and drop it (psso), k 4, k 2 sts together (k 2 tog), k 2, yo, k 1 *; repeat from * to *, ending last repeat with k 2.

Row 2 and all even-numbered rows: Purl.

Row 3: K 2, * yo, k 2, slip 1, k 1, psso, k 2, k 2 tog, k 2, yo, k 3 *; repeat from * to *.

Row 5: K 3, * yo, k 2, slip 1, k 1, psso, k 2, k 2 tog, k 2, yo, k 5 *; repeat from * to *, ending with k 4.

Row 7: K 3, * yo, k 2, slip 1, k 1, psso, k 4, k 2 tog, k 2, yo, k 1 *; repeat from * to *, ending with k 8.

Row 9: K 4, * yo, k 2, slip 1, k 1, psso, k 2, k 2 tog, k 2, yo, k 3 *; repeat from * to *, ending with yo, k 1.

Row 11: K 5, * yo, k 2, slip 1, k 1, psso, k 2 tog, k 2, yo, k 5 *; repeat from * to *, ending with k 2.

Repeat Rows 1 through 12 for pattern.

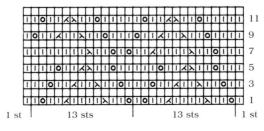

1 st   13 sts   13 sts   1 st

	= k 1
O	= yarn over
⋋	= slip 1, k 1, psso
⋀	= k 2 tog
□	= p 1

CREATIVE STITCHES

Darts

Work with a multiple of 4 stitches, plus 3.

Rows 1, 3, 7, and 11: P 3, * k 1, p 3 *; repeat from * to *.

Row 2 and all even-numbered rows: Work each stitch as it appears on this side of work (k the k sts and p the p sts). Purl long sts, and work twisted p st (p in back loop) over twisted sts of previous row.

Rows 5, 9, and 13: K 3, * work long st as follows: insert needle in corresponding st 3 rows below next st and k 1, drop unworked st above from left needle, letting sts unravel behind long st, p 3 *; repeat from * to *.

Row 15: P 3, * k 1 in back loop for twisted st, p 3 *; repeat from * to *.
Repeat Rows 3 through 16 for pattern.

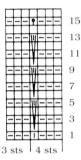

− = p 1

⋎ = 1 long st

φ = 1 twisted k st

☐ = 1 st as shown

3 sts | 4 sts

Staid columns

Work with a multiple of 8 stitches, plus 5.

Row 1: P 1, work (k in back loop of next st for twisted k st) 3 times, * p 2, work bobble on 1 st as follows: purl, knit, purl, knit, purl, and knit in back loop all in next st, then one by one, pass first 5 bobble sts over last one and drop them to complete bobble, p 2, k 3 twisted sts *; repeat from * to *, ending p 1.

Rows 2 and 4: Work each stitch as it appears on this side of work (k the k sts and p the p sts), and work twisted p st (p in back loop) over twisted sts of previous row.

Row 3: P 1, k 3 twisted sts, * p 5, k 3 twisted sts *; repeat from * to *, ending p 1.
Repeat Rows 1 through 4 for pattern.

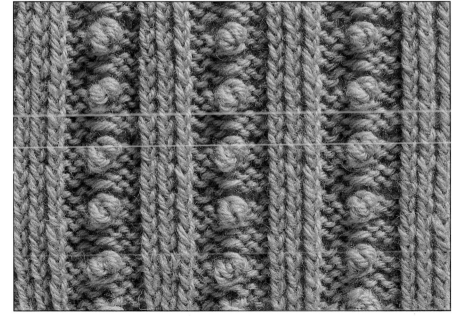

− = p 1

φ = 1 twisted k st

● = bobble

☐ = 1 st as shown

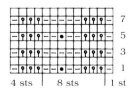

4 sts | 8 sts | 1 st

CREATIVE STITCHES

Winding trail

Work with a multiple of 7 stitches, plus 2.

Rows 1, 3, and 5: K 2, * yarn over (yo), k 1, yo, k 2 sts together through back loops, k 2 sts together (k 2 tog), k 2 *; repeat from * to *.

Row 2 and all even-numbered rows: Purl.

Rows 7, 9, and 11: K 2, * k 2 tog in back loops, k 2 tog, yo, k 1, yo, p 2 *; repeat from * to *.

Repeat Rows 1 through 12 for pattern.

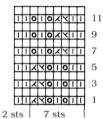

| = k 1
O = yarn over
X = k 2 tog in back loops
X = k 2 tog
□ = p 1

2 sts | 7 sts

Textured knit stitch

Work with a multiple of 5 stitches, plus 3.

Row 1: K 3, * work knot on 3 sts as follows: k 3 sts together through back loops, retaining them on left needle, yarn over and k 3 sts together again, drop original sts from left needle, k 2 *; repeat from * to *.

Row 2 and all even-numbered rows: Purl.

Row 3: K 2, * work knot, k 2 *; repeat from * to *, ending last repeat with k 3.

Row 5: K 1, * work knot, k 2 *; repeat from * to *, ending last repeat with k 4.

Row 7: K 5, * work knot, k 2 *; repeat from * to *, ending last repeat with k 5.

Row 9: K 4, * work knot, k 2 *; repeat from * to *, ending last repeat with k 1.

Repeat Rows 1 through 10 for pattern.

| = k 1
⌃ = 1 knot
□ = p 1

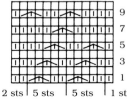

2 sts | 5 sts | 5 sts | 1 st

194

CREATIVE STITCHES

Little mushrooms

Work with a multiple of 6 stitches, plus 1.

Row 1: K 1, * p 2, k 1 *; repeat from * to *.

Rows 2, 8, and 14: P 1, * k 2, p 1 *; repeat from * to *.

Row 3: K 1, * p 2, work knit, purl, knit, and purl all in next st (4 sts worked in 1 st), p 2, k 1 *; repeat from * to *.

Rows 4 and 6: P 1, * k 8, p 1 *; repeat from * to *.

Row 5: K 1, * p 2, k 4, p 2, k 1 *; repeat from * to *.

Row 7: K 1, * p 2, k 4 sts together, p 2, k 1 *; repeat from * to *.

Row 9: Work 4 sts in 1 st as before, * p 2, k 1, p 2, work 4 sts in 1 st *; repeat from * to *.

Rows 10 and 12: K 6, * p 1, k 8 *; repeat from * to *, ending last repeat with k 6.

Row 11: K 4, * p 2, k 1, p 2, k 4 *; repeat from * to *.

Row 13: K 4 sts together, * p 2, k 1, p 2, k 4 sts together *; repeat from * to *.

Repeat Rows 3 through 14 for pattern.

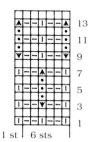

	= k 1
−	= p 1
Ⅴ	= work 4 sts in 1 st
●	= k 4 sts
∧	= k 4 tog
□	= 1 st as shown

Banded columns

Work with a multiple of 6 stitches, plus 2.

Rows 1 and 3 (wrong side): K 2, * p 4, k 2 *; repeat from * to *.

Rows 2 and 4: P 2, * k 4, p 2 *; repeat from * to *.

Row 5: K 2, * work 4 long sts by wrapping yarn twice around needle to purl each st, k 2 *; repeat from * to *.

Row 6: P 2, * k 4 long sts, sliding extra loop for each st off left needle without working it, p 2 *; repeat from * to *.

Repeat these 6 rows for pattern.

	= k 1
−	= p 1
ꙅ	= 1 long st
□	= 1 st as shown

CREATIVE STITCHES

Puffs

Start work with a multiple of 4 stitches, plus 2.

Row 1: P 2, * work knit, yarn over, knit, yarn over, and knit all in next st (5 sts worked in 1 st), work 5 sts in following st, p 2 *; repeat from * to *.

Row 2: K 2, * work 10 long sts by wrapping yarn twice around needle to knit each st, k 2 *; repeat from * to *.

Row 3: P 2, * work (slip 5 long sts to right needle dropping extra loop from each, return these 5 long sts to left needle and k all 5 sts together through back loops) twice, p 2 *; repeat from * to *.

Row 4: Knit.

Row 5: P 1, * work 5 sts in 1 st, p 2, work 5 sts in next st *; repeat from * to *, ending p 1.

Row 6: K 1, * work 5 long sts, k 2, work 5 long sts *; repeat from * to *, ending k 1.

Row 7: P 1, * slip and k 5 sts together as before, p 2, slip and k 5 sts together *; repeat from * to *, ending p 1.

Row 8: Knit.

Repeat these 8 rows for pattern.

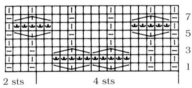

2 sts | 4 sts

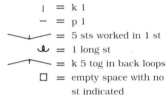

| = k 1
− = p 1
= 5 sts worked in 1 st
= 1 long st
= k 5 tog in back loops
□ = empty space with no st indicated

Canoes

Work with a multiple of 10 sts, plus 5.

Rows 1 through 4: Work in stockinette st (k 1 row, p 1 row).

Row 5: K 5, * work 2 long sts, wrapping yarn twice around needle to knit each st; work 1 double long st, wrapping 3 times to knit it; work 2 more long sts, k 5 *; repeat from * to *.

Row 6: Purl, letting extra loop for long sts and 2 extra loops for double long st slide from needle without working them.

Rows 7 through 10: Work in stockinette st.

Row 11: K 2, * work 1 double long st, 2 long sts, k 5, work 2 long sts *; repeat from * to *, ending with double long st, k 2.

Row 12: Repeat Row 6.

Repeat these 12 rows for pattern.

| = k 1
⎮ = 1 long st
= 1 double long st
□ = p 1 (dropping extra loops for any long sts)

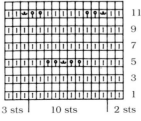

3 sts | 10 sts | 2 sts

LACE STITCHES

Passionflower

Work with a multiple of 17 stitches.
Row 1: K 3, * k 2 sts together (k 2 tog), k 3, yarn over (yo), k 1, yo, k 3, slip 1, k 1, pass slip st over k st and drop it (psso), k 6 *; repeat from * to *, ending last repeat with k 3.
Row 2 and all even-numbered rows: Purl.
Row 3: K 2, * k 2 tog, work (k 3, yo) twice, k 3, slip 1, k 1, psso, k 4 *; repeat from * to *, ending with k 2.
Row 5: K 1, * k 2 tog, k 3, yo, k 5, yo, k 3, slip 1, k 1, psso, k 2 *; repeat from * to *, ending with k 1.
Row 7: * K 2 tog, k 3, yo, k 7, yo, k 3, slip 1, k 1, psso *; repeat from * to *.
Repeat Rows 1 through 8 for pattern.

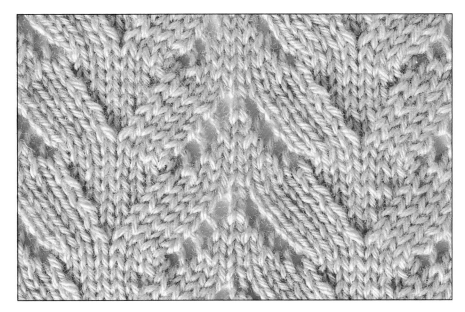

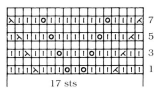

17 sts

$^|$ = k 1
o = yarn over
⋋ = k 2 tog
⋌ = slip 1, k 1, psso
□ = p 1

Bouquet

Work with a multiple of 12 stitches, plus 3.
Row 1: K 5, * yarn over (yo), k 2 sts together (k 2 tog), k 1, slip 1, k 1, pass slip st over k st and drop it (psso), yo, k 7 *; repeat from * to *, ending last repeat with k 5.
Row 2 and all even-numbered rows: Purl.
Row 3: K 4, * yo, k 2 tog, yo, k 3 tog, yo, slip 1, k 1, psso, yo, k 5 *; repeat from * to *, ending last repeat with k 4.
Row 5: K 3, * yo, k 2 tog, k 1, yo, k 3 tog, yo, k 1, slip 1, k 1, psso, yo, k 3 *; repeat from * to *.
Row 7: K 2, * yo, k 2 tog, k 2, yo, k 3 tog, yo, k 2, slip 1, k 1, psso, yo, k 1 *; repeat from * to *, ending last repeat with k 2.
Repeat Rows 1 through 8 for pattern.

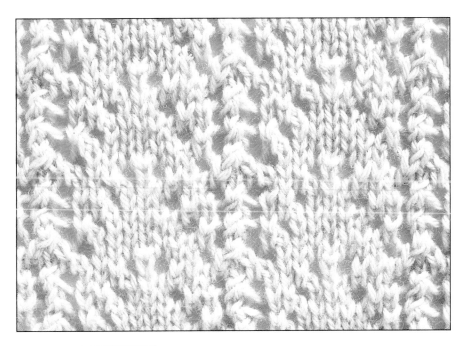

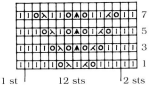

1 st   12 sts   2 sts

$^|$ = k 1
o = yarn over
⋋ = k 2 tog
⋌ = slip 1, k 1, psso
▲ = k 3 tog
□ = p 1

LACE STITCHES

Four-leaf clover

Work with a multiple of 10 stitches, plus 2.

Rows 1 and 5: K 1 for selvage, * k 5, yarn over (yo), slip 1, k 1, pass slip st over k st and drop it (psso), k 1, k 2 sts together (k 2 tog), yo, *; repeat from * to *, ending k 1 for selvage.

Row 2 and all even-numbered rows: Purl.

Row 3: K 2, * yo, k 3 tog, yo, k 1, k 2 tog, yo, k 1, yo, slip 1, k 1, psso, k 1 *; repeat from * to *.

Rows 7 and 15: Knit.

Rows 9 and 13: K 1, * k 2 tog, yo, k 1, yo, slip 1, k 1, psso, k 5 *; repeat from * to *, ending last repeat with k 6.

Row 11: K 1, * yo, slip 1, k 1, psso, k 1, k 2 tog, yo, k 1, yo, k 3 tog, yo, k 1 *; repeat from * to *, ending last repeat with k 2.

Repeat Rows 1 through 12 for pattern.

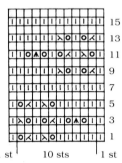

```
I = k 1
o = yarn over
ʎ = k 2 tog
ʌ = slip 1, k 1, psso
ʌ = k 3 tog
□ = = p 1
```

Maple leaf

Work with a multiple of 8 stitches, plus 2.

Row 1: K 1, * yarn over (yo), k 2 sts together through back loops, k 1, k 2 sts together (k 2 tog), yo, k 3 *; repeat from * to *, ending last repeat with k 4.

Row 2 and all even-numbered rows: Purl.

Row 3: K 5, * yo, k 2 tog in back loops, k 1, k 2 tog, yo, k 3 *; repeat from * to *, ending with yo, k 2 tog in back loops, k 3.

Row 5: K 6, * yo, work double decrease on 3 sts as follows: slip 1, k 2 tog, pass slip st over k st and drop it, yo, k 5 *; repeat from * to *, ending last repeat with k 1.

Row 7: K 1, * k 2 tog, yo, k 1, yo, k 2 tog in back loops, k 3 *; repeat from * to *, ending last repeat with k 4.

Row 9: * K 2 tog, yo, k 3, yo, k 2 tog in back loops, k 1 *; repeat from * to *, ending last repeat with k 3.

Row 11: K 1, * yo, k 2 tog in back loops, k 1, k 2 tog, yo, k 3 *; repeat from * to *, ending last repeat with k 4.

Row 13: K 2, * yo, double decrease,

yo, k 5 *; repeat from * to *.

Row 15: K 5, * k 2 tog, yo, k 1, yo, k 2 tog in back loops, k 3 *; repeat from * to *, ending with k 2 tog, yo, k 3.

Repeat Rows 1 through 16 for pattern.

```
I = k 1
□ = p 1
o = yarn over
ʎ = k 2 tog
ʌ = k 2 tog in back loops
ʌ = double dec
```

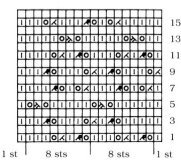

LACE STITCHES

Lace ribbing

Work with a multiple of 3 stitches, plus 2 for selvages.

Row 1: K 1 (selvage), * p 1, k 2 sts together, yarn over * repeat from * to *, ending k 1 (selvage).

Row 2: P 3, * k 1, p 2 *; repeat from * to *; ending k 1, p 1.

Repeat these 2 rows for pattern.

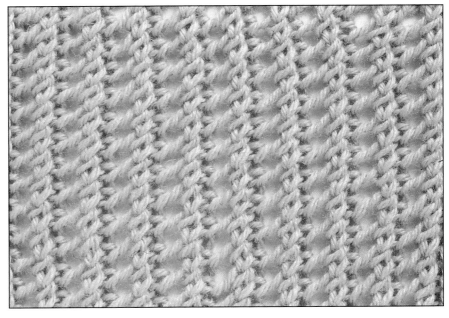

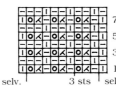

ı = k 1
– = p 1
⋌ = k 2 tog

o = yarn over

selv.   3 sts   selv.

Lace zigzag

Work with a multiple of 5 stitches, plus 1.

Row 1: * P 3, k 2 sts together (k 2 tog), yarn over (yo) *; repeat from * to *, ending p in last st.

Row 2 and all even-numbered rows: Work each stitch as it appears on this side of work (k the k sts and p the p sts). Knit yarn-over loops.

Row 3: P 2, * k 2 tog, yo, p 3 *; repeat from * to *, ending last repeat with p 2.

Row 5: P 1, * k 2 tog, yo, p 3 *; repeat from * to *.

Row 7: P 1, * yo, slip 1, k 1, pass slip st over k st and drop it (psso), p 3 *; repeat from * to *.

Row 9: P 2, * yo, slip 1, k 1, psso, p 3 *; repeat from * to *, ending last repeat with p 2.

Row 11: P 3, * yo, slip 1, k 1, psso, p 3 *; repeat from * to *, ending yo, slip 1, k 1, psso, p 1.

Repeat Rows 1 through 12 for pattern.

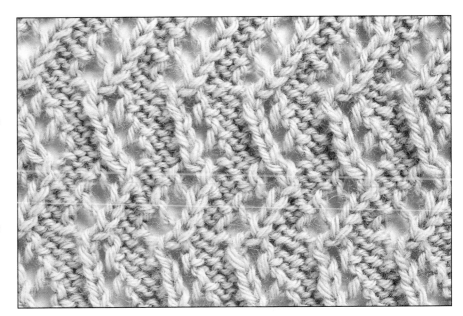

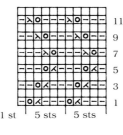

– = p 1
⋌ = k 2 tog

o = yarn over
⋋ = slip 1, k 1, psso
□ = 1 st as shown

1 st   5 sts   5 sts

LACE STITCHES

Rows of eyelets

Work with an even number of stitches.

Row 1: K 1, * k 2 sts together (k 2 tog), yarn over (yo) *; repeat from * to *, ending k in last st.
Row 2: Purl.
Row 3: K 1, * yo, k 2 tog *; repeat from * to *, ending k in last st.
Rows 4 and 5: Purl.
Row 6: Knit.
Row 7: K 1, * yo, slip 1, k 1, pass slip st over k st and drop it (psso) *; repeat from * to *, ending k in last st.
Row 8: Purl.
Row 9: K 1, * slip 1, k 1, psso, yo *; repeat from * to *, ending k in last st.
Rows 10 and 11: Purl.
Row 12: Knit.
Repeat these 12 rows for pattern.

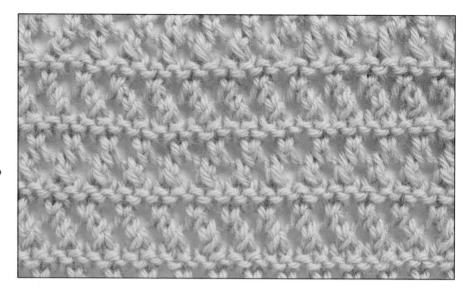

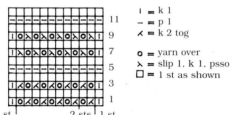

I = k 1
— = p 1
ʎ = k 2 tog

o = yarn over
ʎ = slip 1, k 1, psso
□ = 1 st as shown

Little squares

Work with a multiple of 8 stitches, plus 3.

Rows 1, 3, and 5: K 3, * k 2 sts together, yarn over (yo), k 1, yo, slip 1, k 1, pass slip st over k st and drop it (psso), p 3 *; repeat from * to *.
Row 2 and all even-numbered rows: Work each stitch as it appears on this side of work (k the k sts and p the p sts). Purl yarn-over loops.
Rows 7, 9, and 11: K 2, * yo, slip 1, k 1, psso, p 3, k 2 sts together, yo k 1 *; repeat from * to *, ending last repeat with k 2.
Repeat Rows 1 through 12 for pattern.

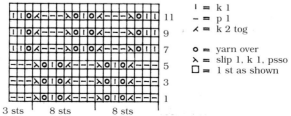

I = k 1
— = p 1
ʎ = k 2 tog

o = yarn over
ʎ = slip 1, k 1, psso
□ = 1 st as shown

LACE STITCHES

Lacy diagonals

Work with a multiple of 3 stitches, plus 2.
Row 1: K 2, * yarn over (yo), slip 1, k 1, pass slip st over k st and drop it (psso), k 1 *; repeat from * to *.
Row 2 and all even-numbered rows: Purl.
Row 3: K 3, * yo, slip 1, k 1, psso, k 1 *; repeat from * to *, ending last repeat with k 3.
Row 5: K 1, * yo, slip 1, k 1, psso, k 1 *; repeat from * to *, ending last repeat with k 2.
Repeat Rows 1 through 6 for pattern.

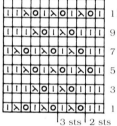

I = k 1
O = yarn over
λ = slip 1, k 1, psso
□ = p 1

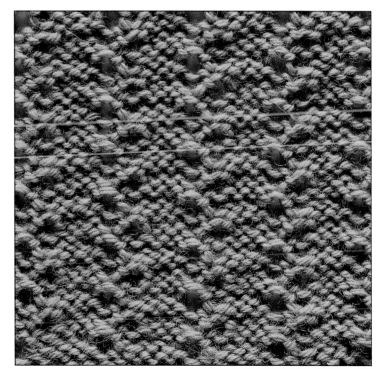

Vertical eyelets

Work with a multiple of 5 stitches, plus 3.
Row 1: P 3, * p 2 sts together, yarn over, p 3 *; repeat from * to *.
Row 2: Knit.
Row 3: P 3, * yarn over, p 2 sts together, p 3 *; repeat from * to *.
Row 4: Knit.
Repeat these 4 rows for pattern.

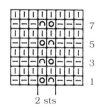

2 sts

I = k 1
− = p 1
∩ = p 2 tog
o = yarn over

LACE STITCHES

Open and closed fans

Work with a multiple of 9 stitches, plus 2.

Row 1: K 2, * yarn over (yo), k 2, slip 1, k 1, pass slip st over k st and drop it (psso), k 2 sts together, k 2, yo, k 1 *; repeat from * to *.

Row 2: Purl.

Row 3: K 1, * yo, k 2, slip 1, k 1, psso, k 2 sts together, k 2, yo, k 1 *; repeat from * to *, ending last repeat with k 2.

Row 4: Purl.

Repeat these 4 rows for pattern.

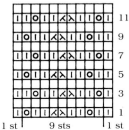

| = k 1
o = yarn over
⅄ = slip 1, k 1, psso
□ = p 1

Lacy points

Work with a multiple of 12 stitches, plus 1.

Row 1: Knit.

Row 2 and all even-numbered rows: Purl.

Row 3: * K 7, yarn over (yo), slip 1, k 1, pass slip st over k st and drop it (psso), k 1, k 2 sts together, yo *; repeat from * to *, ending k in last st.

Row 5: K 8, * yo, work double decrease on 3 sts as follows: slip 1, k 2 sts together, psso, yo, k 9 *; repeat from * to *, ending last repeat with k 2.

Row 7: Knit.

Row 9: K 1, * yo, slip 1, k 1, psso, k 1, k 2 sts together, yo, k 7 *; repeat from * to *.

Row 11: K 2, * yo, double decrease, yo, k 9 *; repeat from * to *, ending last repeat with k 8.

Repeat Rows 1 through 12 for pattern.

| = k 1
o = yarn over
⅄ = slip 1, k 1, psso
⋌ = k 2 tog
⅄ = double dec
□ = p 1

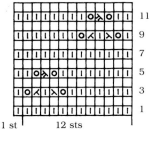

LACE STITCHES

Diamond strips

Work with a multiple of 20 stitches, plus 1.

Row 1: P 1, * k 2, yarn over (yo), slip 1, k 1, pass slip st over k st and drop it (psso), k 1, k 2 sts together (k 2 tog), yo, k 2, p 1, k 3, yo, k 3 tog, yo, k 3, p 1 *; repeat from * to *.

Row 2 and all even-numbered rows: Work each stitch as it appears on this side of work (k the k sts and p the p sts). Purl yarn-over loops.

Row 3: P 1, * k 3, yo, k 3 tog, yo, k 3, p 1, k 2, yo, slip 1, k 1, psso, k 1, k 2 tog, yo, k 2, p 1 *; repeat from * to *.

Row 5: P 1, * k 3, yo, k 3 tog, yo, k 3, p 1, k 1, yo, slip 1, k 1, psso, k 3, k 2 tog, yo, k 1, p 1 *; repeat from * to *.

Row 7: P 1, * k 2, yo, slip 1, k 1, psso, k 1, k 2 tog, yo, k 2, p 1 *; repeat from * to *.

Row 9: P 1, * k 1, yo, slip 1, k 1, psso, k 3, k 2 tog, yo, k 1, p 1, k 3, yo, k 3 tog, yo, k 3, p 1 *; repeat from * to *.

Repeat Rows 1 through 10 for pattern.

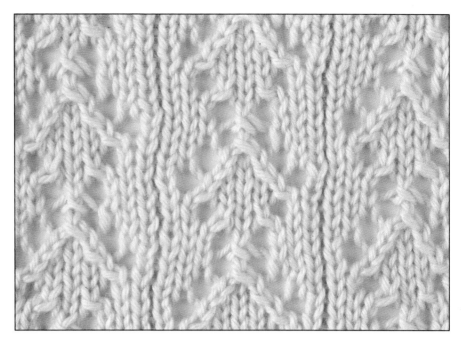

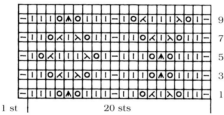

⎮	= k 1
–	= p 1
O	= arn over
⋌	= k 2 tog
⋋	= slip 1, k 1, psso
⋀	= k 3 tog
☐	= 1 st as shown

1 st   20 sts

Little lace strips

Work with a multiple of 6 stitches, plus 2.

Row 1: P 2, * k 2 sts together, yarn over twice, slip 1, k 1, pass slip st over k st and drop it, p 2 *; repeat from * to *.

Row 2: K 2, * p 1, k 1, p 2, k 2 *; repeat from * to *.

Row 3: P 2, * k 4, p 2 *; repeat from * to *.

Row 4: K 2, * p 4, k 2 *; repeat from * to *.

Repeat these 4 rows for pattern.

⎮	= k 1
–	= p 1
O	= yarn over
⋌	= k 2 tog
⋋	= slip 1, k 1, psso

2 sts   6 sts

LACE STITCHES

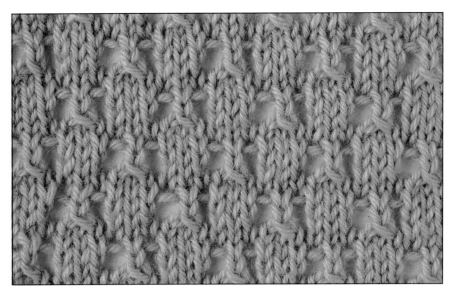

Lacy lozenges

Work with a multiple of 6 stitches, plus 2.

Row 1: Knit.

Row 2 and all even-numbered rows: Work each stitch as it appears on this side of work (k the k sts and p the p sts). Knit yarn-over loops.

Row 3: K 4, * yarn over (yo), work double decrease on 3 sts as follows: slip 1, k 2 sts together, pass slip st over k st and drop it, yo, k 3 *; repeat from * to *, ending last repeat with k 1.

Row 5: Knit.

Row 7: K 1, * yo, double decrease, yo, k 3 *; repeat from * to *, ending last repeat with k 4.

Repeat Rows 1 through 8 for pattern.

| | = k 1
| − = p 1
| o = yarn over
| ⋏ = double dec

1 st   6 sts   1 st

Horseshoe pattern

Work with a multiple of 10 stitches, plus 1.

Rows 1 and 3: K 1, * yarn over (yo), k 2 sts together (k 2 tog), k 5, slip 1, k 1, pass slip st over k st and drop it (psso), yo, k 1 *; repeat from * to *.

Row 2 and all even-numbered rows: Purl.

Row 5: K 1, * yo, k 3, work double decrease on 3 sts as follows: slip 1, k 2 tog, psso, k 3, yo, k 1 *; repeat from * to *.

Row 7: K 2, * yo, k 2, double decrease, k 2, yo, k 3 *; repeat from * to *, ending last repeat with k 2.

Row 9: K 3, * yo, k 1, double decrease, k 1, yo, k 5 *; repeat from * to *, ending last repeat with k 3.

Row 11: K 4, * yo, double decrease, yo, k 7 *; repeat from * to *, ending last repeat with k 4.

Repeat Rows 1 through 12 for pattern.

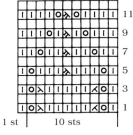

| = k 1
− = p 1
o = yarn over
⋏ = k 2 tog
⋌ = slip 1, k 1, psso
⋏ = double dec
□ = 1 st as shown

1 st   10 sts

LACE STITCHES

Lacy chevrons

Work with a multiple of 9 sts.
Row 1: K 4, * yarn over (yo), slip 1, k 1, pass slip st over k st and drop it (psso), k 7 *; repeat from * to *, ending last repeat with k 3.
Row 2 and all even-numbered rows: Purl.
Row 3: K 2, * k 2 sts together, yo, k 1, yo, slip 1, k 1, psso, k 4 *; repeat from * to *, ending last repeat with k 2.
Row 5: K 1, * k 2 sts together, yo, k 3, yo, slip 1, k 1, psso, k 2 *; repeat from * to *, ending last repeat with k 1.
Row 7: * K 2 sts together, yo, k 5, yo, slip 1, k 1, psso *; repeat from * to *.
Repeat Rows 1 through 8 for pattern.

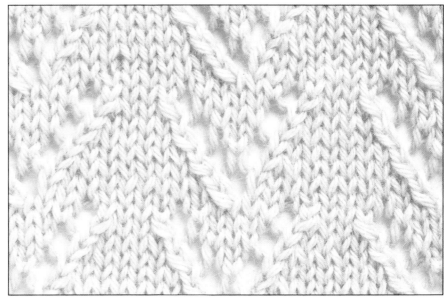

| = k 1
o = yarn over
< = k 2 tog
λ = slip 1, k 1, psso
□ = p 1

| = k 1
− = p 1
o = yarn over
< = k 2 tog
λ = slip 1, k 1, psso
□ = 1 st as shown

Thick and thin zigzags

Work with a multiple of 9 stitches, plus 2.
Row 1: P 3, * k 2 sts together (k 2 tog), yarn over (yo), k 1, k 2 tog, yo, p 4 *; repeat from * to *, ending last repeat with p 3.
Row 2 and all even-numbered rows: Work each stitch as it appears on this side of work (k the k sts and p the p sts). Purl yarn-over loops.
Row 3: P 2, * k 2 tog, yo, k 1, k 2 tog, yo, p 4 *; repeat from * to *.
Row 5: P 1, * k 2 tog, yo, k 1, k 2 tog, yo, p 4 *; repeat from * to *, ending k in last st.
Row 7: P 3, * yo, slip 1, k 1, pass slip st over k st and drop it (psso), k 1, yo, slip 1, k 1, psso, p 4 *; repeat from * to *, ending last repeat with p 3.
Row 9: P 4, * yo, slip 1, k 1, psso, k 1, yo, slip 1, k 1, psso, p 4 *; repeat from * to *, ending last repeat with p 2.
Row 11: P 5, * yo, slip 1, k 1, psso, k 1, yo, slip 1, k 1, psso, p 4 *; repeat from * to *, ending k in last st.
Repeat Rows 1 through 12 for pattern.

LACE STITCHES

Streams

Work with a multiple of 9 stitches,
plus 2.
Row 1: P 2, * k 1, p 1, slip 1, k 1,
pass slip st over k st and drop it
(psso), yarn over (yo), k 3, p 2 *;
repeat from * to *.
Row 2 and all even-numbered rows:
Work each stitch as it appears on this
side of work (k the k sts and p the p
sts). Purl yarn-over loops.
Row 3: P 2, * k 1, p 2, slip 1, k 1,
psso, yo, k 2, p 2 *; repeat from
* to *.
Row 5: P 2, * k 1, p 3, slip 1, k 1,
psso, yo, k 1, p 2 *; repeat from
* to *.
Row 7: P 2, * k 3, yo, k 2 sts together, p 1, k 1, p 2 *; repeat from * to *.
Row 9: P 2, * k 2, yo, k 2 sts together, p 2, k 1, p 2 *; repeat from * to *.
Row 11: P 2, * k 1, yo, k 2 tog, p 3,
k 1, p 2 *; repeat from * to *.
Repeat Rows 1 through 12 for
pattern.

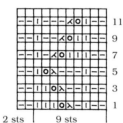

l = k 1
− = p 1
o = yarn over
λ = slip 1, k 1, psso
⟨ = k 2 tog
□ = 1 st as shown

Acorns

Work with a multiple of 6 stitches,
plus 2.
Rows 1 and 3: K 4, * p 3, k 3 *;
repeat from * to *, ending last repeat
with k 1.
Row 2 and all even-numbered rows:
Work each stitch as it appears on this
side of work (k the k sts and p the p
sts). Knit yarn-over loops.
Row 5: K 1, * yarn over (yo), k 3 sts
together, yo, k 3 *; repeat * to *, ending last repeat with k 4.
Row 7: K 1, * p 3, k 3 *; repeat from
* to *, ending last repeat with k 4.
Row 9: K 4, * yo, k 3 sts together, yo,
k 3 *; repeat from * to *, ending last
repeat with k 1.
Repeat Rows 3 through 10 for pattern.

l = k 1
− = p 1
o = yarn over
▲ = k 3 tog
□ = 1 st as shown

206

LACE STITCHES

Zigzag pattern

Work with a multiple of 9 stitches, plus 6.

Rows 1, 3, 5, and 7: K 4, * slip 1, k 1, pass slip st over k st and drop it (psso), k 2 sts together, k 2, yarn over (yo), k 1, yo, k 2 *; repeat from * to *, ending last repeat with k 4.

Row 2 and all even-numbered rows: Purl.

Rows 9, 11, 13, and 15: K 4, * yo, k 1, yo, k 2, slip 1, k 1, psso, k 2 sts together, k 2 *; repeat from * to *, ending last repeat with k 4.

Repeat Rows 1 through 16 for pattern.

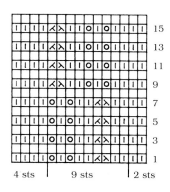

4 sts   9 sts   2 sts

ı = k 1
□ = p 1
o = yarn over
⅄ = slip 1, k 1, psso
⋌ = k 2 tog

Alternating motifs

Work with a multiple of 6 stitches, plus 2.

Rows 1, 3, 5 , and 7: K 1, * yarn over (yo), work double decrease on 3 sts as follows: slip 1, k 2 sts together, pass slip st over k st and drop it, yo, k 3 *; repeat from * to *, ending last repeat with k 4.

Row 2 and all even-numbered rows: Purl.

Rows 9, 11, 13, and 15: K 4, * yo, double decrease, yo, k 3 *; repeat from * to *, ending last repeat with k 1.

Repeat Rows 1 through 16 for pattern.

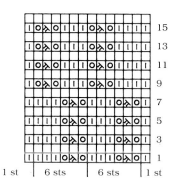

1 st   6 sts   6 sts   1 st

ı = k 1
□ = p 1
o = yarn over
⅄ = double dec

LACE STITCHES

Lace thorns

Work with a multiple of 4 stitches, plus 2.

Row 1: K 3, * yarn over, slip 1, k 1, pass slip st over k st and drop it, k 2 *; repeat from * to *, ending last repeat with k 1.

Row 2: K 1, * p 2, yo, p 2 sts together *; repeat from * to *, ending k in last st.

Repeat these 2 rows for pattern.

ı = k 1
‐ = p 1
o = yarn over
⅄ = slip 1, k 1, psso
∩ = p 2 tog

Easy lace

Work with a multiple of 3 stitches, plus 2.

Row 1: K 2, * yarn over, k 2 sts together, k 1 *; repeat from * to *.

Row 2: P 2, * k 1, p 2 *; repeat from * to *.

Row 3: K 2, * k 2 sts together, yarn over, k 1 *; repeat from * to *.

Row 4: P 1, * k 1, p 2 *; repeat from * to *, ending k 1, p in last 3 sts.

Repeat Rows 1 through 4 for pattern.

ı = k 1
‐ = p 1
o = yarn over
⅄ = k 2 tog

LACE STITCHES

Scattered eyelets

Start work with a multiple of 4 stitches.

Row 1: K 4, * yarn over twice, k 4 *; repeat from * to *.

Row 2: P 2, p 2 sts together, p 1, k 1, * work p 2 sts together twice, p 1, k 1 *; repeat from * to *, ending p 2 sts together, p last 2 sts.

Row 3: K 2, yarn over, * k 4, yarn over twice *; repeat from * to *, ending k 4, yarn over once, k last 2 sts.

Row 4: P 3, * work p 2 sts together twice, p 1, k 1 *; repeat from * to *, ending last repeat with p 3.

Repeat these 4 rows for pattern.

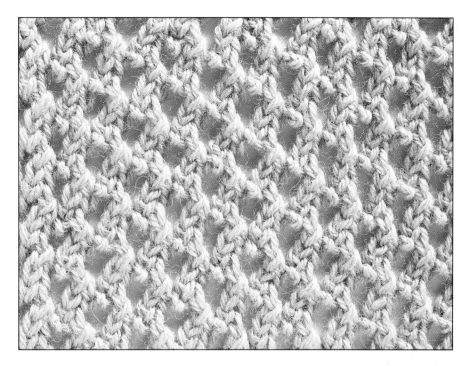

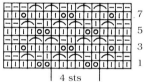

| = k 1
− = p 1
O = yarn over
⌒ = p 2 tog

Overlapping waves

Work with a multiple of 6 stitches, plus 4.

Row 1: K 2, * yarn over (yo), slip 1, k 1, pass slip st over k st and drop it (psso), k 4 *; repeat from * to *, ending yo, slip 1, k 1, psso.

Row 2 and all even-numbered rows: Purl.

Row 3: K 2, * yo, k 1, slip 1, k 1, psso, k 3 *; repeat from * to *, ending yo, slip 1, k 1, psso.

Row 5: K 2, * yo, k 2, slip 1, k 1, psso, k 2 *; repeat from * to *, ending yo, slip 1, k 1, psso.

Row 7: K 2, * yo, k 3, slip 1, k 1, psso, k 1 *; repeat from * to *, ending yo, slip 1, k 1, psso.

Row 9: K 2, * yo, k 4, slip 1, k 1, psso *; repeat from * to *, ending yo, slip 1, k 1, psso.

Repeat Rows 1 through 10 for pattern.

| = k 1
O = yarn over
⋋ = slip 1, k 1, psso
□ = p 1

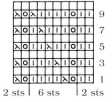

2 sts | 6 sts | 2 sts

LACE STITCHES

Plain and fancy

Work with a multiple of 12 stitches, plus 1.

Row 1: Knit.

Row 2 and all even-numbered rows: Purl.

Row 3: * K 6, yarn over (yo), k 1, slip 1, k 1, pass slip st over k st and drop it (psso), k 1, k 2 sts together, yo *; repeat from * to *, ending k in last st.

Row 5: * K 6, yo, k 2, work double decrease on 3 sts as follows: slip 1, k 2 sts together, psso, k 1, yo *; repeat from * to *, ending k in last st.

Row 7: Knit.

Row 9: K 1, * yo, slip 1, k 1, psso, k 1, k 2 sts together, k 1, yo, k 6 *; repeat from * to *.

Row 11: K 1, * yo, k 1, double decrease, k 2, yo, k 6 *; repeat from * to *.

Repeat Rows 1 through 12 for pattern.

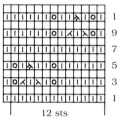

| = k 1
O = yarn over
⋋ = slip 1, k 1, psso
⋌ = k 2 tog
⅄ = double decrease
□ = p 1

12 sts

| = k 1
O = yarn over
⋋ = slip 1, k 1, psso
⋌ = k 2 tog
⋏ = double decrease
□ = p 1

1 st   10 sts

Steeples

Work with a multiple of 10 stitches, plus 1.

Rows 1 and 3: K 1, * yarn over (yo), slip 1, k 1, pass slip st over k st and drop it (psso), k 2 sts together (k 2 tog), yo, k 1, yo, slip 1, k 1, psso, k 2 tog, yo, k 1 *; repeat from * to *.

Row 2 and all even-numbered rows: Purl.

Row 5: K 1, * yo, slip 1, k 1, psso, k 5, k 2 tog, yo, k 1 *; repeat from * to *.

Row 7: K 2, * yo, slip 1, k 1, psso, k 3, k 2 tog, yo, k 3 *; repeat from * to *, ending last repeat with k 2.

Row 9: K 3, * yo, slip 1, k 1, psso, k 1, k 2 tog, yo, k 5 *; repeat from * to *, ending last repeat with k 3.

Row 11: K 4, * yo, work double decrease on 3 sts as follows: slip 2 as if to p, k 1, pass both slip sts over k st and drop them, yo, k 7 *; repeat from * to *, ending last repeat with k 4.

Repeat Rows 1 through 12 for pattern.

LACE STITCHES

Mountain peaks

Work with a multiple of 11 stitches.

Row 1: P 3, * k 2 sts together (k 2 tog), yarn over (yo), k 1, yo, slip 1, k 1, pass slip st over k st and drop it (psso), p 6 *; repeat from * to *, ending last repeat with p 3.

Row 2 and all even-numbered rows: Work each stitch as it appears on this side of work (k the k sts and p the p sts). Purl yarn-over loops.

Row 3: P 2, * k 2 tog, yo, k 3, yo, slip 1, k 1, psso, p 4 *; repeat from * to *, ending last repeat with p 2.

Row 5: P 1, * k 2 tog, yo, k 5, yo, slip 1, k 1, psso, p 2 *; repeat from * to *, ending last repeat with p 1.

Row 7: * K 2 tog, yo, k 1, yo, k 2 tog, k 1, slip 1, k 1, psso, yo, k 1, yo, slip 1, k 1, psso *; repeat from * to *.

Row 9: P 1, * slip 1, k 1, psso, yo, k 2 tog, yo, k 1, yo, slip 1, k 1 psso, yo, k 2 tog, p 2 *; repeat from * to *, ending last repeat with p 1.

Repeat Rows 3 through 10 for pattern.

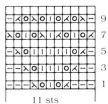

| = k 1
− = p 1
o = yarn over
⋋ = k 2 tog
⋌ = slip 1, k 1, psso
□ = 1 st as shown

11 sts

Larkspurs

Work with a multiple of 9 stitches, plus 2.

Row 1: K 2, * yarn over (yo), slip 1, k 1, pass slip st over k st and drop it (psso), k 3, k 2 sts together (k 2 tog), yo, k 2 *; repeat from * to *.

Row 2 and all even-numbered rows: Purl.

Row 3: K 2, * yo, k 1, slip 1, k 1, psso, k 1, k 2 tog, k 1, yo, k 2 *; repeat from * to *.

Row 5: K 3, * k 2 tog, yo, k 1, yo, slip 1, k 1, psso, k 4 *; repeat from * to *, ending last repeat with k 3.

Row 7: K 2, * k 2 tog, k 1, work (yo, k 1) twice, slip 1, k 1, psso, k 2 *; repeat from * to *.

Repeat Rows 1 through 8 for pattern.

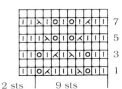

| = k 1
□ = p 1
o = yarn over
⋋ = k 2 tog
⋌ = slip 1, k 1, psso

2 sts | 9 sts

LACE STITCHES

Lace columns

Work with a multiple of 8 stitches, plus 1.

Row 1: P 1, * slip 1, k 1, pass slip st over k st and drop it, yarn over (yo), k 3, yo, k 2 sts together, p 1 *; repeat from * to *.

Rows 2 and 4: Work each stitch as it appears on this side of work (k the k and p the p sts). Knit yarn-over loops.

Row 3: P 1, * k 2, yo, work double decrease on 3 sts as follows: slip 2, slipping each st separately as if to k, k 1, pass both slip sts over k st and drop them, yo, k 2, p 1 *; repeat from * to *.

Repeat Rows 1 through 4 for pattern.

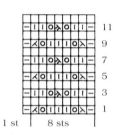

l = k 1
− = p 1
o = yarn over
⋋ = slip 1, k 1, psso
⋌ = k 2 tog
⋏ = double dec
□ = 1 st as shown

Lace triangles

Work with a multiple of 11 sts, plus 6.

Row 1: K 4, * yarn over (yo), slip 1, k 1, pass slip st over k st and drop it (psso), work (yo, slip 1, k 1, psso) 3 times more, k 3 *; repeat from * to *, ending last repeat with k 5.

Row 2 and all even-numbered rows: Purl.

Row 3: K 5, * work (yo, slip 1, k 1, psso) 3 times, k 5 *; repeat from * to * ending with k 6.

Row 5: K 6, * work (yo, slip 1, k 1, psso) twice, k 7 *; repeat from * to *.

Row 7: K 7, * yo, skip 1, k 1, psso, k 9 *; repeat from * to *, ending with k 8.

Row 9: K 1, work (yo, slip 1, k 1, psso) 3 times, * k 3, work (yo, slip 1, k 1, psso) 4 times *; repeat from * to *, ending last repeat with (yo, slip 1, k 1, psso) 3 times, k 1.

Row 11: K 2, work (yo, slip 1, k 1, psso) twice, * k 5, work (yo, slip 1, k 1, psso) 3 times *; repeat from * to *.

Row 13: K 1, * work (yo, slip 1, k 1, psso) twice, k 7 *; repeat from * to *, ending last repeat with k 1.

Row 15: K 2, * yo, slip 1, k 1, psso, k 9 *; repeat from * to *, ending last repeat with k 2.

Repeat Rows 1 through 16 for pattern.

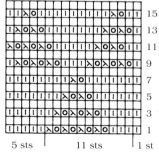

l = k 1
o = yarn over
⋋ = slip 1, k 1, psso
□ = p 1

212

LACE STITCHES

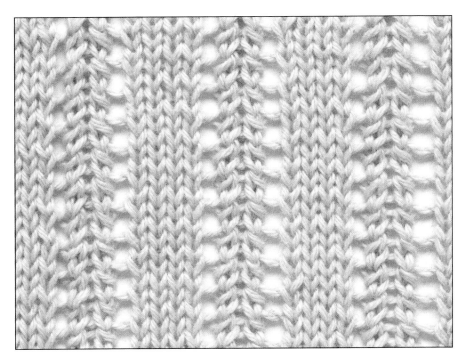

Vertical eyelet rows

Note: Chart shows only the 4 stitches for eyelet pattern.

Work pattern as shown in photograph with a multiple of 8 stitches, plus 4.

Row 1: Knit.

Row 2: Purl.

Row 3: K 4, * yarn over, slip 1, k 1, pass slip st over k st and drop it, k 2 sts together, yarn over, k 4 *; repeat from * to *.

Row 4: Purl.

Repeat these 4 rows for pattern.

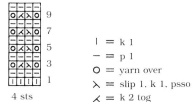

4 sts

| = k 1
− = p 1
O = yarn over
⋋ = slip 1, k 1, psso
⋌ = k 2 tog

Eyelets on the bias

Work a multiple of 9 stitches, plus 1.

Row 1: * P sts tpgether (p 3 tog), yarn over twice (yo twice), k 6 *; repeat from * to *, ending last repeat with k 7.

Row 2 and all even-numbered rows: Work each stitch as it appears on this side of work (k the k sts and p the p sts). On double yarn-over loops work k 1, p 1.

Row 3: K 1, * p 3 tog, yo twice, k 6 *; repeat from * to *.

Row 5: K 2, * p 3 tog, yo twice, k 6 *; repeat from * to *, ending last repeat with k 5.

Row 7: K 3, * p 3 tog, yo twice, k 6 *; repeat from * to *, ending with k 4.

Row 9: K 4, * p 3 tog, yo twice, k 6 *; repeat from * to *, ending with k 3.

Row 11: K 5, * p 3 tog, yo twice, k 6 *; repeat from * to *, ending with k 2.

Row 13: K 6, * p 3 tog, yo twice, k 6 *; repeat from * to *, ending k in last st.

Repeat Rows 1 through 14 for pattern.

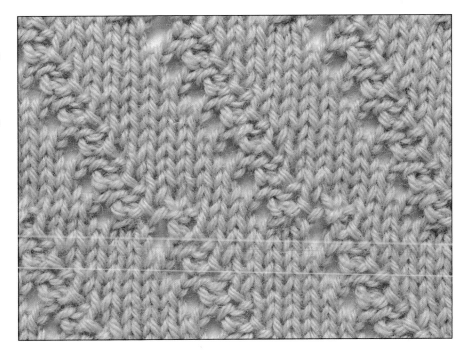

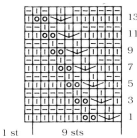

1 st   9 sts

| = k 1
− = p 1
O = yarn over
⋁ = p 3 tog

□ = empty space with no st indicated

LACE STITCHES

Light tulle

Work with an uneven number of stitches.
Row 1: Knit.
Row 2: * K 2 sts together, yarn over *; repeat from * to *, ending k in last st.
Repeat Row 2 for pattern.

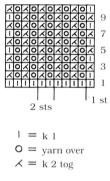

2 sts

1 st

| = k 1
O = yarn over
⋋ = k 2 tog

Kiwi

Start work with a multiple of 14 stitches, plus 1.
Row 1: K 1, * yarn over (yo), k 2 sts together, k 3 tog, work (yo, k 1) 3 times, yo, k 3 tog through back loops, slip 1, k 1, pass skip st over k st and drop it (psso), yo, k 1 *; repeat from * to *.
Row 2 and all even-numbered rows: Purl.
Row 3: K 1, * yo, k 3 tog, yo, k 7, yo, k 3 tog through back loops, yo, k 1 *; repeat from * to *.
Row 5: K 1, * yo, k 2 tog, yo, k 1, yo,

k 2, work double decrease on 3 sts as follows: slip 2 sts together as if to k, k 1, pass both slip sts over k st and drop them, k 2, yo, k 1, yo, slip 1, k 1, psso, yo, k 1 *; repeat from * to *.
Row 7: K 1, * yo, k 2 tog, yo, k 3, yo, k 1, double decrease, k 1, yo, k 3, yo, slip 1, k 1, psso, yo, k 1 *; repeat from * to *.
Row 9: K 1, * yo, k 2 tog twice, k 3, yo, double decrease, yo, k 3, work

(slip 1, k 1, psso) twice, yo, k 1 *; repeat from * to *.
Row 11: K 1, * yo, work (k 2 tog) 3 times, k 1, work (yo, k 1) twice, work (slip 1, k 1, psso) 3 times, yo, k 1 *; repeat from * to *.
Repeat Rows 1 through 12 for pattern.

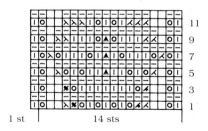

1 st   14 sts

| = k 1
− = p 1
O = yarn over
⋋ = k 2 tog
⋌ = k 3 tog
✖ = k 3 tog in back loops
⋋ = slip 1, k 1, psso
⋀ = double dec
□ = empty space with no st indicated

LACE STITCHES

Geometric forms

Work with a multiple of 7 stitches, plus 2.

Row 1: K 3, * k 2 sts together (k 2 tog), yarn over (yo), k 5 *; repeat from * to *, ending last repeat with k 4.

Row 2: K 1, p 1, * p 2 tog in back loops, yo, p 1, yo, p 2 tog, p 2 *; repeat from * to *, ending last repeat with p 1, k in last st.

Row 3: K 1, * k 2 tog, yo, k 3, yo, slip 1, k 1, pass slip st over k st and drop it (psso) *; repeat from * to *, ending with k in last st.

Row 4: Knit.

Row 5: K 1, * yo, slip 1, k 1, psso, k 5 *; repeat from * to *, ending with k 6.

Row 6: K 1, * yo, p 2 tog, p 2, p 2 tog through back loops, yo, p 1 *; repeat from * to *, ending with k last st.

Row 7: K 3, * yo, slip 1, k 1, psso, k 2 tog, yo, k 3 *; repeat from * to *, ending last repeat with k 2.

Row 8: Knit.

Repeat these 8 rows for pattern.

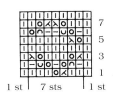

| = k 1
− = p 1
O = yarn over
⋋ = k 2 tog
⋌ = slip 1, k 1, psso
∩ = p 2 tog
∪ = p 2 tog in back loops

Leaves and lines

Work with a multiple of 12 stitches, plus 1.

Row 1: K 1, * p 11, k 1 *; repeat from * to *.

Rows 2, 4, 6, and 8: Work each stitch as it appears on this side of work (k the k sts and p the p sts). Purl yarn-over loops.

Row 3: K 1, * p 3, p 2 sts together (p 2 tog), yarn over (yo), k 1, yo, p 2 tog, p 3, k 1 *; repeat from * to *.

Row 5: K 1, * p 2, p 2 tog, yo, k 3, yo, p 2 tog, p 2, k 1 *; repeat from * to *.

Row 7: K 1, * p 1, p 2 tog, yo, k 5, yo, p 2 tog, p 1, k 1 *; repeat from * to *.

Row 9: K 1, * p 2 tog, yo, k 7, yo, p 2 tog, k 1 *; repeat from * to *.

Rows 10, 12, 14, 16 and 18: Continue to work each stitch as it appears, but now knit yarn-over loops.

Row 11: K 1, * p 2, yo, k 2, work double decrease on 3 sts as follows: slip 1, k 2 tog, pass slip st over k st and drop it, p 2, yo, p 2, k 1 *; repeat from * to *.

Row 13: K 1, * p 3, yo, k 1, double decrease, k 1, yo, p 3, k 1 *; repeat from * to *.

Row 15: K 1, * p 4, yo, double decrease, yo, p 4, k 1 *; repeat from * to *.

Row 17: Repeat Row 1.

Repeat Rows 1 through 18 for pattern.

| = k 1
− = p 1
O = yarn over
∩ = p 2 tog

⋋ = double dec

LACE STITCHES

Eyelet pattern

Work with a multiple of 12 stitches, plus 7.

Rows 1, 3, and 5: Purl.

Row 2 and all even-numbered rows: Knit.

Row 7: P 5, * p 2 sts together (p 2 tog), yarn over (yo), p 5, yo, p 2 tog, p 3 *; repeat from * to *, ending last repeat with p 5.

Row 9: P 4, * p 2 tog, yo, p 7, yo, p 2 tog, p 1 *; repeat from * to *, ending last repeat with p 4.

Row 11: Repeat Row 7.

Row 13: Purl.

Row 15: K 9, * yo, p 2 tog, p 10 *; repeat from * to *, ending last repeat with p 8.

Repeat Rows 3 through 16 for pattern.

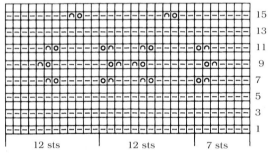

```
15
13
11
 9
 7
 5
 3
 1
```

    12 sts   12 sts   7 sts

- − = p 1
- □ = k 1
- o = yarn over
- ∩ = p 2 tog

Dewdrops

Start work with a multiple of 6 sts, plus 5.

Row 1: P 5, * k 1, yarn over, p 5 *; repeat from * to *.

Rows 2 and 4: K 5, * p 2, k 5 *; repeat from * to *.

Rows 3 and 5: P 5, * k 2, p 5 *; repeat from * to *.

Row 6: K 5, * p 2 sts together, k 5 *; repeat from * to *.

Row 7: P 2, * k 1, yarn over, p 5 *; repeat from * to *, ending k 1, yarn over, p 2.

Rows 8 and 10: K 2, * p 2, k 5 *; repeat from * to *, ending p 2, k 2.

Rows 9 and 11: P 2, * k 2, p 5 *; repeat from * to *, ending k 2, p 2.

Row 12: K 2, * p 2 sts together, k 5 *; repeat from * to *, ending p 2 sts together, k 2.

Repeat these 12 rows for pattern.

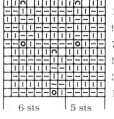

```
11
 9
 7
 5
 3
 1
```

    6 sts   5 sts

- I = k 1
- − = p 1
- o = yarn over
- ∩ = p 2 tog

- □ = empty space with no st indicated

LACE STITCHES

Double arrowheads

Work with a multiple of 10 stitches, plus 5.

Row 1: Knit.

Row 2 and all even-numbered rows: Purl.

Row 3: K 2, * yarn over (yo), slip 1, k 1, pass slip st over k st and drop it (psso), k 8 *; repeat from * to *, ending yo, slip 1, k 1, psso, k 1.

Row 5: K 3, * yo, slip 1, k 1, psso, k 5, k 2 sts together (k 2 tog), yo, k 1 *; repeat from * to *, ending last repeat with k 3.

Row 7: K 4, * yo, slip 1, k 1, psso, k 3, k 2 tog, yo, k 3 *; repeat from * to *, ending last repeat with k 4.

Row 9: K 2, * work (yo, slip 1, k 1, psso, k 1) twice, k 2 tog, yo, k 2 *; repeat from * to *, ending yo, slip 1, k 1, psso, k 1.

Row 11: K 3, * yo, slip 1, k 1, psso, k 1, yo, work double decrease on 3 sts as follows: slip 1, k 2 tog, psso, yo, k 1, k 2 tog, yo, k 1 *; repeat from * to *, ending last repeat with k 3.

Row 13: K 4, * yo, slip 1, k 1, psso, k 1, yo, slip 1, k 1, psso, k 2 tog, yo, k 3 *; repeat from * to *, ending last repeat with k 4.

Row 15: K 5, * yo, slip 1, k 1, psso, k 1, k 2 tog, yo, k 5 *; repeat from * to *.

Row 17: K 6, * yo, double decrease, yo, k 7 *; repeat from * to *, ending

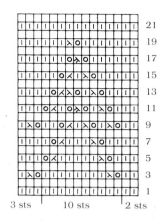

| = k 1
□ = p 1
O = yarn over
⋋ = slip 1, k 1, psso
⋌ = k 2 tog
⋏ = double decrease

last repeat with k 6.

Row 19: K 7, * yo, slip 1, k 1, psso, k 8 *; repeat from * to *, ending last repeat with k 6.

Row 21: Knit.

Repeat Rows 1 through 22 for pattern.

Net to the left

Work with an uneven number of stitches, plus 2 for selvages.

Row 1: P 1, * yarn over (yo), slip 1, k 1, pass slip st over k st (psso) *; repeat from * to *, ending k 1, p last st.

Rows 2 and 4: Purl.

Row 3: P 1, k 1, * yo, slip 1, k 1, psso *; repeat from * to *, ending p 1.

Repeat Rows 1 through 4 for pattern.

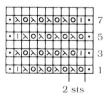

| = k 1
□ = p 1
O = yarn over
⋋ = slip 1, k 1, psso
• = p 1 (selvage)

LACE STITCHES

Net to the right

Work with an uneven numbered of stitches, plus 2 for selvages.

Row 1: P 1, k 1, * k 2 sts together, yarn over (yo) *; repeat from * to *, ending p 1.

Rows 2 and 4: Purl.

Row 3: P 1, * k 2 sts together, yo *; repeat from * to *, ending k 1, p 1.

Repeat Rows 1 through 4 for pattern.

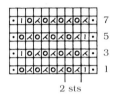

2 sts

| = k 1
□ = p 1
O = yarn over
ᗄ = k 2 tog
• = 1 slip st (selvage)

Rising pathways

Work with a multiple of 12 stitches, plus 1.

Row 1: K 1, * k 2 sts together (k 2 tog), k 3, yarn over (yo), k 1, k 2 tog, yo, k 1, yo, slip 1, k 1, pass slip st over k st and drop it (psso), k 1 *; repeat from * to *.

Row 2 and all even-numbered rows: Purl.

Row 3: K 1, * k 2 tog, k 2, yo, k 1, k 2 tog, work (yo, k 1) twice, slip 1, k 1, psso, k 1 *; repeat from * to *.

Row 5: K 1, * k 2 tog, k 1, yo, k 1, k 2 tog, yo, k 1, yo, k 2, slip 1, k 1, psso, k 1 *; repeat from * to *.

Row 7: K 1, * k 2 tog, yo, k 1, k 2 tog, yo, k 1, yo, k 3, slip 1, k 1, psso, k 1 *; repeat from * to *.

Repeat Rows 1 through 8 for pattern.

| = k 1
□ = p 1
O = yarn over
λ = slip 1, k 1, psso
ᗄ = k 2 tog

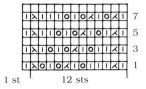

1 st   12 sts

LACE STITCHES

Encores

Work with a multiple of 6 stitches, plus 2.

Row 1: P 2, * k 2, yarn over (yo), slip 1, k 1, pass slip st over k st and drop it (psso), p 2 *; repeat from * to *.

Row 2 and all even-numbered rows: Work each stitch as it appears on this side of work (k the k sts and p the p sts). Knit yarn-over loops.

Row 3: P 2, * k 1, yo, p 1, slip 1, k 1, psso, p 2 *; repeat from * to *.

Row 5: P 2, * yo, p 2, slip 1, k 1, psso, p 2 *; repeat from * to *.

Row 7: P 2, * k 2 sts together, yo, k 2, p 2 *; repeat from * to *.

Row 9: P 2, * k 2 sts together, p 1, yo, k 1, p 2 *; repeat from * to *.

Row 11: P 2, * k 2 sts together, p 2, yo, p 2 *; repeat from * to *.

Repeat Rows 1 through 12 for pattern.

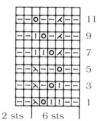

| = k 1
— = p 1
O = yarn over
⅄ = slip 1, k 1, psso
⋌ = k 2 tog
□ = 1 st as shown

2 sts | 6 sts

Simple symmetries

Start work with a multiple of 4 stitches.

Row 1: * K 3, yarn over, k 1 *; repeat from * to *.

Row 2 and all even-numbered rows: Purl.

Row 3: * K 3, yarn over, k 2 *; repeat from * to *.

Row 5: * K 3, yarn over, k 3 *; repeat from * to *.

Row 7: * K 4 sts together, k 3 *; repeat from * to *.

Repeat Rows 1 through 8 for pattern.

| = k1
— = p 1
O = yarn over
= k 4 tog
□ = empty space with no st indicated

4 sts

LACE STITCHES

Trapezoids

Work with a multiple of 10 stitches, plus 2.

Rows 1 and 3: K 1, * k 2 sts together, p 4, yarn over, k 4 *; repeat from * to *, ending last repeat with k 5.

Row 2 and all even-numbered rows: Work each stitch as it appears on this side of work (k the k sts and p the p sts). Purl yarn-over loops.

Rows 5 and 7: K 5, * yarn over, p 4, slip 1, k 1, pass slip st over k st and drop it, k 4 *; repeat from * to *, ending last repeat with k 1.

Repeat Rows 1 through 8 for pattern.

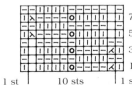

| = k1
− = p 1
○ = yarn over
⼂ = k 2 tog
⼃ = slip 1, k 1, psso
□ = empty space with no st indicated

Lace with loops

Work with a multiple of 9 stitches, plus 2.

Row 1: K 2, * k 3 sts together (k 3 tog), k 3, yarn over (yo), k 1, yo, k 2 *; repeat from * to *.

Row 2 and all even-numbered rows: Purl.

Row 3: K 2, * k 3 tog, k 2, yo, k 1, yo, k 3 *; repeat from * to *.

Row 5: K 2, * k 3 tog, work (k 1, yo) twice, k 4 *; repeat from * to *.

Row 7: Knit.

Row 9: K 6, * work group of 3 long sts as follows: insert needle in eyelet 3 rows below next st, k 1 and draw up long st, yo, k 1 and draw up another long st from same place, then work (k 1 long st, yo, k 1 long st) from eyelet 5 rows below following st (always work in left eyelet of pair), then work (k 1 long st, yo, k 1 long st) in eyelet 7 rows below 3rd st on left needle, k next st on left needle and pass each of the loops over k st to complete group, k 8 *; repeat from * to *, ending with k 4.

Repeat Rows 1 through 10 for pattern.

| = k 1
○ = yarn over
⼂ = k 3 tog
↑ = 1 group of 3 long sts
□ = p 1

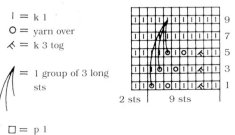

220

LACE STITCHES

Lace V's

Work with a multiple of 8 stitches, plus 6.

Row 1: K 5, * slip 1, k 1, pass slip st over k st and drop it (psso), yarn over (yo), k 6 *; repeat from * to *, ending last repeat with k 7.

Row 2 and all even-numbered rows: Purl.

Row 3: K 4, * slip 1, k 1, psso, yo, k 1, yo, k 2 sts together, k 3 *; repeat from * to *, ending last repeat with k 5.

Row 5: K 3, * slip 1, k 1, psso, yo, k 3, yo, k 2 sts together, k 1 *; repeat from * to *, ending last repeat with k 4.

Rows 7 and 9: Knit.

Repeat Rows 1 through 10 for pattern.

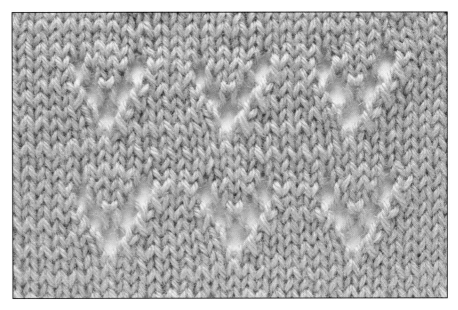

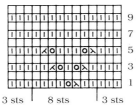

3 sts | 8 sts | 3 sts

| = k 1
⅄ = slip 1, k 1, psso
O = yarn over
⋏ = k 2 tog
□ = p 1

| = k 1
⅄ = slip 1, k 1, psso
O = yarn over
⋏ = k 2 tog
□ = p 1

Upward bound

Work with a multiple of 9 stitches, plus 1.

Row 1: K 7, * yarn over (yo), slip 1, k 1, pass slip st over k st and drop it (psso), k 2, k 2 sts together, yo, k 3 *; repeat from * to *; ending last repeat with k 6.

Row 2 and all even-numbered rows: Purl.

Row 3: K 8, * yo, slip 1, k 1, psso, k 2 sts together, yo, k 5 *; repeat from * to *, ending last repeat with k 7.

Row 5: K 9, * yo, slip 1, k 1, psso, k 7 *; repeat from * to *, ending last repeat with k 8.

Repeat Rows 1 through 6 for pattern.

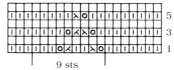

9 sts

LACE STITCHES

Diamonds in lace

Work with a multiple of 14 stitches, plus 2.

Row 1: K 1, * yarn over (yo), slip 1, k 1, pass slip st over k st and drop it (psso), k 2, work (yo, slip 1, k 1, psso) 4 times, k 2 *; repeat from * to *, ending last repeat with k 3.

Row 2 and all even-numbered rows: K 1, p to last st, k last st.

Row 3: K 2, yo, slip 1, k 1, psso, * k 2, work (yo, slip 1, k 1, psso) 3 times, k 2, work (yo, slip 1, k 1, psso) twice *; repeat from * to *, ending k 2, work (yo, slip 1, k 1, psso) 3 times, k 4.

Row 5: K 3, * yo, slip 1, k 1, psso, k 2, work (yo, slip 1, k 1, psso) twice, k 2, yo, slip 1, k 1, psso, k 2 *; repeat from * to *, ending last repeat with k 1.

Row 7: * K 4, yo, slip 1, k 1, psso, k 6, yo, slip 1, k 1, psso *; repeat from * to *, ending k in last 2 sts.

Row 9: K 5, * yo, slip 1, k 1, psso, k 4, yo, slip 1, k 1, psso, k 6 *; repeat from * to *, ending last repeat with k 3.

Row 11: K 2, * work (yo, slip 1, k 1, psso, k 2) 3 times, yo, slip 1, k 1, psso *; repeat from * to *, ending (yo, slip 1, k 1, psso, k 2) twice, yo, slip 1, k 1, psso, k 4.

Row 13: K 1, work (yo, slip 1, k 1, psso) twice, * k 2, work (yo, slip 1, k 1, psso) twice, k 2, work (yo, slip 1, k 1, psso) 3 times *; repeat from * to *, ending last repeat with (yo, slip 1, k 1, psso) once, k 1.

Row 15: K 2, work (yo, slip 1, k 1, psso) twice, * k 2, yo, slip 1, k 1, psso, k 2, work (yo, slip 1, k 1, psso) 4 times *; repeat from * to *, ending with (yo, slip 1, k 1, psso) once, k 2.

Row 17: Repeat Row 13.
Row 19: Repeat Row 11.
Row 21: Repeat Row 9.
Row 23: Repeat Row 7.
Row 25: Repeat Row 5.
Row 27: Repeat Row 3.
Repeat Rows 1 through 28 for pattern.

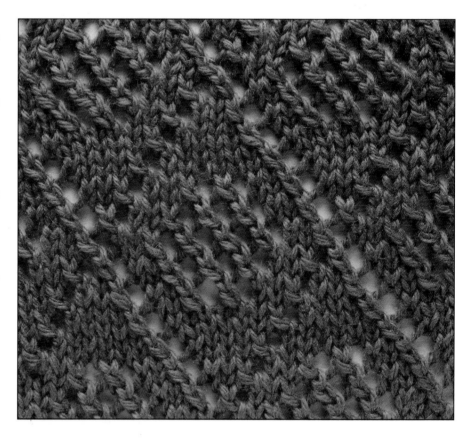

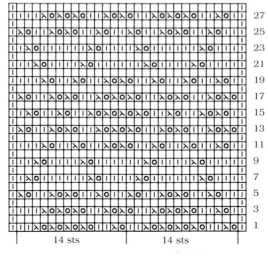

| = k 1
O = yarn over
ㅅ = slip 1, k 1, psso
□ = p 1

LACE STITCHES

Checker games

Work with a multiple of 24 stitches, plus 14.

Rows 1, 5, and 9: K 1, * yarn over (yo), k 2 sts together (k 2 tog), work (k 1, yo, k 2 tog) 3 times, k 13 *; repeat from * to *, ending last repeat with k 2.

Row 2 and all even-numbered rows: Purl.

Rows 3, 7, and 11: K 2, * slip 1, k 1, pass slip st over k st and drop it (psso), yo, work (k 1, slip 1, k 1, psso, yo) 3 times, k 13 *; repeat from * to *, ending last repeat with k 1.

Rows 13, 17, and 21: K 14, * slip 1, k 1, psso, yo, work (k 1, slip 1, k 1, psso, yo) 3 times, k 13 *; repeat from * to *.

Rows 15, 19, and 23: K 13, * yo, k 2 tog, work (k 1, yo, k 2 tog) 3 times, k 13 *; repeat from * to *, ending last repeat with k 14.

Repeat Rows 1 through 24 for pattern.

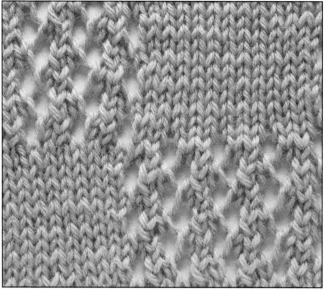

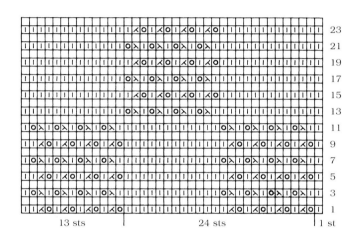

13 sts   24 sts   1 st

| = k 1
O = yarn over
⋋ = slip 1, k 1, psso
∠ = k 2 tog
□ = p 1

Ostrich plumes

Work with a multiple of 13 stitches, plus 2.

Rows 1, 3, and 5: P 2, * k 2 sts together (k 2 tog), k 3, yarn over (yo), k 1, yo, k 3, slip 1, k 1, pass slip st over k st and drop it (psso), p 2 *; repeat from * to *.

Row 2 and all even-numbered rows: Work each stitch as it appears on this side of work (k the k sts and p the p sts). Purl yarn-over loops.

Rows 7 and 17: P 2, * k 2 tog, k 2, yo, k 3, yo, k 2, slip 1, k 1, psso, p 2 *; repeat from * to *.

Row 9: P 2, * k 2 tog, k 1, yo, k 5, yo, k 1, slip 1, k 1, psso, p 2 *; repeat from * to *.

Rows 11 and 13: P 2, * k 2 tog, yo, k 1, k 2 tog, yo, work (k 1, yo, slip 1, k 1, psso) twice, p 2 *; repeat from * to *.

Row 15: P 2, * k 2 tog, k 1, yo, k 5, yo, k 1, slip 1, k 1, psso, p 2 *; repeat from * to *.

Row 19: P 2, * k 11, p 2 *; repeat from * to *.

Repeat Rows 1 through 20 for pattern.

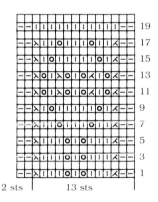

2 sts   13 sts

| = k 1
— = p 1
O = yarn over
∠ = k 2 tog
⋋ = slip 1, k 1, psso
□ = 1 st as shown

223

LACE STITCHES

Dual diamonds

Work with a multiple of 12 stitches, plus 2.

Row 1: P 1, * yarn over (yo), p 2 sts together (p 2 tog), p 10 *; repeat from * to *, ending p in last st.

Row 2: K 12, * p 1, k 11 *; repeat from * to *, ending p 1, k in last st.

Row 3: P 1, * k 1, yo, p 2 tog, p 7, p 2 tog, yo *; repeat from * to *, ending k in last st.

Row 4: P 1, * k 11, p 1 *; repeat from * to *, ending k in last st.

Row 5: P 1, * k 1, p 1, yo, p 2 tog, p 5, p 2 tog, yo, p 1 *; repeat from * to *, ending k in last st.

Rows 6 and 8: P 1, k 1, p 1, * k 7, work (p 1, k 1) twice, p 1 *; repeat from * to *, ending with (p 1, k 1) twice.

Row 7: Work (p 1, k 1) twice, * yo, p 2 tog, p 3, k 2 tog, yo, k 1, work (p 1, k 1) twice *; repeat from * to *, ending with k 1, p 1, k 1.

Row 9: P 1, work (k 1, p 1) twice, * yo, k 2 tog, p 1, k 2 tog, yo, p 1, work (k 1, p 1) 3 times *; repeat from * to *, ending with (p 1, k 1) twice.

Rows 10 and 12: P 1, work (k 1, p 1) twice, * k 3, p 1, work (k 1, p 1) 4 times *; repeat from * to *, ending with (p 1, k 1) 3 times.

Row 11: Work (p 1, k 1) 3 times, * yo, p 3 tog, yo, work (k 1, p 1) 4 times, k 1 *; repeat from * to *, ending with k 1, (p 1, k 1) twice.

Row 13: P 7, * yo, p 2 tog, p 10 *; repeat from * to *, ending with p 5.

Rows 14 and 16: K 6, * p 1, k 11 *; repeat from * to *, ending with k 7.

Row 15: P 5, * p 2 tog, yo, k 1, yo, p 2 tog, p 7 *; repeat from * to *, ending with p 4.

Row 17: P 4, * p 2 tog, yo, p 1, k 1, p 1, yo, p 2 tog, p 5 *; repeat from * to *, ending with p 3.

Rows 18 and 20: K 4, * p 1, work (k 1, p 1) twice, k 7 *; repeat from * to *, ending with k 5.

Row 19: P 3, * p 2 tog, yo, k 1, work (p 1, k 1) twice, yo, p 2 tog, p 3 *; repeat from * to *, ending with p 2.

Row 21: P 2, * p 2 tog, yo, p 1, (k 1, p 1) 3 times, yo, p 2 tog, p 1 *; repeat from * to *.

Rows 22 and 24: K 2, * p 1, work (k 1, p 1) 4 times, k 3 *; repeat from * to *.

Row 23: P 1, p 2 tog, yo, * k 1, work (p 1, k 1) 4 times, yo, p 3 tog, yo *; repeat from * to *, ending last repeat with yo, p 2 tog.

Repeat Rows 1 through 24 for pattern.

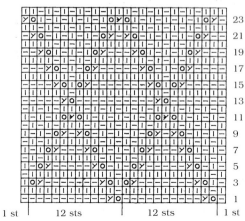

1 st   12 sts   12 sts   1 st

− = p 1
O = yarn over
⅄ = p 2 tog
I = k 1
⅄ = p 3 tog

224

LACE STITCHES

Lace and solid diamonds

Work with a multiple of 12 stitches.
Row 1: K 3, * k 2 sts together (k 2 tog), yarn over (yo), k 2 tog, work increase as follows: pick up and k connecting strand between last st worked and next st, yo, then, on left needle, pass second st over first st, then k first st, k 6 *; repeat from * to *, ending last repeat with k 3.
Rows 2, 4, 8, and 10: Purl.
Row 3: K 2, * k 2 tog, yo, k 4, yo, pass 1 and k 1 on left needle, k 4 *; repeat from * to *, ending with k 2.
Row 5: K 1, * k 2 tog, yo, k 1, k 2 tog, yo, pass 1 and k 1 on left needle, k 1, yo, pass 1 and k 1 on left needle, k 2 *; repeat from * to *, ending with k 1.
Row 6: P 5, * k 1 and p 1 in yo, p 10 *; repeat from * to *, ending with p 6.
Row 7: K 3, * yo, pass 1 and k 1 on left needle, k 2, k 2 tog, yo, k 6 *; repeat from * to *, ending with k 3.
Row 9: K 4, * yo, pass 1 and k 1 on left needle, k 2 tog, yo, k 8 *; repeat

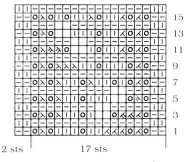

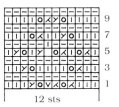

from * to *, ending k 4.
Repeat Rows 1 through 10 for pattern.

| = k 1
− = p 1
O = yarn over
ʎ = k 2 tog
Y = pass 1 and k on left needle
V = 1 increase

□ = empty space with no st indicated

Bellflowers

Work with a multiple of 17 stitches, plus 2.
Row 1: P 2, * yarn over (yo), k 2 sts together (k 2 tog), yo, k 2 tog 3 times, k 2, yo, k 3, yo, slip 1, k 1, pass slip st over k st and drop it (psso), yo, p 2 *; repeat from * to *.
Row 2 and all even-numbered rows: Work each stitch as it appears on this side of work (k the k sts and p the p sts). Purl yarn-over loops.
Row 3: P 2, * yo, k 2 tog, k 3 tog twice, yo, k 1, yo, k 2, work (slip 1, k 1, psso, yo) twice, p 2 *; repeat from * to *.
Row 5: P 2, * yo, k 4 tog, yo, k 3, yo, k 2, work (slip 1, k 1, psso, yo) twice, p 2 *; repeat from * to *.
Row 7: P 2, * yo, k 2 tog, yo, k 1, yo, k 2, slip 1, k 1, psso, yo, k 2, work (slip 1, k 1, psso, yo) twice, p 2 *; repeat from * to *.
Row 9: P 2, * yo, k 2 tog, yo, k 3, yo, k 2, work (slip 1, k 1, psso) twice, work (slip 1, k 1, psso, yo) twice, p 2 *; repeat from * to *.
Row 11: P 2, * work (yo, k 2 tog) twice, k 2, yo, k 1, yo, work (slip 1 as if to k, k 2 tog, psso) twice, slip 1, k 1, psso, yo, p 2 *; repeat from * to *.
Row 13: P 2, * work (yo, k 2 tog) twice, k 2, yo, k 3, yo, slip 1 as if to k, k 3 tog, psso, yo, p 2 *; repeat from

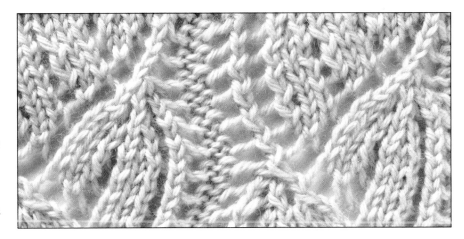

* to *.
Row 15: P 2, * work (yo, k 2 tog) twice, k 2, yo, slip 1, k 1, psso, k 2, yo, k 1, yo, slip 1, k 1, psso, yo, p 2 *

2 sts   17 sts

| = k 1
− = p 1
O = yarn over
ʎ = k 2 tog
⋋ = slip 1, k 1, psso
ʎ = k 3 tog
⋌ = slip 1, k 2 tog, psso
⋘ = k 4 tog
⋋ = slip 1, k 3 tog, psso
□ = empty space with no st indicated

repeat from * to *.
Repeat Rows 1 through 16 for pattern.

LACE STITCHES

Lace and moss stitch bands

Note: For moss stitch, p over k sts (as sts face you) and k over p sts.
Work with a multiple of 10 sts, plus 5.

Row 1: K 1, (p 1, k 1) twice for 5 moss sts, * yarn over (yo), k 2 sts together through back loops, k 1, slip 1, k 1, pass slip st over k st and drop it (psso), yo, work 5 moss sts *; repeat from * to *.

Rows 2 and 4: Work moss st over moss sts (see note above) and purl remaining sts.

Row 3: Work 5 moss sts, * k 1, yo, slip 1, k 2 sts together, psso (double decrease made), yo, k 1, work 5 moss sts *; repeat from * to *.
Repeat Rows 1 through 4 for pattern.

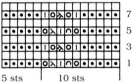

- **•** = 1 moss st
- **O** = yarn over
- **∩** = k 2 tog in back loops
- **I** = k 1
- **⅄** = slip 1, k 1, psso
- **⅄** = double dec
- **□** = 1 st as shown

5 sts   10 sts

Lacy scallops

Work with a multiple of 9 stitches, plus 2.

Row 1: K 2, * yarn over (yo), k 2, slip 1, k 1 pass slip st over k st and drop it (psso), k 2 sts together, k 2, yo, k 1*; repeat from * to *.

Row 2 and all even-numbered rows: Purl.

Row 3: K 1, * yo, k 2, slip 1, k 1, psso, k 2 sts together, k 2, yo, k 1 *; repeat from * to *, ending last repeat with k 2.

Row 5: Knit.
Repeat Rows 1 through 6 for pattern.

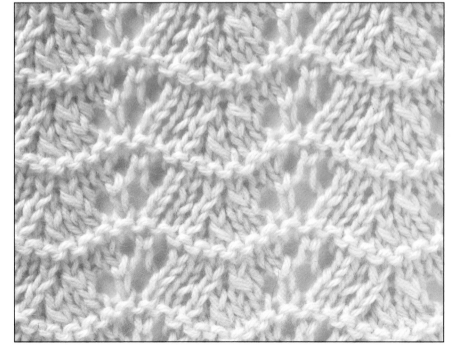

- **I** = k 1
- **□** or **−** = p 1
- **O** = yarn over
- **⅄** = slip 1, k 1, psso
- **⅄** = k 2 tog

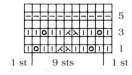

1 st   9 sts   1 st

LACE STITCHES

Amphoras

Work with a multiple of 12 stitches, plus 1.

Row 1: P 1, * slip 1, k 1, pass slip st over k st and drop it (psso), k 3, yarn over (yo), k 1, yo, k 3, k 2 sts together (k 2 tog), p 1 *; repeat from * to *.

Row 2 and all even-numbered rows: Work each stitch as it appears on this side of work (k the k sts and p the p sts). Purl yarn-over loops.

Row 3: P 1, * slip 1, k 1, psso, k 2, yo, k 3, yo, k 2, k 2 tog, p 1 * repeat from * to *.

Row 5: P 1, * slip 1, k 1, psso, k 1, yo, k 5, yo, k 1, k 2 tog, p 1 *; repeat from * to *.

Row 7: P 1, * yo, k 3, k 2 tog, k 1, slip 1, k 1, psso, k 3, yo, p 1 *; repeat from * to *.

Row 9: P 1, * k 1, yo, k 2, k 2 tog, k 1, slip 1, k 1, psso, k 2, yo, k 1, p 1 *; repeat from * to *.

Row 11: P 1, * k 2, yo, k 1, k 2 tog, k 1, slip 1, k 1, psso, k 1, yo, k 2, p 1 *; repeat from * to *.

Repeat Rows 1 through 12 for pattern.

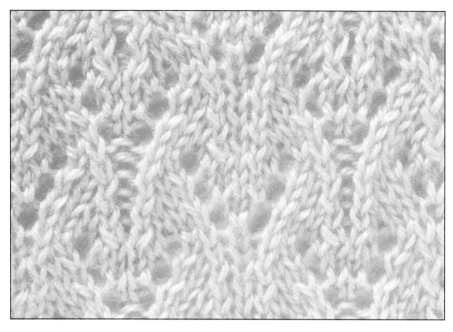

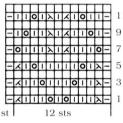

1 st | 12 sts

| = k 1
− = p 1
⋋ = slip 1, k 1, psso
O = yarn over
⋌ = k 2 tog
□ = 1 st as shown

Jumping eyelets

Work with a multiple of 10 stitches, plus 1.

Row 1: P 1, * k 1, yarn over (yo), k 2 sts together, k 1, p 1, k 1, slip 1, k 1, pass slip st over k st and drop it (psso), yo, k 1, p 1 *; repeat from * to *.

Rows 2 and 4: Work each stitch as it appears on this side of work (k the k sts and p the p sts). Purl yarn-over loops.

Row 3: P 1, * k 1, slip 1, k 1, psso, yo, k 1, p 1, k 1, yo, k 2 sts together, k 1, p 1 *; repeat from * to *.

Repeat Rows 1 through 4 for pattern.

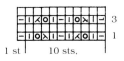

1 st | 10 sts,

| = k 1
− = p 1
⋋ = slip 1, k 1, psso
O = yarn over
⋌ = k 2 tog
□ = 1 st as shown

LACE STITCHES

Hills and valleys

Work with a multiple of 13 stitches.
Rows 1 through 4: Work in moss st (see page 5).
Row 5: P 1, * slip 1, k 1, pass slip st over k st and drop it (psso), k 3, yarn over (yo), k 1, yo, k 3, k 2 sts together (k 2 tog), p 2 *; repeat from * to *, ending last repeat with p 1.
Rows 6, 8, and 10: Purl.
Row 7: P 1, * slip 1, k 1, psso, k 2, yo, k 3, yo, k 2, k 2 tog, p 2 *; repeat from * to *, ending with p 1.
Row 9: P 1, * slip 1, k 1, psso, k 1, yo, k 2 tog, yo, k 1, yo, slip 1, k 1, psso, yo, k 1, k 2 tog, p 2 *; repeat from * to *, ending with p 1.
Row 11: P 1, * slip 1, k 1, psso, yo, k 2 tog, yo, k 3, yo, slip 1, k 1, psso, yo, k 2 tog, p 2 *; repeat from * to *, ending with p 1.
Repeat Rows 1 through 12 for pattern.

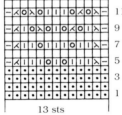

13 sts

□ or — = p 1
| = k 1
λ = slip 1, k 1, psso
⋌ = k 2 tog
○ = yarn over
● = 1 moss st

Old fern

Work with a multiple of 12 stitches, plus 1.

Rows 1, 3, and 5: K 2 sts together (k 2 tog), * k 2, yarn over (yo), slip 1, k 1, pass st over k st and drop it (psso), yo, k 1, yo, k 2 tog, yo, k 2, k 3 tog *; repeat from * to *, ending last repeat with slip 1, k 1, psso.
Row 2 and all even-numbered rows: Purl.
Row 7: K 2 tog, * k 1, yo, k 2 tog, yo, k 3, yo, slip 1, k 1, psso, yo, k 1, k 3 tog *; repeat from * to *, ending last repeat with skip 1, k 1, psso.
Row 9: K 2 tog, * yo, k 2 tog, yo, k 5, yo, slip 1, k 1, psso, yo, k 3 tog *; repeat from * to *, ending last repeat with slip 1, k 1, psso.
Rows 11, 13, and 15: K 1, * yo, k 2 tog, yo, k 2, k 3 tog, k 2, yo, slip 1, k 1, psso, yo, k 1 *; repeat from * to *.
Row 17: K 2, * yo, slip 1, k 1, psso, yo, k 1, k 3 tog, k 1, yo, k 2 tog, yo, k 3 *; repeat from * to *, ending last repeat with k 2.
Row 19: K 3, * yo, slip 1, k 1, psso, yo, k 3 tog, yo, k 2 tog, yo, k 5 *; repeat from * to *, ending last repeat with k 3.
Repeat Rows 1 through 20 for pattern.

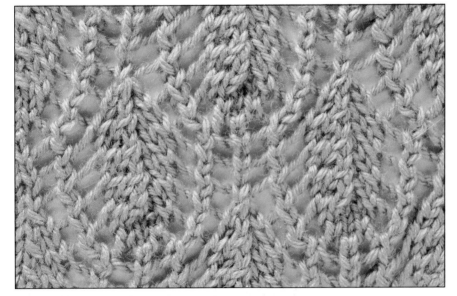

| = k 1
⋌ = k 2 tog
○ = yarn over
λ = slip 1, k 1, psso
⋏ = k 3 tog
□ = p 1

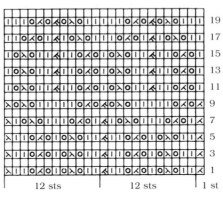

12 sts   12 sts   1 st

LACE STITCHES

Snowdrops

Work with multiple of 10 sts, plus 3.
Row 1: K 3 sts in back loop (k 3 tw sts), * p 1, k 2 sts together in back loops (k 2 tw sts tog), yarn over (yo), k 1 tw st, yo, on left needle pass 2nd st over first, k first st in back loop, p 1, k 3 tw sts *; repeat from * to *.
Row 2 and all even-numbered rows:
Work each stitch as it appears (k the k sts and p the p sts), working tw p st over tw k sts; purl yo loops.
Rows 3 and 5: K 3 tw sts, * p 1, pass and k on left needle as before, yo, k 1 tw st, yo, k 2 tw sts tog, p 1, k 3 tw sts *; repeat from * to *.
Row 7: K 2 tw sts, * yo, pass and k on left needle, p 1, k 3 tw sts, p 1, k 2 tw sts tog, yo, k 1 tw st *; repeat from * to *, ending last repeat with k 2 tw sts.
Rows 9 and 11: K 2 tw sts, * yo, k 2 tw sts tog, p 1, k 3 tw sts, p 1, pass and k on left needle, yo, k 1 tw k st *; repeat from * to *, ending with k 2 tw sts.
Repeat Rows 1 through 12 for pattern.

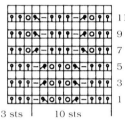

3 sts | 10 sts

- ♀ = 1 twist k st
- O = yarn over
- ♠ = k 2 tog in back loops
- ⅂ = pass and k on left needle
- — = p 1
- ☐ = 1 st as shown

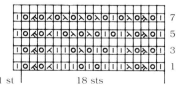

1 st | 18 sts

- I = k 1
- O = yarn over
- ⅄ = double dec
- ⅄ = slip 1, k 1, psso
- ⋌ = k 2 tog
- ⋌ = k 3 tog
- ☐ = p 1

Little lace ladders

Work with a multiple of 18 stitches, plus 1.
Row 1: K 1, * yarn over (yo), make double decrease: slip 1, k 2 sts together (k 2 tog), pass slip st over k st and drop it (psso), yo, slip 1, k 1, psso, k 3, yo, k 1, yo, k 3, k 2 tog, yo, k 3 tog, yo, k 1 *; repeat from * to *.
Row 2 and all even-numbered rows:
Purl.
Row 3: K 1, * yo, slip 1, k 2 tog, psso, yo, slip 1, k 1, psso, k 2, yo, k 1, yo, slip 1, k 1, psso, yo, k 2, k 2 tog, yo, k 3 tog, yo, k 1 *; repeat from * to *.
Row 5: K 1, * yo, slip 1, k 2 tog, psso, yo, slip 1, k 1, psso, work (k 1, yo) twice, work (slip 1, k 1, psso, yo) twice, k 1, k 2 tog, yo, k 3 tog, yo, k 1 *; repeat from * to *.
Row 7: K 1, * yo, slip 1, k 2 tog, psso, yo, slip 1, k 1, psso, yo, k 1, yo, work (slip 1, k 1, psso, yo) 3 times, k 2 tog, yo, k 3 tog, yo, k 1 *; repeat from * to *.
Repeat Rows 1 through 8 for pattern.

LACE STITCHES

Gothic lace

Work with a multiple of 6 stitches, plus 3.

Row 1: Knit.

Row 2 and all even-numbered rows: Purl.

Row 3: * K 4, yarn over (yo), slip 1, k 1, pass slip st over k st and drop it (psso) *; repeat from * to *, ending k in last 3 sts.

Row 5: K 2, * k 2 sts together, yo, k 1, yo, slip 1, k 1, psso, k 1 *; repeat from * to *, ending last repeat with k 2.

Row 7: K 1, k 2 tog, yo, * k 3, yo, slip 1, k 2 sts together, psso, yo *; repeat from * to *, ending last repeat with yo, slip 1, k 1, psso, k in last st.

Row 9: Repeat Row 5.

Row 11: Repeat Row 3.

Repeat Rows 1 through 12 for pattern.

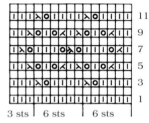

| | = k 1
O = yarn over
⋋ = slip 1, k 1, psso
⋌ = k 2 tog
⋏ = slip 1, k 2 tog, psso
□ = p 1

Lace-trimmed stripes

Work with a multiple of 9 stitches, plus 1.

Row 1: K 1, * yarn over (yo), slip 1, k 1, pass slip st over k st and drop it (psso), k 1, yo, slip 1, k 1, psso, yo, k 3 sts together, yo, k 1 *; repeat from * to *.

Row 2 and all even-numbered rows: Purl.

Row 3: * K 2, yo, slip 1, k 1, psso, k 2, yo, k 3 sts together, yo *; repeat from * to *, ending k in last st.

Row 5: * K 3, yo, slip 1, k 1, psso, k 1, yo, k 3 sts together, yo *; repeat from * to *, ending k in last st.

Repeat Rows 1 through 6 for pattern.

| | = k 1
O = yarn over
⋋ = slip 1, k 1, psso
⋏ = k 3 tog
□ = p 1

230

LACE STITCHES

Triangles with lace hypotenuse

Work with a multiple of 15 stitches, plus 1.

Row 1: * P 13, k 2 sts together (k 2 tog), yo *; repeat from * to *, ending k in last st.

Row 2 and all even-numbered rows: Work each stitch as it appears on this side of work (k the k sts and p the p sts). Purl yarn-over loops.

Row 3: * P 12, k 2 tog, yo, k 1 *; repeat from * to *, ending last repeat with k 2.

Row 5: * P 11, k 2 tog, yo, k 2 *; repeat from * to *, ending with k 3.

Row 7: * P 10, k 2 tog, yo, k 3 *; repeat from * to *, ending with k 4.

Row 9: * P 9, k 2 tog, yo, k 4 *; repeat from * to *, ending with k 5.

Row 11: * P 8, k 2 tog, yo, k 5 *; repeat from * to *, ending with k 6.

Rows 13 and all right-side rows through 27: Continue in this manner, moving the (k 2 tog, yo) 1 st to the right each right-side row, working Row 27 as follows: * K 2 tog, yo, k 13 *; repeat from * to *, ending with k 14.

Repeat Rows 1 through 28 for pattern.

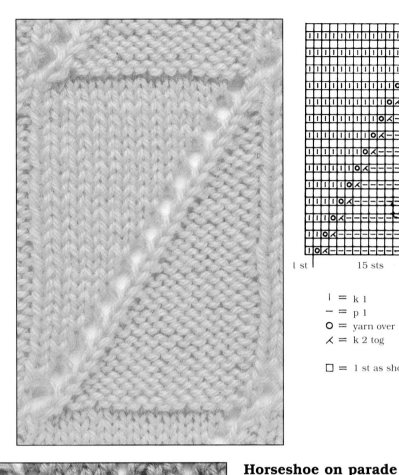

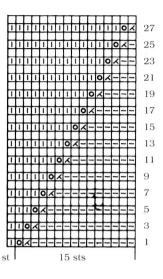

| | = k 1
| — = p 1
| O = yarn over
| ⋋ = k 2 tog

| □ = 1 st as shown

Horseshoe on parade

Work with a multiple of 10 sts, plus 1.

Row 1: K 1, * yarn over (yo), k 3, slip 1, k 2 sts together, pass slip st over k st and drop it (double decrease made), k 3, yo, k 1 *; repeat from * to *.

Row 2 and all even-numbered rows: Purl.

Row 3: K 2, * yo, k 2, double decrease, k 2, yo, k 3 *; repeat from * to *, ending last repeat with k 2.

Row 5: K 3, * yo, k 1, double decrease, k 1, yo, k 5 *; repeat from * to *, ending last repeat with k 3.

Row 7: K 4, * yo, double decrease, yo, k 7 *; repeat from * to *, ending last repeat with k 4.

Repeat Rows 1 through 8 for pattern.

| = k 1
O = yarn over
⋋ = double dec
□ = p 1

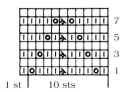

LACE STITCHES

Lighted torches

Work with a multiple of 12 stitches, plus 11.

Row 1: K 3, * yarn over (yo), slip 1, k 1, pass slip st over k st and drop it (psso), k 7, k 2 sts together (k 2 tog), yo, k 1 *; repeat from * to *, ending last repeat with k 6.

Row 2 and all even-numbered rows: Purl.

Row 3: K 3, yo, k 1, * slip 1, k 1, psso, k 5, k 2 tog, k 1, work (yo, k 1) twice * repeat from * to *, ending skip 1, k 1, psso, k 5.

Row 5: K 3, yo, * k 2, slip 1, k 1, psso, k 3, k 2 tog, k 2, yo, k 1, yo *; repeat from * to *, ending with k 4.

Row 7: K 3, yo, * k 3, slip 1, k 1, psso, k 1, k 2 tog, k 3, yo, k 1, yo *; repeat from * to *, ending with k 3.

Row 9: K 3, yo, * k 4, slip 1, k 2 sts together, psso (double decrease made), k 4, yo, k 1, yo *; repeat from * to *, ending k 4, slip 1, k 1, psso, k 2.

Row 11: K 6, * k 2 tog, yo, k 1, yo, slip 1, k 1, psso, k 7 *; repeat from * to *, ending k 2 tog, yo, k 3.

Row 13: * K 5, k 2 tog, k 1, work (yo, k 1) twice, slip 1, k 1, psso *; repeat from * to *, ending k 5, k 2 tog, k 1, yo, k 3.

Row 15: K 4, * k 2 tog, k 2, yo, k 1,

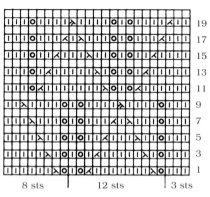

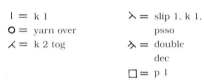

8 sts · 12 sts · 3 sts

yo, k 2, slip 1, k 1, psso, k 3 *; repeat from * to *, ending k 2 tog, k 2, yo, k 3.

Row 17: K 3, * k 2 tog, k 3, yo, k 1, yo, k 3, slip 1, k 1, psso, k 1*; repeat from * to *, ending k 2 tog, k 3, yo, k 3.

Row 19: K 2, k 2 tog, * k 4, yo, k 1, yo, k 4, double decrease *; repeat from * to *, ending k 4, yo, k 3.
Repeat Rows 1 through 20 for pattern.

Double zigzag

Work with a multiple of 9 stitches, plus 5.

Row 1: K 3, * yarn over (yo), slip 1, k 1, pass slip st over k st and drop it (psso), yo, slip 1, k 1, psso, k 5 *; repeat from * to *, ending last repeat with k 7.

Row 2 and all even-numbered rows: Purl.

Row 3: K 4, * work (yo, slip 1, k 1, psso) twice, k 5 *; repeat from * to *, ending with k 6.

Row 5: K 5, * (yo, slip 1, k 1, psso) twice, k 5 *; repeat from * to *.

Row 7: K 6, * (yo, slip 1, k 1, psso) twice, k 5 *; repeat from * to *, ending with k 4.

Row 9: K 7, * (yo, slip 1, k 1, psso) twice, k 5 *; repeat from * to *, ending with k 3.

Row 11: K 6, * k 2 sts together (k 2 tog), yo, k 2 tog, yo, k 5 *; repeat from * to *, ending with k 4.

Row 13: K 5, * work (k 2 tog, yo) twice, k 5 *; repeat from * to *.

Row 15: K 4, * (k 2 tog, yo) twice, k 5

3 sts · 9 sts · 2 sts

*; repeat from * to *, ending with k 6.

Row 17: K 3, * (k 2 tog, yo) twice, k 5 *; repeat from * to *, ending with k 7.

Row 19: K 2, * (k 2 tog, yo) twice, k 5 *; repeat from * to *, ending with k 8.
Repeat Rows 1 through 20 for pattern.

LACE STITCHES

Peach blossoms

Work with a multiple of 13 stitches.
Row 1: K 5, * yarn over (yo), slip 1, k 1, pass slip st over k st and drop it (psso), k 11 *; repeat from * to *, ending last repeat with k 6.
Row 2 and all even-numbered rows: Purl.
Row 3: K 6, * yo, slip 1, k 1, psso, k 11 *; repeat from * to *, ending with k 5.
Row 5: K 2, * yo, slip 1, k 1, psso, k 3, yo, slip 1, k 1, psso, k 6 *; repeat from * to *, ending with k 4.
Row 7: K 1, * work (yo, slip 1, k 1, psso) twice, k 3, yo, slip 1, k 1, psso, k 4 *; repeat from * to *, ending with k 3.
Row 9: K 2, * yo, slip 1, k 1, psso, k 3, k 2 sts together (k 2 tog), yo, k 6 *; repeat from * to *, ending with k 4.
Row 11: K 6, * k 2 tog, yo, k 11 *; repeat from * to *, ending with k 5.
Row 13: K 5, * k 2 tog, yo, k 11 *; repeat from * to *, ending with k 6.
Row 15: K 4, * k 2 tog, yo, k 3, yo, slip 1, k 1, psso, k 6 *; repeat from * to *, ending with k 2.
Row 17: K 3, * k 2 tog, yo, k 3, work (yo, slip 1, k 1, psso) twice, k 4 *;

repeat from * to *, ending with k 1.
Row 19: K 4, * yo, slip 1, k 1, psso, k 3, yo, slip 1, k 1, psso, k 6 *; repeat from * to *, ending with k 2.
Repeat Rows 1 through 20 for pattern.

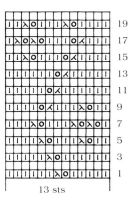

13 sts

| = k 1
O = yarn over
✕ = k 2 tog

⅄ = slip 1, k 1, psso

□ = p 1

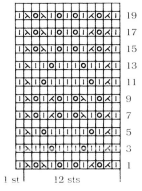

1 st   12 sts

| = k 1
O = yarn over
✕ = k 2 tog

⅄ = slip 1, k 1, psso

□ = p 1

Filigree

Work with a multiple of 12 stitches, plus 1.
Rows 1, 15, 17, and 19: K 1, * k 2 sts together (k 2 tog), yarn over (yo), k 2 tog, k 1, work (yo, k 1) twice, slip 1, k 1, pass slip st over k st and drop it (psso), yo, slip 1, k 1, psso, k 1 *; repeat from * to *.
Row 2 and all even-numbered rows: Purl.
Rows 3 and 13: K 1, * k 2 tog, k 2, yo, k 3, yo, k 2, slip 1, k 1, psso, k 1 *; repeat from * to *.
Rows 5 and 11: K 1, * k 2 tog, k 1, yo, k 5, yo, k 1, slip 1, k 1, psso, k 1 *; repeat from * to *.
Rows 7 and 9: K 1, * k 2 tog, yo, k 1, slip 1, k 1, psso, yo, k 1, yo, k 2 tog, k 1, yo, slip 1, k 1, psso, k 1 *; repeat from * to *.
Repeat Rows 1 through 20 for pattern.

233

LACE STITCHES

Lace oval

Work with multiple of 16 sts, plus 3.

Rows 1 and 9: K 3, *slip 1, k 1, pass slip st over k st (psso), k 2 in back loop for twisted sts (k 2 tw), yarn over (yo), k 5, yo, k 2 tw, k 2 sts together (k 2 tog), k 3 *; repeat from * to *.

Row 2 and all even-numbered rows: Work each stitch as it appears (k the k and p the p sts); work p tw st above tw sts and purl yo loops.

Rows 3 and 7: K 4, * slip 1, k 1, psso, k 2 tw, yo, k 3, yo, k 2 tw, k 2 tog, k 5 *; repeat from * to *, ending with k 4.

Row 5: K 5, * slip 1, k 1, psso, k 2 tw, yo, k 1, yo, k 2 tw, k 2 tog, k 7 *; repeat from * to *, ending with k 5.

Row 11: K 4, * k 2 tw, yo, k 2, slip 2 tog as if to k, k 1, pass both slip sts over k st (double decrease), k 2, yo, k 2 tw, k 5 *; repeat from * to *, ending k 4.

Row 13: K 3, * k 2 tw, yo, k 2, slip 1, k 1, psso, k 1, k 2 tog, k 2, yo, k 2 tw, k 3 *; repeat from * to *.

Row 15: K 4, * yo, k 2 tw, slip 1, k 1, psso, k 3, k 2 tog, k 2 tw, yo, k 5 *; repeat from * to *, ending with k 4.

Row 17: K 5, * yo, k 2 tw, slip 1, k 1,

psso, k 1, k 2 tog, k 2 tw, yo, k 7 *; repeat from * to *, ending with k 5.

Row 19: K 6, * yo, k 2 tw, double decrease, k 2 tw, yo, k 9 *; repeat from * to *, ending with k 6.

Repeat Rows 1 through 20 for pattern.

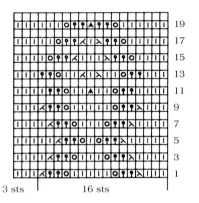

3 sts | 16 sts

I	= k 1
⅄	= slip 1, k 1, psso
☥	= 1 twisted k st
O	= yarn over
⅄	= k 2 tog
⋏	= double dec
□	= 1 st as shown

Wandering lace

Work with a multiple of 16 stitches.

Row 1: * P 7, yarn over (yo), k 1 in back loop (twisted st), yo, k 1, slip 1, k 1, pass slip st over k st and drop it (psso), p 3, p 2 sts together (p 2 tog) *; repeat from * to *.

Row 2 and all even-numbered rows: Work each stitch as it appears on this side of work (k the k sts and p the p sts); work twisted p st over twisted sts.

Row 3: * P 7, yo, k 1 twisted st, p 1, yo, k 1, slip 1, k 1, psso, p 2, p 2 tog *; repeat from * to *.

Row 5: * P 7, yo, k 1 twisted st, p 2, yo, k 1, slip 1, k 1, psso, p 1, p 2 tog *; repeat from * to *.

Row 7: * P 7, yo, k 1 twisted st, p 3, yo, k 1, slip 1, k 1, psso, p 2 tog *; repeat from * to *.

Row 9: * P 2 tog, p 3, k 2 tog, k 1, yo, k 1 twisted st, yo, p 7 *; repeat from * to *.

Row 11: * P 2 tog, p 2, k 2 tog, k 1, yo, p 1, k 1 twisted st, yo, p 7 *; repeat from * to *.

Row 13: * P 2 tog, p 1, k 2 tog, k 1,

yo, p 2, k 1 twisted st, yo, p 7 *; repeat from * to *.

Row 15: * P 2 tog, k 2 tog, k 1, yo, p 3, k 1 twisted st, yo, p 7 *; repeat * to *.

Repeat Rows 1 through 16 for pattern.

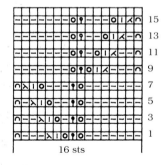

16 sts

−	= p 1
O	= yarn over
☥	= 1 twisted k st
⅄	= slip 1, k 1, psso
∩	= p 2 tog
⋏	= k 2 tog
I	= k 1
□	= 1 st as shown

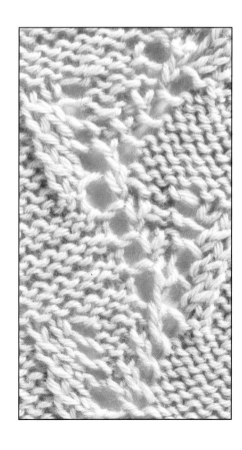

LACE STITCHES

Diamond edging

Start work with 25 stitches.

Row 1: K 1, yarn over (yo), k 2 sts together (k 2 tog), k 19, yo, k 1, k 2 tog.

Row 2: Yo, k 2, p 1, k to end of row. Rows are now increasing in width.

Row 3: K 1, yo, k 2 tog, k 18, yo, k 2 tog, yo, k 1, k 2 tog.

Row 4: Yo, k 2, p 3, k to end of row.

Row 5: K 1, yo, k 2 tog, k 17, work (yo, k 2 tog) twice, yo, k 1, k 2 tog.

Row 6: Yo, k 2, p 5, k to end of row.

Row 7: K 1, yo, k 2 tog, k 16, work (yo, k 2 tog) 3 times, yo, k 1, k 2 tog.

Row 8: Yo, k 2, p 7, k to end of row.

Row 9: K 1, yo, k 2 tog, k 15, work (yo, k 2 tog) 4 times, yo, k 1, k 2 tog.

Row 10: Yo, k 2, p 9, k to end of row.

Row 11: K 1, yo, k 2 tog, k 14, work (yo, k 2 tog) 5 times, yo, k 1, k 2 tog.

Row 12: Yo, k 2, p 11, k to end of row.

Row 13: K 1, yo, k 2 tog, k 13, work (yo, k 2 tog) 6 times, yo, k 1, k 2 tog.

Row 14: Yo, k 2, p 13, k to end of row.

Row 15: K 1, yo, k 2 tog, k 12, work (yo, k 2 tog) 7 times, yo, k 1, k 2 tog.

Row 16: Yo, k 2, p 15, k to end of row.

Row 17: K 1, yo, k 2 tog, k 11, work (yo, k 2 tog) 8 times, yo, k 1, k 2 tog.

Row 18: Yo, k 2, p 17, k to end of row.

Row 19: K 1, yo, k 2 tog, k 10, work (yo, k 2 tog) 9 times, yo, k 1, k 2 tog.

Row 20: Yo, k 2, p 19, k to end of row.

Row 21: K 1, yo, k 2 tog, k 9, work (yo, k 2 tog) 10 times, yo, k 1, k 2 tog.

Row 22: Yo, k 2, p 21, k to end of row.

Row 23: K 1, yo, k 2 tog, k 8, work (yo, k 2 tog) 11 times, yo, k 1, k 2 tog.

Row 24: Yo, k 2, p 23, k to end of row.

Row 25: K 1, yo, k 2 tog, k 8, work (k 2 tog, yo) 11 times, work k 2 tog twice. Rows are now decreasing in width.

Row 26: Yo, k 2, p 21, k to end of row.

Row 27: K 1, yo, k 2 tog, k 9, work (k 2 tog, yo) 10 times, work k 2 tog twice.

Row 28: Yo, k 2, p 19, k to end of row.

Rows 29 through 48: Continue in this manner, reducing the number of sts worked for diamond as indicated on chart. Work until Row 48 is completed. There should be 25 stitches, counting yarn over, on needle at the end of Row 48.

Repeat Rows 1 through 48 for pattern.

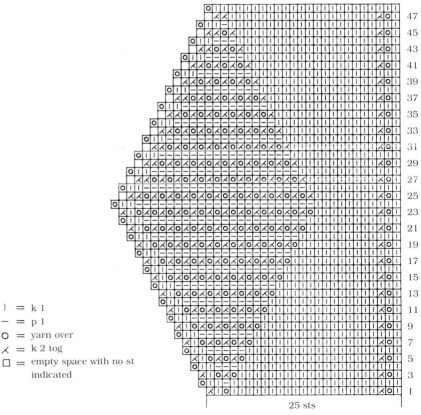

| = k 1
− = p 1
O = yarn over
⟋ = k 2 tog
□ = empty space with no st indicated

25 sts

LACE STITCHES

Lace edging
Start work with 12 stitches.
Row 1: K 3, yarn over (yo), k 5, yo, k 2 sts together (k 2 tog), yo, k 2.
Row 2: K 2, p 12.
Row 3: K 4, work double decrease: slip 1, k 2 tog, pass slip st over k st and drop it (psso), k 2, work (yo, k 2 tog) twice, k 1.
Row 4: K 2, p 10.
Row 5: K 3, slip 1, k 1, psso, k 2, work (yo, k 2 tog) twice, k 1.
Row 6: K 2, p 9.
Row 7: K 2, slip 1, k 1, psso, k 2, work (yo, k 2 tog) twice, k 1.
Row 8: K 2, p 8.
Row 9: K 1, slip 1, k 1, psso, k 2, work (yo, k 2 tog) twice, k 1.
Row 10: K 2, p 7.
Row 11: Slip 1, k 1, psso, k 2, yo, k 1, yo, k 2 tog, yo, k 2.
Row 12: K 2, p 8.
Row 13: Work (k 3, yo) twice, k 2 tog, yo, k 2.
Row 14: K 2, p 10.
Repeat these 14 rows for pattern.

| | = k 1
| — = p 1
| O = yarn over
| ⋋ = slip 1, k 1, psso
| ⋌ = k 2 tog
| ⋏ = double dec

12 sts

Little buds
Work with a multiple of 8 stitches, plus 3.
Row 1: K 1, * yarn over (yo), slip 1, k 1, pass slip st over k st and drop it (psso), k 6 *; repeat from * to *, ending last repeat with k 8.
Row 2 and all even-numbered rows: Purl.
Rows 3, 5, and 7: K 2, * yo, k 2, work double decrease on 3 sts as follows: slip 2 sts together as if to k, k 1, pass both slip sts over k st and drop them; k 2, yo, k 1 *; repeat from * to *, ending last repeat with k 2.
Row 9: K 5, * yo, slip 1, k 1, psso, k 6 *; repeat from * to *, ending with k 4.
Rows 11, 13, and 15: K 1, k 2 sts together, * k 2, yo, k 1, yo, k 2, double decrease *; repeat from * to *, ending last repeat with slip 1, k 1, psso, k 1.
Row 16: Purl.
Repeat Rows 1 through 16 for pattern.

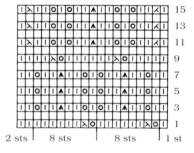

2 sts | 8 sts | 8 sts | 1 st

| | = k 1
| □ = p 1
| O = yarn over
| ⋋ = slip 1, k 1, psso
| ⋏ = double dec
| ⋌ = k 2 tog

LACE STITCHES

Lace wedges

Work with a multiple of 8 stitches, plus 1.

Rows 1 through 10 (moss st): K 1, * p 1, k 1 *; repeat from * to *.

Row 11: K 1, * yarn over (yo), slip 1, k 1, pass slip st over k st and drop it (psso), k 3, k 2 sts together, yo, k 1 *; repeat from * to *.

Rows 12, 14, and 16: Purl.

Row 13: K 2, * yo, slip 1, k 1, psso, k 1, k 2 sts together, yo, k 3 *; repeat from * to *, ending last repeat with k 2.

Row 15: K 3, * yo, slip 1 as if to k, k 2 sts together, psso (double decrease), yo, k 5 *; repeat from * to *, ending last repeat with k 3. Repeat Rows 1 through 16 for pattern.

• = 1 moss st

| = k 1

O = yarn over

⅄ = slip 1, k 1, psso

⋌ = k 2 tog

⋋ = double dec

□ = 1 st as shown

Ribs and eyelets

Work with a multiple of 20 stitches, plus 4.

Row 1: P 4, * k 1, p 4 *; repeat from * to *.

Row 2 and all even-numbered rows: Knit.

Rows 3, 7, 11, 15, and 19: P 4, * for double st, insert needle into corresponding st 1 row below next st and k 1, drop unworked st above from left needle, p 4 *; repeat from * to *.

Row 5: * P 1, p 2 sts together (p 2 tog), yarn over (yo), p 1, double st, work (p 4, double st) 3 times *; repeat from * to *, ending p in last 4 sts.

Row 9: P 4, * double st, p 1, p 2 tog, yo, p 1, work (double st, p 4) 3 times *; repeat from * to *.

Row 13: Work (p 4, double st) twice, * p 1, p 2 tog, yo, p 1, work (double st, p 4) 3 times, double st *; repeat from * to *, ending last repeat with p 4, double st, p 4.

Row 17: * Work (p 4, double st) 3 times, p 1, p 2 tog, yo, p 1, double st *; repeat * to *, ending p in last 4 sts.

Row 21: * P 1, p 2 tog, yo, p 1, work (double st, p 4) 3 times, double st *; repeat from * to *, ending p 1, p 2 tog, yo, p 1.
Repeat Rows 7 through 22 for pattern.

| = k 1

V = 1 double st

∩ = p 2 tog

O = yarn over

□ = 1 st in reverse stockinette st

LACE STITCHES

Little roses

Work with a multiple of 11 stitches.
Row 1: K 3, * yarn over (yo), slip 1, k 1, pass slip st over k st and drop it (psso), k 9 *; repeat from * to *, ending last repeat with k 6.
Row 2 and all even-numbered rows: Purl.
Row 3: K 4, * yo, slip 1, k 1, psso, k 9 *; repeat from * to *, ending with k 5.
Row 5: K 5, * yo, slip 1, k 1, psso, k 9 *; repeat from * to *, ending with k 4.
Row 7: K 3, * k 2 sts together (k 2 tog), yo, k 1, yo, slip 1, k 1, psso, k 6 *; repeat from * to *, ending with k 3.
Row 9: K 2, * k 2 tog, yo, k 3, yo, slip 1, k 1, psso, k 4 *; repeat from * to *, ending with k 2.
Row 11: Repeat Row 7.
Row 13: Repeat Row 9.
Row 15: K 4, * yo, slip 1, k 2 tog, psso (double decrease made), yo, k 8 *; repeat from * to *, ending with k 4.
Repeat Rows 1 through 16 for pattern.

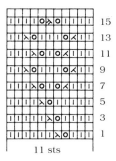

| = k 1
O = yarn over
⋋ = slip 1, k 1, psso
⋌ = k 2 tog
⋏ = double dec
□ = p 1

Plantation

Work with a multiple of 10 stitches, plus 1.
Rows 1, 3, and 5: K 1, * yarn over (yo), k 2, slip 1, k 1, pass slip st over k st and drop it (psso), k 1, k 2 sts together (k 2 tog), k 2, yo, k 1 *; repeat from * to *.
Row 2 and all even-numbered rows: Purl.
Row 7: K 2, * yo, k 2, work double decrease on 3 sts as follows: slip 2 sts together as if to k, k 1, pass both slip sts over k st and drop them; k 2, yo, k 3 *; repeat from * to *, ending last repeat with k 2.
Row 9: K 3, * yo, k 1, double decrease, k 1, yo, k 5 *; repeat from * to *, ending with k 3.
Row 11: K 4, * yo, double decrease, yo, k 7 *; repeat from * to *, ending with k 4.
Row 13: * K 2 tog, yo *; repeat from * to *, ending k 1 in last st.
Row 14: Knit.
Repeat these 14 rows for pattern.

| = k 1
O = yarn over
⋋ = slip 1, k 1, psso
⋌ = k 2 tog
⋏ = double dec
□ = p 1

LACE STITCHES

Knotted threads

Work with a multiple of 4 stitches, plus 3.

Row 1: K 1, yarn over (yo), slip 1, k 2 sts together (k 2 tog), pass slip st over k st and drop it (psso), * yo, k 1, yo, slip 1, k 2 tog, psso *; repeat from * to *, ending yo, slip 1, k 1, psso, yo, k 1.

Row 2: Purl.

Row 3: K 1, yo, k 2 tog, * yo, slip 1, k 2 tog, psso, yo, k 1 *; repeat from * to *.

Row 4: Purl.

Repeat these 4 rows for pattern.

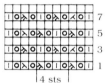

| = k 1
O = yarn over
⋋ = lip 1, k 2 tog, psso
⋋ = lip 1, k 1, psso
⋌ = k 2 tog
☐ = p 1

Irish net

Work with a multiple of 3 stitches.

Row 1: K 2, * yarn over (yo), slip 1, k 2, pass slip st over both k sts and drop it *; repeat from * to *, ending k in last st.

Row 2: Purl.

Row 3: K 1, * slip 1, k 2, pass slip st over both k sts, yo *; repeat from * to *, ending k in last 2 sts.

Row 4: Purl.

Repeat these 4 rows for pattern.

| = k 1
O = yarn over
V = 1 slip st
⌒ = psso k 2

☐ = p 1

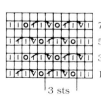

LACE STITCHES

Tiny diamond mesh

Work with a multiple of 5 stitches, plus 3.

Row 1: K 4, * yo, slip 1, k 2 sts together, pass slip st over k st and drop it (double decrease made), increase between sts by picking up connecting yarn between last st worked and next st, place strand on left needle and k 1 in back loop, k 2 *; repeat from * to *, ending last repeat with k 1.

Row 2 and all even-numbered rows: Purl.

Row 3: K 3, * yo, double decrease, increase, k 2 *; repeat from * to *.

Row 5: K 2, * yo, double decrease, increase, k 2 *; repeat from * to *, ending last repeat with k 3.

Row 7: K 1, * yo, double decrease, increase, k 2 *; repeat from * to *, ending with k 4.

Row 9: K 5, * yo, double decrease, increase, k 2 *; repeat from * to *, ending with k 5.

Repeat Rows 1 through 10 for pattern.

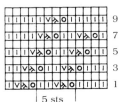

| = k 1
O = yarn over
⅄ = double dec
∨ = 1 increase

□ = p 1

Ripples

Work with a multiple of 5 stitches, plus 2.

Row 1: K 1, * p 1, slip 2 with yarn at front of work, p 2 sts together (p 2 tog), yarn over (yo) *; repeat from * to *, ending k in last st. *Note*: Slip sts with yarn in front throughout pattern.

Row 2 and all even-numbered rows: Purl.

Row 3: K 1, * slip 2, p 2 tog, yo, p 1 *; repeat from * to *, ending k in last st.

Row 5: K 1, slip 1, * p 2 tog, yo, p 1, slip 2 *; repeat from * to *, ending last repeat with slip 1, k in last st.

Row 7: K 1, * p 2 tog, yo, p 1, slip 2 *; repeat from * to *, ending k in last st.

Row 9: K 1, p 2, * slip 2, p 2 tog, yo, p 1 *; repeat from * to *, ending slip 2, p 1, k in last st.

Repeat Rows 1 through 10 for patterns.

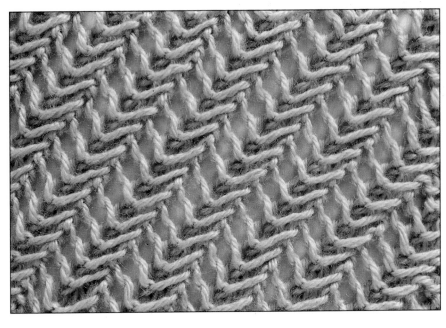

| = k 1
□ or − = p 1
O = yarn over
∧ = 1 slip st
∩ = p 2 tog

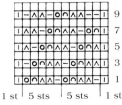

LACE STITCHES

Rippling water

Work with a multiple of 8 stitches, plus 5.

Rows 1, 3, 5, 9, and 11 (right side): Purl.

Row 2: K 5, * yarn over (yo), slip 1 as if to k, k 2 sts together, pass slip st over k st and drop it (double decrease), yo, k 5 *; repeat from * to *.

Rows 4, 6, 10, and 12: Knit.

Row 7: P 6, * insert needle in corresponding st 4 rows below next st and k 1, drop unworked st above from left needle, letting sts unravel down to worked st (long st made), p 7 *; repeat from * to *, ending last repeat with k 6.

Row 8: K 1, * yo, double decrease, yo, k 5 *; repeat from * to *, ending last repeat with k 1.

Row 13: P 2, * work long st below next st, p 7 *; repeat from * to *, ending last repeat with p 2.

Repeat Rows 2 through 13 for pattern.

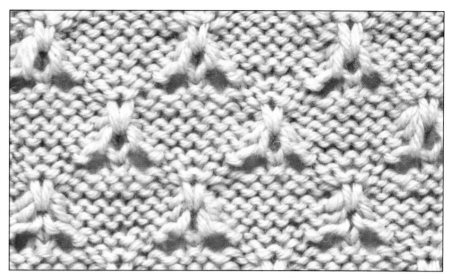

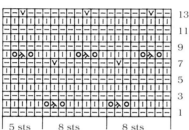

−	= p 1
I	= k 1
O	= yarn over
⋋	= double dec
V	= 1 long st

Alternating eyelets and ribs

Work with a multiple of 6 stitches, plus 5.

Rows 1 and 5: P 5, * k 1 in back loop (twisted k st), p 5 *; repeat from * to *.

Rows 2, 4, and 6: K 5, * p 1 in back loop (twisted p st), k 5 *; repeat from * to *.

Row 3: * P 1, p 2 sts together, yarn over (yo), p 2, k 1 twisted st *; repeat from * to *, ending last repeat with p 2.

Rows 7 and 11: P 2, * k 1 twisted st, p 5 *; repeat from * to *, ending last repeat with p 2.

Rows 8, 10, and 12: K 2, * p 1 twisted st, k 5 *; repeat from * to *, ending last repeat with k 2.

Row 9: P 2, * k 1 twisted st, p 1, p 2 sts together, yo, p 2 *; repeat from * to *, ending last repeat with p 2.

Repeat Rows 1 through 12 for pattern.

−	= p 1
?	= 1 twisted st
∩	= p 2 tog
O	= yarn over
□	= k 1

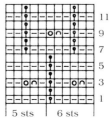

LACE STITCHES

Shaped diamonds

Work with a multiple of 14 stitches.
Row 1: * Slip 1, k 1, pass slip st over k st and drop it (psso), k 4, yarn over (yo), p 2, yo, k 4, k 2 sts together (k 2 tog) *; repeat from * to *.
Row 2: * P 2 tog, p 3, yo, k 4, yo, p 3, p 2 tog through back loops, *; repeat from * to *.
Row 3: * Slip 1, k 1, psso, k 2, yo, p 6, yo, k 2, k 2 tog *; repeat from * to *.
Row 4: * P 2 tog, p 1, yo, k 8, yo, p 1, p 2 tog through back loops *; repeat from * to *.
Row 5: * Slip 1, k 1, psso, yo, p 10, yo, k 2 tog *; repeat from * to *.
Row 6: K 1, * yo, p 4, p 2 tog through back loops, p 2 tog, p 4, yo, k 2 *; repeat from * to *, ending last repeat with k 1.
Row 7: P 2, * yo, k 3, k 2 tog, slip 1, k 1, psso, k 3, yo, p 4 *; repeat from * to *, ending last repeat with p 2.
Row 8: K 3, * yo, p 2, p 2 tog through back loops, p 2 tog, p 2, yo, k 6 *; repeat from * to *, ending with k 3.
Row 9: P 4, * yo, k 1, k 2 tog, slip 1,

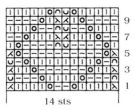

14 sts

$\curlywedge$ = slip 1, k 1, psso
$|$ = k 1
O = yarn over
$-$ = p 1
$\curlywedge$ = k 2 tog
$\cup$ = p 2 tog
$\cap$ = p 2 tog in back loops

k 1, psso, k 1, yo, p 8 *; repeat from * to *, ending last repeat with p 4.
Row 10: K 5, * yo, p 2 tog through back loops, p 2 tog, yo, k 10 *; repeat from * to *, ending k 5.
Repeat Rows 1 through 10 for pattern.

Portholes

Work with a multiple of 8 stitches, plus 6.
Note: To work double slip sts, shown as vv on chart, always carry yarn on right side of work.
Rows 1 and 7 (right side): Purl.
Row 2: P 2, * with yarn at back, slip 2, p 6 *; repeat from * to *, ending last repeat with p 2.
Row 3: K 2, * slip 2, k 1, k 2 sts together (k 2 tog), yarn over twice, slip 1, k 1, pass slip st over k st and drop it (psso), k 1 *; repeat from * to *, ending slip 2, k 2.
Row 4: P 2, * slip 2, p 3, k 1 in back loop, p 2 *; repeat from * to *, ending slip 2, p 2.
Row 5: K 2, * slip 2, k 6 *; repeat from * to *, ending slip 2, k 2.
Row 6: Knit.
Row 8: P 6, * slip 2, p 6 *; repeat from * to *.
Row 9: K 3, yarn over (yo), * slip 1, k 1, psso, k 1, slip 2, k 1, k 2 tog, yo twice *; repeat from * to *, ending last repeat with single yo, k last 3 sts.
Row 10: P 6, * slip 2, p 3, k 1 in back loop, p 2 *; repeat from * to *, ending slip 2, p 6.

Row 11: K 6, * slip 2, k 6 *; repeat from * to *.

Row 12: Knit.
Repeat these 12 rows for pattern.

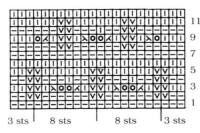

3 sts   8 sts   8 sts   3 sts

$|$ = k 1
$-$ = p 1
$\vee$ = 1 slip st
$\curlywedge$ = k 2 tog
$\curlywedge$ = slip 1, k 1, psso
O = yarn over

LACE STITCHES

Clusters

Work with a multiple of 4 stitches, plus 1.

Row 1: K 1, * yarn over (yo), k 2 sts together (k 2 tog), k 2 *; repeat from * to *.
Row 2: P 1, * p 2 tog, yo, p 2 *; repeat from * to *.
Row 3: K 3, * yo, k 2 tog, k 2 *; repeat from * to *, ending yo, k 2 tog.
Row 4: P 1, * yo, p 2 tog, p 2 *; repeat from * to *.
Row 5: K 1, * k 2 tog, yo, k 2 *; repeat from * to *.
Row 6: P 3, * yo, p 2 tog, p 2 *; repeat from * to *, ending yo, p 2 tog.
Repeat these 6 rows for pattern.

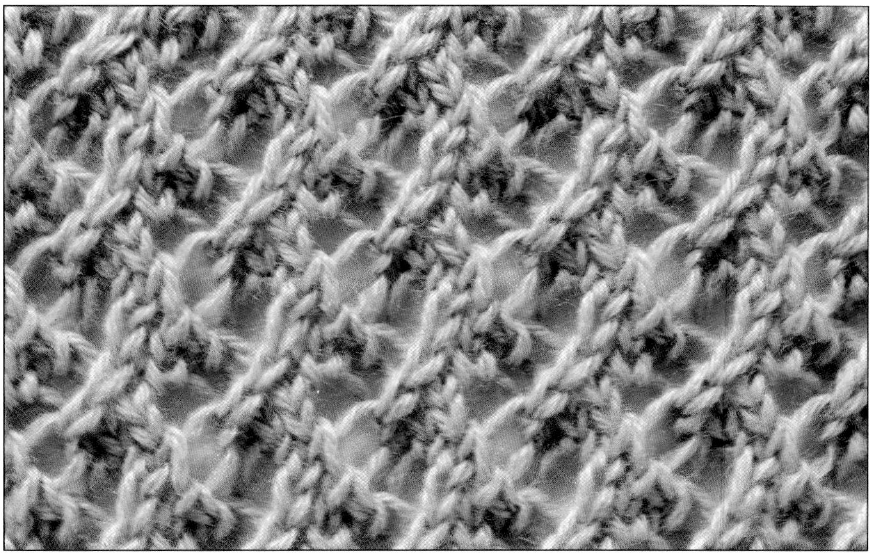

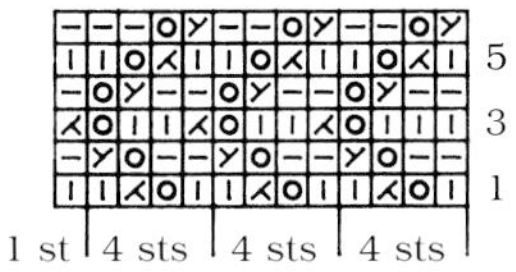
5
3
1
1 st
4 sts
4 sts
4 sts

| = k 1
O = yarn over
⋌ = k 2 tog
– = p 1
Y = p 2 tog

Vertical lace bands

Work with a multiple of 11 stitches.

Row 1: * Slip 1, k 1, pass slip st over k st and drop it (psso), k 3 in back loop for twisted k sts, yarn over (yo), k 1, yo, k 3 twisted sts, k 2 sts together (k 2 tog) *; repeat from * to *.
Row 2 and all even-numbered rows: Purl.
Row 3: * Slip 1, k 1, psso, k 2 twisted sts, yo, k 1, yo, slip 1, k 1, psso, yo, k 2 twisted sts, k 2 tog *; repeat from * to *.
Row 5: * Slip 1, k 1, psso, k 1 twisted st, yo, k 1, yo, work (slip 1, k 1, psso, yo) twice, k 1 twisted st, k 2 tog *; repeat from * to *.
Row 7: * Slip 1, k 1, psso, yo, k 1, yo, work (slip 1, k 1, psso, yo) 3 times, k 2 tog *; repeat from * to *.
Repeat Rows 1 through 8 for pattern.

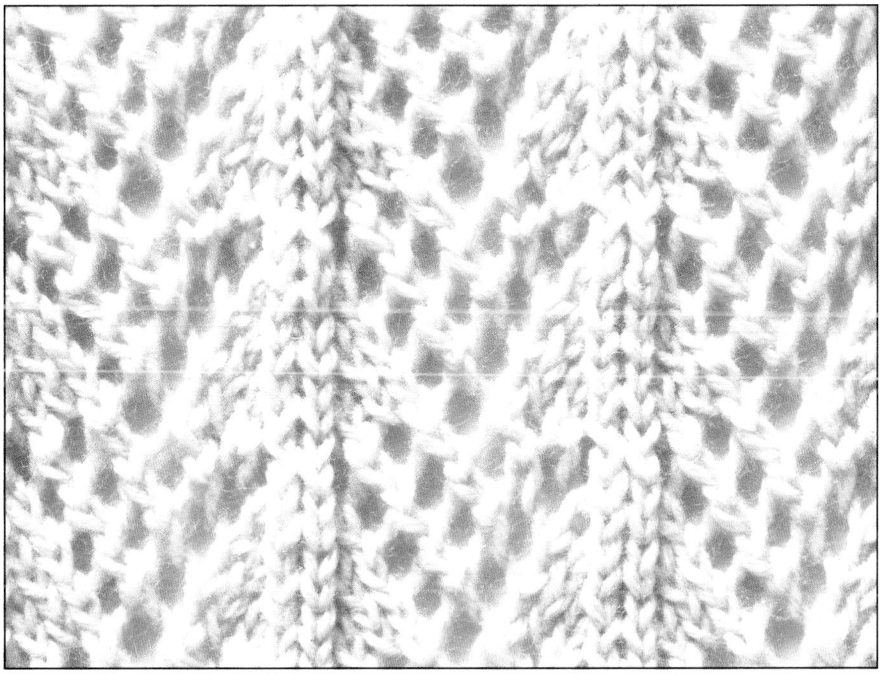

| = k 1
♀ = 1 twisted k st
O = yarn over
⋋ = slip 1, k 1, psso
⋌ = k 2 tog
– = p 1

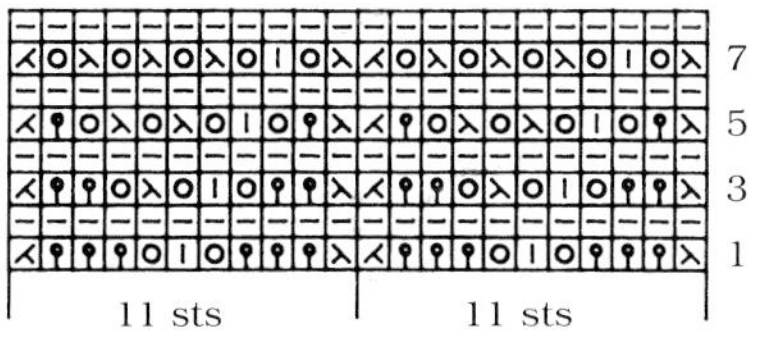
7
5
3
1
11 sts
11 sts

LACE STITCHES

Kites

Work with a multiple of 8 stitches, plus 1.

Rows 1, 3, 5, 17, 19, and 21: K 3, * yarn over (yo), work double decrease: slip 1, k 2 sts together (k 2 tog), pass slip st over k st and drop it (psso), yo, k 5 *; repeat from * to *, ending last repeat with k 3.

Row 2 and all even-numbered rows: Purl.

Row 7: K 2, * k 2 tog, yo, k 1, yo, slip 1, k 1, psso, k 3 *; repeat from * to *, ending last repeat with k 2.

Row 9: K 1, * k 2 tog, yo, k 3, yo, slip 1, k 1, psso, k 1 *; repeat from * to *.

Row 11: K 7, * yo, double decrease, yo, k 5 *; repeat from * to *, ending last repeat with k 7.

Row 13: K 1, * yo, slip 1, k 1, psso, k 3, k 2 tog, yo, k 1 *; repeat from * to *.

Row 15: K 2, * yo, slip 1, k 1, psso, k 1, k 2 tog, yo, k 3 *; repeat from * to *, ending last repeat with k 2.
Repeat Rows 1 through 22 for pattern.

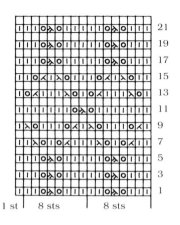

I = k 1
O = yarn over
⅄ = double dec
⟋ = k 2 tog
⟍ = slip 1, k 1, psso
□ = p 1

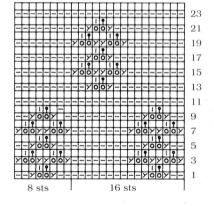

− = p 1
O = yarn over
⅄ = p 2 tog
I or □ = k 1
ꝗ = k 1 in back loop

Floweret

Work with a multiple of 16 stitches, plus 8.

Rows 1, 5, and 9: P 2, * p 2 sts together (p 2 tog), yarn over twice (yo twice), p 2 tog, p 12 *; repeat from * to *, ending last repeat with p 2.

Row 2 and all even-numbered rows: Work each stitch as it appears on this side of work (k the k sts and p the p sts). K 1 and k 1 in back loop on double yarn-over loops.

Rows 3 and 7: * Work (p 2 tog, yo twice, p 2 tog) twice, p 8 *; repeat from * to *, ending (p 2 tog, yo twice, p 2 tog) twice.

Rows 11 and 23: Purl.

Rows 13, 17, and 21: P 10, * p 2 tog, yo twice, p 2 tog, p 12 *; repeat from * to *, ending last repeat with p 10.

Rows 15 and 19: K 8, * work (p 2 tog, yo twice, p 2 tog) twice, p 8 *; repeat from * to *.
Repeat Rows 1 through 24 for pattern.

LACE STITCHES

Agave

Work with a multiple of 24 stitches, plus 5.

Row 1: K 1, yarn over (yo), work double decrease: slip 1, k 2 sts together (k 2 tog), pass slip st over k st and drop it (psso), yo, k 1, * p 5, k 4, yo, k 3, slip 1, k 1, psso, p 5, k 1, yo, double decrease, yo, k 1 *; repeat from * to *.

Row 2 and all even-numbered rows: Work each stitch as it appears on this side of work (k the k sts and p the p sts). Purl yarn-over loops.

Row 3: K 1, yo, double decrease, yo, k 1, * p 4, k 2 tog, k 3, yo, k 1, yo, k 3, slip 1, k 1, psso, p 4, k 1, yo, double decrease, yo, k 1 *; repeat from * to *.

Row 5: K 1, yo, double decrease, yo, k 1, * p 3, k 2 tog, work (k 3, yo) twice, k 3, slip 1, k 1, psso, p 3, k 1, yo, double decrease, yo, k 1 *; repeat from * to *.

Row 7: K 1, yo, double decrease, yo, k 1, * p 2, k 2 tog, k 3, yo, k 5, yo, k 3, slip 1, k 1, psso, p 2, k 1, yo, double decrease, yo, k 1 *; repeat from * to *.

Row 9: K 1, yo, double decrease, yo, k 1 *; p 1, k 2 tog, k 3, yo, k 7, yo, k 3, slip 1, k 1, psso, p 1, k 1, yo, double decrease, yo, k 1 *; repeat from * to *.

Row 2 and all even-numbered rows: Work each stitch as it appears on this side of work.

Repeat Rows 1 through 10 for pattern.

I	=	k 1
—	=	p 1
O	=	yarn over
⋋	=	slip 1, k 1, psso
⋌	=	k 2 tog
⋏	=	double dec
☐	=	1 st as shown

5 sts   24 sts

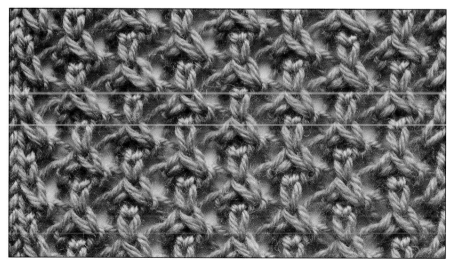

I	=	k 1
O	=	yarn over
⋏	=	double dec
Y	=	p 2 tog
—	=	p 1
⋌	=	k 2 tog
⋋	=	slip 1, k 1, psso

6 sts   6 sts   3 sts

Clovers

Work with a multiple of 6 stitches, plus 3.

Row 1: K 3, * yarn over (yo), work double decrease on 3 sts as follows: slip 1, k 2 sts together (k 2 tog), pass slip st over k st and drop it (psso), yo, k 3 *; repeat from * to *.

Row 2: P 2, * p 2 tog, yo, p 1, yo, p 2 tog, p 1 *; repeat from * to *, ending last repeat with p 2.

Row 3: K 1, k 2 tog, yo, * k 3, yo, double decrease, yo *; repeat from * to *, ending last repeat with slip 1, k 1, psso, p last st.

Row 4: P 2, * yo, p 2 tog, p 1, p 2 tog, yo, p 1 *; repeat from * to *, ending last repeat with yo, p 2.

Repeat Rows 1 through 4 for pattern.

LACE STITCHES

Column of leaves

Start work with a multiple of 23 stitches, plus 2.

Row 1: P 2, * k 7, k 2 sts together (k 2 tog), yarn over (yo), k 1, yo, p 1, yo, k 1, yo, slip 1, k 1, pass slip st over k st and drop it (psso), k 7, p 2 *; repeat from * to *.

Row 2: K 2, * p 6, p 2 tog in back loops, p 3, k 1, p 3, p 2 tog, p 6, k 2 *; repeat from * to *.

Row 3: P 2, * k 5, k 2 tog, k 1, work (yo, k 1) twice, p 1, k 1, work (yo, k 1) twice, slip 1, k 1, psso, k 5, p 2 *; repeat from * to *.

Row 4: K 2, * p 4, p 2 tog in back loops, p 5, k 1, p 5, p 2 tog, p 4, k 2 *; repeat from * to *.

Row 5: P 2, * k 3, k 2 tog, k 2, yo, k 1, yo, k 2, p 1, k 2, yo, k 1, yo, k 2, slip 1, k 1, psso, k 3, p 2 *; repeat from * to *.

Row 6: K 2, * p 2, p 2 tog in back loops, p 7, k 1, p 7, p 2 tog, p 2, k 2 *; repeat from * to *.

Row 7: P 2, * k 1, k 2 tog, k 3, yo, k 1, yo, k 3, p 1, k 3, yo, k 1, yo, k 3, slip 1, k 1, psso, k 1, p 2 *; repeat from * to *.

Row 8: K 2, * p 2 tog in back loops, p 9, k 1, p 9, p 2 tog, k 2 *; repeat from * to *.

Repeat these 8 rows for pattern.

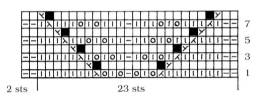

	= p 1
|	= k 1
⊀	= k 2 tog
O	= yarn over
⅄	= slip 1, k 1, psso
⋎	= p 2 tog in back loop
Y	= p 2 tog
□	= 1 st as shown
■	= empty space with no st indicated

2 sts   23 sts

Little lace diamonds

Work with a multiple of 9 stitches.

Rows 1 and 5: K 2, * k 2 sts together (k 2 tog), yarn over (yo), k 1, yo, slip 1, k 1, pass slip st over k st and drop it (psso), k 4 *; repeat from * to *, ending last repeat with k 2.

Row 2 and all even-numbered rows: Purl.

Row 3: K 1, * k 2 tog, yo, k 3, yo, slip 1, k 1, psso, k 2 *; repeat from * to *, ending last repeat with k 1.

Rows 7 and 11: K 1, * yo, slip 1, k 1, psso, k 3, k 2 tog, yo, k 2 *; repeat from * to *, ending last repeat with k 1.

Row 9: K 2, * yo, slip 1, k 1, psso, k 1, k 2 tog, yo, k 4 *; repeat from * to *, ending last repeat with k 2. Repeat Rows 1 through 12 for pattern.

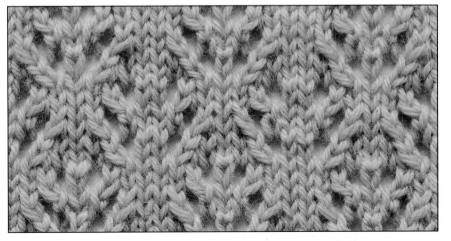

|	= k 1
⊀	= k 2 tog
O	= yarn over
⅄	= slip 1, k 1, psso
□	= p 1

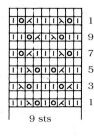

9 sts

LACE STITCHES

Pearls

Work with a multiple of 6 stitches, plus 5.

Rows 1 and 3: K 4, * p 3, k 3 *; repeat from * to *, ending last repeat with k 4.

Row 2: P 4, * k 2 sts together, yarn over (yo), k 1, p 3 *; repeat from * to *, ending last repeat with p 4,

Rows 4 and 8: Knit.

Rows 5 and 7: K 1, * p 3, k 3 *; repeat from * to *, ending p 3, k in last st.

Row 6: P 1, * k 2 sts together, yo, k 1, p 3 *; repeat from * to *, ending last repeat with p 1.

Repeat Rows 1 through 8 for pattern.

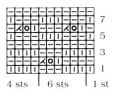

4 sts | 6 sts | 1 st

| = k 1
− = p 1
O = yarn over
⋌ = k 2 tog

Amber

Work with a multiple of 18 stitches, plus 3.

Row 1: P 2, * yarn over (yo), k 1, yo, work bobble on 1 st as follows: purl, knit, purl, knit, and purl all in next st, pass first 4 sts, one at a time, over 5th st to complete bobble; k 3, slip 1, k 2 sts together, pass slip st over k st and drop it (double decrease made), p 1, k 3 sts together (k 3 tog), k 3, bobble, yo, k 1, yo, p 1 * repeat from * to *, ending last repeat with p 2.

Row 2 and all even-numbered rows: Work each stitch as it appears on this side of work (k the k sts and p the p sts). Purl yarn-over loops.

Row 3: P 2, * yo, k 1, yo, k 3, double decrease, bobble, p 1, bobble, k 3 tog, k 3, yo, k 1, yo, p 1 *; repeat from * to *, ending last repeat with p 2.

Row 5: P 2, * yo, k 1, yo, k 2, double decrease, bobble, k 1, p 1, k 1, bobble, k 3 tog, k 2, yo, k 1, yo, p 1 *; repeat from * to *, ending last repeat with p 2.

Row 7: P 2, * work (yo, k 1) twice, double decrease, bobble, k 2, p 1, k 2, bobble, k 3 tog, work (k 1, yo) twice, p 1 *; repeat from * to *, ending last repeat with p 2.

Row 9: P 2, * k 3 tog, k 3, bobble, yo, k 1, yo, p 1, yo, k 1, yo, bobble, k 3, double decrease, p 1 *; repeat from * to *, ending last repeat with p 2.

Row 11: P 2, * bobble, k 3 tog, k 3, yo, k 1, yo, p 1, yo, k 1, yo, k 3, dou-ble decrease, bobble, p 1 *; repeat

from * to *, ending last repeat with p 2.

Row 13: P 2, * k 1, bobble, k 3 tog, k 2, yo, k 1, yo, p 1, yo, k 1, yo, k 2, double decrease, bobble, k 1, p 1 *; repeat from * to *, ending last repeat with p 2.

Row 15: P 2, * k 2, bobble, k 3 tog, work (k 1, yo) twice, p 1, work (yo, k 1) twice, double decrease, bobble, k 2, p 1 *; repeat from * to *, ending last repeat with p 2.

Repeat Rows 1 through 16 for pattern.

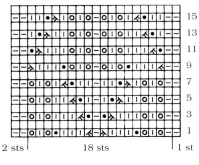

2 sts | 18 sts | 1 st

− = p 1
| = k 1
O = yarn over
⋋ = slip 1, k 2 tog, psso
⋏ = k 3 tog
● = 1 bobble
□ = 1 st as shown

LACE STITCHES

Gentle curves

Work with a multiple of 14 stitches, plus 1.

Rows 1, 3, 11, and 13: Knit.

Row 2 and all even-numbered rows: Work each stitch as it appears from this side of work (k the k sts and p the p sts). Purl yarn-over loops.

Rows 5, 7, and 9: P 1, * yarn over (yo), k 4, slip 1, k 1, pass slip st over k st and drop it (psso), p 1, k 2 sts together, k 4, yo, p 1 *; repeat from * to *.

Rows 15, 17, and 19: P 1, * k 2 tog, k 4, yo, p 1, yo, k 4, slip 1, k 1, psso, p 1 *; repeat from * to *.

Repeat Rows 1 through 20 for pattern.

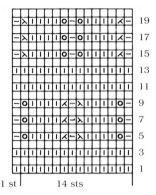

| = k 1
— = p 1
⅄ = slip 1, k 1, psso
⋌ = k 2 tog
O = yarn over
□ = 1 st as shown

Movement

Start work with a multiple of 13 sts, plus 2.

Row 1: K 3, * work bobble on 1 st as follows: knit, purl, knit, purl, and knit all in next st, turn work, k 5, turn, p 5 sts together to complete bobble; k 2, yarn over (yo), k 1, yo, k 5, k 2 sts together (k 2 tog), k 2 *; repeat from * to *, ending last repeat with k 2 tog, p 1.

Rows 2, 4, 6, 8, and 10: P 1, * p 2 tog, p 12 *; repeat from * to *, ending p last st.

Row 3: K 7, * yo, k 1, yo, k 4, k 2 tog, k 6 *; repeat from * to *, ending last repeat with k 2 tog, k 1.

Row 5: K 8, * yo, k 1, yo, k 3, k 2 tog, k 7 *; repeat from * to *, ending last repeat with k 2 tog, k 1.

Row 7: K 9, * yo, k 1, yo, k 2, k 2 tog, k 8 *; repeat from * to *, ending last repeat with k 2 tog, k 1.

Row 9: K 10, * work (yo, k 1) twice, k 2 tog, k 9 *; repeat from * to * ending last repeat with k 2 tog, k 1.

Row 11: K 1, * slip 1, k 1, pass slip st over k st and drop it (psso), k 5, yo, k 1, yo, k 2, bobble, k 2 *; repeat from * to *, ending k in last st.

Rows 12, 14, 16, 18, and 20: K 13, * p 2 tog in back loops, p 12 *; repeat from * to *, ending last repeat with p 1.

Row 13: K 1, * slip 1, k 1, psso, k 4, yo, k 1, yo, k 6 *; repeat from * to *, ending k in last st.

Row 15: K 1, * slip 1, k 1, psso, k 3, yo, k 1, yo, k 7 *; repeat from * to *, ending k in last st.

Row 17: K 1, * slip 1, k 1, psso, k 2, yo, k 1, yo, k 8 *; repeat from * to *, ending k in last st.

Row 19: K 1, * slip 1, k 1, psso, work (k 1, yo) twice, k 9 *; repeat from * to *, ending k in last st.

Repeat Rows 1 through 20 for pattern.

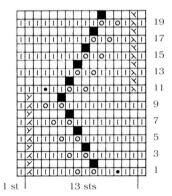

| = k 1
● = 1 bobble
O = yarn over
⋌ = k 2 tog
⅄ = p 2 tog
⅄ = slip 1, k 1, psso
⋋ = p 2 tog in back loop
□ = p 1
■ = empty space with no st indicated

LACE STITCHES

Chessboard

Work with a multiple of 14 stitches, plus 7.

Rows 1 and 9: P 7, * k 7, p 7 *; repeat from * to *.

Row 2 and all even-numbered rows: Work each stitch as it appears on this side of work (k the k sts and p the p sts). Purl yarn-over loops.

Rows 3 and 7: P 7, * k 3, yarn over (yo), k 2 sts together (k 2 tog), k 2, p 7 *; repeat from * to *.

Row 5: P 7, * k 1, k 2 tog, yo, k 1, yo, k 2 tog, k 1, p 7 *; repeat from * to *.

Rows 11 and 19: K 7, * p 7, k 7 *; repeat from * to *.

Rows 13 and 17: K 3, yo, k 2 tog, k 2, * p 7, k 3, yo, k 2 tog, k 2 *; repeat from * to *.

Row 15: K 1, k 2 tog, yo, k 1, yo, k 2 tog, k 1, * p 7, k 1, k 2 tog, yo, k 1, yo, k 2 tog, k 1 *; repeat from * to *. Repeat Rows 1 through 10 for pattern.

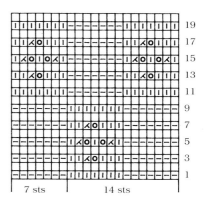

7 sts   14 sts

- − = p 1
- I = k 1
- O = yarn over
- ⊼ = k 2 tog
- □ = 1 st as shown

Folk lace

Work with a multiple of 8 stitches, plus 5.

Row 1: Knit.

Row 2 and all even-numbered rows: Purl.

Row 3: K 2, k 2 sts together (k 2 tog), yarn over (yo), * k 1, yo, work (slip 1, k 1, pass slip st over k st and drop it, yo) twice, slip 1, k 2 tog, pass slip st over k st (psso) for double decrease, yo *; repeat from * to *, ending k 1, work (yo, slip 1, k 1, psso) 3 times, k 2.

Row 5: K 4, * work (yo, slip 1, k 1, psso) 3 times, k 2 *; repeat from * to *, ending last repeat with k 3.

Row 7: K 5, * work (yo, slip 1, k 1, psso) twice, k 4 *; repeat from * to *.

Row 9: * K 6, yo, slip 1, k 1, psso *; repeat from * to *, ending k last 5 sts.

Row 11: K 4, * k 2 tog, yo, k 1, yo, slip 1, k 1, psso, k 3 *; repeat from * to *, ending last repeat with k 4.

Row 13: K 3, * k 2 tog, yo, k 1, yo, slip 1, k 1, psso, yo, slip 1, k 1, psso, k 1 *; repeat from * to *, ending last repeat with k 3. Repeat Rows 3 through 14 for pattern.

- I = k 1
- ⅄ = slip 1, k 1, psso
- ⅄ = double dec
- O = yarn over
- ⼂ = k 2 tog
- □ = p 1

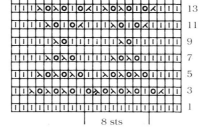

8 sts

LACE STITCHES

Bands of alternating eyelets

Work with a multiple of 4 stitches, plus 2.

Row 1: Knit.
Row 2: Purl.
Row 3: K 1, * yarn over, k 2 sts together, k 2 *; repeat from * to *, ending last repeat with k 3.
Rows 4 and 5: Knit,
Row 6: Purl.
Row 7: K 3, * yarn over, k 2 sts together, k 2 *; repeat from * to *, ending last repeat with k 1.
Row 8: Knit.
Repeat these 8 rows for pattern.

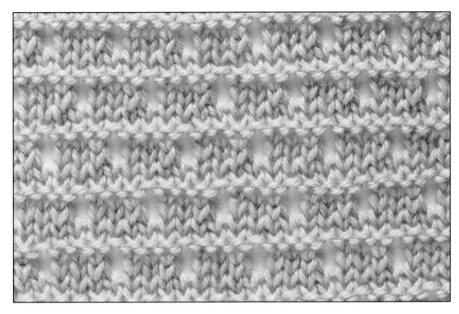

| = k 1
− = p 1
O = yarn over
⟋ = k 2 tog

Upsweep pattern

Work with a multiple of 5 stitches, plus 2.

Row 1: K 1, * p 3, k 2 sts together, yarn over *; repeat from * to *, ending k last st.
Row 2 and all even-numbered rows: Work each stitch as it appears on this side of work (k the k sts and p the p sts). Purl yarn-over loops.
Row 3: K 1, * p 2, k 2 sts together, k 1, yarn over *; repeat from * to *, ending k last st.
Row 5: K 1, * p 1, k 2 sts together, k 2, yarn over *; repeat from * to *, ending k last st.
Row 7: K 1, * k 2 sts together, k 3, yarn over *; repeat from * to *, ending k last st.
Repeat Rows 1 through 8 for pattern.

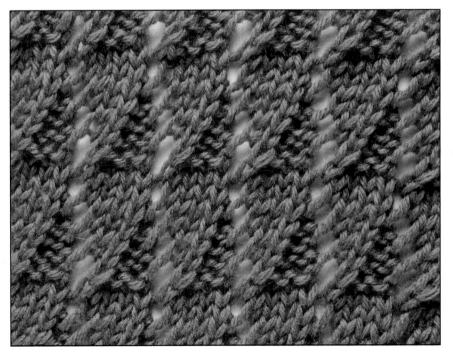

| = k 1
− = p 1
O = yarn over
⟋ = k 2 tog
□ = 1 st as shown

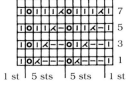

LACE STITCHES

Lace diamond edging

Start work with 17 stitches.

Row 1: K 1, yarn over (yo), k 2 sts together (k 2 tog), yo, k 1, yo, slip 1, k 1, pass slip st over k st (psso), k 5, p 2 tog, yo, p 4.

Row 2 and all even-numbered rows: P 2, p 2 tog, yo, p to end of row.

Row 3: K 1, yo, k 2 tog, yo, k 3, yo, slip 1, k 1, psso, k 4, p 2 tog, yo, p 4.

Row 5: K 1, yo, k 2 tog, yo, k 5, yo, slip 1, k 1, psso, k 3, p 2 tog, yo, p 4.

Row 7: K 1, yo, k 2 tog, yo, k 3, work (yo, slip 1, k 1, psso, k 2) twice, p 2 tog, yo, p 4.

Row 9: K 1, yo, k 2 tog, yo, k 3, work (yo, slip 1, k 1, psso) twice, k 2, yo, slip 1, k 1, psso, k 1, p 2 tog, yo, p 4.

Row 11: K 1, yo, k 2 tog, yo, k 3, work (yo, slip 1, k 1, psso) 3 times, k 2, yo, slip 1, k 1, psso, p 2 tog, yo, p 4.

Row 13: Slip 1, k 1, psso, work (yo, slip 1, k 1, psso) twice, k 2, work (yo, slip 1, k 1, psso) twice, k 1, k 2 tog, yo, k 2, p 2 tog, yo, p 4.

Row 15: Slip l, k 1, psso, work (yo, slip 1, k 1, psso) twice, k 2, yo, slip 1, k 1, psso, k 1, k 2 tog, yo, k 3, p 2 tog, yo, p 4.

Row 17: Slip 1, k 1, psso, work (yo, slip 1, k 1, psso) twice, k 3, k 2 tog, yo, k 4, p 2 tog, yo, p 4.

Row 19: Slip 1, k 1, psso, work (yo, slip 1, k 1, psso) twice, k 1, k 2 tog, yo, k 5, p 2 tog, yo, p 4.

Row 21: Slip 1, k 1, psso, yo, slip 1, k 1, psso, k 1, k 2 tog, yo, k 6, p 2 tog, yo, p 4.

Repeat Rows 3 through 22 for pattern.

Start with 17 sts

| $=$ k 1
O $=$ yarn over
⊀ $=$ k 2 tog
⋋ $=$ slip 1, k 1, psso
∩ $=$ p 2 tog
☐ $=$ p 1

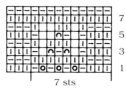

7 sts

| $=$ k l
– $=$ p 1
O $=$ yarn over
∩ $=$ p 2 tog
☐ $=$ empty space with no st indicated

Yo-yo

Start work with a multiple of 7 stitches, plus 3.

Row 1 (wrong side): K 3, * p 1, work (yarn over, p 1) 3 times, k 3 *; repeat from * to *.

Rows 2, 4, and 6: Work each stitch as it appears on this side of work (k the k sts and p the p sts). Knit yarn-over loops.

Row 3: K 3, * p 1, work (p 2 sts together, p 1) twice, k 3 *; repeat from * to *.

Row 5: K 3, * p 2, p 2 tog, p 1, k 3 *; repeat from * to *.

Row 7: Knit.

Row 8: Purl.

Repeat these 8 rows for pattern.

LACE STITCHES

Ascending lace pattern

Work with a multiple of 10 stitches, plus 2.

Row 1: P 2, * work (yarn over, skip 1, k 1, pass slip st over k st and drop it) twice, k 2, k 2 sts together (k 2 tog), yarn over (yo), p 2 *; repeat from * to *.

Row 2 and all even-numbered rows: Work each stitch as it appears on this side of work (k the k sts and p the p sts). Purl yarn-over loops.

Rows 3 and 7: P 2, * k 1, yo, slip 1, k 1, pass slip st over k st (psso), k 2, k 2 tog, yo, k 1, p 2 *; repeat from * to *.

Row 5: P 2, * yo, slip 1, k 1, psso, k 2, work (k 2 tog, yo) twice, p 2 *; repeat from * to *.

Repeat Rows 1 through 8 for pattern.

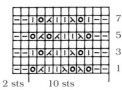

	= k 1
-	= p 1
O	= yarn over
⋋	= slip 1, k 1, psso
⋌	= k 2 tog
□	= 1 st as shown

2 sts   10 sts

Eyelet diamond pattern

Work with a multiple of 10 stitches.

Row 1: P 4, * k 4, p 6 *; repeat from * to *, ending last repeat with p 2.

Row 2 and all even-numbered rows: Work each stitch as it appears on this side of work (k the k sts and p the p sts). Purl yarn-over loops.

Row 3: P 3, * k 2, k 2 sts together (k 2 tog), yarn over (yo), k 2, p 4 *; repeat from * to *, ending last repeat with p 1.

Row 5: * P 2, k 2, work (k 2 tog, yo) twice, k 2 *; repeat from * to *.

Row 7: P 1, * k 2, work (k 2 tog, yo) twice, k 2, p 2 *; repeat from * to *, ending last repeat with p 1.

Row 9: * K 2, work (k 2 tog, yo) twice, k 2, p 2 *; repeat from * to *.

Row 11: P 1, * k 2, k 2 tog, yo, k 2, p 4 *; repeat from * to *, ending last repeat with p 3.

Row 13: P 2, * k 4, p 6 *; repeat from * to *, ending last repeat with p 4.

Row 15: P 3, * k 2, p 8 *; repeat from * to *, ending last repeat with p 5.

Row 17: P 4, * k 2, p 8 *; repeat from * to *, ending last repeat with p 4.

Row 19: P 5, * k 2, p 8 *; repeat from * to *, ending last repeat with p 3.

Repeat Rows 1 through 20 for pattern.

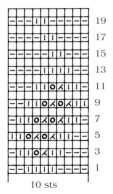

10 sts

	= k 1
-	= p 1
O	= yarn over
⋌	= k 2 tog
□	= 1 st as shown

TEXTURED STITCHES

Fabric stitch

Work with an even number of stitches, plus 2 for selvages.
Row 1: * K 1, bring yarn to front of work, slip 1 as if to p *; repeat from * to *, ending k last 2 sts.
Row 2: Purl.
Row 3: K 2, * slip 1 with yarn in front, k 1 *; repeat from * to *.
Row 4: Purl.
Repeat these 4 rows for pattern.

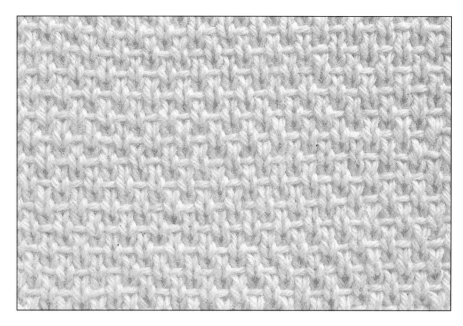

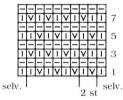

selv.   2 st   selv.

ı = k 1
– = p 1
V = 1 slip st

Fabric stitch rib

Work with a multiple of 6 stitches, plus 3, plus 2 for selvages.
Row 1: K 1, * bring yarn to front of work, slip 1 as if to p, k 1, slip 1 with yarn in front, p 3 *; repeat from * to *, ending (slip 1 with yarn in front, k 1) twice.
Row 2: Purl.
Row 3: K 2, * slip 1 with yarn in front, k 1, p 3, k 1 *; repeat from * to *, ending slip 1 with yarn in front, k 2.
Row 4: Purl.
Repeat these rows for pattern.

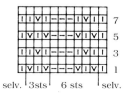

selv. 3sts   6 sts   selv.

ı = k 1
□ or – = p 1
V = 1 slip st

253

TEXTURED STITCHES

Knotted stitch

Work with an even number of stitches, plus 2 for selvages.

Row 1: Knit.

Row 2: Purl.

Row 3: K 1, * work k 2 sts together *; repeat from * to *, ending k last st.

Row 4: P 1, * k 1, work increase st between sts as follows: with tip of right needle, lift connecting strand between last st worked and next st, place strand over left needle, k 1 in back of strand *; repeat from * to *, ending p last st.

Repeat these 4 rows for pattern.

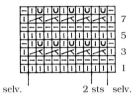

```
= k 1
- = p 1
= k 2 tog
U = 1 increase
```

selv.   2 sts selv.

Soft stitch

Work with an even number of stitches, plus 2 for selvages.

Row 1 (wrong side): K 2, * yarn over, bring yarn to front of work, slip 1 as if to p, yarn over (yo), k 1 *; repeat from * to *.

Row 2: K 1, * working on slip st and yarn-over of previous row, k 2 sts together through back loops, k 1 *; repeat from * to *, ending last repeat with k 2.

Repeat these 2 rows for pattern.

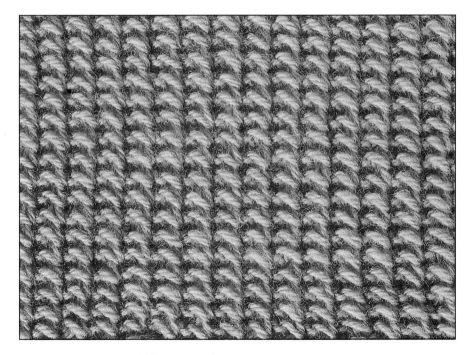

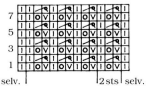

```
= k 1
V = 1 slip st

o = yarn over
= k 2 tog in back loops
```

selv.   2 sts selv.

TEXTURED STITCHES

Fabric stitch in reverse

Work with an uneven number of stitches.

Row 1: P 1, * with yarn in front, slip 1 as if to p, p 1 *; repeat from * to *.
Row 2: Knit.
Row 3: With yarn in front, slip 1 as if to p, * p 1, with yarn in front, slip 1 as if to p *; repeat from * to *.
Row 4: Knit.
Repeat these 4 rows for pattern.

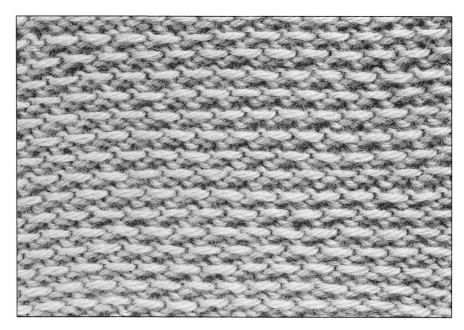

l = k 1
− = p 1
v = 1 slip st

Tightly-worked fabric stitch

Work with an even number of stitches.

Row 1 (right side): * K 1, bring yarn forward, slip 1 as if to p *; repeat from * to *, ending k last 2 sts.
Row 2: * P 1, with yarn at back, slip 1 as if to p *; repeat from * to *, ending p last 2 sts.
Repeat these 2 rows for pattern.

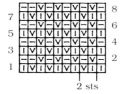

l = k 1
− = p 1
v = 1 slip st

TEXTURED STITCHES

Small zigzag pattern

Work with an even number of
stitches.

Row 1: K 1, * work left cross on 2 sts
as follows: slip 1 to dp needle, k 1,
k 1 from dp needle *; repeat from * to
*, ending k in last st. *Note*: The left
cross can also be worked as follows:
retaining sts on left needle, reach tip
of right needle behind work to knit
second stitch, keeping yarn behind
work, then knit first st and slide both
original stitches off left needle. Use
the method more comfortable for you.

Row 2: P 1, * work right cross on 2
sts as follows: skip 1 st, reaching in
front of work, p second st, then p
skipped st and drop both original sts
from left needle *; repeat from * to *,
ending p in last st.

Repeat these 2 rows for pattern.

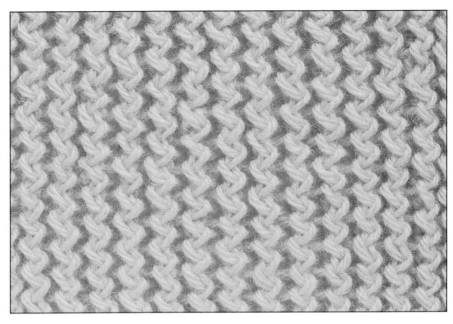

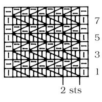

ı = k 1
– = p 1
= 2-st left cross
= 2-st right cross

2 sts

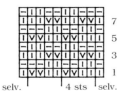

selv.   4 sts   selv.

ı = k 1
– = p 1
v = 1 slip st

Slip stitch pattern

Work with a multiple of 4 stitches,
plus 2 for selvages.

Row 1: K 3, * bring yarn to front of
work, slip 2 as if to p, k 2 *; repeat
from * to *, ending last repeat with
k 1.

Row 2: P 3, * k 2, p 2 *; repeat from
* to *, ending last repeat with p 1.

Row 3: K 1, * with yarn in front, slip
2 as if to p, k 2 *; repeat from * to *,
ending last repeat with k 3.

Row 4: P 1, * k 2, p 2 *; repeat from
* to *, ending last repeat with p 3.
Repeat these 4 rows for pattern.

TEXTURED STITCHES

Pebbled stitch

Work with an uneven number of stitches.

Row 1: P 1, * k 1, p 1 *; repeat from * to *.

Row 2: K 1, * bring yarn to front of work, slip 1 as if to p, k 1 *; repeat from * to *.

Row 3: K 1, * p 1, k 1 *; repeat from * to *.

Row 4: K 2, * with yarn in front, slip 1 as if to p, k 1 *; repeat from * to *, ending slip 1, k 2.

Repeat these 4 rows for pattern.

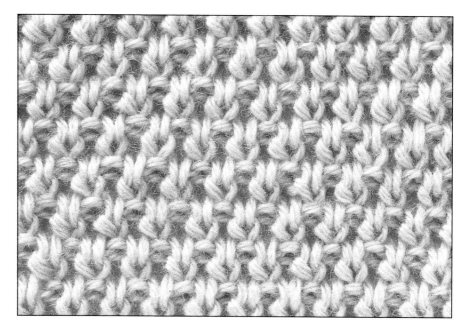

I = k 1
− = p 1
V = 1 slip st

2 sts

Basket weave

Work with a multiple of 4 stitches, plus 2.

Row 1: Knit.

Row 2 and all even-numbered rows: Purl.

Row 3: * Work right crossover on 4 sts as follows: slip 2 sts to dp needle and hold in back of work, k 2, k 2 from dp needle *; repeat from * to *, ending k last 2 sts.

Row 5: K 2, * work left crossover on 4 sts as follows: slip 2 to dp needle and hold in front of work, k 2, k 2 from dp needle *; repeat from * to *. Repeat Rows 3 through 6 for pattern.

I = k 1
□ = p 1
⌐⌐⌐ = 4-st right crossover

⌐⌐⌐ = 4-st left crossover

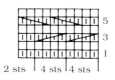

2 sts   4 sts   4 sts

TEXTURED STITCHES

Crossed bridges

Work with a multiple of 6 sts, plus 5.
Row 1 (right side): K 4, * k 3 long sts, wrapping yarn twice around needle for each st, k 3 *; repeat from * to *, ending last repeat with k 4.
Rows 2 and 10: P 4, * with yarn on wrong side, slip 3 long sts, dropping extra loop from each, p 3 *; repeat from * to *, ending last repeat with p 4.
Rows 3, 4, 7, 8, 11, and 12: With yarn on wrong side to slip the slip sts, work each remaining st as it appears on this side of work.
Row 5: K 1, * work crossover on 6 sts as follows: slip 3 to dp needle and hold in back, k 3 long sts, wrapping yarn twice around needle, k 3 from dp needle, * repeat from * to *, ending k 3 long sts, k 1.
Row 6: P 1, * slip long sts, dropping extra loop, p 3 *; repeat from * to *, ending slip 3, p 1.
Row 9: K 4, * crossover on 6 sts *; repeat from * to *, ending k in last st. Repeat Rows 5 through 12 for pattern.

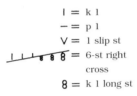

```
I   = k 1
—   = p 1
V   = 1 slip st
      = 6-st right
        cross
8   = k 1 long st
```

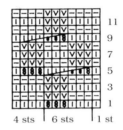

4 sts | 6 sts | 1 st

Little twisted ribs

Work with a multiple of 6 stitches, plus 1.
Row 1: * Work (k 1 in back loop for twisted st, p 1) twice, k 2 for garter st * repeat from * to *, ending k 1 twisted st.
Row 2 and all even-numbered rows: P twisted st (p in back loop) over twisted sts of previous row and k all remaining sts (garter sts and p sts of previous row).
Row 3: K 1 twisted st, * p 1, k 1 twisted st, k 3 garter sts, k 1 twisted st *; repeat from * to *.
Row 5: K 1 twisted st, * p 1, k 3 garter sts, p 1, k 1 twisted st *; repeat from * to *.
Row 7: K 1 twisted st, * k 3 garter sts, k 1 twisted st, p 1, k 1 twisted st *; repeat from * to *.
Row 9: K 1 twisted st, * k 2 garter sts, work (p 1, k 1 twisted st) twice *; repeat from * to *.
Row 11: K 1 twisted st, * k 1 garter st, work (k 1 twisted st, p 1) twice, k 1 twisted st *; repeat from * to *.
Row 13: K 1 twisted st, * work (p 1, k 1 twisted st) twice, k 1 garter st, k 1 twisted st *; repeat from * to *.
Repeat Rows 1 through 14 for pattern.

1 st | 6 sts

```
I   = k 1
—   = p 1
ᕳ   = k 1 twisted st
∩   = k 1 (garter
        st)
□   = 1 st as shown
```

SLIP STITCH PATTERNS

Right diagonals

Work with a multiple of 6 stitches, plus 3.

Row 1 (right side): K 3, * bring yarn to front of work, slip 3 as if to p, k 3 *; repeat from * to *. *Note*: To slip sts, always carry yarn on right side of work.

Row 2: P 4, * slip 3 with yarn at back, p 3 *; repeat from * to *, ending last repeat with p 2.

Row 3: K 1, * slip 3, k 3 *; repeat from * to *, ending last repeat with k 5.

Row 4: P 6, * slip 3, p 3 *; repeat from * to *, ending last repeat with p 6.

Row 5: K 5, * slip 3, k 3 *; repeat from * to *, ending last repeat with k 1.

Row 6: P 2, * slip 3, p 3 *; repeat from * to *, ending last repeat with p 4.

Repeat these 6 rows for pattern.

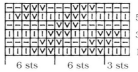

I	= k 1
–	= p 1
V	= 1 slip st

Left diagonals

Work with a multiple of 6 stitches, plus 3.

Row 1 (right side): K 3, * bring yarn to front of work, slip 3 as if to p, k 3 *; repeat from * to *. *Note*: For slip sts, always carry yarn on right side of work.

Row 2: P 2, * slip 3 with yarn in back, p 3 *; repeat from * to *, ending last repeat with p 4.

Row 3: K 5, * slip 3, k 3 *; repeat from * to *, ending last repeat with k 1.

Row 4: P 6, * slip 3, p 3 *; repeat from * to *, ending last repeat with p 6.

Row 5: K 1, * slip 3, k 3, *; repeat from * to *, ending last repeat with k 5.

Row 6: P 4, * slip 3, p 3 *; repeat from * to *, ending last repeat with p 2.

Repeat these 6 rows for pattern.

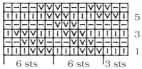

I	= k 1
–	= p 1
V	= 1 slip st

SLIP STITCH PATTERNS

Slip stitch triangles

Work with a multiple of 6 stitches, plus 1

Row 1 (right side): Knit.

Row 2: Purl.

Rows 3 and 13: K 1, * bring yarn to front of work, slip 5, k 1 *; repeat from * to *. *Note*: For slip sts, always carry yarn on right side of work.

Rows 4 and 12: * P 2, slip 4 with yarn in back *; repeat from * to *, ending slip 4, p 1.

Rows 5 and 11: K 1, * slip 3, k 3 *; repeat from * to *.

Rows 6 and 10: * P 4, slip 2 *; repeat from * to *, ending last repeat with p 1.

Rows 7 and 9: K 1, * slip 1, k 5 *; repeat from * to *.

Rows 8 and 14: Purl.

Repeat Rows 3 through 14 for pattern.

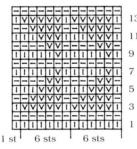

I = k 1
− = p 1
V = 1 slip st

Textured bands

Work with a multiple of 8 stitches, plus 3.

Row 1: Knit.

Row 2 and all even-numbered rows: Purl.

Row 3: P 1, k 1, p 1, * with yarn in front, slip 5 as if to p, p 1, k 1, p 1 *; repeat from * to *.

Row 5: P 1, k 1, p 1, * with tip of right needle lift yarn carried in front of slip sts below and place it onto left needle, work (k 1, yarn over and k 1) all in this yarn loop, then bind off first 3 sts on left needle, (a 4th st remaining from binding-off process is on right needle), work (k 1, p 1) twice *; repeat from * to *.

Repeat Rows 3 through 6 for pattern.

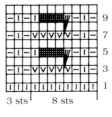

I = k 1
□ or − = p 1
V = 1 slip st
⫽ = 3 sts worked on carried yarn
▦ = 1 bound-off st

SLIP STITCH PATTERNS

Stripes and bands

Work with a multiple of 3 stitches, plus 2.

Row 1: P 2, * with yarn in back, slip 1 as if to k, p 2 *; repeat from * to *.

Row 2: K 2, * with yarn in front, slip 1 as if to p, k 2 *; repeat from * to *.

Row 3: Knit.

Row 4: Purl.

Repeat these 4 rows for pattern.

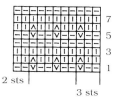

| = k 1
− = p 1
V = slip 1 as if to k
Λ = slip 1 as if to p

2 sts
3 sts

Mock ribbing

Work with a multiple of 3 stitches, plus 1.

Row 1: Knit.

Row 2: P 1, * with yarn in front, slip 2 as if to p, k 1 *; repeat from * to *.

Repeat these 2 rows for pattern.

| = k 1
V = 1 slip st

3 sts

SLIP STITCH PATTERNS

Slip stitch diamonds

Work with a multiple of 16 stitches, plus 3.

Note: To work slip sts throughout, carry yarn on right side of work.

Row 1 (right side): K 4, * with yarn in front, slip 2 as if to p, k 3, slip 1, k 3, slip 2, k 5 *; repeat from * to *, ending last repeat with k 4.

Row 2 and all even-numbered rows: Purl.

Rows 3 and 15: K 3, * slip 2, k 3, slip 3, k 3, slip 2, k 3 *; repeat from * to *.

Rows 5 and 13: K 2, * slip 2, k 3, slip 2, k 1, slip 2, k 3, slip 2, k 1 *; repeat from * to *, ending last repeat with k 2.

Rows 7 and 11: K 1, slip 2, * work (k 3 , slip 2) twice, k 3, slip 3 *; repeat from * to *, ending last repeat with slip 2, k in last st.

Row 9: K 1, * slip 1, k 3, slip 2, k 5, slip 2, k 3 *; repeat from * to *, ending slip 1, k in last st.

Repeat Rows 1 through 16 for pattern.

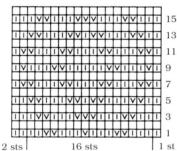

I = k 1
V = 1 slip st
□ = p 1

2 sts | 16 sts | 1 st

I = k 1
V = 1 slip st
□ = p 1

4 sts | 11 sts | 1 st

Steps and ladders

Work with a multiple of 11 stitches, plus 5.

Note: To work slip sts throughout, carry yarn on right side of work.

Row 1 (right side): K 1, * with yarn in front, slip 3 as if to p, k 8 *; repeat from * to *, ending slip 3, k in last st.

Row 2 and all even-numbered rows: Purl.

Row 3: K 1, * slip 3, k 5, slip 2, k 1 *; repeat from * to *, ending slip 3, k 1.

Row 5: K 1, * slip 3, k 4, slip 2, k 2 *; repeat from * to *, ending slip 3, k 1.

Row 7: K 1, * slip 3, k 3, slip 2, k 3 *; repeat from * to *, ending slip 3, k 1.

Row 9: K 1, * slip 3, k 2, slip 2, k 4 *; repeat from * to *, ending slip 3, k 1.

Row 11: K 1, * slip 3, k 1, slip 2, k 5 *; repeat from * to *, ending slip 3, k 1.

Repeat Rows 1 through 12 for pattern.

MULTICOLORED STITCHES

Little dashes

Work with a multiple of 6 stitches.
Row 1 (right side): With color A, knit.
Row 2: With color A, purl.
Rows 3 and 4: With color B, k 2, * slip 2 (carry yarn on wrong side of work throughout), k 4 *; repeat from * to *, ending last repeat with k 2.
Rows 5 and 6: Repeat Rows 1 and 2.
Rows 7 and 8: With color B, slip 1, * k 4, slip 2 *; repeat from * to *, ending last repeat with slip 1.
Repeat these 8 rows for pattern.

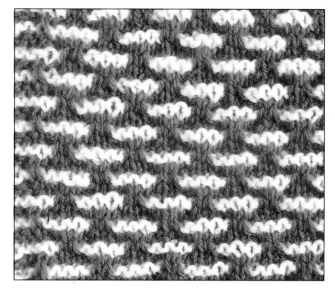

6 sts

ɪ = k 1
− = p 1
v = 1 slip st

A = shown as green
B = shown as white

6 sts

ɪ = k 1
− = p 1
v = 1 slip st

A = shown as dark green
B = shown as light green

Wide honeycomb

Work with a multiple of 6 stitches.
Rows 1, 2, 5, and 6: With color A, knit.
Row 3: With color B, k 2, * slip 1 (carry yarn on wrong side of work throughout), k 5 *; repeat from * to *, ending last repeat with k 3.
Row 4: With B, p 3, * slip 1, p 5 *; repeat from * to *, ending with p 2.
Row 7: With B, * k 5, slip 1 *; repeat from * to *.
Row 8: With B, * slip 1, p 5 *; repeat from * to *.
Repeat these 8 rows for pattern.

Two-color stripes

Work with a multiple of 8 stitches, plus 6.
Row 1 (right side): With color A, k 2, * slip 2 (carry yarn on wrong side of work throughout), k 6 *; repeat from * to *, ending slip 2, k last 2 sts.
Row 2: With A, p 2, * slip 2, p 6 *; repeat from * to *, ending slip 2, p 2.
Rows 3 and 4: With color B, k 6, * slip 2, k 6 *; repeat from * to *.
Repeat these 4 rows for pattern.

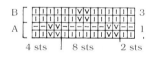

4 sts   8 sts   2 sts

ɪ = k 1
− = p 1
v = 1 slip st

A = shown as pink
B = shown as green

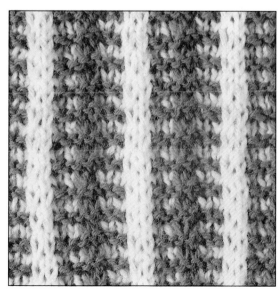

MULTICOLORED STITCHES

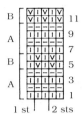

1 st   2 sts

ı = k 1
− = p 1
v = 1 slip st

A = shown as light blue
B = shown as dark blue

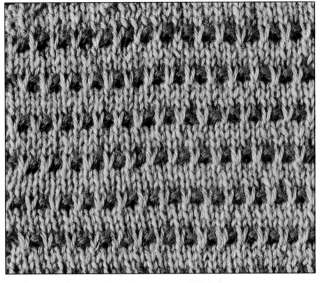

Little seed stitch

Work with an uneven number of stitches.
Rows 1 and 3 (right side): With color A, knit.
Rows 2 and 4: With A, purl.
Rows 5 and 6: With color B, k 1, * slip 1 (carry yarn on wrong side of work throughout), k 1 *; repeat from * to *.
Rows 7 and 9: With color A, knit.
Rows 8 and 10: With A, purl.
Rows 11 and 12: With color B, slip 1, * k 1, slip 1 *; repeat from * to *.
Repeat these 12 rows for pattern.

Linen stitch

Work with a multiple of 6 stitches.
Row 1 (right side): With color A, purl.
Row 2: With color B, k 3, * slip 1 (carry yarn on wrong side of work throughout), k 5 *; repeat from * to *, ending last repeat with k 2.
Row 3: With B, k 2, * slip 1, k 5 *; repeat from * to *, ending with k 3.
Row 4: With color A, * slip 1, k 1; * repeat from * to *.
Row 5: With A, * k 1, slip 1; * repeat from * to *.
Repeat Rows 2 through 5 for pattern.

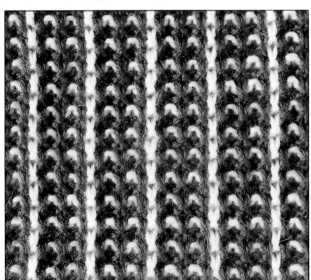

6 sts

ı = k 1
− = p 1
v = 1 slip st

A = shown as white
B = shown as blue

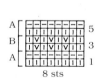

8 sts

ı = k 1
− = p 1
v = 1 slip st

A = shown as blue
B = shown as pink

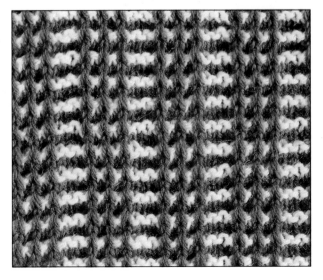

Triple stripes

Work with a multiple of 8 stitches.
Row 1 (right side): With color A, knit.
Row 2: With A, purl.
Row 3: With color B, k 2, * slip 1 (carry yarn on wrong side of work throughout), work (k 1, slip 1) twice, k 3 *; repeat from * to *, ending last repeat with k 1.
Row 4: With B, k 1, * work (slip 1, k 1) twice, slip 1, k 3 *; repeat from * to *, ending last repeat with k 2.
Repeat these 4 rows for pattern.

MULTICOLORED STITCHES

Slip stitch

Work with a multiple of 4 stitches, plus 2.

Row 1 (right side): With color A, k 2, * slip 2 (carry yarn on right side of work throughout), k 2 *; repeat from * to *.

Row 2: With A, p 2, * slip 2, p 2 *; repeat from * to *.

Row 3: With A, knit.

Row 4: With A, purl.

Row 5: With color B, k 4, * slip 2, k 2 *; repeat from * to *, ending last repeat with k 4.

Row 6: With B, p 4, * slip 2, p 2, *; repeat from * to *, ending last repeat with p 4.

Row 7: With B, knit.

Row 8: With B, purl.

Repeat these 8 rows for pattern.

I = k 1
− = p 1
v = 1 slip st
A = shown as pink
B = shown as fuchsia

Grain slip stitch

Work with an even number of stitches, and work on a base of 2 rows of stockinette st (k 1 row, p 1 row) made with color A.

Row 1 (right side): With color B, k 2, * slip 1 (carry yarn on wrong side of work throughout), k 1 *; repeat from * to *.

Row 2: With B, * k 1, slip 1 *; repeat from * to *, ending with k last 2 sts.

Use these 2 rows of pattern for trim on stockinette st piece, or, for pattern as shown, alternate these 2 rows of pattern (worked with B) with 4 rows of stockinette st (worked with A).

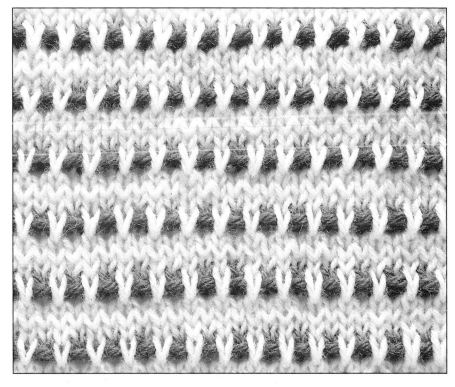

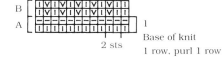

Base of knit
1 row, purl 1 row

I = k 1
v = 1 slip st
A = shown as white
B = fuchsia

MULTICOLORED STITCHES

Two-color festoons

Work with a multiple of 6 stitches, plus 1.

Row 1: With color A, k 2 sts together, * k 1, work double increase as follows: with tip of right needle, lift connecting strand between last st worked and next st and place strand over left needle, k 1 in back loop of this strand, k 1 st; work another increase between stitches to complete double increase, k 1, work double decrease on 3 sts as follows: slip 2 sts together as if to k, k 1, slip both sts over k st and drop them *; repeat from * to *, ending k 1, double increase, k 1, slip 1, k 1, pass slip st over k st and drop it.

Row 2: With A, purl.
Row 3: With color B, repeat Row 1.
Row 4: With B, purl.
Repeat these 4 rows for pattern.

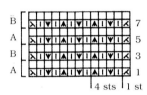

I = k 1
⋏ = k 2 tog
v = double inc
⋀ = double dec
⋋ = slip 1, k 1, psso
□ = p 1
A = shown as white
B = shown as orange

Two-color peacock's tail

Work with a multiple of 15 stitches, plus 2.

Rows 1 and 3: With color A, k 2, * work (slip 1, k 1, pass slip st over k st and drop it) twice, k 1, work (yarn over, k 1) 4 times, k 2 sts together twice, k 2 *; repeat from * to *.

Rows 2 and 4: With A, purl.
Rows 5 and 6: With color B, purl.
Repeat these 6 rows for pattern.

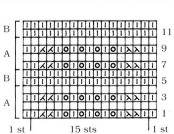

I = k 1
o = yarn over
⋏ = k 2 tog
⋋ = slip 1, k 1, psso
□ = p 1
A = shown as yellow
B = shown as orange

MULTICOLORED STITCHES

Two-color hedges

Work with a multiple of 6 stitches, plus 2 for selvages.

Row 1: With color A, knit.

Row 2 and all even-numbered rows: Working in the same color as previous row, purl.

Row 3: With A, k 2, * work right cross on 2 sts as follows: skip 1, k 1, k skipped st and drop both original sts from left needle; k 1, work left cross on 2 sts as follows: slip 1 to dp needle and hold in front of work, k 1, k 1 from dp needle, k 1 *; repeat from * to *.

Row 5: With color B, knit.

Row 7: With B, k 2, * left cross, k 1, right cross, k 1 *; repeat from * to *.

Row 9: With color A, k 4, * work long st as follows: insert needle into corresponding st 5 rows below next st and k 1, drop unworked st above from left needle, letting it unravel down to where long st was worked, k 5 *; repeat from * to * , ending last repeat with k 3.

Row 11: With A, repeat Row 3.

Row 13: With color B, k 1, * long st, k 5 *; repeat from * to *, ending k last st.

Repeat Rows 7 through 14 for pattern.

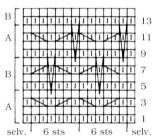

¹	=	k 1
⤢	=	2-st right cross
⤡	=	2-st left cross
⋁	=	1 long st
□	=	p 1
A	=	shown as yellow
B	=	shown as orange

Two-color mock rib stitch

Work with an even number of stitches, plus 2 for selvages.

Row 1 (right side): With color A, knit.

Row 2: With A, k 2, * slip 1 as if to p (carry yarn on wrong side of work throughout), k 1 *; repeat from * to *.

Row 3: With color B, knit.

Row 4: With B, work as for Row 2.

Repeat these 4 rows for pattern.

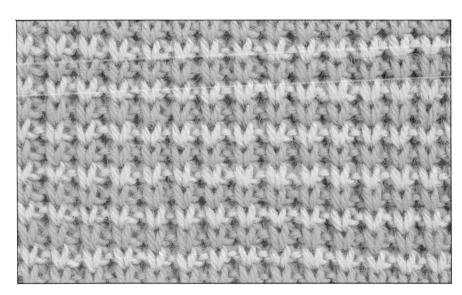

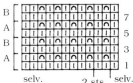

¹	=	k 1
∩	=	1 slip st
A	=	shown as green
B	=	shown as yellow

MULTICOLORED STITCHES

Two-color wrapped stripes

Work with an even number of stitches.

Row 1: With color A, k 1, * yarn over (yo), k 2, pass yo over 2 k sts and drop it (wrap made) *; repeat from * to *, ending k last st.

Row 2: With A, purl.

Row 3: With color B, work as for Row 1.

Row 4: With B, purl.

Repeat these 4 rows for pattern.

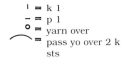

| | = k 1
− = p 1
o = yarn over
⌣ = pass yo over 2 k sts

A = shown as pale blue
B = shown as blue

2 sts

Creative reliefs

Work with an uneven number of stitches.

Row 1: With color A, knit.

Row 2: With A, purl.

Row 3: With color B, k 1, * k 2 sts together *; repeat from * to *.

Row 4: With B, k 1, * work increase as follows, with tip of left needle lift connecting strand between last st worked and next st, k 1 in back loop of this strand, k 1 *; repeat from * to *.

Repeat these 4 rows for pattern.

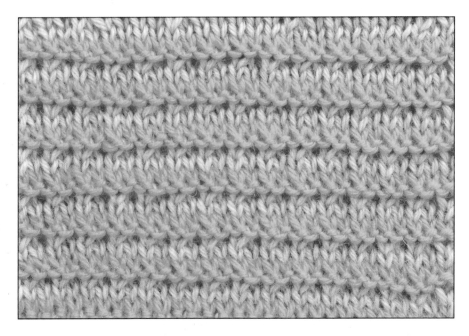

| = k 1
− = p 1
⋌ = k 2 tog

V = 1 increase

□ = empty space with no st indicated

A = shown as pale blue
B = shown as yellow

2 sts

MULTICOLORED STITCHES

Daisies

Work with a multiple of 4 stitches, plus 1.

Row 1: With color A, k 3, * work daisy as follows: k 3 sts together retaining them on left needle, p the 3 sts together again, then k them together again, drop original sts from left needle, k 1 *; repeat from * to *, ending last repeat with k 3.

Row 2 and all even-numbered rows: With same color as on previous row, purl.

Row 3: With color B, k 1, * work daisy, k 1 *; repeat from * to *.

Row 5: With color C, work as for Row 1.

Row 7: With color A, work as for Row 3.

Row 9: With color B, work as for Row 1.

Row 11: With color C, work as for Row 3.

Repeat Rows 1 through 12 for pattern.

I = k 1
– = p 1
⌄ = 1 daisy
A = shown as fuchsia
B = shown as salmon
C = shown as pale pink

Three-color honeycomb

Work with a multiple of 6 stitches, plus 2.

Rows 1 and 7 (right side): With color A, knit.

Rows 2 and 8: With A, purl.

Rows 3 and 5: With color B, k 4, * slip 1 as if to p (carry yarn on wrong side of work throughout), k 5 *; repeat from * to *, ending last repeat with k 3.

Rows 4 and 6: With B, p 3, * slip 1, p 5 *; repeat from * to *, ending with p 4.

Rows 9 and 11: With color C, k 1, * slip 1, k 5 *; repeat from * to *, ending last repeat with k 6.

Rows 10 and 12: With C, p 6, * slip 1, p 5 *; repeat from * to *, ending last repeat with p 1.

Repeat these 12 rows for pattern.

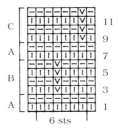

I = k 1
– = p 1
V = 1 slip st
A = shown as blue
B = shown as pale lilac
C = shown as light blue

MULTICOLORED STITCHES

Little flowers

Work with a multiple of 4 stitches, plus 3.

Note: Work flowers by attaching contrasting color (CC) at beginning of flower row (shown as Rows 1 and 5 on chart) and fastening it off at end of that row. Work 1, 2 (as shown), or more different colors for flower rows, using only one CC on any one flower row.

Row 1 (flower row): With main color (MC), k 3, * with CC, work flower as follows: in next st k 1, yarn over and k 1, k 3 MC (carry CC on wrong side of work across row) *; repeat from * to *.

Row 2 (wrong side): With MC, p 3, * slip 3 flower sts, carrying yarn on wrong side of work, p 3 *; repeat from * to *.

Row 3: With MC, k 2, *k 2 sts together (1 background st and first flower st), k 1, slip 1 (last flower st), k 1, pass slip st over k st and drop it, k 1 *; repeat from * to *, ending last repeat with k 2.

Row 4: With MC, purl.

Repeat these 4 rows for pattern.

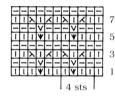

I = k 1
— = p 1
♥ = 1 flower
V = 3 slip sts in contrasting color

⋏ = k 2 tog
⋋ = slip 1, k 1, psso

Garter stitch

Work with a multiple of 4 stitches, plus 2.

Row 1 (right side): With color A, k 4, * slip 1 as if to p (carry yarn on wrong side of work throughout), k 3 *; repeat from * to *, ending slip 1, k 1.

Row 2: With A, p 1, * slip 1, k 3 *; repeat from * to *, ending p last st.

Row 3: With color B, k 3, * slip 1, k 3 *; repeat from * to *, ending slip 1, k 2.

Row 4: With B, p 1, k 1, * slip 1, k 3 *; repeat from * to *, ending slip 1, k 2, p last st.

Row 5: With color C, k 2, * slip 1, k 3 *; repeat from * to *.

Row 6: With B, p 1, k 2, * slip 1, k 3 *; repeat from * to *, ending slip 1, k 1, p last st.

Repeat these 6 rows for pattern.

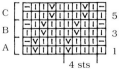

I = k 1
— = p 1
V = 1 slip st
A = shown as blue
B = shown as yellow
C = shown as pale lilac

MULTICOLORED STITCHES

Two-color ribbing

Work with a multiple of 4 stitches.
Row 1 (right side): With color A, * k 2, p 2 *; repeat from * to *.
Rows 2 through 5: With color B, work each stitch as it appears on this side of work (k the k sts and p the p sts).
Row 6: Moving both yarns forward to purl or backward to k and catching yarn not in use in sts of contrasting color, * k 2 A, p 2 B *; repeat from * to *.
Row 7: Moving both yarns and catching yarn not in use in sts of contrasting color, * k 2 B, p 2 A *; repeat from * to *.
Rows 8 and 9: With color B, * k 2, p 2 *; repeat from * to *.
Repeat Rows 2 through 9 for pattern.

♦ = k 1 A   – = p 1 B

♠ = p 1 A   □ = 1 color B st as shown

I = k 1 B

A = shown as green
B = shown as yellow

4 sts

Texture in two colors

Work with a multiple of 3 stitches, plus 2.
Rows 1 through 4: With color A, k 2, * slip 1 as if to p (carry yarn on wrong side of work [in back for Row 1] throughout), k 2 *; repeat from * to *.
Row 5: With color B, k 1, * slip 1, k 2 *; repeat from * to *, ending last repeat k 3.
Row 6: With B, k 3, * slip 1, k 2 *; repeat from * to *, ending slip 1, k last st.
Row 7: Repeat Row 5.
Row 8: Repeat Row 6.
Repeat these 8 rows for pattern.

I = k 1
V = 1 slip st
A = tan
B = green

2 sts   3 sts

MULTICOLORED STITCHES

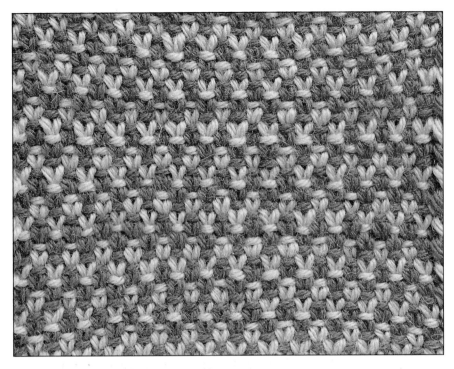

Tweed

Work with an even number of stitches.

Row 1 (right side): With color A, *
k 1, slip 1 as if to p (carry yarn on
right side of work throughout) *;
repeat from * to *, ending k last 2 sts.

Row 2: With A, * p 1, slip 1 *; repeat
from * to *, ending p last 2 sts.

Row 3: With color B, work as for
Row 1.

Row 4: With B, work as for Row 2.
Repeat these 4 rows for pattern.

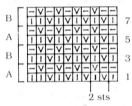

```
B  - V - V - V - V -    7
A  I I V I V I V I V I
   - V - V - V - V -    5
B  I I V I V I V I V I
A  - V - V - V - V -    3
   I I V I V I V I V I
   - V - V - V - V -    1
   I I V I V I V I V I
        2 sts
```

I = k 1
− = p 1
V = 1 slip st
A = shown as pink
B = shown as fuchsia

Double stitch, double color

Work with a multiple of 3 stitches,
plus 1.

Row 1 (wrong side): With color A,
purl.

Row 2: With A, knit.

Row 3: With color B, knit.

Row 4: With B, * k 2, insert needle
into st below next st and k 1, drop
unworked st above it (double st
made) *; repeat from * to *, ending k
last st.

Repeat these 4 rows for pattern.

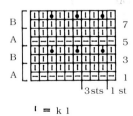

```
B    7
A    5
B    3
A    1
   3 sts  1 st
```

I = k 1
− = p
= 1 double st
A = shown as yellow
B = shown as fuchsia

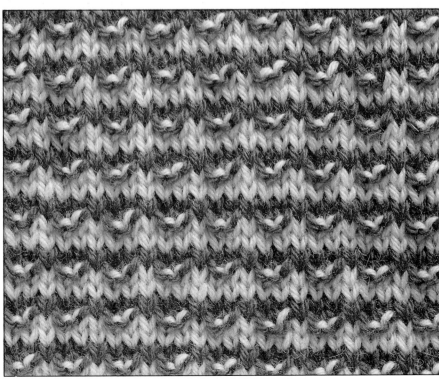

MULTICOLORED STITCHES

Rainbow strands

Work with a multiple of 6 stitches, plus 3.

Rows 1, 3, and 7 (right side): With color A, knit.

Row 2: Bringing color forward as needed to purl, and carrying color not in use in back (on right side of work), p 3 A, * p 3 B, p 3 A *; repeat from * to *.

Rows 4, 6, and 8: With color A, purl.

Row 5: Taking color to back as needed to knit and carrying color not in use in front (on right side of work), k 3 A, * k 3 B, k 3 A *; repeat from * to *.

Repeat Rows 1 through 8 for pattern.

I = k 1 A

— = p 1 A

✦ = k 1 B

•— = p 1 A

A = shown as teal
B = shown as pink

Long stitch and stripes

Work with a multiple of 4 stitches, plus 5.

Row 1 (right side): With color A, knit.

Row 2: With A, k 2, * p 1 wrapping yarn twice around needle to make long st, k 3 *; repeat from * to *, ending last repeat with k 2.

Row 3: With color B, p 2, * with yarn in back of work (on wrong side), slip long st as if to k, letting extra loop drop from needle, p 3 *; repeat from * to *, ending last repeat with p 2.

Row 4: With B, k 2, * with yarn in front (on wrong side), slip 1 as if to p, k 3 *; repeat from * to *, ending slip 1, k 2.

Row 5: With color A, p 2, * k 1 (long st), p 3 *; repeat from * to *, ending k 1, p 2.

Row 6: With A, k 2, * p 1, k 3 *; repeat from * to *, ending p 1, k 2.

Row 7: With color B, knit.

Row 8: With B, purl.

Repeat these 8 rows for pattern.

I = k 1 A

— = p 1 A

✦ = k 1 B

•— = p 1 B

~ = p 1 long st

V = slip long st as if to k

Λ = slip as if to p

A = shown as teal
B = shown as pale blue

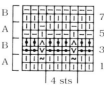

MULTICOLORED STITCHES

Patterned ribs

Work with a multiple of 8 stitches, plus 2.

Row 1 (wrong side): With color A, k 2, * p 6, k 2 *; repeat from * to *.

Row 2: With A, p 2, * with yarn in back, slip 1 as if to p (carry yarn on wrong side of work throughout), k 4, slip 1, p 2 *; repeat from * to *.

Rows 3 and 5: With color B, k 2, * with yarn in front, slip 1, p 4 , slip 1, k 2 *; repeat from * to *.

Row 4: With B, work as for Row 2.

Row 6: With B, p 2, * work left cross on 3 sts as follows: slip 1 to dp needle and hold in front of work, k 2, k 1 from dp needle; work right cross on 3 sts as follows: slip 2 to dp needle and hold in back of work, k 1, k 2 from dp needle, p 2 *; repeat from * to *.
Repeat these 6 rows for pattern.

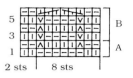

I = k 1

— = p 1

∧ = slip 1 with yarn in back

∨ = slip 1 with yarn in front

⊤⌐ = 3-st left cross

⌐⊤ = 3-st right cross

A = shown as green

B = shown as yellow

Three-color stripes

Work with a multiple of 14 stitches.

Row 1: With color A, knit.

Note: On following rows, move colors forward to purl or back to knit as needed, twisting yarns when you change colors to prevent holes in work. Carry color not in use on wrong side of work throughout.

Row 2 (wrong side): * K 7 sts with B, p 7 sts with A *; repeat from * to *.

Row 3: * K 7 A, p 7 B *; repeat from * to *.

Row 4: * K 7 C, p 7 A *; repeat from * to *.

Row 5: * K 7 A, p 7 C *; repeat from * to *.

Row 6: * P 7 A, k 7 B *; repeat from * to *.

Row 7: * P 7 B, k 7 A *; repeat from * to *.

Row 8: * P 7 A, k 7 C *; repeat from * to *.

Row 9: * P 7 C, k 7 A *; repeat from * to *.
Repeat Rows 2 through 9 for pattern.

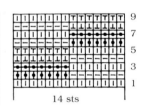

I = k 1 A

— = p 1 A

♦ = k 1 B

•– = p 1 B

⊥ = k 1 C

⊤ = p 1 C

A = shown as yellow

B = shown as blue

C = shown as pink

MULTICOLORED STITCHES

Violets

Work with a multiple of 8 stitches, plus 1.

Note: Have a crochet hook handy to crochet leaves and bobble.

Rows 1 and 3 (right side): With color A, k 4, * slip 1 as if to p (carry yarn on wrong side of work throughout), k 7 *; repeat from * to *, ending slip 1, k 4.

Rows 2, 4, and 18: With A, p 4, * slip 1, p 7 *; repeat from * to *, ending slip 1, p 4.

Row 5: With A, k 2, * p 5, k 3 *; repeat from * to *, ending p 5, k 2.

Rows 6, 11, and 14: With A, work each stitch as it appears on this row.

Row 7: K 2 A, * with B work leaf: insert crochet hook into slip st 3 rows below 3rd st on left needle, make slip knot on hook (hold B yarn behind work and work through slip st to wrap yarn on hook for sts), chain (ch) 3 sts, work double crochet in ch at base of ch-3, transfer last loop on hook to right needle, p 5 A, make 2nd leaf in same slip st, k 3 A *; repeat from * to *, ending with k 2.

Row 8: With A, p 2, * p 2 sts together, k 3, p 2 tog, p 3 *; repeat from * to *, ending with p 2.

Row 9: With A, k 4, * with C, work bobble: insert crochet hook into next st and draw up C loop (hold C yarn behind work), yarn over and draw up 4 more loops, yarn over and draw through all loops on hook, ch 1 to

complete bobble, transfer loop on hook to right needle, k 3 A, slip 1, k 3 A *; repeat from * to *, ending bobble, k 4.

Rows 10 and 12: With A, p 8, * slip 1, p 7 *; repeat from * to *, ending p last st.

Row 13: With A, k 6, * p 3, k 3 *; repeat from * to *, ending with k 6.

Row 15: With A, k 6, work leaf as before, p 5, work 2nd leaf, k 3 *;

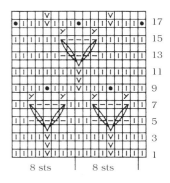

repeat from * to *, ending with k 6.

Row 16: With A, p 5, * p 2 tog, k 3, p 2 tog, p 3 *; repeat from * to *, ending with p 6.

Row 17: With C, work bobble, * k 3 A, slip 1, k 3 A, work C bobble *; repeat from * to *.

Repeat Rows 3 through 18 for pattern.

| = k 1
— = p 1
V = 1 slip st
/ = 1 leaf

Y = p 2 tog
● = bobble
□ = 1 st as shown
    A = shown as pale pink
    B = shown as fuchsia
    C = shown as blue

Imitation embroidery

Work with an uneven number of stitches.

Row 1: K 1 A, * work 1 B flake as follows: with B, work (k 1, yarn over [yo], pass k st over yo and return remaining yo st to left needle) 3 times, leaving last yo st on right needle, k 1 A *; repeat from * to *.

Row 2: With A, purl.

Row 3: With C, work 1 flake as before, * k 1 A, work 1 C flake *; repeat from * to *.

Row 4: With A, purl.

Repeat these 4 rows for pattern.

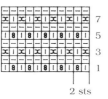

| = k 1 A
8 = 1 B flake
— = p 1 A
ᐅ = 1 C flake
A = shown as pale green
B = shown as fuchsia
C = shown as teal

MULTICOLORED STITCHES

Multicolored beehive

Work with an even number of stitches.

Rows 1 and 2: With color A, knit.

Row 3: With color B, k 1, * work double st by inserting needle into st below next st to k 1, drop unworked st above from left needle, k 1 *; repeat from * to *, ending last repeat with k 2.

Row 4: With B, knit.

Rows 5 and 9: With color A, k 2, * double st, k 1 *; repeat from * to *.

Rows 6 and 10: With A, knit.

Row 7: With color C, work as for Row 3.

Row 8: With C, knit.

Repeat Rows 3 through 10 for pattern.

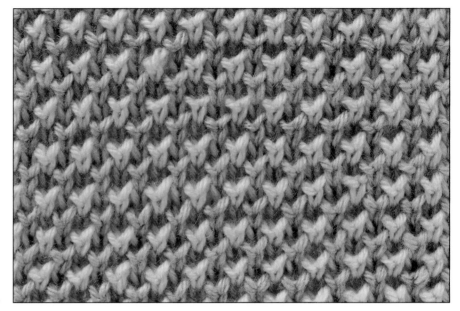

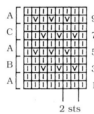

I = k 1
V = double stitch
A = shown as yellow
B = shown as lilac
C = shown as green

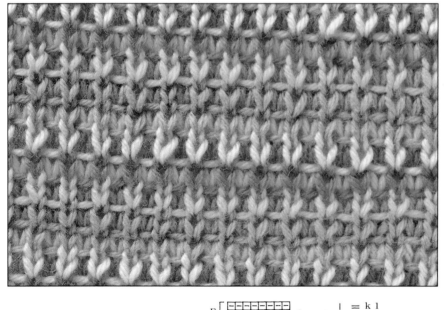

Joyous stripes

Work with an even number of stitches.

Row 1: With color A, k 2, * slip 1 with yarn in front, k 1 *; repeat from * to *.

Row 2 and all even-numbered rows: With same color as previous row, purl.

Row 3: With color B, work as for Row 1.

Row 5: With color C, work as for Row 1.

Row 7: With color D, work as for Row 1.

Row 9: With color E, work as for Row 1.

Repeat Rows 1 through 10 for pattern.

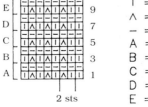

I = k 1
∧ = 1 slip st
— = p 1
A = shown as yellow
B = shown as orange
C = shown as pink
D = shown as lilac
E = shown as green

MULTICOLORED STITCHES

Rows of circles

Work with a multiple of 6 stitches, plus 5.

Row 1 (right side): With color A, knit.

Row 2: With A, k 1, * p 3, k 3 *: repeat from * to *; ending p 3, k last st.

Row 3: With color B, k 1, * slip 3 with yarn at back (carry yarn on wrong side throughout), k 3 *; repeat from * to *, ending slip 3, k 1.

Row 4: With B, p 2, *slip 1 with yarn in front, p 5 *; repeat from * to *, ending slip 1, p 2.

Row 5: With color B, knit.

Row 6: With B, k 4, * p 3, k 3 *; repeat from * to *, ending p 3, k 4.

Row 7: With color A, k 4, * slip 3, k 3 *; repeat from * to *, ending slip 3, k 4.

Row 8: With A, p 5, * slip 1, p 5 *; repeat from * to *.

Repeat these 8 rows for pattern.

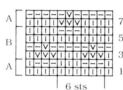

	= k 1
—	= p 1
V	= 1 slip st
A	= shown as teal
B	= shown as yellow

6 sts

Alternating colored bands

Work with a multiple of 4 stitches, plus 2.

Rows 1 and 5 (right side): With color A, knit.

Rows 2 and 6: With A, purl.

Row 3: With color B, k 1, slip 1 with yarn in back (carry yarn on wrong side of work throughout), * k 2, slip 2 *; repeat from * to *, ending k 2, slip 1, k 1.

Row 4: With B, p 1, slip 1 (with yarn in front), * p 2, slip 2 *; repeat from * to *, ending p 2, slip 1, p 1.

Rows 7 and 11: With B, knit.

Rows 8 and 12: With B, purl.

Row 9: With color A, k 2, * slip 2, k 2 *; repeat from * to *.

Row 10: With A, p 2, * slip 2, p 2 *; repeat from * to *.

Repeat Rows 1 through 12 for pattern.

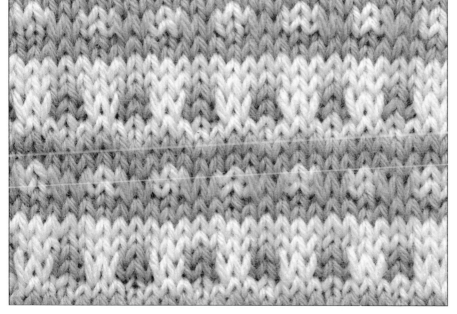

	= k 1
—	= p 1
V	= 1 slip st
A	= shown as teal
B	= shown as pink

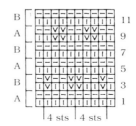

4 sts   4 sts

MULTICOLORED STITCHES

Dots and dashes

Work with a multiple of 10 stitches, plus 7.

Rows 1 and 5 (right side): With color A, knit.

Rows 2 and 6: With A, purl.

Row 3: With color B, k 6, * slip 2 with yarn in back (carry yarn on wrong side of work throughout), k 1, slip 2, k 5 *; repeat from * to *, ending last repeat with k 6.

Row 4: With B, k 6, * slip 2 (with yarn in front), k 1, slip 2, k 5 *; repeat from * to *, ending last repeat with k 6.

Rows 7 and 8: With color B, k 1, * slip 2, k 1, slip 2, k 5 *; repeat from * to *, ending last repeat with k 1. Repeat these 8 rows for pattern.

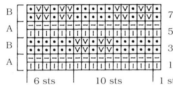

I	=	k 1 A
−	=	p 1 A
•	=	k 1 B
V	=	1 slip st
A	=	shown as red
B	=	shown as pink

Tile design

Work with a multiple of 4 stitches, plus 3.

Rows 1 and 2 (moss st): With color A, p 1, * k 1, p 1; repeat from * to *.

Row 3: With color B, k 1, * slip 1 with yarn in back, k 3 *; repeat from * to *, ending slip 1, k 1.

Row 4: With B, p 1, * slip 1 with yarn in front, p 3 *; repeat from * to *, ending slip 1, p 1.

Rows 5 and 6: Repeat Rows 1 and 2.

Row 7: With color B, k 3, * slip 1 with yarn in back, k 3 *; repeat from * to *.

Row 8: With B, p 3, * slip 1 with yarn in front, p 3 *; repeat from * to *. Repeat these 8 rows for pattern.

•	=	1 moss st
I	=	k 1 B
−	=	p 1 B
V	=	1 slip st
A	=	shown as blue
B	=	shown as pink

MULTICOLORED STITCHES

Chains in relief

Work with a multiple of 2 stitches, plus 1.

Rows 1 and 5: With color A, knit.

Rows 2 and 6: With A, purl.

Row 3: With color B, p 2, * with yarn in front, slip 1 as if to p, p 1 *; repeat from * to *, ending slip 1, p 2.

Row 4: With B, k 1, * with yarn in back, slip 1 as if to p, k 1 *; repeat from * to *.

Repeat rows 1 through 6 for pattern.

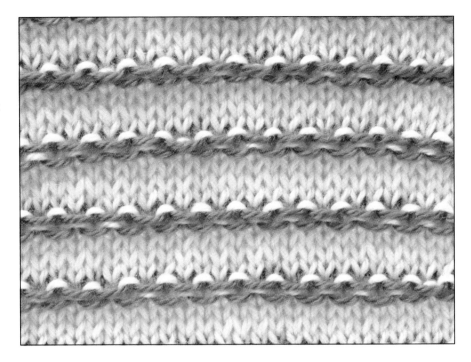

I = k 1
— = p 1
V = 1 slip st
A = shown as white
B = shown as green

Columns of bells

Work with a multiple of 6 stitches, plus 3.

Row 1 (right side): With color A, k 1, * slip 1 with yarn in back (carry yarn on wrong side of work throughout), k 5 *; repeat from * to *, ending slip 1, k 1.

Row 2: With A, p 1, * slip 1 (yarn in front), p 5 *; repeat from * to *, ending slip 1, p 1.

Row 3: With color B, k 3, *slip 3, k 3 *; repeat from * to *.

Row 4: With B, p 3, * slip 3, p 3 *; repeat from * to *.

Row 5: With color A, k 1, slip 2, * k 3, slip 3 *; repeat from * to *, ending k 3, slip 2, k 1.

Row 6: With A, p 1, slip 2, * p 3, slip 3 *; repeat from * to *, ending p 3, slip 2, p 1.

Row 7: With color B, k 4, * slip 1, k 5 *; repeat from * to *, ending slip 1, k 4.

Row 8: With B, p 4, * slip 1, p 5 *; repeat from * to *, ending slip 1, p 4.

Repeat these 8 rows for pattern.

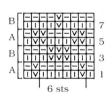

I = k 1
— = p 1
V = 1 slip st
A = shown as white
B = shown as orange

MULTICOLORED STITCHES

Two-color beehive

Work with an uneven number of stitches.

Rows 1 and 2: With color A, knit.

Row 3: With color B, k 1, * work double st as follows: insert needle into st just below next st and k 1, drop unworked st above from left needle, k 1 *; repeat from * to *.

Row 4: With B, knit.

Row 5: with color A, k 2, * double st, k 1 *; repeat from * to *, ending double st, k 2.

Row 6: With A, knit.

Repeat Rows 3 through 6 for pattern.

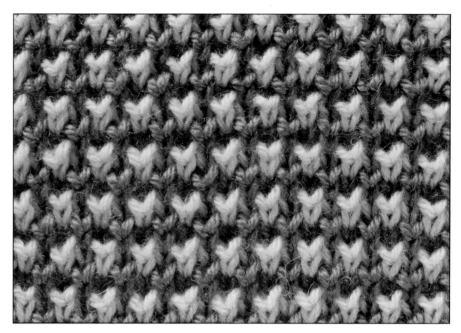

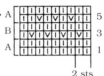

I = k 1
− = p 1
V = 1 double st
A = shown as tan
B = shown as yellow

I = k 1
− = p 1
∧ = double p st
V = double k st
A = shown as teal
B = shown as purple

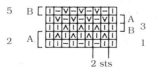

Two-color brioche rib

Work with an uneven number of stitches on double-pointed (dp) needles or a circular needle.

Row 1: With color A, k 2, * p 1, k 1 *; repeat from * to *, ending p 1, k 2. Turn work.

Row 2: With color A, k 1, * work double p st as follows: insert needle from back into st just below next st, p 1, drop unworked st above from left needle, k 1 *; repeat from * to *. Turn work.

Row 3: With color B, k 2, * double p st, k 1 *; repeat from * to * ending double p st, k 2. Do not turn work.

Row 4: Starting at beginning of last row with color A, k 1, * work double k st as follows: insert needle from front into st just below next st and k 1, drop unworked st, p 1 *; repeat from * to *, ending double k st, k 1. Turn work.

Row 5: With color B, k 1, p 1, * double k st, p 1 *; repeat from * to *, ending k last st. Do not turn work. Begin next row at start of one just worked.

Repeat Rows 2 through 5 for pattern.

MUTLICOLORED STITCHES

Two-toned texture

Work with a multiple of 3 stitches, plus 2.

Row 1 (right side): With color A, k 1, * with yarn in back, slip 1 as if to p (carry yarn on wrong side of work throughout), work 1 group as follows: slip 1 as if to k (slip 1 k), k 1, yarn over (yo), pass slip st over k st and yo *; repeat from * to *, ending k 1.

Row 2: With A, p 3, * with yarn in front, slip 1 as if to p (slip 1 p), p 2 *; repeat from * to *, ending slip 1 p, p 1.

Row 3: With color B, k 2, * slip 1 p, work group *; repeat from * to *, ending slip 1 p, k 2.

Row 4: With B, p 2, * slip 1 p, p 2 *; repeat from * to *, ending slip 1 p, p 2.

Row 5: With color A, k 3, * slip 1 p, work group *; repeat from * to *, ending slip 1 p, k 1.

Row 6: With A, p 1, * slip 1 p, p 2 *; repeat from * to *, ending slip 1 p, p 3.

Row 7: With color B, k 1, * slip 1 p, work group *; repeat from * to *, ending k 1.

Row 8: With B, p 3, * slip 1 p, p 2 *; repeat from * to *, ending slip 1 p, p 1.

Row 9: With color A, k 2, * slip 1 p, work group *; repeat from * to *, ending slip 1 p, k 2.

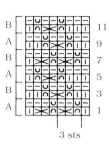

3 sts

| | = k 1
− | = p 1
∩ | = slip 1 with yarn in back
∪ | = slip 1 with yarn in front
✕ | = 1 group

Row 10: With A, p 2, * slip 1 p, p 2 *; repeat from * to *.

Row 11: With color B, k 3, * slip 1 p, work group *; repeat from * to *, ending slip 1 p, k 1.

Row 12: With B, p 1, * slip 1 p, p 2 *; repeat from * to *, ending slip 1 p, p 3.

Repeat these 12 rows for pattern.

Sparrow's track

Work with a multiple of 3 stitches, plus 1.

Row 1: With color A, knit.

Row 2: With A, purl.

Row 3: With color B, k 1, * with yarn in back, slip 1 as if to p, k 2 *; repeat from * to *.

Row 4: With B, purl.

Row 5: With color A, * k 2, slip 1 as before *; repeat from * to *, ending k 1.

Row 6: With A, purl.

Repeat Rows 3 through 6 for pattern.

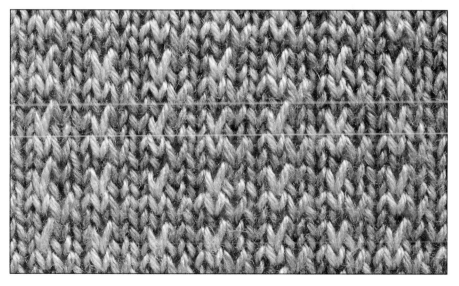

| | = k 1
− | = p 1
V | = 1 slip st

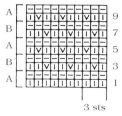

3 sts

MULTICOLORED STITCHES

Squares

Work with a multiple of 12 stitches, plus 1.

Rows 1 and 9 (right side): With color A, k 3, * with yarn in back, slip 1 as if to p (carry yarn on wrong side of work throughout), work (k 2, slip 1) twice, k 5 * repeat from * to *, ending last repeat with k 3.

Rows 2 and 10: With A, p 3, * slip 1 (with yarn in front), work (p 2, slip 1) twice, p 5 *; repeat from * to *, ending last repeat with p 3.

Rows 3 and 7: With color B, k 2, * slip 1, k 2, slip 1, k 1, slip 1, k 2, slip 1, k 3 *; repeat from * to *, ending last repeat with k 2.

Rows 4 and 8: With B, p 2, * slip 1, p 2, slip 1, p 1, slip 1, p 2, slip 1, p 3 *; repeat from * to *, ending last repeat with p 2.

Row 5: With color A, k 1, * slip 1, k 2, slip 1, k 3, slip 1, k 2, slip 1, k 1 *; repeat from * to *.

Row 6: With A, p 1, * slip 1, p 2, slip 1, p 3, slip 1, p 2, slip 1, p 1, *; repeat from * to *.

Rows 11 and 15: With color B, k 1, * slip 1, k 3, slip 1, k 1, slip 1, k 3, slip 1, k 1 *; repeat from * to *.

Rows 12 and 16: With B, p 1, * slip 1, p 3, slip 1, p 1, slip 1, p 3, slip 1, p 1 *; repeat from * to *.

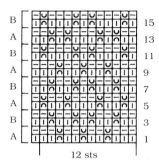

12 sts

| = k 1
− = p 1
∩ = slip 1 with yarn in back
∪ = slip 1 with yarn in front
A = shown as pale green
B = shown as turquoise

Row 13: With color A, k 2, * slip 1, k 1, slip 1, k 3, slip 1, k 1, slip 1, k 3 *; repeat from * to *, ending last repeat with k 2.

Row 14: With A, p 2, * slip 1, p 1, slip 1, p 3, slip 1, p 1, slip 1, p 3 *; repeat from * to *, ending last repeat with p 2.

Repeat Rows 1 through 16 for pattern.

Clovers in garter stitch

Work with a multiple of 4 stitches, plus 3.

Row 1: With color A, k 3, * with yarn in back, slip 1 as if to p, k 3 *; repeat from * to *.

Row 2: With A, knit.

Row 3: With color B, k 1, * slip 1 with yarn in back, k 3 *; repeat from * to *, ending slip 1, k 1.

Row 4: With B, knit.

Repeat these 4 rows for pattern.

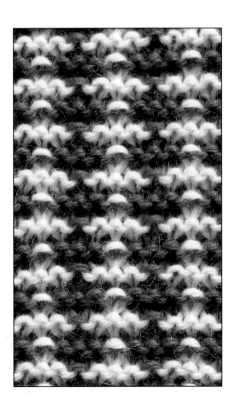

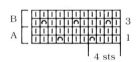

4 sts

| = k 1
∩ = slip 1 with yarn in back

JACQUARD PATTERNS

Blue waters

Work with a multiple of 6 stitches.
Work as follows: Work in stockinette st, following chart for colors and design. Read chart right to left on knit rows and left to right on purl rows, starting at bottom and working up to top. Carry color not in use somewhat loosely across back of work to keep stitches from puckering. Twist (crossover) yarns with each change of color to avoid holes in work.
Catch carried yarn in back of stitches if yarn is to be carried for more than 3 or 4 sts.

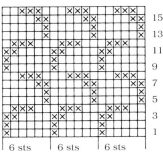

□ = color A, shown as white
✕ = color B, shown as blue
    Knit in stockinette st.

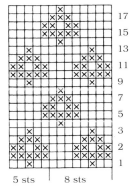

5 sts | 8 sts

□ = color A, shown as white
✕ = color B, shown as wine
    Knit in stockinette st.

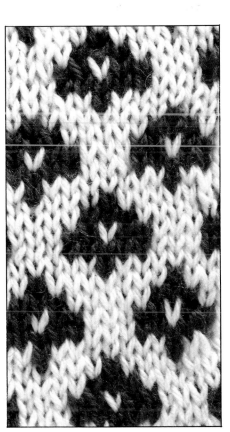

Little flowers

Work with a multiple of 8 stitches, plus 5.
Work as follows: Work in stockinette st, following chart for colors and design. Read chart right to left on knit rows and left to right on purl rows, starting at bottom and working up to top. Carry color not in use somewhat loosely across back of work to keep stitches from puckering. Twist (crossover) yarns with each change of color to avoid holes in work.
Catch carried yarn in back of stitches if yarn is to be carried for more than 3 or 4 sts.

JACQUARD PATTERNS

Dogs

Work with a multiple of 12 stitches, plus 1.

Work as follows: Work in stockinette st, following chart for colors and design. Read chart right to left on knit rows and left to right on purl rows, starting at bottom and working up to top. Carry color not in use somewhat loosely across back of work to keep stitches from puckering. Twist (crossover) yarns with each change of color to avoid holes in work.

Catch carried yarn in back of stitches if yarn is to be carried for more than 3 or 4 sts.

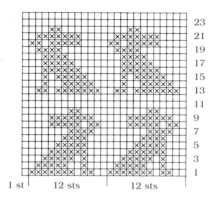

1 st   12 sts   12 sts

☐ = color A, shown as white

✕ = color B, shown as green

Knit in stockinette st.

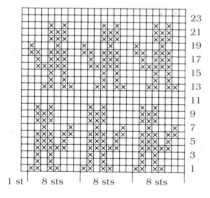

1 st   8 sts   8 sts   8 sts

☐ = color A, shown as white

✕ = color B, shown as tan

Knit in stockinette st.

Cats

Work with a multiple of 12 stitches, plus 1.

Work as follows: Work in stockinette st, following chart for colors and design. Read chart right to left on knit rows and left to right on purl rows, starting at bottom and working up to top. Carry color not in use somewhat loosely across back of work to keep stitches from puckering. Twist (crossover) yarns with each change of color to avoid holes in work.

Catch carried yarn in back of stitches if yarn is to be carried for more than 3 or 4 sts.

JACQUARD STITCHES

Multicolored design

Work with a multiple of 19 stitches.
Work as follows: Work in stockinette st, following chart for colors and design. Read chart right to left on knit rows and left to right on purl rows, starting at bottom and working up to top. Carry only colors used on the particular row you are working. As you work the row, carry color currently not in use somewhat loosely across back of work to keep stitches from puckering. Twist (crossover) yarns with each change of color to avoid holes in work. Catch carried yarn in back of stitches if yarn is to be carried for more than 3 or 4 sts.

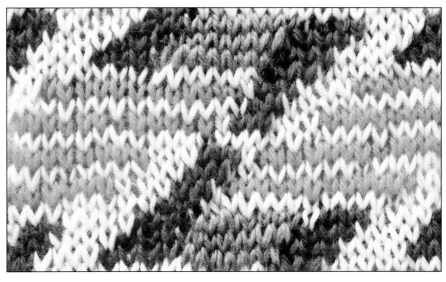

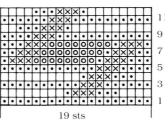

• = color A, shown as white
□ = color B, shown as yellow
X = color C, shown as green
O = color D, shown as pink

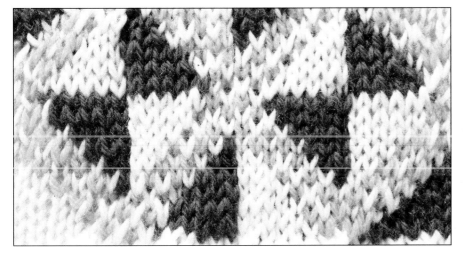

□ = color A, shown as white
• = color B, shown as green
X = color C, shown as yellow

Butterflies

Knit in stockinette st.
Work with a multiple of 16 stitches.
Work as follows: Work in stockinette st, following chart for colors and design. Read chart right to left on knit rows and left to right on purl rows, starting at bottom and working up to top. Carry color not in use somewhat loosely across back of work to keep stitches from puckering. Twist (crossover) yarns with each change of color to avoid holes in work.
Catch carried yarn in back of stitches if yarn is to be carried for more than 3 or 4 sts.

JACQUARD PATTERNS

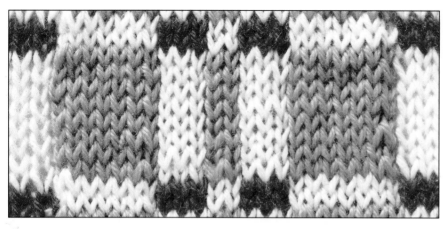

Plaid

Work with a multiple of 15 stitches, plus 7.

Work as follows: Work in stockinette st, following chart for colors and design. Read chart right to left on knit rows and left to right on purl rows, starting at bottom and working up to top. Carry only colors used on the particular row you are working. As you work the row, carry color currently not in use somewhat loosely across back of work to keep stitches from puckering. Twist (crossover) yarns with each change of color to avoid holes in work. Catch carried yarn in back of stitches if yarn is to be carried for more than 3 or 4 sts.

□ = color A, shown as white
o = color B, shown as turquoise
× = color C, shown as bright pink

Penguins

Work with a multiple of 32 stitches.

Work as follows: Work in stockinette st, following chart for colors and design. Read chart right to left on knit rows and left to right on purl rows, starting at bottom and working up to top. Carry only colors used on the particular row you are working.

As you work the row, carry color currently not in use somewhat loosely across back of work to keep stitches from puckering. Twist (crossover) yarns with each change of color to avoid holes in work. Catch carried yarn in back of stitches if yarn is to be carried for more than 3 or 4 sts.

□ = color A, shown as white
V = color B, red (trim)
× = color C, yellow
• = color D, black

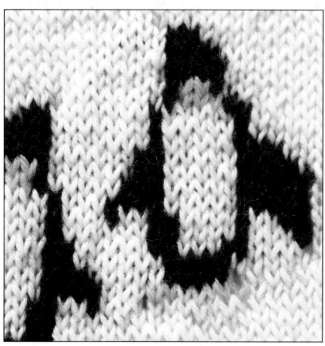

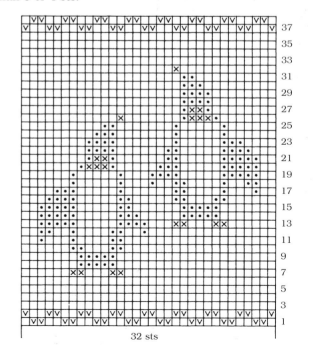

JACQUARD PATTERNS

Columns and diagonals

Work with a multiple of 12 stitches, plus 8.

Work as follows: Work in stockinette st, following chart for colors and design. Read chart right to left on knit rows and left to right on purl rows, starting at bottom and working up to top. If you wish, you can use small bobbins for separated colors to avoid carrying colors. Otherwise, as you work the row, carry any color currently not in use somewhat loosely across back of work to keep stitches from puckering. Twist (crossover) yarns with each change of color to avoid holes in work. Catch carried yarn in back of stitches if yarn is to be carried more than 3 or 4 stitches.

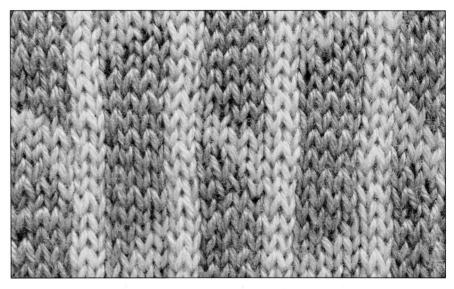

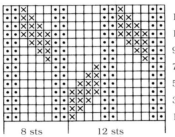

□ = color A, shown as lilac
● = color B, shown as yellow
✕ = color C, shown as green

Geometric shapes

Work with a multiple of 14 stitches.

Work as follows: Work in stockinette st, following chart for colors and design. Read chart right to left on knit rows and left to right on purl rows, starting at bottom and working up to top. If you wish, you can use small bobbins for separated colors to avoid carrying colors. Otherwise, carry only colors used on the particular row you are working. As you work the row, carry color currently not in use somewhat loosely across back of work to keep stitches from puckering. Twist (crossover) yarns with each change of color to avoid holes in work. Catch carried yarn in back of stitches if yarn is to be carried for more than 3 or 4 sts.

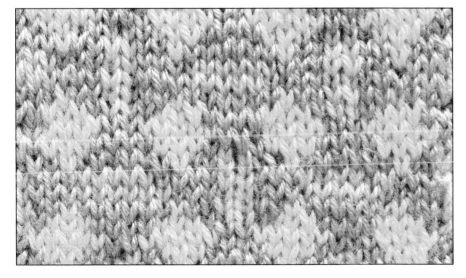

□ = color A, shown as lilac
✕ = color B, shown as yellow
● = color C, shown as green
○ = color D, shown as pink

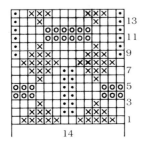

JACQUARD PATTERNS

Arches

Work with a multiple of 4 stitches, plus 1.

Work as follows: Work in stockinette st, following chart for colors and design. For a softer texture, a mohair blend was used for color B yarn in photograph. Read chart right to left on knit rows and left to right on purl rows, starting at bottom and working up to top. Carry only colors used on the particular row you are working. As you work the row, carry color currently not in use somewhat loosely across back of work to keep stitches from puckering. Twist (crossover) yarns with each change of color to avoid holes in work. Catch carried yarn in back of stitches if yarn is to be carried for more than 3 or 4 sts.

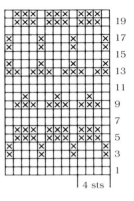

$\square$ = color A, shown as white
$\times$ = color B, shown as green

Loops

Work with a multiple of 6 stitches, plus 1.

Work as follows: Work in stockinette st, following chart for colors and design. For a softer texture, a mohair blend was used for color B yarn in photograph. Read chart right to left on knit rows and left to right on purl rows, starting at bottom and working up to top. Carry only colors used on the particular row you are working. As you work the row, carry color currently not in use somewhat loosely across back of work to keep stitches from puckering. Twist (crossover) yarns with each change of color to avoid holes in work. Catch carried yarn in back of stitches if yarn is to be carried for more than 3 or 4 sts.

$\square$ = color A, shown as white
$\times$ = color B, shown as pink

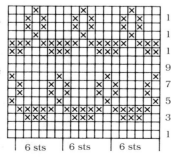